Marg's World
© *Monos www.monos-art.be*

PURRING ANGELS

© Copyright 2007
Marguerite Vlielander

ISBN: 978-1-4251-2202-7

Order this book online at www.trafford.com/07-0604
or email orders@trafford.com

Stichting De Rietkat (Reed Cat)
Postal address: Mishagen 43, 2930 Brasschaat
Tel: +32-3-633.29.71 Fax: +32-3-633.03.96
Email: info@rietkat.be
Site: www.rietkat.be

Books by the same author:

Eindelijk Lucht
Ik heb een sleutel
Wonderen op pootjes
Spinnende Bengeltjes

Cover and illustrated by: Anne Versteyne
Photography by: Marguerite Vlielander
Translated by: Jozef Gommeren
Printed by: Trafford Publishing
Printed in Victoria, BC, Canada.

Note for Librarians: A cataloguing record for this book is available from Library and Archives Canada at www.collectionscanada.ca/amicus/index-e.html

www.trafford.com

10 9 8 7 6 5 4 3

THE RAINBOW BRIDGE

"Just this side of Heaven is a place called Rainbow Bridge. When an animal dies that has been especially close to someone here, that pet goes to the Rainbow Bridge.

There are meadows and hills for all our special friends so they can run and play together. There is plenty of food, water and sunshine, and our friends are warm and comfortable.

All the animals who had been ill or old are restored to health and vigour those who were hurt or maimed are made whole and strong again, just as we remember them in our dreams of days gone by.

The animals are happy and content, except for one small thing; they each miss someone very special to them who had to be left behind.

They all run and play together, but the day comes when one suddenly stops and looks into the distance. His bright eyes are intent. His eager body quivers. Suddenly he begins to run from the group, flying over the green grass, his legs carrying him faster and faster.

You have been spotted, and when you and your special friend finally meet, you cling to each other in joyous reunion, never to be parted again.

The happy kisses rain upon your face, your hands again caress the beloved head, and you look once more into the trusting eyes of your pet. So long gone from your life but never absent from your heart. Then you cross Rainbow Bridge together! "

Author - Unknown

Preface

I dedicate this book first and foremost to my seven Purring Angels: Puddie, Donsje, Mickje, Daimke, Catje and Chummy, the co-authors of this book and to my black Angelcat Tommeke, who joined us after the Dutch version of Purrring Angels was finished.

Next, I dedicate my work to all the poor abandoned cats, forced to live the life of a tramp and having a tough time.

Then, I dedicate my book to all the fantastic men and women who - each in his or her own way - devote themselves with heart and soul to these poor stray cats. Day and night they are there to help the strays. Wonderful people! How I admire them!

It is my profound wish that 'Purring Angels' will help reduce feline suffering by spreading facts and knowledge about cats, and by showing the beauty and intelligence of this very special animal.

With my whole heart I want to thank my dear friends Maria and Gé for their friendship. Indeed, Maria is like a 'soulsister' to me and it is a tremendous pleasure to discuss cat-problems with her. If Maria doesn't know the answer, nobody knows the answer!

True friends are very important. Another friend, Anne, owner of 'de kat z'n viool' has made the beautiful drawings you'll find in this book. I am sure that the success of my first cat-book 'Miracles on little Feet', which is not translated in English, is also due to Anne's excellent drawings. I am so glad that she agreed to illustrate 'Purring Angels' as well. I also want to thank Irene and Dede, the mama's of tomcat Stapper for reading the manuscript over and my wonderful friend Phil for helping me to choose the best photos. She is such a wonderful cat-photographer. I am extremely grateful to my dear friend Sheelagh who offered to correct the manuscript. As I am Dutch I don't speak English like an English person of course. I do really appreciate her assistance, it was a big job. 'Thank you, Dear Sheelagh, you are wonderful!'

I want to thank Arie den Toom for his interesting cd-rom 'Animals in the Bible' and the moving story about the St Elisabeth's flood. I am also very glad to include the beautiful piece on St Francis from Hans Sevenhoven. I would like to thank Marilyn and Elyse for the permission to include their wonderful stories about Ophelia, Tarzan and Foo Foo and Wayne for the permission to use his two lovely stories 'Kitty's best Christmas' and 'In the beginning'. Many thanks also to Cats Confidential who permitted me to put some of their lovely stories in this book. I am so grateful for the beautiful poems my friends allowed me to use. They are so sweet!

I am extremely grateful to the Feline Advisory Bureau for allowing me to use their Catfacts sheets for chapter 17 and the information about dangerous plants for cats for chapter 18. FAB is the leading source of information about cat illnesses in England. They are wonderful.

I owe also thanks to Doctor Allard who sent me his write-up on urethral obstructions.

And then there is my dear friend Paul, the computer-guru. Even from afar he can call my computer to order! Paul, you are a dear. It's unbelievable what you are doing for us. What with all those viruses trying to break into my computer. I am so happy with the virus-shield you installed for me. It intercepts all of them smoothly.

Also I owe a really big 'Thank You' to Jef who translated this book. He did a wonderful job. Thank you, dear Jef! To all these dear friends as well as to many others who helped me: thank you from the bottom of my heart. Indeed, without them 'Purring Angels' wouldn't have been finished by now.

VERNON COLEMAN'S PRAYER FOR CATS

Thank you, God...

Thank you, God, for allowing me to share my life with an Upright Who loves and cares for me. Thank you, God, for giving me a life where I am protected from deliberate cruelty and hardship and thank you, God, for providing me with an Upright who will always ensure that I have enough food to eat and a warm, dry place to sleep.

But please God, permit me to remind you of the many cats and kittens who are not as fortunate as I; the cats who face each day with fear in their hearts, and who must deal with cruelty and pain without love to sustain them.

Please, God, remember, care for and love those cats and kittens who live in laboratory cages and who are imprisoned and tortured by Uprights.

Please God, teach those Uprights the error and pointlessness of their ways.

Please God, turn my thanks to you for your kindness to me, into love for those poor creatures who are not as fortunate as I am.

Thank you, God.

© *Written by Vernon Coleman, on behalf of cats everywhere.*

This beautiful poem comes out of the lovely book: Cats' Own Annual written by Vernon Coleman. All information is available on the site www.vernoncoleman.com
In Chapter 22 I will give all the titles of the books Doctor Coleman has written about cats, you will find his address in chapter 21.

Contents

It's just a matter of cause and effect, this sequel to our first cat book 'Miracles on little Feet.' 'Only natural', Puddie concluded philosophically. 'There is no way around it: Daimke, Catje and Chummy are also entitled to 'their book'.

PUDDIE, THE OLDEST AND WISEST WILL INTRODUCE US.

Puddie: born on 25-3-1995

Pudje

I am a splendid grey tabby, er...I-lost-something-at-the-vet-cat, with big black spots. Everybody says I am 'oriental', that I look like a Bengal. I have big, communicative green eyes, which have earned me many prizes in America. (It is very hard to be humble when one is such a winner as I). Mama and me, we have a very strong bond. An eternal bond. In the beginning there were just the two of us: Marg (= mama) and me. How I enjoyed that! We were inseparable. We still are inseparable but we are no longer two. More fluffies came our way, you see.

1

First came **Luckje:**

On a rainy night he walked into our life. He stayed exactly for one year. Marg loved him very much. But I, to be frank, I didn't love him. Maybe that's why he left? Well, Luckje sometimes attacked me and he wanted to claim Marg all for himself. I didn't want any of that, of course. I did understand him, though. He strayed in here and had a very difficult time behind him. Put it like this: Luckje was some kind of sailor looking for a job ashore for a change. He wanted a roof to sleep under and longed for love and affection and he found that with us. But Marg was mine and he couldn't accept that. Further, having to stay indoors made matters worse for Luck, the desperado used to the Great Outdoors. We didn't have open-air runs at that time where we could play. Running around free is something Marg found (and still finds) too dangerous. In short, after lots of thinking and grieving, Luckje was allowed to go outdoors and he didn't have to share the room with me any more. Slowly, very slowly I calmed down. Luck's territory was the entire garden, the upper floor of our house and a small house in the garden where our cat-dwarfs live. Yes, we do have little dwarfs around here. Cat-dwarfs of course, they take care of cats in distress. Just like the Poezenbel Foundation does.

So, exactly one year after his sudden appearance in our world, Luckje left. All of a sudden he was gone. Mama is still looking for him. I know he is happy somewhere, probably living with people who need his help. You see, when Luck came here, mama had a lot of sadness and trouble because of some straightup-walker misfit who was trying to spoil her life. I think that's Luckje's mission here on earth: comforting and healing people who are feeling down. You know, like his patron, Doctor Luke, the Healer of the Bible. Sure, I am very grateful to him for that, but, mind you, hoping for his return is another matter!

So you can understand, I have had a difficult time each time another fluffy has come into our lives. Yet, now I don't mind so much any more being with more cats. I have observed that mama's love for me hasn't changed a bit, she still loves me as much as before. And, I do enjoy playing with the 'newcomers' (and showing them who's the boss around here).

LUCKY BOY

You came,
You saw,
And conquered.
You acted like an emperor.
To rule was your nature.

You came out of nowhere.
Where have you been before?
Too much a free spirit to stay.
You comforted somebody
Who really needed it.

But you got your freedom.
And suddenly
You were gone.
On your way to somebody
Who might need you too.

God Bless dear Lucky
Safe journey.

© Margreet van der Wart

Donsje: born 6-8-1997.

Donsje

She is grey/beige and white. She is a very cute, lovely, soft and fluffy girl who came to live with us thanks to Aunt Maria from Poezenbel. She was found in a wheatfield when the farmer was baling hay with a huge machine. She was cosily resting with her mother, brothers and sisters in her nest, when that monster came rattling along, smashing everything in its way, including Donsje's warm nest. Her mother panicked and rushed off. Her brothers and sisters were killed. Only Donsje survived. Luckily for her a caring woman living close to the field picked her up and brought her to Maria from Poezenbel. When she had grown big and strong she joined the family.

I love her very much. But I must admit that Mickje and I like to tease her a lot. We have fun watching her running away shrieking noisily to safety under the cabinet. Mostly however, she runs to mama to complain with a pathetic face: 'Mama, they are at it again, hellleeeppp meee!' Mama then scolds us and we promise never to do it again...till next time, that is. Still, we really don't want to hurt Donsje, and mama knows that. Donsje has a special place in mama's heart. Her name means fluffy.

Mickje: probably also born on 6-8-1997.

We don't know the exact date. She was dumped in our garden around St Nicholas. She was just skin and bones and had a big umbilical hernia. She had been badly abused. I think some mean man must have kicked her, because whenever a male straightup-walker enters our house, Mickje will hide under a chair and always keeps her eyes on his feet. Mickje and I sleep in the living room and we enjoy each other's company. We love each other in a 'decent' way. You see, I am engaged to Asselijntje from Poezenbel. But Mickje is a fine friend. She is very happy that she can stay with us. Whenever she talks about her terrible experiences I start shivering and my tail fluffs up from anger. Mickje can't retract her claws, so she has some difficulty walking, but we do play a lot and you should see her now! Her fur shining like a mirror. I think (and hope) she has forgotten the horror she has experienced.

Daimke: born on 24-5-1999

Daimke

The famous painter Renate Leijen saved this small pussy-girl. Renate found five newly born kittens in the bushes close to a hotel under construction. The mother had fled. Immediately Renate took the poor things to Maria. The two male kittens soon crossed over to the Rainbow Bridge, but the girls made it here. Daimke lacks some kind of enzyme and has to have a pinch of tryplase with every meal to make up for this lack. She has a lot of Oriental blood in her veins, so we resemble each other. When she was small I was her idol and I liked that very much. I am a bit of an ego-tripper, you see. But now she is mature (and not so easy to fool any more). Mama often calls her 'Our little Elf'.

Catrientje (Catje): probably born on 17-6-1999.

Catje

She was dumped together with her little brothers when she was about six weeks old. Holiday-time or no-more-welcome? Her brothers were found and brought to Maria two days before Catje was rescued. Catje had taken refuge high up in a tree and lived there for two days. How happy she was when she arrived at Maria's place and felt Maria's love, warmth and security! Catje and Daimke are very close friends.

And last but not least, **Chummy**: born on 13-5-2001.

He is the youngest of us. He was born on Mother's Day. For three months we closely followed his growing up. And how he grew! After five months he was

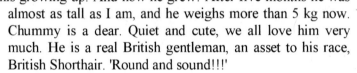

almost as tall as I am, and he weighs more than 5 kg now. Chummy is a dear. Quiet and cute, we all love him very much. He is a real British gentleman, an asset to his race, British Shorthair. 'Round and sound!!!'

And then (although he was not yet with us when Purring Angels was written in Dutch) our beautiful 'wild' **Tommeke** joined us. He looks like a Norwegian Forest Cat. He is a lovely black boy with a long waterproof fur coat. We will write about him later on. He is such a dear and mummy calls him her guardian angel. But that's what we all are!

We live together with three little dogs. Horry is the oldest, he must be eighteen years old by now, at least. We don't know his date of birth. He looks like a dachshund.

Next we have **Kirby**.

She is a Cardigan Corgi and was born on 25-12-92.
She was grandma's favourite dog. She still misses her dear
mummy. Luckily Femke is there to comfort her.

Femke: born on...8-98.

She is a cross between a Labrador and a Border Collie, black
with white spots and very tall. Femke is a real dear. Because
she went through a lot of misery when she was a puppy, she
is afraid of strangers. She is a very good watchdog. No
stranger can enter the garden or Femke knows and spreads
the news!

There were also six big geese who hissed at us and fifteen chickens and a proud
cock. When the bird-influenza came too near and we had to kill all domestic
birds we took the geese to the river and let them go. We could not protect them
any more. They were so happy to be free. It's not good to have geese if you
don't have enough water for them to have a good swim. Now we have 6 ducks.
They are so sweet and funny. Also two lovely mountain goats came to live
with us. Treeske and Mekkie. They were meant to be eaten and we are so glad
they are safe now. They are so funny and sweet and play with Femke and
Kirby. Very rarely a few deer come to visit us. We love them! They are so
elegant and gentle natured. It's incredible with how much ease they jump over
the 1.50 high fence. They are nearly as lithe as we are!

And then there is mama, of course. We have a very dear friend, Mariette, who
took fantastic care of grandma and who is very nice to mama and to all of us.
Mariette lives upstairs since grandma passed away. So nice and cosy! We all
love her very much. Mama and Mariette are close friends.
So, now you know us. We have two big open-air runs where we have super
fun. What a delight to run and play under the sun! Whenever the weather is
fine, Mama stays outdoors with her laptop too.

I have to go now, mama needs the PC, you see.
Many ppprrrrrrreetinggggsss from Puddie, secretary of the Rietkat.

Marg: born on 19-2-47.

Yes, my dear Puddie is right.
I had better tell my 'own' story, having been born some time before Puddie. I grew up on a huge farm: the Manor Cromstrijen in Numansdorp, the Netherlands. My father managed it as steward. I had a wonderful youth. I had lots of animal friends and 1800 hectares of fenced-in farmlands to play in. It was a real garden of Eden. When I was about to study to be a veterinarian, my father fell ill and I stayed at his side and looked after him. We all moved, first to France and then to Belgium. All this happened during the past thirty years of my life. I will not go further into this now because I wrote in detail about these years in my book 'Miracles on little Feet.'

During the thirty years that I helped and cared for my parents I had Anorexia Nervosa. Nowadays there is much talk about this illness and countless books have been written on it. But at that time it was still very much 'Terra Incognita'. Sure, my parents saw me growing thinner and thinner, but nobody realized that the Anorexia-devil - Satano is my 'nickname' for him - was slowly but steadily taking control of every move and moment of my life. If you haven't been in 'Anorexia-land' it is next to impossible to understand what a hell it is. Yet, for me, it was also a way to survive. I don't regret my long residence there. It has taught me a lot and in spite of my illness I did succeed in taking care of my parents. Now, I am an experienced consultant and assist other girls struggling to get out of the horrible hell of anorexia.

Thanks to the Lord, I am 'healed' and the 'living proof' that it is possible indeed to leave Anorexia-land, even after a 'residence' there of thirty long years. Of course it was not easy. I told the Lord all about my sorrows and fears. I gave them to Him and felt His reply: 'Have faith in Me, you will make it. Just trust Me!' This bond with Him is very important to me. My mother was still alive then and, oh, how happy she was when she saw me growing healthier and stronger again. I got also tremendous support from my dietician Marleen and Rudi, her father. And then there were the animals. Without them I would not have won the battle! They were my reason to live. For them I wanted to live and get strong, they needed me! They taught me to eat again, to live again, to enjoy living again. They loved me unconditionally and I could count on them twenty-four hours a day. My dear Shorthair Collie Karma, mama's Cardigan

Corgi Ferntje, Horry and Puddie. The other animal friends were not there at that time.

Together with Rudi I wrote my first book 'Free at Last'. It is an autobiography about my youth and ano-years. This book brought me in contact with many girls suffering from anorexia. I tried to help and support them during their climb out of the terrible ano-well. 'Free at Last' was widely read, so I decided to write a second book, also with Rudi. This time a book of advice and counsel for girls wanting to heal from anorexia. I titled this new book 'I have a key'.

I was and still am infinitely grateful that I defeated Satano. Anorexia is a lifelong addiction. Even when Satano has been put securely behind bars, he still rattles his chains and shouts threats at me. I just have to remain on the alert forever. But now I do enjoy life and its opportunities that are still within my reach. That's what I call being 'healed'. You don't have to join the world's 'rat race'. It is possible to take the good things from Anoland with you when you move to your 'own' land. Yes, there are some good things there too of course, otherwise so many girls would not go to live there. From your new place - as soon as you feel really safe and in control – you can think about what you are going to do in your new life. Never mind if you hang on to certain peculiar habits from the past. That is your choice and your right. The most important thing is that you are happy and that you can bring that happiness and help to other living beings. That's what really matters here on earth. In Chapter 13 I will discuss anorexia in more detail.

When my Donsje came to live with us, I decided to keep some sort of diary to record all the nice happenings and things we, the fluffies and I, experienced. Out of this, the concept for my third book 'Miracles on little Feet' gradually evolved. When I started writing Miracles, I gave it the working title Donsbook, as the idea of writing a book about my pussy-children was born on the day Donsje arrived. Consequently, I titled this book Daimbook for the time being because Daimke (and Catje) were the next miracles after Donsje who came to live with us. Chummy came much later.

How could I ever have expected that 'Miracles' would be such a miraculous success? A dream come true. Luckily dreams often do, if you really visualise them and feel deep down inside you that they will become true. I include a summary at the back of this book.

How proud we were when the book was printed! To write a book is almost the same as having a baby. Printing it is like the birth of the baby. When Miracles came into the 'big world' I felt as worried as a mother feels when her teenagers are going to their first party. How was my baby going to be received by the people? Would these people love her? Would my book succeed in its purpose: sensitising people into more love and concern for their cats and for stray cats? Would my book help in convincing them that cats are really miracles on little feet? That they are animals who need lots of love and attention? It is not true that cats prefer to be left alone so that they can go their own way. Some cats are forced to live that way but of all animals it is the cat that needs most warmth, love, security and appreciation. Cats are as loyal as dogs, but you have to deserve their friendship and loyalty. They do not give it just like that to everyone.

Now, two years later I dare say: 'Yes, indeed, that's exactly what Miracles has brought about.' We have received many lovely letters with positive reactions. I keep them all in a special file, so that later, when I am very old, I can read them again, sitting cosily close to the heater surrounded by my fluffies!

We hear and see many bad news bulletins on radio and television. The newspapers are filled with horror stories. All this bad news almost makes us forget that there are lots of very kind people out there, men and women going out of their way to help animals and who love their cats very, very much. Sometimes I hear heartbreaking stories. But also I hear beautiful and tender stories. About a little cat who meant everything in the life of an old woman. 'Only because she still had her cat, she had a purpose in her life.' Another woman refused to go to a home for the elderly because then she would have had to leave her sixteen-year-old pussycat behind, so she just didn't report when she had a chance of a room. Very moving!

Of course, I also received bad telephone calls: My cat has to go, not tomorrow but immediately! She scratches my furniture, she urinates inside the house. My child is allergic to cats. Any excuse would do, the decision having been taken already. How did I know that? Very simple. I offered help such as, for instance, advising how to cure cats from scratching furniture and received the reply that it was no use. Or I mailed information about the protein causing allergy for cats and what to do about it – something can indeed be done about it, I include details about the book in the bibliography at the end of this book – and I heard 'No, that doesn't interest me.' Well, as I don't shelter cats myself, all I can do then is give the addresses of some friends who do. But their shelters are already full. Oh, if only everyone took his or her responsibility seriously, how simple life would be and what a huge reduction in sorrow and sadness!

We've been on television. An adventure by itself. How surprised I was when we actually appeared on the screen and the reactions kept my telephone ringing! The 'aftermath': more than one hundred 'Miracles on little Feet' sold in just a couple of days. A miracle! We also appeared in newspapers and magazine. It was a marvellous and thrilling time. I think that the wonderful drawings of my friend Anne Versteyne also induced people to buy the book. I am very happy that Anne consented to illustrating this book as well. Also I will borrow some illustrations from 'Miracles' for 'Purring' and some stories too.

Let me now talk a bit about the Poezenbel Foundation. You will find all the details at the end of this book. My dear friend Maria, who is like a sister to me, founded the Poezenbel Foundation in 1995. She dedicates herself in all possible ways to help cats in distress. She is the middle woman between people and cats, trying to balance 'supply and demand'. She shelters tiny abandoned kittens. She gives information and assistance in the rearing of motherless kittens. She helps cats in distress, has strays neutered and is always available for questions related to cats. I don't know how many starved, abandoned kitties she has saved and nursed to maturity! And that's not all. The 'Poezenbel-cat' breed is the most 'cuddlable' cat-breed that ever existed! They are super miracles and I am enormously grateful to Maria and of course also to her husband Gé who assists and supports her tremendously, for my three splendid cat-girls, Donsje, Catje and Daimke.

'TO BE(E) OR NOT TO BE(E)!'

Pussies or cats? That's the question.

'These days, when you are a tomcat, it is really difficult to keep the 'to be'. I heard straightup-walking Tomcats presently also grumble about it.' Puddie told Mickje when both were watching the sunset.

True: Out of the abundance of the heart, the mouth speaketh.

TOO BEE OR NOT TOO BEE

© *Anne Versteyne*

Indeed, I do talk a lot about...pussies. (In Dutch that means mostly she-cats). Once Puddie came to me with very sad eyes. 'Mama, you don't love me any more?' I was flabbergasted. 'Whatever gave you that idea?', I asked him. 'Weeeell, you are always talking about pussies and I, I'm a tom**cat**, so you're not talking about me then! Why, don't I belong any more? You don't find me 'sweet' any more? You don't love me any more then?' I had never thought about that. You see, I prefer the word pussy, it sounds cute and lovely to my ears. The Dutch word "Kat" sometimes has a negative connotation. 'Oh, my dear Puddie,' I replied, 'You know very well that you are my "firstborn", my big, wise, bosom-buddy, and I love you with heart and soul.' I picked him up and hugged him closely. 'Come, lay down next to me, let us do some research and find out more about it.'

One says:

In Afrikaans:	kat
In Arabic:	kitte
In Basque:	gatua
In Chinese:	miu or mau
In German:	Katze (male) and Katti (female)
In Danish:	kat
In Dutch:	kat (male and female), poes (female) kater (male)

In English:	cat
In Egyptian:	mau
In Eskimo:	pussi
In French:	chat (male) and chatte (female)
In Finnish:	kissa
In Flemish:	kat (male and female), poes, katinneke (female) Kater (male)
In Gaelic:	pishyakan
In Greek:	catta or kata
In Hawaiian:	popoki
In Italian:	gatto (male) and gatta (female)
In Irish:	cat (male) and cait (female)
In Japanese:	neko
In Latin:	felis or cattus
In Norwegian:	katt (male) a katta (female)
In Portuguese:	gato
In Polish:	kot or gatto
In Russian:	kots (male) and koshka (female)
In Spanish:	gato (male) and gata (female)
In Turkish:	kedi
In Welsh:	kath
In Icelandic:	köttur
In Swedish:	katt

'So, indeed, Puddie, you are right. What shall we do? You know what we'll do? When I talk about cats in general I'll use the word "cat". But in the comfort of my furry circle I will talk about "fluffies" or "my pussy-children". And that word includes you, don't ever doubt that! I like "fluffies", it's such a cosily "fluffy" word. And you are really fluffy, all of you.' Puddie felt completely reassured and rushed off to tell the rest of the gang. Well, Puddie is right, grammar and gender do matter, and deliberately using a word wrongly creates confusion. So, cats they are, cats they shall be, purr, purr...

WONDERFUL CAT:

The Siamese is a wonderful cat,
a good companion, if you fancy that!
Warm and snuggly, with a rumbling purr,
smooth and sleek, soft velvety fur.

Clear and bright, those sapphire eyes,
watching you, they can hypnotize!
Dark little faces, all full of fun,
tails held high as they leap and run.

For entertainment, you can't ask for more,
don't need TV, that is for sure!
With deep wowly voices, they try to convey,
it would be nice, if you'd join in their play!

Then when you are sleepy, and gone to your bed,
often you'll find, they'll curl up by your head!
Looking just like a big furry hat,
a Siamese is a wonderful cat!

© Sue Wingett

'You know what Pudje? Let us tell Mickje's story first before we go on. Then the readers will understand why she is still scared of strangers and they will love her even more. You go and fetch her'.

Here's Mickje's story or better our reconstruction of the things she has been through.

I HAVE A DREAM,
A BEAUTIFUL DREAM!

Once upon a time...that's how most fairy tales start, but what follows is not a fairy tale, it's a true story. At first Mickje didn't want to talk about it, it had been too bad. She pushed them away, the thoughts about

17

those terrible things that had come her way, and hid them. She had tucked them away deep down under her thick brown beautifully golden-flamed fur. But little by little she regained her strength and risked thinking about them now and then. Donsje and Puddie, who know how to deal with cat-reticence, managed to coax the secret out of Mickje by asking lots of tactful questions. Also they could read her unspoken thoughts. Cats are very good at that. At night, when Mickje was asleep, they came to me and told me all, and so I was able to reconstruct Mickje's story. Mickje, who on a cold and wintry day stepped into our life and warmed our hearts which were chilled by sorrow about Luckje who had left us. Yes, that was what Mickje did and as she has the same endearing traits as Luckje had, I am sure he taught them to her.

September '98. It's autumn and the time of falling leaves, it is marvellous to look at the splendidly coloured trees and that's what Mijntje, an old woman, and her beautifully golden brown flamed cat were doing while sitting before the window in the late summer sun, which still was really warm. 'Yes, only behind the glass', Mijntje said to herself with a smile, for outside the temperature was already quite low. She was used to sitting in front of the window like this, her beloved cat friend on her lap, enjoying the view over the park and each other's company. What greater happiness could there be? She used to think of past times then. Times long, long ago. Of memories most of which were not very clear in her mind any more. Except for one thing which she would never forget, the years when her only son, John, was a lovely little blond-haired toddler. Oh, what a charming and enterprising little fellow he had been! Everybody loved him and she most of all.

Yet, those were tough times. John's father had walked out on them when the child was barely four years old. She had had to work hard to make ends meet. 'But', Mijntje mused, 'I managed! Look at our flat and the nice surroundings! True, it is small, but we have a nice view over the park, and, anyway, what's the use of living in a big house when we're just two, isn't it, Mickje?' That's how she called her favourite friend who had suddenly appeared in her lonely life about a year ago. They had become instant friends. They loved each other and had an intimate bond, so that they sensed each other's feelings without need of words. Mickje was the only reason she wanted to live for after all the unhappiness she'd been through.

Shame, what kind of thinking was this? A frown covered her forehead. So, what had happened to that nice little fair-haired toddler who had been the joy of her life, ages ago? Well, that can happen to the best of us. Of course, it was her fault, what with always being out working and he left behind, alone in the house. So, in his teens, he got into bad company, tried drugs and drink, got addicted and ran away from home. For years she neither saw nor heard anything from him. Then, a couple of years ago, he suddenly appeared at her front door with a woman! She remembered thinking to herself:' Thank you, Lord, now he'll calm down and get settled!' But nothing was farther from the truth. His drinking problem had only become worse. 'Still, deep down inside, he is a good boy,' Mijntje thought with love.' Why, did he not visit me twice last month, even bringing a bunch of flowers, something he'd never done before?' Usually he only came around once yearly, at Christmas.

But Mickje, who sensed mama's thoughts, trembled. That John, how she feared him! And his wife with her shrill voice was worse still. She smelled the evil that hung around them. But Mickje couldn't get her misgivings across to Mijntje. A mother won't accept any shadows of evil in her child. Mickje sensed the danger that hovered above her head like a dark cloud. It made her restless, she wagged her tail. There was something bad in the offing; something nasty was about to happen. That's what she inferred from the couple's last visit, especially from their parting words. Merrily they had shouted on leaving the house: 'We'll be back soon and with a nice surprise, just look forward to our next visit! Mickje shuddered. Something 'nice' from such people? Impossible!

One week later John and his wife returned. 'Mama, we have very good news for you, just listen. We've been able to arrange a nice, cosy flat for you in an old people's home. It is a dream of a flat, and you can move into it next month, isn't that just wonderful?' At first, Mijntje didn't understand. 'Son, I don't want to leave this place. We are all right here, Mickje and I. Why should I leave?' But the couple nagged on about all the advantages of the home, the professional care she would receive there, the cosiness and sociability. When Mijntje continued to object, John lost his temper. He looked her angrily in the eyes and said: 'Mother, what is getting into you? We've done our very best to arrange everything for you and you don't show any appreciation! You are not even happy that I care. It's for your own good.' Mijntje definitely couldn't feel happy about the new home, but John had shown he cared for her, surely. She did not want to disappoint him, that lovely boy of hers, so, she hesitatingly consented. One week before she was to move to her new flat, she learned that Mickje could not come with her. 'Under no condition! Totally out of the question! No, mama, impossible! Just imagine…an animal in the home, the hygiene, the trouble a cat brings! The nursing staff have their hands full with the people living there, they have no time left for pets. Now, don't worry about that cat, we'll find a nice place for her. You just think of the cosy little room you're about to move into. Enjoy the prospect of that!' Tears welled up in Mijntjes eyes and that night she sat for long hours with Mickje curled up in her arms. 'My dear girl', she whispered, 'if you are not around, I am through with life. From now on I'll pray and plead with the Lord to come and fetch me away from here. Life without you will be impossible. What are they going to do with you? Why can't we just stay here and live our lives of peace and quiet as we did?' Well, Mickje very well knew the answer to the last question: 'Dear son John' had thought it all out very well. He wanted to sell mama's place and get hold of the money. Didn't he need lots of money to keep up his expensive hobby of boozing and bumming? His wife, of course, wouldn't object to some extra money, so she gladly went along with her husband's wicked scheme. Once, when mama was busy in the kitchen and Mickje was in the living-room, she had actually heard them whisper to each other:' Who knows, she won't live much longer, and then it's all ours and ours only!' How they had laughed then, like devils welcoming another lost soul into hell! How united they were in their devious little plan!

The last week in their apartment was like mourning. Mickje could only watch her mama getting worse from day to day. She just sat and most of the time wept quietly. Mickje tried to comfort her, but there was not much she could do to help. She put her little paws around Mijntjes neck, rested her little head against her cheek and purred and purred. She had been able to comfort her kittens that way and maybe it would relieve some of her beloved mama Mijntje's distress as well. Very softly she licked Mijntje's tears, rubbed her paws over her face, but to no avail. 'Oh, dear little Mickje', Mijntje would cry out once in a while, 'why don't they just kill me or throw me in prison. I don't care what happens to me as long as you are with me.' Of course, no doubt about it, Mickje would have followed her mama to prison without a moment's hesitation, but there was nothing to do about it. 'Dear John' had placed her in a home and that's where she was going! Mijntje was too old and too tired to put up a real fight against this decision 'for her own good'.
And then, all of a sudden, the day of departure arrived. They came to take her away. All her things had been moved ahead of her and Mijntje had even handed the keys to John already. Mickje was desperate. Desperate because of

20

the sudden departure of her beloved mama who told her just before going outside to the car that was waiting to take her to the home:' Mickje, please always remember me, I am so sorry to have to leave you behind. I just can't help it, those are the rules and I am too weak to fight them. Please take care of yourself, I have to go now, but we'll meet again.' When the car drove off, Mickje felt panic rise up in her. She ran through the room, tried to find a way out to escape, but everything was closed. She had been locked in. After a while, John returned and she tried to escape through the door when he entered, but he gave her a hard kick in the stomach so that she was flung against the door frame. He picked the dazed Mickje up and threw her in a big cardboard box. 'Good riddance', she faintly heard him sneer.

Stunned, she lay in the box. She heard doors slam, felt how the box was dumped in the boot of a car and then she felt the starting of an engine. She had experienced this before, when she had been to a veterinarian, but that had been very different. Then she had sat on mama Mijntje's lap while now...Suddenly the car stopped somewhere, rough hands picked up the box and flung it down a staircase leading into a damp and musty-smelling cellar. Then silence, a terrorising silence. Mickje tried to squeeze herself out of the box, but it took all night before she finally freed herself. My golly, how her belly was hurting from that vicious kick and the fall down the stairs! And thirst! Fortunately she found a leaking water-tap somewhere in that awful place so that she could quench the worst of her thirst. Two days and two nights she was left there.

Then, suddenly, she heard the shrill voice of that awful woman. She shrieked: 'If you think I will accept the presence of that cat, you must be out of your mind. I am not going to run after that beast, removing her filthy hairs scattered about everywhere, placing cat's boxes and dishes! I won't even consider it! It's her out or I go, and if I go, you'll be living in an empty house, because most of the things here are mine and I'll take them with me. So, take your pick!' Scared, Mickje hid in the darkest corner she could find in her prison. She sensed danger coming close. John came down and found her behind a pile of garbage. 'Hey, bitch, I found you, no use hiding. What? Making my nice cellar dirty, are you? You just wait, I'll teach you some manners! ' Quickly John grabbed poor Mickje by her neck.
There was nothing she could do to defend herself. Helpless she hung in the air. Ugh, the smell of strong drink that wafted out of the mouth of her jailor!

21

She felt like fainting. Again she was dropped in a cardboard box · and dumped in the boot of a car. Again a ride in complete darkness to some awful place. A shrieking stop, the opening of the boot, the rough handling of the box. Again a flight through the air and the painful impact when the box hit the ground. Dazed, Mickje heard the car zooming away, leaving her hungry, thirsty, sick and scared in some unknown place. She dozed and dreamed, or was it a hallucination or reality?

Suddenly a handsome black and white he-cat stood in front of her. Goodness and love seemed to radiate from him like sunrays breaking through a black cloud. Tenderly he touched her shoulder and licked her ear. 'Listen, Mickje,' said he, 'my name is Luckje and I am going to help you from now on. Don't be afraid, everything will be all right. Just trust me!' When Mickje woke up, Luckje was gone of course, and she still found herself in the box. Meanwhile it had started to rain and she felt how her box was slowly getting wet and soft. She started scratching and digging around and soon she managed to worm herself out of it. Motionless, she observed her new surroundings. She listened and sensed and sniffed around. Where was she? It was dark and it was raining. It was cold and there was a peculiar sound. 'Wind rustling the leaves?' From deep down in her subconscious cat-mind, feelings she had never known before rose up. It was as if her ancestors were telling her something. Suddenly she knew what to do. Slowly she got up and started prowling about like a tiger. She looked in the bushes for a safe place to rest. She found a hole under a tree, dry and well covered by grass and branches. There she curled herself up for a refreshing sleep, far away from the dangerous world full of horrible Johns, shrieking wives and damp cellars.

She had barely dozed off when Big Luckje was there again. He nestled himself down close to her so that Mickje would feel warm and whispered: 'Listen, Mickje, I have been looking around for a long time to find a lovely, sweet cat who could be my deputy. I think I found the one I am looking for and I feel intensely grateful for that. See, the Almighty has sent me to assist living beings in distress here on earth. For a period I was allowed to comfort someone who had been unfairly treated in her life. It was a splendid time of joy for both of us. A pity, I had to leave her as other living beings were claiming my company. She was terribly grieved by my departure. She kept on looking and calling for me. That's why I went looking for a little cat in distress who could take my place. A she-cat, 'cause Marg, that's the name of the girl I'm talking about, has two cats living in her house. Puddie, a proud he-cat who won't accept another 'he' next to him, and cute Donsje who wouldn't mind having another girl-mate to play with. Now, I 'm sure you would be all right there. In fact you won't find a better home than Marg's place. And on top of that you'll help my beloved Marg getting over the sorrow my sudden disappearance has caused her. So Mickje, please go there. You'll do Marg and me a big favour, if you did. Really, kid, you won't regret it! And don't worry how to get there. I'll guide you, even if you might not see me.'

The next morning when she opened her eyes to a bright day, Mickje felt the urge to take a long walk. And through the bushes and the woods she went. She walked over the fields, until she came to the edge of a wide and deep ditch. There she stopped and brooded irresolutely about crossing or not, for though dry, it was deep, dark and wide. The memory of what could happen to cats in deep and dark places was still very fresh on her mind. 'Just go on, cross this ditch,' she suddenly heard Luckje whisper in her ear. ' Cross here and continue your walk, because you are close now to a little house. A warm and cosy place where dwarfs like to dwell. They will help you. God bless you, Mickje, I wish you Godspeed. I know you will take good care of Marg.' And again Luckje vanished. Mickje did as Luckje had told her, crossed the ravine-like ditch and continued to walk straight ahead. Indeed, she soon came to the little house Luckje had talked about. There was a staircase running up to a door, which was ajar. Slowly, because she was exhausted by now and nearly starving, Mickje climbed the steps and went inside where she soon found a warm spot under a mishmash of disused objects. This became her new 'base' from which she would organise her daily excursions for food and drink. But food was hard to come by, except for a mouse now and then. She was still too weak to use her hunting skills properly, and besides, mean John's kick still hurt, especially when she moved fast. Still, she felt less afraid now.

She sensed the presence of someone watching over her like a guardian angel.

One freezing cold winter morning she heard footsteps coming up the stairs and quickly she hid herself. Silently and full of fear again she waited. Nothing happened except that suddenly the door was closed with a loud bang. Locked in again! Fortunately, her prison was warm and cosy this time, but there was no leaking water-tap to quench her thirst either! After one day of imprisonment she nearly went mad with thirst. She licked the windows where some water vapour had condensed, but that hardly helped. That night Luckje appeared. 'Dear Mickje, tomorrow everything will be all right. Marg is sleeping now and I will appear in her dreams and give her the message to visit this place tomorrow. Believe me, she'll know that you are here and she'll take you in her heart without any hesitation. Just trust me!'

And that's exactly what happened. Next day, Mickje heard a voice coming up the stairs. The door was opened and Marg with Donsje on her shoulder entered the house. 'Say, Donsje, do you have any idea why I suddenly had to come here this morning?' Marg asked her companion. Then complete silence. Did she sense something? 'There is someone here, Donsje.' Mickje heard Marg whisper. Mickje couldn't prevent a mew of fear escaping her clenched jaws. Or was it a mew of desperate hope and survival because she was badly in need of something to drink? It was more a sigh than a real cat's mew but Marg and Donsje had heard it. 'Did you hear that, Donsje dear? I thought so, there must be a pussycat living here. Oh dear, she must be very thirsty, locked in as she is! Well we'll solve that in a jiffy, won't we, Donsje?' 'Mieeuw', Donsje answered, let's go quickly mummy, she is so thirsty and weak!' And the voices went away, closing the door behind them. But they were soon back bringing a bowl with something smelling like...Mickje couldn't believe her nose...'Milk! Could it be real warm tasty cat milk, like only cats know how to savour?' There, she saw Marg crouching, putting the bowl with the delicious liquid in front of her and then she heard her talking friendly and softly, yes, even mewing a disarming mew. 'The girl knows how to speak our language', Mickje thought. She started to feel relaxed. Slowly, very slowly she got up and moved in the direction whence came that irresistible aroma of real cat milk. Real comforting, life giving and reinforcing nourishment for a cat who had been without food for so long like Mickje had. And suddenly she was guzzling the milk down! My golly, how it tasted, there was no stopping her now! She finished it all and felt how the warmth and the strength was returning to her exhausted body.

And Marg let her be, just encouraged her with friendly words and nerve-relaxing mews. When Mickje was through with the milk, she saw a dish of chicken-meat appear. 'You take your time and enjoy yourself, I'll be back later, dear little pussycat' Mickje heard Marg tell her while leaving.

She helped herself to the juicy bits of chicken and then curled up for a relaxed after-dinner nap. Yes, Luckje was right! And indeed, Marg came every day more than once to see how the visitor was doing. Mickje slowly lost her distrust and at a given moment found herself in Marg's arms. 'Oh, poor dear, what are you doing here? What happened to you? You're so thin!' Mickje pressed herself to Marg's body in reply to these questions from her new friend. She thought of her mama Mijntje. Where would that dear old lady be now? Would she still remember her Mickje? For a moment she felt utterly desolate again. Marg caressed her and felt the bruise on Mickje's belly. The souvenir from mean John, the result of the parting kick he had given her. Marg shuddered: 'Dear girl, what is that?' She put Mickje down and went to fetch something. A kind of box, a cat-carrier in which she put Mickje. Mickje suddenly felt afraid again. She sensed another betrayal. To her boxes meant hurt and sorrow. But her panic didn't last long. Luckje had told her that everything would be all right, so why worry? She sensed him near her.

That night, while nicely stowed away in a cosy room upstairs, Mickje listened to Marg's reassuring explanation why she had to take her to a veterinarian: 'We have to check that swelling on your belly, dear, it's for your own good! I guess you got a bad kick, girl, but that kick brought you to me, so I kick the 'k' from 'kick' and replace it by the 'm' from 'me', and that will be your name, Mickje. Yes, that's how I will call you. Nice name, isn't it?' How did Marg know about the kick from mean John? How did she guess her name? Luckje, of course, Luckje must have told her!

So, next morning, Mickje was taken in a motorised 'thing' to another house and there placed on a table. There were two other women with Marg and also a cute cat with little 'feathers' in its ears and long grey hair. A Norwegian Forest Cat, Marg told her later. He watched her kindly and with confidence, closing his eyes now and then like cats do when they meet each, other to say: 'I am O.K, you are O.K. and everything is fine.' Mickje felt at ease. Suddenly she got a little prick and then all went black. When she woke up she felt very lousy. Marg sat next to her and softly stroked her fur. 'It is over now, Mickje, everything is all right. Time now to meet your new friends, Puddie and Donsje. You are one of us now!'

25

From then on things worked out all right for Mickje and she felt very happy. Of course, like in every family, she had to quarrel once in a while to defend her little spot in the house. In the beginning Puddie and Donsje would spit when she came too near, but in the end they became friends. Marg was so happy with her newfound friend. Many times she was amazed at the behaviour of Mickje which was very much like Luckje's. 'Mickje dear, that's exactly how Luckje would react, how come you know his ways?' 'Well Marg, 'Mickje would then think, 'we cats know a lot about each other. We know how to communicate even if we don't use the wordy contraptions you human beings seem not to be able to do without.' That's how I learned Luckje's style of cuddling. But one thing was always on Mickje's mind: 'If only I could tell mama Mijntje that I have found a new friend and a new home.

That I am so happy!'

So one night – those things always happen during the night when our subconscious becomes active and guides us - Luckje appeared again. He beamed with joy, because he felt that his beloved friend Marg's grief about his sudden departure had lessened since Mickje had come in her life. He gave Mickje some licks on her little head out of gratefulness. 'Now, Mickje, don't you worry any more about your mama Mijntje. The Lord has taken her off this world. She is now on the Rainbow Bridge and knows everything that happened to you and she knows too where you are. She is very happy amidst all the cats she has taken care of in her life and which went to the Rainbow Bridge before her. As soon as she is rested, she will visit you herself, but now she can't as she is still adjusting to her new surroundings.' And then Luckje took a huge leap and was gone again. Mickje sighed with happiness. So, everything was all right now! Thanks to that beautiful black-and-white he-cat, her guardian angel Luckje!

But Mickje is not the only one to have nice dreams. Puddie, Donsje and I also have them. We picture ourselves a home for the elderly. It is standing in beautiful surroundings. We see many small rooms with large windows behind which are sitting happy old people each in the company of a cat. The whole building radiates warmth and security. Arrangements have been made, fixed by contracts, as to who will take care of the pets when their old friends are ill or can't look after them for some reason. There is a veterinarian who has a contract with the home and regularly calls to check the health of the cats or can be relied on to come at once in case he is needed. There are volunteers who love animals in the service of the home. They have been professionally trained to look after the pets and to clean the cat's boxes when the old people cannot do that. The health of the home's occupants is conspicuously good. 'A miracle!', the scientists say. 'How could it be, could it be thanks to the...?' It is really a happy home, not at all one of these 'storage-spaces' where people 'dump' their parents, when they want to get rid of them. The old people have lively conversations about their pets. There are even competitions to select the 'kindest cat of the home'. There is some kind of magazine in which the occupants publish their 'cat-stories'. A dream? Not really. In many homes in Holland this dream is reality. Thanks to the enormous dedication of the LSOH, a foundation managed by Hans and Corry Bergman who dedicate themselves to older people and their pets. Not a dream any more for some 'homes'. But here in Belgium? Still a vision for the future, but it will also here become reality. That is our dream!

'Like those great sphinxes lounging through eternity in noble attitudes upon the desert Sand, they gaze incuriously at nothing, calm and wise.'

Charles the Baudelaire 1821-1867

Chapter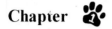

A sad Spring

What a greater gift than the love of a cat...

Charles Dickens (1812-1870)

March 1999

In my diary I had noted at Christmas 1998 that I feared mama would not be among us very much longer. 'I anticipate her crossing to the next world in March. Maybe on daddy's crossing day?', I wrote. And exactly on March 18, 1999 - the day of my father's death nine years before - my mother quietly passed away. She had just turned ninety; we had celebrated her birthday in February. A day of gold full of sun, cosiness, cheerfulness and lots and lots of flowers. Her room was completely filled with flowers. Puddie and Donsje had their joy trying to rearrange them! Mama beamed with joy and I cherish the pictures of her on that day. After that day she quickly went from bad to worse.

I am so happy mama could stay at home in peace and quiet where we could take care of her. Mariette, Emmy, Rik, Doctor Jef who treated her so well, dear Marc my close pharmacist-friend and Sister Lea, they were always available for mama and me. With infinite love and patience they tried to make mama's last days as comfortable as possible. I am profoundly grateful to them! It must be terrible to cross over to your next life alone, in a cold clinic, without the people and the animals that are very dear to you.

Mama slept most of the time during her last weeks. In fact she had lapsed into a kind of coma. She was far, far away. Kirby, her cherished little dog, never left her. She knew, of course, just like Puddie and Donsje knew. Although mama didn't seem awake, she felt it when I put Kirby on the bed. I saw her face beginning to shine and relax when Kirby nestled herself close to her.
Mama did not suffer much and if she had pain I was allowed to give her morphine which was very effective. Such a medicine really is a blessing!

Mama and I had talked much about the hereafter. She was not afraid of crossing. Yet, the nights were rather terrible. She was very restless then. I had fixed an intercom connection to my room, so I could always hear her, but I tried to be at her side as much as possible. After three sleepless nights I was so exhausted that I fainted in the kitchen with the result that I had two shiny black eyes and several cuts and bruises. I scrambled to my feet and wanted only one thing: to go to my secure den, to Puddie, Donsje and Mickje. When I reached my bed and fell down on it, Puddie and Donsje shouted: 'There you are, we told you this was going to happen! Come, let us take care of you, purr purr.'

And take care of me they did! They crawled on top of me and purred and licked the blood on my face away. So lovely and, oh, so comforting and calming. After half an hour I was able to go back to mama. But I did get assistance for the following nights. Raymonde, my dear friend from France, arrived a couple of days before mama died. It was a very moving moment when Raymonde came into the room and softly said: 'Bonjour Madame, ici Raymonde' (Good day, Madame, Raymonde is here). Mama awoke from her near-coma, smiled intensely and answered: 'Bonjour Raymonde, comme je suis contente que tu es venue, merci, merci!' (Good day, Raymonde, I am so happy you have come, thank you, thank you.) Mama had immediately recognised Raymonde and spoke French! Indeed, mama was very happy she had come. Mostly for my sake.

How tremendously my fluffies have supported me! Puddie understood and knew everything. I could see in Puddie's eyes mama's condition. Now and then Puddie checked up on mama and returned to me, his big green eyes full of worry. 'Grandma is not well, is she?', was his comment. We both knew it, the end was near. On March 18, early in the morning, mama quietly passed away, while Raymonde was at her side. I know for sure that papa and her father together with her most cherished dogs Ferntje and little Peter, were waiting for her. Her crossing on papa's day of dying was a clear message to me that from now on it was papa who would take care of mama again. 'Child', I heard him say, 'now I will look after your mother, don't worry, she will be happy! That's why she died on my dying day. That's the sign!'

The morning of the funeral I got into the car. When I started the engine, the radio said: 'Ici Radio Bleu!' This was mama's favourite radio station, to which she used to listen every morning. I always had my breakfast with her and we both enjoyed listening to those nice old-fashioned French chansons. I always tune in to Radio Two, and my car radio was programmed accordingly. So, this was again a clear message from mama. 'Be strong today, my child, I really am still with you!' The funeral was very beautiful and serene and the presence of Maria and Gé was a big support to me. They had come from far-away Huissen in the Netherlands. Indeed, Maria is a true sister to me! In such moments you realize the importance of friends, real friends!

The next weeks were of course very difficult. There were also lots of things to be arranged. I felt immensely grateful for all the help I received then. Slowly we resumed our routines. Spring came, flowers and young birds. Yes, life and death, they are inseparable. Yet, it is true what that beautiful poem says:

'You are not gone, you who in my heart still lives.
 It is the silence around here that me sorrow gives.'

And indeed it was silent around me, very silent, even though for a long time I still heard the ring of mama's bell. Of course, mama was not "dead" in the sense we usually give to that word: no more here, gone forever. Yes, her body was gone but mama herself, her spirit had just moved to another place: the hereafter. There she has been received with love. There she is being cared for until she is rested and used to her new life. I knew that for a fact, and that made me happy. Yet I missed my dear mother and longed to take her once again in my arms, hug her and tell her: 'Mama, I love you.' The smile I received then! But after a few weeks I felt her presence around me. Especially when playing the piano. Now she regularly visits me. I feel her presence, even stronger than when she was still physically here. She was too tired then and heard almost nothing. Now she is young again and 'Holland's most beautiful girl' as papa used to say with pride. I can see her playing the piano on top of a little cloud. Her little dogs frolicking around her and papa enjoying her music. She was at the Academy of Music but had not had the opportunity to continue playing her beloved piano. It had caused her a lot of sorrow, but that's how it was in the old days. The husband led and the woman had to follow. Marriage for a woman meant giving up her ambitions. Yet mama was a virtuoso on the piano.

Springtime!

The best way to come to terms with grief is to work hard. Fortunately I had a lot of work to do. I had to prepare the glasshouse for the new season. Vegetables had to be sown and planted. I always enjoy this job. Only, I still suffered pain from that sudden fall. Later, after I had X-rays taken, it was found that some bones had been fractured. 'What about Velpon-glue?' Donsje suggested when I came home. Good suggestion! But the bones had repaired themselves. There you see, don't rush too soon to the clinic; nature often is the best healer! Besides, pain releases endorphins, the body's own morphine. Things just don't happen without a reason. So I was a bit sedated and didn't feel the pain of mama's crossing over too much.

I decided, together with Puddie, Donsje and Mickje to transform our living room into a real 'Cat room'. I had mama's newly bought waterbed moved to my room. My bed was worn and torn because Puddie had used it as a scratching post. The new bed could not serve for that. 'Oh mama', cried Donsje elated, ' how nice, now we have space for the climbing pole.' How stupid of me to forget our travel-happy climbing pole! An acquaintance of me had sold it to me for a low price. A splendid thing, really big and high. So big and high that I could find no place for it then. I gave the pole to my friend Jerrie, but it was too high for her place as well. So it moved to Jerrie's neighbour, a woman also fond of cats. But she put the poor pole in her loft. When I heard that, I got it back. This climbing pole travelled quite some kilometres!

Quickly we set it up and what a splendid sight it was! Mickje especially, who prefers watching the world from above, is always lying on it. I also put some scratching posts and lots of baskets, balls and toy-mice in the room. A real garden-of-Eden for feline fellows! Now I didn't feel sad any more when entering the living room to play the piano. How some re-arranging can make a lot of difference!

The weather was not nice but in between the showers we did enjoy the run. Puddie and I went to see our friend Erik, the 'tree-doctor' to select trunks with 'feline-friendly' rough bark. Trunks of about one metre high, with a diameter of also about one metre. Delightful to sit on. I had three longer trunks positioned at an angle against the wall and I fixed them securely with wire so that they could not slide. The fluffies found it terrific. Much nicer than the climbing pole inside. They fly up and down one trunk, then up and down the second one, which stands a bit further away. Fun and fun again! The rough bark is ideal for sharpening their claws. I also planted catnip in some stand-up ends of drainpipes. How my fluffies love lying in them!

Fortunately Puddie and Donsje have now fully accepted Mickje's presence. Sure, Puddie, once in a while will still swear at Mickje if she comes too close, but that's only his way of telling that he prefers to keep distance. He has had some unpleasant experiences when he was a kitten and so he will always have this nervousness when others are around. He had to leave his mother much too soon, he was only five weeks old. Yet I had no choice. Either I took him then or he risked an accident. The kittens were in a garage where my friend Rudi's son and his friends were trying out motorbikes. Noise and oil all around. Besides, Rudi's wife wanted the kittens gone. Oh, what a cute little ball of love and warmth he was when he cuddled up to me. We were inseparable and we still are. Yes, Puddie is very special to me and he is my 'firstborn'!

In the first years it was just the two of us. When Luckje strayed in, Puddie got some thrashings. Not the way to get to like other cats. Those attacks have terrified him, but slowly he regains confidence. Donsje is a great help in that, so tender and cute. Puddie's fear shows in his wanting to be the boss and his habit of reminding the others, like a strict pasha, that there is only one boss now and forever and that's Puddie! That's why he regularly has to chase Donsje and Mickje away. Mickje has a super thick fur coat and she is almost as tall as Puddie. But Donsje's fur is soft and silky and she is only half Puddie's size. Therefore I must prevent him "over-teasing" her.

32

How nice to see how the three fluffies secure their place. They really try out how far they can go. Yes, Puddie teases Donsje, but she usually doesn't mind too much. When she can't bear it any more she'll fly to 'mama' and lies on my shoulders, just like a small grey fur scarf. Anyway my shoulders are her favourite spot. When I'm cooking she always lies there, probably much to Mickje's annoyance. She has at last found her mama and for keeps!!! I've never met a pussycat as thin and dehydrated as Mickje was. I watched her trying to catch a little mouse in the heather garden, but when she jumped she fell from weakness. The first days she was here she ate everything she could lay her paws on. A full box of breadcrumbs vanished in a couple of minutes. A slice of bread disappeared without a trace. I couldn't blame her, she was really starving. I can't help thinking of Mickje as an ex-ano patient. Ex-anorexics have often been starving for so many years that when, at last, they have mastered their fear to eat they exaggerate, overeat and get bulimia. (That's why it is very important to get the assistance of a dietician when you are about to take the life-saving decision to eat).

No news from Luckje, my handsome black and white desperado. Luckje strayed into my life on my father's birthday, August 6 1997. A time in which I had to confront aggression and anger. I am sure he came because of those tense days. He was like a little sun chasing dark thunderhead clouds. And he did! Luckje was very special. A super cuddlable street tough, but always good-tempered. Full of adventure stories. He only had to see me and he started some street yarn. So nice! Puddie and I had noticed his presence in the garden before, but we thought he lived somewhere in the neighbourhood. After a while Luckje allowed me to cuddle him. That's when I felt that he was much thinner than I'd expected. He had a rather thick fur. I was delighted of course that this cute desperado wanted to stay, but there was one condition: Puddie and he had to come to terms. Much to my regret they didn't. I don't know who is to blame, but from day one those two hated each other. Maybe Luckje wanted me all for himself? True, he was a stray used to fighting for his survival. Puddie became tense and nearly ill from stress. I consulted Maria and we decided to give Luckje his freedom again. I have a large garden and it's relatively quiet around here, but nowadays it is too dangerous to let your cats roam around free. He had a heated little house for himself and yes, he loved to be free again.

At the end of September 1998 Luckje suddenly vanished. Never, never do I want to experience that again. There is nothing worse than the uncertainty of

33

not knowing what happened to your pussy-child. I have tried everything and more to find him. Even now I hope that some day he'll be back here. It does happen that years later, cats come back! I have consulted some friends who are mediums. Both told me the same thing: 'Luckje is alive and happy. He is a born roamer cat. He is like a sailor who can't live without the sea. Now and then he will go ashore for a while, but in the end the call of the sea makes him restless again and then he just has to move on.' Miguella from Sittard, the daughter of my dear friend Jos said after studying a picture of Luckje: 'Luckje came to you on one of his wanderings. He looks for adventure and his extreme charming character ensures that all people receive him with love and warmth. People consider it an honour if Luckje will stay with them. Luckje will always be all right. Maybe he'll come back to you, maybe not, but one fact is sure: he is happy!' I have to, want to believe that now! Well, let's be honest: Luckje warned me. He removed his collar twice in the week before he left. The first time I found his collar in front of my house. Just to be sure, I put a new collar around his neck; the other one was probably too old. A couple of days later I noticed he was not wearing it any more. One hour later he was gone. Of course I didn't want to realise it, but his message was loud and clear: 'Mama, I am very sorry but my time has come. I have to move on. Don't cry for me, don't be sad. It's my nature, an urge I have to follow. But don't you ever forget it, you are in my heart and I take you with me. And I know I will always be in your heart too.' 'Yes, Luckje, so be it! You will always be in my heart.'

The first time I saw Mickje in the garden I thought: 'There you are, Luckje has sent a friend to me because he knows how much I miss him.' I still believe that. Indeed, Mickje has the same 'cuddlability' as Luckje! She hides her cute little head in my neck just like Luckje. She rubs her head so hard against mine that my nose turns blue. She chats all day long. You can almost call it singing, with lots of beautiful rollers, a sign of affection. When she sees me she flies in my arms. In short, she does exactly the same things Luckje did. Because Luckje taught her! I am so sure!

In a few more days Puddie, Donsje and Mickje will be able to bask and play in their own herb garden. You can bet that their mama will be close by. We all long for the sun.

What about Donsje? As I wrote in 'Miracles on little Feet', Donsje is a very special pussycat, indeed!!! We have a very strong bond. Oh, how I love her!

She is so lovely and tender. I think that's why the others tease her so much. It has nothing to do with love. All three fluffies are equally dear to me, but Donsje has some super lovability that is almost unbelievable. In the morning she accompanies me alone to the office now. Puddie and Mickje remain in the living room, where Mickje also wanted to sleep at night. She likes her rest, she says. There is also a run for them there and they are close buddies now. They even play together. It's fun to watch them, I enjoy it tremendously. So Donsje has peace and quiet. Outside office hours, we are all together of course.

Since Donsje is alone with me in the office she, has changed completely. Before, she used to sit outside in the run but now she sits on a nice soft cushion in the drawer of my desk. When she thinks I am working too hard – which is mostly the case according to her - she grips my shoulder and nestles her body against my arm, her diesel engine purring in fourth gear. If I don't kiss or cuddle at once, she will take firmer action. She rubs her little head against my cheek, gives me licks and rubs her paw over my face. Sometimes she softly bites my nose, 'Whiiieww whiieww, oh, nice isn't it, mama, just the two of us here, purr purr'! I would like to record this on film. It is so cute. Of course, she then gets some tasty titbits and lots of cuddles. In the beginning of our walk through the garden, she usually sits on my shoulder, purring and rubbing her head against mine. That's why she became a star. During the Television recordings for 'Miracles on little Feet' and during the interviews for our book, she really was the centre of attraction, always on my shoulder, always in the spotlight. Indeed, she is now an FFF, a Fabulous Flemish Feline.
Yes, she is a Poezenbel pussy! Indeed, Maria really adds love to the milk she feeds her kittens. A secret recipe, because love can't be bought. And luckily so. Besides, Puddie was calm towards Donsje during the weeks mama was so ill. Very peculiar. Yes, our cats do know so much more than most people think. Puddie sensed that it was not the time to make trouble.

But now it's spring and then he gets the heebie-jeebies. Fortunately this only lasts a few weeks and then it's over. The skin on his back quivers like the skin of a horse does when there is a fly sitting on it. Puddie then will look with fright to that spot, rush off and start biting himself. We racked our brains to find the cause. Allergy to
fleas? But I give my fluffies Frontline monthly. I never miss. Nervous twitches? Hormones? The veterinarian doesn't know either.

Our cats have their own pen club: The Feline Scribes Club FSC for short. Members are: Asselijntje, Puddie's fiancée - when our children were still small Maria and I decided that they should become engaged – The BEE's, the cats living with Nick and Noush, my two Rotterdam friends. Tedje who lives with Chantal and Ron. Then there is Tomcat Stapper who wrote the beautiful poem: 'Not Ideal' in 'Miracles'. ('I have the most fantastic mama, only...she never licks me!') And there is Tomcat Slaapmuts, but he is rather a 'sleeping' member. Meaning he will receive letters but never replies. Simply because he lacks the time to reply, in view of his many activities for 'de kat z'n viool',

Anne Versteyne's shop in Zwolle. Beautiful cat-paintings, cards and other 'pussy' things are on sale there. Anne has made the lovely drawings for 'Purring Angels' as well. I am very grateful to her. Her address is in chapter 21, addresses.

The following nice poem is by Tomcat Stapper:

LITTER TRAY

When my Mom has cleaned my litter tray,
She always calls:" Stapper, your tray is clean!"
Then I open my eyes carefully
While my Mom is waiting patiently
And I arise slowly from the chair where I am lying.
While my Mom is waiting patiently
I walk, at ease, in the direction of my tray.
While my Mom is waiting patiently
On my way, I have a nice long stretch
While my Mom is waiting patiently
Then I step in my tray with dignity
While my Mom is waiting patiently
There I dig extensively until I have a deep hole
While my Mom is waiting patiently
Finally, I squat cautiously and do what is necessary
While my Mom is waiting patiently
After that, I bury my performance carefully

While my Mom is waiting patiently
And I declare the session ended.
Then my Mom removes my superfluous
From the tray
While I am waiting patiently
Then she says: "You are a good boy!
And so it is..

© *Stapper (Stapper is the Dutch name for Strider, nickname for Aragorn, used*
by the hobbits in Tolkiens 'The Lord of the Rings')

Out of despair Puddie wrote a letter to his friend Stapper. Although Stapper looks like Luckje - Stapper also is black and white - he is Puddie's pen friend.

Dear Stapper,

Do you also get that? Ehhh, ladies: don't tire your eyes on this, nothing interesting for you, please! (I bet my evening's meal, Stap, that the ladies will read this now with even more attention!). Ok, let's discuss this from man to man. It's the same whenever spring comes: I get the heebie-jeebies. I quiver and I twitch! I want something but I can't do anything about it, because I miss something. You get it? I get tense, testy, and itchy. Yep, I frankly admit that I take it out on Donsje. I know it's not fair but I just can't control it, sometimes I am so tense I just have to chase her. What shall I do about it? It sounds very stupid but that's how it is. Of course Donsje gets the shivers from my 'antics'. She starts swearing at me, flies away, but her reaction makes me even wilder. I must catch her! She climbs to the top of the cabinet where I can't reach her. My body is then very nervous and my tail fluffs out. It is worse when Donsje rushes to mama, jumps triumphantly on her shoulder and challenges me: 'Mieeuweee, what are you waiting for, come and get me, I am here!' Then Mama gets sad and scolds me. That's the worst thing for me, 'cause I love her so much. Strange though, Mickje does not make me behave so out-of-orderly. Maybe 'cause Mickje's doesn't dash off so funnily like dear Donsje? Yesterday it was too much. I followed Donsje even when she jumped onto the little wall outside and

37

I caught her. Mama was frightened when she noted my anger. Donsje was all right, only very scared.

Afterwards, I felt very confused, of course. I regretted my behaviour very much. I didn't know what to do to make amends. My punishment was that I had to stay alone in the bedroom for one hour while Mickje and Donsje went to the office with mama and got some delicious milk. I cried softly: 'Mama, mama, I didn't mean to be bad. Please, don't be angry. I will not do it again, really. I don't understand what happened to me.' Luckily Marg heard it and we had a serious talk. 'My dear Puddie, she said, 'you can't behave like this. Donsje and you are the best of friends and all of a sudden you act like crazy. Why, what's the matter with you? But I guess it's something you can't do much about. It's something that sometimes just gets in males like you. Luckily Donsje doesn't mind too much. She just flies away and waits somewhere out of your reach till you have calmed down. But I do mind. Last year around springtime you also acted like this. I gave you Bach flower remedies then and that helped. So, I'll give you that medicine again so that you'll calm down and feel better.'
'I do hope so, mama,' I softly replied while two tears ran over my cheeks. 'All I want is to be lovely and companionable to you. I hate it when you are angry with me. Please don't be mad at me any more, I sincerely apologise!' Quickly I shoved my head under her arm and purred. I was so shocked that I promised myself once and for all to count till ten before acting like that again. And you know... I can count very well. Mama was glad, she said: 'Puddie, I missed you during that hour as much as you missed me. You see, I had to let you calm down first and think about what you had done. But now everything is forgotten.' Oh, how happy I was. I could not stop purring. Do you have that kind of problems too Stapper, in the spring?

Lots and lots of prrrreetings from your friend
Puddie.'

So far Puddie's letter. But it is indeed not nice for Donsje. Therapy with Bach flower remedies is good. I use it myself as well and it works! I heard there was a course in June in the Information Centre 'De Walnut' right here in Brasschaat. I decided to follow it. The teacher, Jef Strubbe was fantastic. I found it so interesting that I followed the next course in September as well. I regret that the course deals only with the treatment of human beings, but I bought some books about Bach flower therapy for animals. There is not much difference anyway.

The Most important thing is to transform yourself mentally into a cat and then try to see through 'their' eyes, hear through 'their' ears and feel 'their' feelings. For me, being half a cat already, that is not difficult!

At the end of this book you will find a bibliography with books about that subject. I will also include a chapter on Bach flower remedies that Carina Smeets, a homeopathic veterinarian and a close friend of Maria and me, wrote for me.

Sometimes he sits at your feet looking into your face with an expression so gentle and caressing that the depth of his gaze startles you. Who can believe that there is no soul behind those luminous eyes!

Theophile Gautier

Chapter 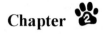 2

Little Princess

How you behave toward cats here below, determines your status in heaven.

Robert Heinlein

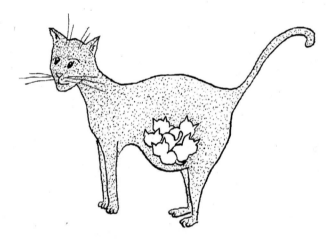

Whit Sunday, May 23, 1999

It is still very early on Whit Sunday of the year 1999. Little Princess, in the last days of her pregnancy, walks around restlessly. She feels something...she seeks something...she is not sure what, but she is afraid. For a couple of years she has been living, together with many other stray cats, in an industrial park in Spijkenisse. There is a hotel nearby and so it's not too hard to find something to eat. Yet the place has its dangers. It's close to an exit of the busy motorway to Rotterdam. That road is jammed from morning till evening with noisy, impatient and frustrated motorists. Not so long ago the road was relatively safe outside the rush hours, but now the hotel is expanding. A couple of days ago heavy equipment came rolling in and foundations were laid. The strays were terrified. Some moved on. A wise decision since the actual construction is scheduled to start after the weekend.

Little Princess, that's the nickname the other strays teased her with, did not know what to do. She sensed it was high time to find a quiet place to deliver her kittens, but where? And where had everybody gone? She got the nickname Little Princess because she felt herself better than the other strays. Her grandmother had been a real Siamese princess. And, indeed, Little Princess looked very Oriental, she had lovely long legs and a beautiful little face. She thought about the days when things were quiet and easy and she and her lover had a thrilling time. Yes, she was indeed loved by the male strays when she was on heat. They turned and turned around her and fought for her. Seemingly unimpressed she sat down and watched this 'tomcat foolery', meanwhile deliberating on the lover she'd select. 'What a lot of nonsense,' she observed silently, but nature called.

In the end only two big macho cats remained. Furiously growling and snarling, they circled each other. Soon the moment of reckoning would come. She didn't have any feeling for these boorish lovers. Suddenly she noticed a small tomcat behind the two rivals. He was smaller in size but had beautiful black-and-white fur. "There, someone who has manners", Little Princess suddenly thought and she felt tickles in her belly. She looked again. He blinked at her! Bingo! Together they vanished into the night. It was beautiful, very beautiful. He was kind and tender. She wondered where he would be at this moment. Moved on like the others? She felt very lonely and vulnerable.

But her babies wanted to get into the world and they wanted to come **now**! Fortunately it was the weekend and so all was quiet. Quickly Little Princess disappeared into the bushes close to the hotel. She scratched a hole in the ground and lay down. It was her third litter, so she knew what was going to happen. Without too much difficulty her kittens were born. Little Princess bit the navel cords through and licked the kitties clean. She ate the placenta - excellent proteins for a cat-mother and good for the milk yield - and purred her kittens to her milk sources.

Relieved, she took a nap. Maybe everything would be all right? A couple of hours later a walker and his dog passed. She was startled and ran away. Fortunately the dog followed her, away from her kittens. Of course that had been her intention, but the dog did not give up and chased her very far away.

When she had at last got rid of him and was on her way back to her babies, she noticed more walkers coming her way. She decided that she had better wait till this 'traffic' stopped. 'Tonight I'll find us a better place,' she promised herself.

Rob, the husband of Renate Leijen, the famous painter who makes beautiful paintings of cats, returned home from his job at five o' clock. He drove close to the spot where the kittens were crying helplessly for their mama. Rob used to go to the office in the weekend, when he could work there in peace and quiet. So also that Whit Sunday. He heard the kittens but could not see them. As soon as he arrived home he told Renate who immediately jumped in the car to go and find them.

Little Princess had just returned to her kittens when Renate arrived. Again Little Princess had to speed away, so Renate knew at once the location of the litter. Oh dear, she found five kittens on the cold ground. It looked like one had already died. Ants were crawling over its body and they even came out of its little mouth. That little kitten lay a bit away from the others.

Renate hesitated, what to do? Take the kittens home? What about the mother then? But how could they survive there, in an industrial park, close to a hotel under construction? Along a hectic motorway? And when the kittens grew up, how would they survive among all the heavy equipment in their territory? No, there was just no other alternative, she had to take them with her. Or…Renate called the animal ambulance on her mobile phone, asking for a cat trap to catch the mother so she could be neutered, and for shelter for the kittens. Renate was willing to pay the expenses. The reply made her sad, 'Lady, mind your own business, just leave those kittens alone! Now, the mother is gone and maybe for good. We'll go there in an hour and euthanase those kittens.' Renate got angry and asked again for a cat trap. 'No, Missus, we won't have anything to do with that. We don't know of anyone to take the kittens, and a cat trap? Why? To have the mother spayed? No, no way!' Was it for such 'service' that Renate had paid membership fees all those years???

Quickly she picked up the kittens and put them in the cat-carrier she brought along in her car. One kitten was ice-cold. Dead already? But she didn't want to leave it behind. She cleaned its mouth. Soil and dirt and some ants came out. Suddenly it seemed to gasp for air. It was alive! Renate called Rob, her husband, and asked him to prepare a tray with lukewarm water and some towels. While quickly driving home with one hand, she held the ice-cold kitten under her T-shirt against her warm body.

Having put the kittens in the lukewarm water, so they warmed up a bit, she laid them on a heated pillow and took them upstairs. There she fed them kitten colostrum so that their insides also warmed up. Quickly she ate some food and discussed with Rob what next to do. One of Renate's beautiful Norwegian Forest Cats, Wuppie, came to take a look at the kittens. Wuppie had had a litter of three herself a week before and would certainly not mind being a substitute mother, kind as she is. Now, would that not be an option?

Renate phoned Maria from the Poezenbel Foundation. Maria had only three kittens in her care and said immediately: 'Come here, don't put the foundlings with your healthy kittens'. Renate was startled. She had not thought about that. She, always so super careful, always concerned about disinfecting and cleaning. She even ordered everyone entering the house to wash their hands first when her kittens were present! She had completely forgotten to think about the fact that these little kittens could have some illness under their cute and soft fur. Rescuing them had wiped out all other considerations from her mind. Her feelings had taken control.

Around coffee-time she arrived at Maria's house. Everything was ready for the kittens. The smallest tomcat, the cold kitten, was still blue. Maria did not like it either. The kittens received their names. The girls were called Daimy, Daatje and Dotje, the boys Spikey (found at Spijkenisse) and Robbedoesje.

As Renate and Maria expected, Spikey very soon left for the Rainbow Bridge and a couple of days later Robbedoesje followed him. The three girls survived. Day and night Maria sat up with them and tube fed them. The kittens had diarrhoea as well and had to have fluid injections under their skin.

When Renate visited Maria after nine weeks she noticed immediately the enormous difference in weight and size of the kittens as compared to her own kittens at home. They weighed 500 grams now! 'What a difference in starting your life', she mused, driving back home. 'A cold damp spot on the ground under some bushes or a cosy, soft, flannel-lined basket! What a difference, a mother running away in terror or a mother having full confidence in her 'human mum'. What a difference!' But no difference in the amount of love

43

with which they are raised. They will grow into real cuddle-cats that will get a first class home. Thank God for people like Maria, how fortunate for these kittens that they exist!

Renate kept thinking about the poor mother. 'What right did I have to take her kittens away from her? Maybe she has kittens again? Did she miss them?' Yet, those kittens wouldn't have had a chance. Renate has returned more than once to the place where she found the kittens, but she has never met the mother cat again. She had borrowed a cat trap from Maria and Poezenbel would have paid the expenses for spaying, but it was no use. She had gone.

One year later, there was a campaign to capture all strays around the hotel and to bring them, of all places, to the animal shelter belonging to the ambulance that refused to help. That was equal to a one-way ticket to the Rainbow Bridge. Renate learned this from the lady who looked after the cats and saw to it that the strays were captured, neutered, wormed, vaccinated and chipped.

Thanks to the Lord, Little Princess was not one of them. She had been spotted, but our heroine had out-smarted them. She just moved on to a better place. Maybe she lives together with her lover again? It goes beyond saying that Renate cancelled her membership to the Animal Protection Society.

And so it was that Daimke appeared in our life.

The purity of a person's heart can be quickly measured by how he regards cats.

(Anonymous)

Chapter

Daimke, Daatje, Dotje

Confront a child, a puppy and a kitten with a sudden danger. The child will turn instinctively for assistance. The puppy will grovel in abject submission ... the kitten will brace its tiny body for a frantic resistance.
Saki.

When the kittens arrived at Maria's place, what a sight they were! So small and frail! Yes, they were hardly more than half a day old. Daimke weighed only 92 grams, Daatje 97 grams, Dotje 103 grams, Robbedoesje 80 grams and Spikey 103 grams. Maria had prepared everything for the arrival of the kittens and soon they slept snugly in a warm cradle. They were too weak to drink, so Maria tube fed them for the first two days and nights. They were real survivors though and on the third day they drank from the bottle. Still, Maria was worried about Robbedoesje, Spikey and Daimke. She has an infallible feeling for such matters.

Their bowels hardly functioned and they got terrible diarrhoea. On day nine, Maria found Robbedoesje dead in the cradle. Her premonition had warned her. Probably he had swallowed some amniotic fluid. It was also strange that his eyes were already open after four days, so that he contracted an eye-infection. The other four seemed to do well for a while, but Daimke didn't grow and Spikey got worse by the day. On June 8 he didn't want to drink any more and so Maria had to tube feed him again. Elly, Maria's friend who is a medium came over to magnetise him. For a while he drank again by himself but on June the fifteenth Maria had to let him go. The kitten was worn out. Very sad, but at least he was not suffering any more. Now he was on the Rainbow Bridge, together with Robbedoesje.

I feel a very close bond with Poezenbel, so Maria and I phoned or faxed each other every day. This litter touched me deeper than usual. Maybe because mama had crossed over to her next life so shortly before and I had to face death again?

Together with Daimke's birth an idea was born in my mind. Wouldn't it be nice for Donsje if she got a lovely friend to play with? Mickje and Puddie teased her mainly because of her 'funny' way of dashing off, but Donsje had no choice. Those 'bullies' were just too big and strong for her. What if Donsje had a friend? Two are stronger than one and Donsje would get more self-confidence. This idea kept on coming back. Just a small hunch that developed into a plan. If Daimke made it, could she not come to us? Oh, how I longed to make her happy! She had been through such hard times in her very short life so far. I wanted the rest of her life to be all happiness. Of course, that is impossible, but yes, we do have lots of fun here. The fluffies have spacious runs. We are outdoors whenever the weather is fine and I am always at home.

Deep down in my heart I knew that Daimke and I belonged together. I had only one little picture of her, a very blurred one at that. I always carried it with me. But...what about Puddie, Donsje and Mickje? How would they react? Well, that was a bridge to cross when I came to it. First things first! Daimke had to grow strong and healthy.

Daatje and Dotje did well. They drank their bottle obediently and gained weight. But Daimke, my dear Daimke, she suffered from a persistent diarrhoea and her bottom was all red and inflamed. Poor little kitty, my little elf, who had such a hard time. She had such a sad expression on her little face, as if she carried all the sufferings of the world and, who knows, probably she did. Oh, how Maria and Daimke fought for her life! Maria really is a fantastic woman! With unbelievable love and patience she often succeeds in saving 'given-up' kittens, but this time it was extraordinarily difficult.

Whatever Maria tried, Daimke's stools remained watery and thin. She even tried an intestinal cleanser, some Isogel-like medicine, but more powdery so it can easily be diluted and administered in the milk bottle. It gives some bulk to the stools and spreads a protective lining on the intestinal wall. Daimke fought and fought and certainly had no intention of giving up the battle, but when the body does not absorb any food, how can one grow big and strong?

More and more I longed for Daimke to come and live with us, once she was well. I could not postpone it any longer, I had to cross the bridge and ask my trio what they thought about my plan. Puddie had already experienced problems when Luckje had come into his cosy life here. Puddie is a real loner, just like his 'mother' and that's why I understand him so well. Now things were all right with Donsje and Mickje, what would happen when again another pussy-child joined the family? Could he handle that? How about Mickje, what would she say? Would she not feel abandoned again? And Donsje? Well, Donsje wouldn't mind at all. Donsje was Donsje. A little furry ball all made up of love and satisfaction. Was it fair to them? Of course, the fluffies already suspected that something was bothering their mama.

Puddie came to me with a serious face. 'Mama, do you have a moment? I want to talk to you.' 'Of course, my dear Puddie, for you I always have time. And I also have something very important to discuss with you three. What if you get Donsje and Mickje while I get something delicious to eat while we talk?' And so it happened that within a quarter of an hour the four of us were cosily sitting together in the run. The weather was fine for the first time in weeks. Wonderful!

'Mama, there is something. I sense that you are thinking and brooding about something for days now. And I guess I know what about too! ' Well, this did not surprise me at all; Puddie can read my mind as if it were an open book. 'Right, Puddie,' I said, 'You hit the nail on the head. OK, what would you three think about another pussy-girl joining us?' Mickje was startled, her tail grew very bristly. Donsje looked very surprised. Puddie said nothing, he just gave me a piercing look. 'Mama, I've overheard many of your conversations with those anorexia-girls you're helping so well, so, let me now ask you the question you always ask those girls: Why?'

I thought deeply about the 'Why'? The big advantage of our 'meetings' is that we hold them in feline style, meaning we insert long spells of silence and take our time to think things out. Why? Good question. 'I think it is a longing for a young living creature, a little pussy-child I can hug close to me and cuddle like a mother her baby. A little pussy-girl that I can teach and tell about everything. We've had so much grief and gloom around here this last winter: Luckje gone, Karma who went to the Rainbow Bridge and my mama who also crossed over to her new life. I do miss it a lot, the caring and being 'nice' to mama.' The fluffies looked at each other. I could hear them thinking: 'There you are, we thought so!' 'But mama,' Donsje softly said, 'what about us? We are there for you. We always hug and cuddle you, don't we? Are we not enough?' Mickje bowed her head; I saw a small tear run down her nose. 'Mickje, what would you say?' I asked, 'Wouldn't you like it to have a lovely little kitten to bring up just like you once brought up your own kittens?' Dr. Liliane had told us that Mickje had once had little ones. Sadly she replied: 'But then you are going to love me less than before and just now I need your love and attention so much! I've had so much sorrow and violence in my life. Now that I am here with you, I feel how I get calmer by the day and my self-confidence gets stronger. I really get confidence in your love and affection for me now. You know that I've been abandoned in my life before. Please don't stop loving me! Please!' She softly sobbed.

Puddie's eyes were sad and pensive. 'I don't think mama wants another child because the three of us are not enough for her. No, I know that mama loves us with heart and soul. But I know too that there is still more than enough room in her heart for a fourth fluffy and even more. But yes, I am afraid too and I don't like it. Still, I do understand mama very well. I sense her restlessness. Mama is still unsettled by the disappearance of grandma. I have heard that it's a part of the mourning process, even a very important and necessary part. But is it than the right moment to take such an important decision as the one we are discussing here? I doubt that very much.'

Yes, my little man had a point there. I also had strong doubts. Puddie resumed his argument. He would make an excellent lawyer. 'You hope and think that little Daimke, who Maria is bringing up so lovingly right now, will be the ideal friend for Donsje, Mickje and me. I can see you, in your dreams going everywhere with Daimke on the harness. You take her with you whenever you go car driving. She is not afraid at all. She likes taking rides in the car and she plays for hours and hours with the three of us. Donsje and she will become buddies in no time. OK, that's the positive side. Now, what if things won't work out that way? What if Daimke, just like Donsje, is afraid of visitors and won't like car driving? What if she won't like the harness? Donsje loves walking on a leash. She always returns delighted from her garden-walks. I don't like it any more myself. Yes, I know what you think: Then Daimke will stay cosily with you and Mickje. But what if we don't like her? I know very well you don't like the way we treat Donsje sometimes. We can't help it, it 's an "urge", which nature sometimes imposes on us. We don't mean any harm, but that's how we fluffies communicate. Agreed, sometimes we downright harass her. But mama,' proudly and happily Puddie looked at me, 'didn't you notice that we have had a truce for four days already? That there 's peace now without the least breath of a hiss? If we promise to try to stop teasing Donsje altogether won't you stop thinking about asking another Fluffie to come and live with us?'

I hugged them. 'Oh, guys, you don't know how happy I am because of your behaviour! How come there's peace?' 'Well Mum' Pudje said: 'It's you! Didn't you calm down and feel happier since last Sunday when we tried out those new Bach flower remedies? Remember? I sat next to you when we selected them. **You** have changed. All three of us have felt it and that makes us calmer as well. Otherwise Mickje and I would take our agitation out on Donsje, but now we feel relaxed so why should we do that?' Yes, the Bach flower therapy! I had forgotten it but now Puddie brought it back to my mind. I had selected Olive to rest and regain my inner balance. Oak, to allow myself to take some rest and recreation in time. I just hadn't been able to do that lately. Rockwater to tone down my obsessive adherence to schemes. And Star of Bethlehem for comfort and pain relief. There was an immediate positive reaction. I felt very relaxed and happy again.

How wonderful that the fluffies reacted at once and calmed down when I calmed down. And how great that they didn't quarrel any more. 'You know,' Puddie said, we are not so happy to welcome another little one, because we know that you'll have to attend to her most of the time. That we understand. She is still small and helpless. I've experienced it with Donsje and with Mickje. But I don't know if we can handle that situation. We need you too, you know. I know I am very special to you, but will Mickje be able to cope? And what about Donsje, who now accompanies you wherever you go. Will she still be able to do that? Otherwise she'll be sad.
And there is more. We were planning for this autumn, when the days are shortening and we have to be inside, to finish our book. How can you work on that when your mind and your heart are for a great part occupied by the new arrival?' And with a smart face he played his last trump. 'On your desk there are pictures of Sheelagh's lovely Traditional Siamese cats. I know that for years now, you have wanted such a cute applehead relative of mine. Well that's different because it is planned for in a couple of years, not now. Maybe, by that time we three will be on such good terms that we'd welcome a new playmate. But now Mama, it is too soon. Please could you wait?' With imploring looks, my trio watched me. So, what now? The fluffies had a point there, but their reaction was inspired by fear and fear is a bad counsellor. My intuition assured me that things would work out when Daimke came to live here. Of course, she and Donsje would become friends. Two super soft fluffies, it would click

immediately between them.

'OK, guys,' I said, 'I'll make an agreement with you. You know, next week I'm going to Maria. I will think deeply about everything you have said to me. I am glad that we can talk so openly and freely about this. Of course I want you all to agree. But I haven't seen Daimke yet, and Daimke hasn't met me. I don't know if she will love me as I love her already. But if I really still want her after having met her 'live', I trust you'll accept that. For I do indeed long very strongly for her. For a long time now I have this wish to form a clover with four fluffy leaves and I have a strong feeling that Daimke is the missing leaf.'

Mickje heaved a sigh of relief. 'So, you still love us very much!' Happily she jumped up and started rubbing her head against me. Puddie purred loudly. Yes, we really understand each other. I gave him a big hug. 'Thank you, my sweet guy, for your wise and nice advice. What if we two hadn't met?' Puddie agreed completely. And Donsje? Donsje jumped cheerfully on my lap and rubbed her soft front paws over my cheek. 'So I remain mama's dearest, nearest girl? Yippee, come Puddie, let's go for a run.' Merrily she bounced away. Yes, she is a very special pussy and my dear little girl. Oh, how I love her! And maybe, just a little maybe...

Next day we received wonderful news. I always know at once when there 's cat-mail among my letters. Puddie will sit on them! Yes, yippee, the promised pictures of Maria's kitties. The fluffies watched with interest while I opened the envelope. They sensed the importance? Oh, how nice! For the first time I saw a clear picture of Daimke. I melted like ice in the sun: what a cute head, what sweet eyes! So loving and sad. She looked a bit like Donsje. 'Look guys, this is Daimke. 'Full of attention they sniffed at the picture. 'Oh, how small,' Donsje said. Puddie looked at her and then he looked at the picture again. 'Yes, mama, now I can see how hard it is. Indeed, Daimke is a cutie. Well, I'd better tell you what we decided. You see, we did realise after our conversation that you were not really happy. We three talked things over again. And yes, it could be nice for us, to have another little sister. Especially for Donsje, because I do realise that we are not always very nice to her. Fortunately she doesn't mind.' Playfully, he gave her a shove. Donsje looked at the picture again. 'Gosh, mama, she really looks like me. Will she play with me? Would she be willing to play tag and hide-and-seek and hit-the-ball? Would she like me? Imagine the fun we will have on the new climbing pole. Both of us flying through the room and then swoosh swoosh to the top.' And she was gone. Pudje and I looked at each other full of surprise: What's going on here?

'Yes mama,' Donsje said when she returned, 'I too have thought very much about it and the more I think about it the more I like it. This morning I had to go with you in the car. I do enjoy being with you and the new car is not as terrifying as the old one. But, oh, I got it again! All of a sudden I was so afraid. I just can't help it. I will never forget that huge monstrous machine which destroyed our litter. The desperate cry of my first mother when she ran away and had to leave us behind. As a matter of fact, I will never really like cars. I suppose Daimke will get used to the car very quickly when you take her with you everywhere. She'll enjoy it and then I can stay at home.' Puddie nodded. 'Yes, indeed it's like that. I don't like to accompany mama in the car either. I don't mind the ride, but I hate waiting alone in the car.

I burst out laughing. Those fluffies of mine, so wise and so shrewdly sensing what I think and feel. Yes, I had had a feeling of loss and estrangement after the first conversation with my trio. A feeling of regret. I am still sorry I did not bring Madeliefje home with me last time I went to Maria. The little rescuee, who had only one eye. Sometimes you cannot afford not to take a risk, because that would be the biggest risk! I felt a ray of excitement and happiness passing through me. Maybe, just maybe, it would be possible? 'You know what we're going to do, guys? We are going to wait and see. This Saturday I'll go to see Daimke. The most important thing is that she will love me as well. She comes first. If Maria entrusts her to us, it is good, because my 'sister' would never do that if she had any doubts. So I can indeed look forward immensely to it.
As you know I received bad news yesterday, the result of my bone scan. It worries me a lot. Sure, I know now why I have pain, but that doesn't take it away. I cannot take longer walks than I am doing now. You know how I love and need to exercise. So, let us prepare for a cosy winter inside the house with five. In our big 'cat'-room we will have fun playing together and enjoy the fluffies'tree! Let us write our book and read it out aloud to Daimke? Oh boy, we'll tell her some stories!' Puddie's eyes started sparkling. He is fond of story telling. Meanwhile Mickje had joined us. 'Mama, do you really promise that you will still love me and cuddle me as much as you do now if Daimke lives with us?' 'And will I remain your dearest and nearest pussy-girl?' Donsje's voice had a mousy squeak from fear. Puddie and I looked at each other. 'Of course, guys, don't ever doubt it again. You are in my heart and I am in yours.

51

We belong to each other and we are there for each other. That will never change. I'm sure Daimke is very soft and sweet.' Puddie looked at Donsje. 'Girl, I have an inkling that you're going to have a little sister soon. Let's take a bet?' 'No way, boy! Donsje refused, 'I won't even think about it. I never bet when I know I will lose!' The four of us burst out laughing. Oh, if only it was Saturday!

Quickly I phoned Maria and asked her if Daimke could come to live with us. Of course she agreed wholeheartedly. Maria also had good news, for Daatje and Dotje were going to live with very nice people who live close to Maria. We could keep in touch with them. Great! Later Daimke and her sisters started writing letters to each other and Diny and Hans and Mariëlle have become fantastic friends of ours. We are bonded by the three sisters.

I wrote to Daimke:

Dear, dear Daimke of mine,

Oh, little girl, did you get the news? Maybe you will come and live with us. Would you like that? What do you think, would you be happy here with us? Tomorrow we'll see each other and we'll cuddle each other. I give you herewith lots of purrings from your brother Puddie, your big sister Mickje and little Donsje. I'm sure you'll get a strong bond with Donsje. She is very soft, fluffy and cute. That's no wonder because she too was saved by your mother and brought up with lots of love mixed with the milk. I'll tell you all about it later. Puddie is Asselijntje's fiancé. You can ask her anything you want to know about your brother-to-be. Mickje had a hard life before she came to me. She has experienced the shady side of human beings. I will do my utmost to prevent anything bad happening to you, because there are really cruel and mean people in this world.

But we are four to protect you. I am so proud of you that you are eating well now. Please continue eating well so that soon you will be big and strong, then you can come and live here. Maybe we can work out something on the sly so that you can come with me tomorrow. I might hide you in my waistcoat pocket. You can tell the other fluffies there that I'm bringing delicious chicken titbits. See you tomorrow. Oh, how I look forward to meeting you! Lots of love from Pudje, Mickje, Donsje and your Belgian mama, Marg.'

At last it was 'tomorrow'. How happy I was! Waiting lasts long and I was burning up with curiosity. Before leaving I gave my trio an extra cuddle. Puddie and Mickje were sitting cosily together in the living room. It's good they are there, so I could be sure that Donsje would not be attacked. She is completely relaxed and happy when we are together in the office. She doesn't like being alone of course, but at least she'll be left in peace. Sometimes Puddie comes to me at night and asks permission to go to 'his' room. 'In all peace and quiet together with Mickje, prr purrr,' he says then. A good idea maybe, but I'll miss him during the night. In the morning I always take him with me when I exercise on my home trainer. He and Mickje then fly through the room, enjoying each other's company.

It was a marvellous ride in my small jeep. What a difference from the Ford I had before. It was too much of a luxury car for me. This jeep was exactly the vehicle I had always wanted to have. Listening to beautiful cowboy-music and filled with feelings of freedom and expectation I drove to Huissen. When I entered Maria and Gé's house - suspecting nothing of the surprise reception - Daimke was there to welcome me, sitting snugly in the pocket of Maria's trousers. Fortunately I was standing with both feet firmly planted on the floor or I would have fallen like a stone for that moving little fluffy mass. How sweet were her little eyes! What a dear! She had put one little foot on the rim of the pocket and was watching me so lovingly.

At last! Never shall I forget the first time I held Daimke in my arms. That teensy-weensy fluffy curled herself up against me. She put her head in my neck and purred. Although very weak and ill, she purred and knew that we belonged to each other. Oh, what a pitiful sight she was! Her little face was dirty and her little bottom was red and inflamed. Maria cleaned her more than once daily but quickly she dirtied herself again. Still she tried to play with the others. Brave little girl!

But I was not the only one who had lost her heart. Daimke played with me and stayed on my lap all morning. We recorded it all on video, so that Puddie, Donsje and Mickje would be able to take part in our joy. Yes, they really watch videotapes. When I arrived home, many joy-filled hours later, Donsje embraced me and lay on my shoulder. 'Now, you stay here or if not, I am going with you!' So funny. She licked my face, put her little arms around me and purred. Puddie and Mickje were happy as well, of course, but Donsje was also very curious to know everything about her new little sister. Daimke had been resting in my camera bag. Donsje went in there to sniff and rubbed her head many times on that spot. A welcome?

'Now, mama, come on, tell us everything!' Even after I took a shower and changed clothes, they still smelt and pinpointed exactly where I had been and that it was a place full of fluffies. Moreover they could read my mind. 'Oh guys, she is so lovely, so fluffy, so small, so moving', I started my report. 'All small pussies are like that,' Mickje grumbled edgily. 'I have had kittens myself, you know, and they were also lovely.' 'Yes, but this little one is special, really special. She has something in her eyes that makes you feel terribly happy and protective towards her. Just believe me. When I arrived there I played for a long time with Daimke on the floor. She had a little toy-mouse. You also like to play with your toy-mouse, don't you Donsje? We had lots and lots of fun. I told her everything about you, and also I told her that she will become your special friend. You two look much alike anyway.' 'So, I am also very lovely, small and moving,' Donsje squeaked, glancing at Puddie. 'I love you three with all my heart, you three are movingly lovely and my sweet little pussy-children. Never think that I love Daimke more because I talk a lot about her. When she is here I will be attending to her very much in the beginning. I also gave you all the attention you needed when you were still small. You know, all babies need that attention, care and love. But you'll get my attention as well and you won't

54

lack anything. Besides, aren't we going to take care of her, the four of us?' The eyes of Donsje shone. ' Yes, it will actually be quite fun having a baby-fluffy around here. As long as she won't swear at me and be angry with me, you know I can't stand such behaviour. But you promised me, mama, she will play nicely with me?'

'I promise you that you are going to get the most tender, loveliest sister I could ever find for you. Aunt Maria also says so and she is (almost) always right.' 'When is she coming?' Puddie asked. 'I hope early August, maybe on the sixth. On the birthday of Papa, Donsje, Mickje and Asje.' 'Did you meet my sweet Asselijntje?' Puddie asked, (Puddie and Asselijntje are engaged) and he started to beam. 'Was she nice and did she stay much with you?' 'Yes, I have to give you her sweetest greetings; she insisted I told you especially. Sure she sat on my lap and we talked about you. She is so cute! But I spent most of my time on the floor, with Daimke on my lap, so Asje and I haven't seen so much of each other as we usually do.

If only you could come with me! It is so wonderful there in Aunt Maria's place. If you just could see how harmoniously her own sixteen fluffies live together with the rescuees, you wouldn't say that we are 'full house'.' Startled, Mickje looked up and Puddie frowned. 'No, don't worry, I promised you, for the time being it will be just the five of us. A fluffy four-leaf clover and its stalk, that makes five.' (Sometimes one makes promises one can't keep). 'You know what?' Puddie said with a pensive look, 'Let's be honest, we have known for a long time now that another fluffy was coming to join us. It was in the air and I think we may thank our lucky stars that Daimke is so sweet and small. My grandma used to say: 'Count your blessings and be happy with what you have.' She was right. Maybe we are the happiest fluffies in Belgium. A warm bed, good food, security, love, a run so that we can play outside and the dearest mama in the world.'

All three nodded happily. 'Right you are, Puddie, now let's count the days.' Donsje shoved her head against me and said dreamily:' A playmate, how nice!' With mischief in her eyes she suddenly challenged Mickje and Pudje, ' Together we'll be a good match for you two!' 'We'll see about that!' They replied and exchanged glances of connivance.'Well, let the young ones play, so that we can talk, philosophise and groom ourselves in peace.'

PLAYTIME:

Three yawning kittens at the start of the day,
are stretching long limbs, getting ready to play.
Almond-shaped eyes of deep sapphire blue,
peer sleepily from masks of varying hues.

Breakfast is over, and ablutions are done,
three naughty kittens are searching for fun.
An oval paw, the colour of heather,
prods warily at a dark-brown nose leather.

From under the table there suddenly appears
a triangle face, and triangle ears!
A rascal clad in velvety-blue,
climbs up the curtains for a better view!

Downstairs and upstairs the three race around,
on chairs and on tables, not touching the ground.
Jumping on beds, hiding under the covers,
then leaping right out and surprising the others.

Soon they are weary, their playing is done,
they head for their basket, placed in the warm sun.
Soft silken bodies, entwine in a heap,
and three worn out kittens fall fast asleep!

© Sue Wingett

Some weeks have passed. Wonderful weeks. To be 'expecting' is a fantastic feeling. But also weeks full of worries. I felt so powerless. There was nothing I could do to help Daimke and I was very worried. Her diarrhoea didn't stop. Every time I visited my dear fluffy girl I fell more in love with her and she with me. Oh yes, I am sure she received the thoughts and positive energy I sent to her. She came to cuddle me at once when she saw me.

I wrote to her:

'Dear, dear Daimke,

You have stolen my heart and now you ran off with it! How marvellously sweet it was to cuddle each other, to play and to talk! Oh, I have had such fun and I am so glad that you will come and live with us. You are really very special and a cute little miracle. Weren't you a bit frightened when the car did vroom-vroom? I can imagine you were. Cars are very dangerous things, but when you're inside you're safe.
Fourteen days more! Let's count them. I have received a beautiful toy for you: three little balls in a ring standing on a big ball, everything moves and keeps on moving. Donsje, Pudje, Mickje and I have played with it last night but now we'll put it aside until your arrival. May I ask you a favour for your sisters and brother? Do you have some toy or piece of cloth that smells very much of you? If you could send it to me, I will give it to them, so they will get familiar with your smell and you'll already be here in some way. Just ask mama Maria to sent it to us. That's still a bit too complicated for you, going to the post office and things like that. Of course only when Maria has time, because I know she is super busy now with the little farm cats which have just arrived.

Let's dream about each other and sleep soundly. Many close cuddles and kisses from Pudje, Donsje, Mickje and Marg.

PS Tasty, isn't it, chicken meat? You'll get much of that when you are here. Donsje is completely hooked on it.

Yes, I was so happy because Daimke had indeed grown and how nice she played. But her faeces were still thin and watery. If Maria gave her intestinal cleanser it was a bit better, but without it she had diarrhoea. As scheduled, Maria and Elly would bring her to us on August 6. Donsje's birthday. A nicer present was not possible! But the day after my visit to Daimke she had very watery faeces and of course she has to be vaccinated before coming to us. If she was not completely well, vaccination would not be possible. I tried not to show Maria how much I wanted her to be with me here, but of course, Maria and I are just like sisters, so she knew. It was also very hard for her. On the one hand she wanted very much to give Daimke to me as soon as possible, but on the other hand Daimke's health had priority and Maria wanted to spare me the grief should Daimke...but I didn't want to think about that.

And so Maria and I tried to spare each other.

Donsje and I were sitting and reading snugly together after dinner. That's always our 'happy hour'. She lies cosily in my lap then, enjoying the world on her back, and I tickle her belly while reading out loud. We had the following conversation: 'Donsje, listen, you have been through all this a long time ago. Do you remember the day you arrived here? How was it? Where you very tense and tired? Was the change hard?' She thought deeply for a moment before nodding: 'Yes, mama, I had a very hard time. Of course I was happy to be with you, because even then I loved you deeply, although I hadn't met you in person before. But I remember that long horrible ride in the car and Puddie who didn't exactly "welcome" me enthusiastically. I was very afraid then. I remember it as if it was yesterday. What about you, do you remember how I nestled myself very close to you that first night and at last found some warmth and peace?'

'What do you think, girl, aren't we behaving a bit rashly by letting Daimke run a risk just because of some stupid date we fixed for her? Would it not be better to tell Aunt Maria tomorrow we don't mind waiting a couple of weeks longer so that Daimke is better prepared? You know about the difficult days Daimke has behind her. You have read all letters and faxes, do you really think she'll be able to take on next week's trip? It is so soon, isn't it?' Donsje is wise, very wise, so she firmly replied: 'If I were you I'd wait for a while. Let her grow stronger first so she'll better be able to adjust. Besides, if she is stronger I'll be able to play more with her and that will put her mind off worrying about the change any newcomer has to go through.'

Maria had mailed me a funny card showing two pussy-parents madly in love with the child they were holding in between them. 'Expecting? *So ... many more days waiting and the time has come! Thrilling, isn't it?'* Maria wrote: *'Patience, dear sister, Daimke is doing her very best, but sometimes time must run its course.'* Indeed, no matter how hard it was, waiting was the wisest thing to do. That night I faxed Maria my suggestion that it was probably better to leave Daimke with her for a while longer. I got a return-fax at once from...indeed, our Daimke:

58

'Dear Mama,

Of course I want very much to come and live with you. But I am still a bit small and sometimes even a bit ill. I talked it over with mama here, of course. She has explained me that I have to stay here with her for the time being, because she can give me jabs that make me feel better. Also because she has to tube-feed me if I cannot eat. Changes now are not good, she says. 'You must grow really strong first before you can step into the big wide world.' I understand.
'So, Mama', I then said, 'if I am not mistaken both of my mamas are feeling very miserable at the moment. One mama wants me very much to be with her this very moment, but is afraid to ask. The other mama doesn't want to let me go before I am really ready for it, but doesn't want to tell this to my mama in Belgium because she doesn't want to hurt her. Funny persons mamas are! That's not going to get us anywhere. So I, as the smallest being involved, will have to show the most sense. Now, you two listen to me please. Mama in Belgium should know that I want to come to her very much but that my mama in Holland can only allow me to go without worry if the right moment is there. Even if this means that you will have to wait for maybe one month or more. And I don't want mama Maria to feel guilty about this delay. Even if she knows that mama Marg is waiting anxiously for me to come.

Now, what if you two promise me to just take your time and stop all brooding over this, then I promise to do my best to grow strong and healthy? Anyway I am already doing my best for that. I hope you funny mamas got my point. Purr prrr! This morning I didn't feel well again. Mama knows me very well and she can see it at once in my eyes. I didn't have any appetite at all and my bottom was leaking again. I hate that because I make a real mess then. Everywhere I drop dirty drips of diarrhoea. Papa and mama have to wipe me with tissues all the time. Mama has bathed my bottom. I don't like water and certainly not that messing around my bottom. But I do like the hot wind blowing from that noisy thing-that-dries. Yes, I do enjoy that.

Yeah, I couldn't help it, though. Ten minutes after the bath I broke wet wind and again I had a dirty bottom and hind legs. I didn't want to drink the milk and intestinal cleanser. I didn't feel like eating or drinking anything at all. Then Mama put the thermometer in my... I had a slight temperature. When I had been sitting looking so forlornly for an hour, mama gave me an injection against the pain and a fluid-injection. That made me feel better. I've eaten a

59

slice of roast beef and some tasty titbits and played for a while with a toy mouse. I felt better but, it is true, I am not strong enough to travel. I promise you, dear mama in Belgium, I shall come! Now I will go to bed and sleep. I am so tired. I love you all, much, much love from your Daimchild.'

Wise, wise Daimke. Of course, not for all the gold in the world did I want my baby to run the slightest risk and it would be very risky for her if she came too soon.

I wrote her:

'Dear Daimke,

You are right. You are the wisest of us all! Let's do it your way. Let's just wait and see. First you must grow strong and we must find a way to stop you leaking before you can come and live here. From now on the fluffies and I will send you only positive energy and thoughts and we will stop whining about when you are coming. What does it matter if you come later? I very much prefer a strong, healthy and cheerful Daimke later than a sad and ill Daimke now. If my love could heal, you'd be strong and healthy by now, because I keep on sending love to you. Mama Maria also gives you lots of love, anyway. But it is the jabs that you need most. And Maria knows best how to look after you.

Anyway, you belong to both of us already. Let us see it that way? And when you feel strong and well and judge the time ready for moving on, then you'll just tell us, ok? I am more than happy with your letter. I knew already you are a wise girl, I could see that in your eyes, but that wise! No, I hadn't figured that! Little girl, I am so happy that you are there with mama Maria. There is no better place for you in the world. That's a tremendous comfort for me.

Of course, we long for you, but fortunately I have my dear Donsje, Puddie and Mickje. They realize that I am sad. All day long they check up on me, asking me how I am and if they can do something to help me. And that they can do indeed! There is no better comfort than their purring and snuggling up against me. You know what I am going to do now? I am going to throw that ball of sorrow that I have been carrying around these past days, in the toilet and flush it down the drain. Have you ever seen a toilet? Funny thing, Donsje once fell into it and how we laughed! But that's nothing for you, because you already get wet often enough.

Next week we'll know more when we'll have sent a sample of your stools to Utrecht. You know what I'm hoping? Maybe you're just allergic to something. Nothing serious of course, we only have to find out to what. The best medicine is sleeping, eating and no more brooding. Everything will be fine, I know that for sure! We are sitting outside now. There is a rabbit running around here. Mickje is soooooo thrilled. They are about equal in size. Let's agree this: Tomorrow you celebrate Asje's birthday and I the one of Donsje and Mickje. I have a cute grey toy mouse on wheels for Mickje. It really runs. I am so curious what she will think of it. Donsje gets a nice fishing rod with a feather on the end. And Puddie will receive a packet of catnip. After all, it's also a bit his birthday. I will send many loving thoughts to grandpa. He also celebrates his birthday, but he is now on the Rainbow Bridge together with mama. How nice that your mama and aunt Elly are coming. Lots of love and cuddles and I do hope you'll sleep sound. I love you.

Many purrings and love from Puddie, Donsje, Mickje and especially Marg.'

What was wrong? Why still that horrible diarrhoea? Why did she not gain weight? She was drinking well but something was definitely wrong. Something did not function well. I considered that it might be protein-intolerance. Diabetes? A dysfunctional pancreas? Maria had sent some of Daimke's faeces to Utrecht. While waiting for the results Maria tried all kinds of food, but it went from bad to worse.

I still felt very tired. A mourning process has several phases. Because of the pain from my fall immediately before mama's crossing, I hadn't really got around to mourning yet. More and more I missed mama and I had to face the familiar manifestations of the mourning process. The guilt-feelings, should I have done more for mama? Should I have been by her side more during those last days? Should I...Fortunately I had my fluffies to talk these negative thoughts out of my head, but still. Fighting those thoughts did consume energy as well, and, also, yes, simply put I missed mama. I missed caring for her, I missed being there for her.

Elly the medium, who I had met at Maria's place, had told me something very beautiful. We had a nice coffee-chat and I, blissfully happy, attended with

61

Daimke in my arms. 'Marg,' Elly suddenly said, 'I see your mother standing at your side. She is happy and beaming with joy and so glad she can walk again and all her pain is gone. She has already spoken a couple of times with your father and she is going to help mediums once she is rested. She smiles and shakes her head because she knows you're going to receive another pussy-child, but she is moved by Daimke. She is also very happy because you are surrounded with some very nice friends. Really very happy, because that has always been her biggest worry, 'What will happen to Marg once I am gone?'

Yes, that is indeed mama. Elly could not know about mama's preference of dogs over cats. But she learned to love cats once she knew more about them. Donsje especially was her favourite but she loved Luckje very much too. Such a marvellous feeling that mama is still close to me and knows everything that's happening. I had already sensed her presence very clearly, but it was good to hear it confirmed by Elly.

Maria suggested that I went to a friend of Elly's in Nijmegen to have myself tested, by Jeroen of the Centre for Vitality and Health. He practises orthomolecular medicine and knows how to take a Vega test. This test is done to find out whether you have allergies to something or whether you need certain food supplements. Next time I visited Maria I made an appointment with Jeroen. I asked Maria if we could take Daimke too, maybe Jeroen could also test her then. And thus Maria, Elly, Daimke and I went to Nijmegen, about a quarter of an hour from Huissen.

While Daimke was lying snugly against my breast, Jeroen did the test. It appeared **that we had both a fat-deficiency**. I could believe this in my case - although I use two spoonfuls of olive oil for frying and, for my idea quite a lot linseed-oil on my bread, it is probably not enough - but Daimke? Isn't cat milk full of fats? Jeroen advised to add some evening primrose oil to Daimke's food. Would that make the difference? If so, it was easy. Still, it was a good thing that Maria listened to her intuition and added only a few drops, because Daimke's diarrhoea immediately got much worse.

When I telephoned Maria next day, she told me that Daimke simply had the runs. Everything she ate passed like an express train through her body and came out like water, within a quarter of an hour. Like a tap which had not been turned off. Maria never doubted about Daimke's chances to make it, but how long can a little body keep on fighting? I was afraid, so afraid! Tears ran over my cheeks. I tried to send her strength and love by way of her picture. I visualized that very soon she would be running around here. I really tried to feel it intensely. The happiness I would feel when she and Donske were basking together here. I could not give up now. Hope lost, all lost and Maria really had hope!

Daimke could not run free any more but had to stay in the big indoor kennel in the room most of the time. There was no other way but it was very unpleasant for her. Elly came every day to magnetise her. It always helped. She sent me a nice fax:

'Dear Marg, it is 21.30 now and I just finished magnetising Daimke. There is no reason at all to be so worried. Now and then the energy channels are blocked.
She has eaten very well and her faeces were rather normal. Presently she is dismantling a box with the help of her sisters. She looks lively and does not feel pain. I hope you feel a bit relieved now. Please go to bed and sleep now. Everything will be fine, for sure. Lots of love and see you soon,
Elly'

Yes, this fax made me very happy.

A cat has absolute emotional honesty. Human beings, for one reason or another, may hide their feelings, but a cat does not.
Ernest Hemingway.

Chapter 4

Catje

If a man could be crossed with a cat, it would improve man, but it would deteriorate the cat.

MarkTwain

The results of the faeces-tests arrived on 8 August! At last! They showed that Daimke could not digest fats. The veterinarian replacing Doctor Allard - the Vet from Poezenbel-foundation who was on vacation - looked up in the books what she could eat. A diet low in fats, soft curd cheese, yoghurt, chicken breast etc. she advised. Maria went to a pharmacy in Arnhem to buy special milk, but nothing helped. Besides, Daimke turned up her nose for all this stuff.

On Monday the 16th, Doctor Allard came back and then there was a change. Doctor Allard said at once that a cat cannot live without fats. The solution was to add to every meal a special enzyme that would digest the fats for her. It is called Tryplase. Of course Daimke also had a deficiency of some vitamins that are only soluble in fat. She got them from a spray. Wonderful stuff! Daimke got better, she started gaining weight! Oh, how happy we were! But she had a lot of catching up to do.

So, Jeroen had been right, indeed! Daimke's body was short on fat. Quite logical as she did not absorb the fats in her food. But feeding her fat was wrong. It made her leak even more. But that didn't alter the fact that Daimke was very low on fats. Especially the essential fatty acids, according to Jeroen.

On 26 August we received the following and relieving letter from Daimke:

Hi, dear Mama, Puddie, Mickje and Donsje,

At last I feel a bit better and strong enough to write you a few lines. For the last couple of days I have been feeling better, yes! But first I had to catch up on playing. I have here so many boyfriends and girlfriends. Catrientje is my dearest buddy, we are always together, but I like to play with all of them. When I was sickly, I couldn't play, I could only sleep and sleep. Now mama puts enzymes in my food and yes, things are better. Sure, there is still some dirt sticking on my bottom now and then. I don't mind that so much, but my bottom turns red from it and then I still have a bit aauuwww too much.

This morning I played outside. There is a very high climbing pole in the run and I climbed all the way to the top, and that was fun, guys! From there I can see everything. The big fluffies told me that our neighbour has huge fishes in his pond.
Mama told me that you may cheer up a little bit now, because I am little bit better. I know that mama in Belgium is very fond of country music, so I suggest that instead of a cheer you guys make a square dance or so. That's why I include a CD with dance music with this letter.

Mama says she wants to find out first how to turn my dirt drips into little turdies. And then, when I have grown a bit bigger I will come and live with you. When that will be, we don't know yet. Maybe I'll be your Christmas child. Er...will I then get a cradle full of straw? And will Puddie and Donsje play Joseph and Maria? Mickje can be a sheep and you mama in Belgium hm...a donkey? I will be the ox? Wieehh wiehh, there you see, I am indeed better, I want to be naughty for a change! Now I go to sleep for playing outside makes me very tired.

Big cuddles for all of you, also from my mama in Holland, lick lick prrrr

Your Daimke.'

About every two weeks I had visited Daimke and I had seen her getting from bad to worse. When I visited her again she had become a totally different fluffy. Her bottom was not so red any more. She played more and her satin soft fur started to shine. No speck of dirt any more, she was gorgeous! She had made it. Oh, how wonderful! How happy Maria, Gé and I were!

Maria made a birthday card for us:

Hurray, another fluffy came our way
Daimke is her name.
She is small, cute and very game!

Pudje, Donsje, Mickje and Marg Vlielander.'

There is a picture of Daimke when she was still a teensy-weensy little kitten with under it the following beautiful words:

'Round, hazy blue eyes stare forlornly from a wicker basket. 'Love me,' they say, 'feed me, keep me warm, take care of me'!

This is Daimke, she has had a formidable struggle to survive. We have come a long way, but all our efforts have been rewarded. She is a first class cuddler and knows how to purr with purrfection. Our little brave girl, we are so proud of her!'

Meantime my life had continued, in spite of Daimke's problems. I followed a Bach Flower remedies course and found it very interesting. Sure, it was hard work but it kept me from worrying as I could not do that and study at the same time. I was very happy when I received the certificate. I registered also for the following course, scheduled for September. The weather was fine and the fluffies and I stayed outdoors all day. A fantastic invention, a laptop!

Maria had lots of kittens, all abandoned. She always tries not to have more than two or three litters at the same time as the danger of infection is always there. Panleucopenia especially is a terrible risk. If the kittens get it, they often die one after the other. On the other hand it is so hard to say 'no' to kittens. Where would they go then? Fortunately Maria and Gé have acquaintances who are willing to help if necessary. Provided they, in turn, do not have too many kittens.

Every visit to Maria and Gé is a time of joy and happiness for me. Merely entering their house means being embraced by cat-love. Literally! 'Little Tiger', a very sweet old lady, often lies in a hammock at the front door and she will at once clasp her little arms around me. On another visit to Daimke I saw a beautiful shiny white-grey kitten trotting through the room. Daimke? Was it her? I just had seen a flash. Maria burst out laughing. 'No, that was Catrientje.' Of course, I had heard her story.

It is one of those stories that return every year. 'Holiday-time! What to do with your kittens? Why not just dump them? Easy come, easy go and after the holiday we'll get another cat.' Sometimes I am ashamed to be a human! To be honest, I feel more like a cat.

It was on a Sunday night, August 1. Maria and Gé were sitting cosily in the garden. There was a 06-call, an alarm call. Kittens in distress! Walkers had taken two kittens out of a tree during the evening walk with their dog. A quarter of an hour later the kittens were with Maria. They were about six weeks old. Maria christened them Ronnie and Rinus. They smelled of 'living room' and must have been dumped not long before. They looked healthy. Of course they were terrified, but not wild. Maria put them in quarantine. Thankfully they ate the food Maria gave them.

Two days later there was a fair in Huissen. Maria was there and sold cat things on a stand for the benefit of the Poezenbel Foundation. Around three o'clock in the afternoon there was another 06-call. A kitten had been found close to the Technical School. That's just opposite the spot where Ronnie and Rinus were found. The kitten sat in a tree. Another one of the same litter? Quickly Maria phoned Gé and gave him the necessary instructions. This kitten too must be put in the quarantine room. She borrowed a bicycle and rushed home. Indeed, this kitten was the sister of Ronnie and Rinus. Poor little one, she was very thin. No wonder considering the fact that she had spent two days in the bushes all by herself. When Maria entered the quarantine room the kitten moved immediately to the door of her cage. 'Miauwww, oh how wonderful of you to come, I'm so afraid and so starved. Mieeuwww!'

Maria picked her up and the kitten immediately nestled against her. Maria could hear her thinking: 'Oh, how great, I feel cuddles again, safe at last!' What kind of people are they that simply dump such kittens? It is certain that these kittens were treated well. People used to play with them. They were clearly used to humans. They have been hugged and cuddled and then, all of a sudden, all love vanished? I could think of one or two things I'd like to do such people!!! Hairballs they are, all of them!

The little cutie was called Catrientje.

As soon as the three little kittens were allowed to leave quarantine, Catje, as I called her, became close to Daimke. Those two became inseparable. How happy we were for Daimke that she had a dear friend now. Strange however, Catje never left me when I visited Daimke. 'Of course,' I thought, 'she stays with me because I'm staying with Daimke,' but that was not the truth. Even when Daimke was playing with the other kittens, Catje stayed at my side. So I started loving her more and more and toyed with the idea of taking them both with me. That would certainly be very good for Daimke, but what would Puddie, Donsje and Mickje think about it? But then hadn't I promised Daimke that I would do everything to make her happy? So, what if Daimke just brought her bosom-buddy with her? Wouldn't that be a nice present? After all, whether one or two joined us, no big difference for us, but very different for Daimke. She would have someone to hang on to and together they'd be stronger.

On September 26, when she was 17 weeks old, Daimke weighed 1616 grams. She was finally healthy and now we could plan for real. One more week and Maria and Gé would bring her to me.

'Dear, dear Daimke,

Dear girl of mine, another seven long days and nights and you will be here! Now, it is really going to happen! What will you say of your sisters Donsje and Mickje and your brother Puddie? What will you think of the garden, the run, the doggies? We are so happy that you are better now! And how well you are growing! You have such shiny fur on the pictures!
Donsje also is very happy and thrilled to meet you. Don't be afraid if at first she swears a little. She is so used to suffering from Puddie and Mickje's wild games that she can't help being afraid in the beginning. She loves 'Daimke'

*because mama is happy when she is talking about her. But she will not yet fully realise that **that** 'Daimke' and the strange fluffy, all of a sudden appearing in her life are one and the same. In the beginning you may have to stay in the big indoor kennel when I have to go out. I'll make a cosy nest for you in the cage.*

Mickje often finds being inside the indoor kennel safer than being outside when there is something scaring her. How many times a day do you eat? And what kind of food? Well, I'll learn all about it next Sunday. Maybe you could tell mama Maria to bring some food for you, so you don't have a change of food and a change of environment at the same time. I would like to give you tasty titbits, but I will follow Maria's instructions. Oh, the fun we will have! How we will cuddle and play, together with the others! And when they swear or hiss, we'll pretend there is some breeze blowing. You know, they don't mean it really, they are just scared.

You know what I have been pondering about for quite some time now? Well, I've grown very fond of your cute friend, Catje. Would you like to bring her when you move to our place? Is there still some place in your suitcase? So you will not be so lonely here, see? Would you mind asking mama Maria about this? I guess I already know the answer. And what does Catje think? Would she like to come with you? Lots and lots of love and sweet dreams! We will dream of you, too.

Lots of love from your mama in Belgium and from Puddie, Donsje and Mickje, who love you very much!

And then, just when everything seemed under control, a terrible serial killer sneaked into Maria and Gé's house. It is too bad to write much about it. My eyes still fill with tears when I think back to those horrible days. A friend of Maria, a soon-to-be-vet, brought two kittens who belonged to a drug addict. The kittens seemed all right but Maria's intuition kept on flashing warning signals. Watch out!! Be careful!! There's something fishy going on here!! The kittens had had sudden surges in temperature, which is often a bad sign. Yet, there was no room for them elsewhere, so what can one do then? The kittens were six weeks old and weighed only 300 grams. They were infested with fleas. Two little heaps of misery, so sad to see. Instead of putting them in the quarantine room, Maria prepared an indoor kennel for them in the guestroom. The Cats never enter that place, not even Maria's own cats do. Watch out!!! This warning kept on flashing in Maria's mind. From the very first minute she was super careful. She disinfected anything that had been in contact with the kittens. She washed all their things separately. Things like thermometers, needles, anything used for nursing the kittens was kept upstairs. Used cotton wool and other dirty materials were enclosed in a plastic bag and immediately discarded in the waste container outside. Maria wore a surgeon's gown, which reached down to her shoes. She disinfected her hands upstairs in the room and as soon as she came downstairs she washed them again with Betadine. She wore special shoes.

This is the usual precautionary routine Maria follows whenever new kittens arrive in her house, but now she double-checked everything. A couple of days later the little tomcat died. Maria immediately went to Doctor Allard to find out the cause. Panleucopaenia? It looked like that. Indeed, that was the killer! The parvo test confirmed it. On Tuesday the female kitten died, so Maria got rid of anything used by the kittens or if not, she disinfected it thoroughly! Baskets, hot-water bottles, Vet beds, everything was washed at 95° C. The virus cannot stand this high temperature. As a matter of fact the things themselves could not stand it either, so Maria had to throw everything away.

But - really terrible - somehow the virus had reached the kittens downstairs. Probably through a flea who jumped off the kittens when they entered the hall? Who knows, but one by one the other kittens died. A real trauma. Only one kitten, Marjoleintje, did not get the horrible disease. She was moved to an acquaintance to get her out of the danger zone. Ten dear little kittens departed to the Rainbow Bridge.

Doctor Egberink was a big help. At all times he was ready to advise and assist Maria. He is a wonderful veterinarian! He is the Department head of Virology at Utrecht University. He admitted that Maria had done everything, really everything to prevent the spread of the disease, but that nothing can withstand Panleucopaenia. The kittens can survive only if they have traces of maternal immunity transferred with the mother's milk to their bodies. Probably that was the case with Marjoleintje. Doctor Egberink mailed me information on Panleucopaenia and other serious feline diseases. In the Dutch version of Purring Angels I was allowed to use this information, but for the English version of my book I asked the permission of FAB, the Feline Advisory Bureau to use their sheets. I am so grateful they gave them to me. At the end of my book you will find more details on Panleucopaenia and other serious diseases.

How about Daimke and Catje? Thanks to the Lord, both had already been vaccinated. Catje had received only one vaccination but that was sufficient. Both were protected.

The decision whether to let Catje accompany Daimke was quickly taken now. Of course she had to come with Daimke. She should leave the danger zone as soon as possible. On Sunday Maria and Gé brought them to us. I had converted mama's room upstairs into a kitten room. It made sense to keep them separate and in quarantine for a couple of weeks. That way they could settle down and that was of the utmost importance under the circumstances. Stress weakens the immune system and we certainly didn't want that.

The day my little kitties came should have been a day of celebration but it turned out to be a day of sadness, because we were all deeply touched. Still, Daimke and Catje were like rays of sunshine piercing through clouds of darkness. Oh, how I enjoyed their presence! Now it was my turn to change clothes and shoes and disinfect my hands each time I had been in contact with them. But I had to follow this procedure for only two weeks. Sure, Puddie, Donsje and Mickje had been vaccinated, so there was no real danger, but it made sense to remain on guard. It amazed me how difficult that is! One quickly forgets something. Washing your hands before removing 'dirty clothes' is wrong. You have to wash your hands again. One has to think constantly. I felt like I had to be two persons. When I was upstairs I worried about my trio waiting downstairs. When I was downstairs I wondered how my two little 'quarantinees' upstairs were doing. My admiration for Maria grew by the day. She has to do this on a regular basis!

These days were very bleak for Maria and Gé. Everything in their home reminded them of the tragedy. Thanks to the Lord, their own cats had been spared. They also received letters of support from many people. That helped. Nevertheless, it was a big trauma. I couldn't do much to help them. I was also afraid to show my happiness now that I had my two new children with me. And I was happy! So happy I almost felt guilty about it. What a thrill to go upstairs and see their cheerful faces when I entered the room. They rushed at me, somersaulting with delight and mewing loudly. Daimke has a lovely 'silent mew'. She'll open her mouth very wide but I can't hear anything. Catje has a very special direct gaze and stares intently at me. One of her eyes seem smaller than the other one but that's the effect of the 'mascara'. One of her ears has a

71

cute white rim. Catje is just gorgeous. Her fur is a bit rougher than Daimke's. Maria says she has never has seen a kitten with such super soft fur as Daimke's.

I had to proceed carefully or they would run past me when I opened the door. Catje especially was super fast. I always took some acorns with me when I went upstairs. I threw these to the opposite corner of the room before opening the door to leave, otherwise they would get ahead of me. Catje had a funny way to show that she was fed up staying upstairs with Daimke. She would sit up and rub her front feet very fast against the door, as if she was planning to pounce on it. It was great to hear that rubbing. I could hear it when I was downstairs in the hall. Even now she sometimes still performs this ritual against the door of the bathroom. I guess it calms her down.

Mama's room was indeed an ideal quarantine room. Next to it there was a small bathroom where I prepared their meals and washed up their trays. The wallpaper was made of a material easy to climb up. It was easy for my kids to reach the top of the big mahogany cabinet by way of the wallpaper, so they used to sit up there. Getting down was more of a problem but that's when mamas come in handy.

When I was sitting with them, Daimke crawled cutely into my arms and rubbed her little front paws over my cheek. Her way of looking at me was heavenly; it almost brought tears in my eyes. Catje would often deposit herself on the very edge of the table and wanted to be cuddled for a long time. Of course they romped and played a lot. I suppose they slept when I was not there so that they were well rested when I came in. They followed me like puppies. Especially Catje. Maybe the best moment for them was when I worked in the bathroom. I allowed them to come with me and they both watched me, front legs on the wash basin, while I was washing and rinsing dishes, trays and things.

When the dogs barked, outside in the garden, Daimke jumped on the windowsill to observe what was going on. I promised them to take them down with me after twelve days. From their window upstairs they had a superb view over the garden. As they were alone most of the time I was afraid to put on their collars with the little bells. I was not always there to intervene if something went wrong.

Maria warned me strongly about the electrical wires lying everywhere

downstairs. When Donsje was still small I had not taken any notice of them. True, it is much easier to keep your eyes on one pussy-child than on two. Especially because then one kitten can move the wire and the other will be tempted to bite it. So I bought some kind of plastic spiral at the electrical shop and wound it around the wires, so that they could never bite them. I am very grateful to Maria for warning me. I have had enough nastiness for the time being!

I had put a big rocking chair in the room and the radio was always on, so it wasn't too bad for them after all. At night I read the newspaper with them, even though I 'read' more paws and faces in and out of the newspaper than news. As Daimke had to have Tryplase mixed in her food, she could eat only a couple of times every day. Anyway I never leave food standing for the fluffies, because I think it is better to give them three meals every day. If they feel like eating in between the meals they just come and ask for some dry food. I always have some with me. That way I am the mother cat providing food for them. That way I also know whether they are hungry or ill. Every night I invented other games. Our bond grew very strong in that short period. We were not very often together but when we were it was indeed 'quality time'! How happy I was that Catje and Daimke were together! If Daimke had been alone upstairs it would have caused her a lot of unnecessary stress.

A kitten is more amusing than half the people one is obliged to live with.

Lady Sidney Morgan

Chapter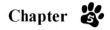

Downstairs

There are two means of refuge from the miseries of life: Music and Cats

Albert Schweitzer

Today Daimke, Catje and I have been to Doctor Liliane, our veterinarian. At last! The last two weeks really lasted longer than usual! This morning, when I opened the curtains in the kids' room and didn't go to the refrigerator to get food as I usually do, two pairs of very surprised eyes looked up to me: 'Mama, what's the matter? Won't you give us our breakfast? Why? Are you angry with us?' I really had to force myself not to give them a tiny bit. I explained the reason why there was no breakfast. We were going to Doctor Liliane. She would do some blood tests and they would get the vaccination. To be on the safe side they should be starved in case they had to be sedated. Fortunately it didn't come to that.

It was a real adventure anyway. For two weeks they had been alone upstairs in the room and now, all of a sudden, they saw the big outdoors! Wauw! They saw the sun, trees, birds and the dogs. They smelled delicious and thrilling things. They felt the wind. Catje found it really scary, but Daimke didn't mind. She didn't interrupt her purring and enjoyed the car ride. Funny to see, she pushed her little paw through the cat carrier and took my hand. And so we rode to the Doctor. Like a proud mother I introduced my 'babies' to Liliane. She found them gorgeous, especially Daimke. She had never felt a fur like hers before, as soft as satin, she said. I wanted both kitties tested for FeLV and FIV. I was quite sure they didn't have these diseases, but if I did not have the tests done the tests of Puddie, Donsje and Mickje would have no value any more. When Luckje came to live with us, the vet we had then had not considered it necessary to test him for those diseases. I never felt at ease. There is much FeLV in the neighbourhood.

Besides, we could send Daimke's blood to the laboratory for a thorough analysis. Should she ever have problems again we could use that analysis as a calibration point. To Doctor Liliane's great amazement Daimke kept on purring when the needle was jabbed in her foreleg. Unbelievable! She really was plucky and remained calm. Afterwards she received a microchip and could return to her cage, which she did but not very enthusiastically. Poor Catje, she really cried when it was her turn. Small wonder as a matter of fact. First she lived in a family where she received many cuddles. Suddenly she was pushed into a car and dumped somewhere along the roadside where she hid for two days and two nights before she was found. Your confidence gets a big knock then. And now? What bad things were going to happen to her again?

Poor little girl, I can read it all in her eyes when she sets herself in front of me to talk. She is such a pensive and wise girl. Fortunately the jab went well and after the chip and the vaccination she could join Daimke in the cat carrier. Daimke was watching everything with big question marks in her eyes. She was very frightened when Catje cried and quivered on her legs. At once she went to Catje to lick and comfort her. Fortunately Catje was herself again pretty soon. I cuddled her for a while and her diesel engine ran once more. Daimke put herself cosily in my lap while her medical file was updated. Catje said she preferred staying in the cat-carrier but she rested her head on my hand. 'Mama, I am very afraid but I'm so happy you are with me.' When we arrived home - they knew where they were when we stopped at the gate - it was celebration time! Once back in the room they jumped out of the cage, looked at each other and me and shouted: 'Yippee...we're home!!!'

To make up for the foodless morning I prepared them an extra tasty meal, which they ate with relish. It had been quite an adventure! One hour later I checked on them to see if everything was all right and found them sleeping in the big balance, paws around each other. How cute! Thank God, this is over. We really got fed up with the cumbersome procedures of clothes on, clothes off, clothes on again, wash hands, change shoes. On Sunday they can come downstairs. My dear plucky fluffies, they have been so brave. I am very proud.

Whenever I leave my trio I always tell them where I'm going and when I'll be back. I charge Puddie, the oldest and the only 'man' in the house, with the task of watching over everything. I think it is important to do this. That way they don't feel lonely, they have something to do and they know I won't belong. I had a lot of explaining to do this time. Donsje, Puddie and Mickje were waiting for me in the run. They knew all too well where Daimke, Catje and I had been. 'I'm so happy we didn't have to go with them,' Mickje whispered in Puddie's ear, for she very well remembered the day she was spayed. 'Two more days, guys' I happily told them, ' and our kids will come downstairs. Then I won't have to leave you any more. Are you going to be nice to Daimke and Catje? They are still very small and they have had a hard life so far. Hey Puddie, I rely on you! I expect you to teach them everything and guide them like a wise uncle. And Mickje you will

be their sweet aunt. You will teach them everything that girls should know. And you Donsje, you'll be their special playmate, you are the lightest and the youngest.' Puddie promised at once. Donsje said she would want to reserve some time for herself but found it thrilling anyway. Only Mickje still had a look of suspicion in her eyes. What trouble was hanging over her beautiful brown head now? Well, she could only wait and see...

KITTEN CALLING

Kitten, Kitten, on the call,
Who is fairest of them all?
Use your time to play awhile,
With your antics make us smile.

Seasons pass and time will come,
To practice skills you've learned from mum.
'Kittenhood' is short and sweet,
All too soon the rooms stay neat.

Time goes by on silent wings,
Soon you'll give up kitten things,
Time enough for adult love,
So save your breath, - have fun my dove!

© *Maureen Eadon-Mills*

And then Sunday came...

A radiant sun. A real beautiful autumn day. It's cold but there is no wind on the terrace in front of the living room. Today is **the day!** This morning when Daimke and Catje were still quietly upstairs, I placed all trays, dishes and so on in a basin with Parvotec, a disinfectant. I disinfected my clothes as well. Then I put everything in the dishwasher and washing machine. From now on everything will be back to normal. I went out to feed the chickens and took the doggies and Donsje for a walk. Those routines finished, I could spend all the time with the fluffies.

I first brought Daimke down. I showed her the office, the bedroom, the litter trays and the run. I told her where she could find water to drink. She purred and kept on purring. Oh, she found it so thrilling! Then it was Catje's turn. She found it rather horrible but remained calm. I fixed the collars with the little bells around their necks, so I can hear where they are. I placed a big indoor-kennel in the living room. That way they could get used to each other in peace and quiet. Of course, all five of them felt strange. The little kids were sitting on their bottoms in the middle of the indoor-kennel and watched everything with big black eyes and flabbergasted faces. 'Where are we now all of a sudden? Are those cats watching us Puddie, Mickje and Donsje?', they asked me. I went to the piano to play some music or rather, I tried to play… as I was watching the fluffies more than the keys. When things had settled down, I took Donsje for another walk in the garden. The weather was so fine. Then I fed the kids. Afterwards, I simply opened the indoor-kennel. Daimke, the bravest and always in front, walked out first. Catje followed. Calmly they strolled around. When they came too close to the others, they got some 'hissy welcomes' but the kids didn't mind. They shrugged their little shoulders and continued their walk. No time for trouble now!

In fact, not much happened. Of course I had introduced both of them to Puddie, Mickje and Donsje and explained that these two were our long expected little fluffy girls. Our kids! I am sure the three of them understood and realised that Catje and Daimke were part of the family now. Soon Daimke and Catje started exploring the room for real. It was wonderful to watch. Mickje and Donsje moved to higher regions. Within five minutes the kids were happily playing busily with all the thrilling new toys. How they enjoyed it! The run especially was a big success. It's so nice playing there. For fourteen days there had been no sun and now this wonderful weather. Soon Catje hung high up in the wire netting. Of course, we've a long way to go yet, a way laced with 'hissy' asides before we'll reach Harmony Home, but things worked out better than I had expected. I immensely enjoy the fun they have running freely through the living room. They are so cute and lovely! Indeed, it is wonderful to be all together!

When we went to my bedroom-kitchen to eat, everything was new to them again. Again they had to explore everything. I sat down on my bed for a while to write down everything so that I could report it to Maria. At once Daimke came to me to see what I was doing. She nuzzled herself against me. Catje also came to report and shoved her head against my hand. They really kept an eye on me, it was all so strange and new here. If mama is not afraid, why should we be?

It's indeed an advantage that they are a bit older now. They can cope better. Daimke rolls herself on her back for a close and cosy cuddle. How soft she is! Catje runs out into the run. She finds the outdoors fantastic. A run is a real delight. A pity though that winter is coming. But after winter there is spring again. Even now the trees are already budding. It goes without saying that Puddie and Mickje stay in the sitting room when I go out for a walk. I wanted to stay around these first days when they are together.

A couple of hours later we're all together in the office. The kids are running and playing around with toy mice and acorns. Puddie, Mickje and Donsje are watching them. They are tense but who wouldn't be? It's great fun to observe them. Now we're really getting acquainted with each other. They seem inexhaustible. All morning they have been running around the living room. They did sleep for a while on the climbing post in my bedroom. A very handy spot, I could see them when I was walking the dogs in the garden, white fluffies on a grey post, very conspicuous. They should be dead tired but I don't see any sign of that yet. Daimke's face clearly shows a 'what-mischief-shall-I-do-next'- intention. Her eyes are so expressive that I can easily read in them what's on her mind.

We slept wonderfully well that night. As I suspected that Mickje would have some difficulties with the arrival of the kids and might work it out on Donsje during the night, I decided to let her sleep in the living room. She asked for it herself, anyway, by positioning herself against the door. I felt sad about it, but at least now she has a big space all to herself. To give Puddie his peace and quiet I did put Daimke and Catje in the indoor-kennel. Maria is very smart! She trains the kittens to sleep in the indoor-kennel at night. As she puts it herself: 'Giving more liberty to kittens later is easier than giving them freedom in the beginning and taking it back when they grow older.' I found it a bit hard, as I eagerly wanted to take them to bed with me. But that would come later, no doubt.

I'm writing this while Daimke sits on my lap. She often comes to me to curl herself in my arms, very close to me. Donsje sits in the drawer nearby watching us. Fortunately she is not jealous. Daimke had her teensy-weensy harness on this morning, for the first time. I am going to take her out in the pouch-bag to show her the garden and I consider it safer to hold on to her. She has some small wounds on her shoulder, probably from the many injections she has received. I put some disinfectant on them. Now she has a red-brown back. 'You are a calico-cat now,' Catje shouted teasingly to her. 'Mieeaauwww, calicos bring good luck!' Daimke replied. She is never lost for words!

A thrilling moment: Daimke entering the garden. There is wind and leaves fly about. That's fun! Quietly she remains sitting in the pouch bag, even when cars pass on the road. Most amusing for her are the chickens. I put her down. She sits and watches those funny-feathered cats that 'mew' so funnily: 'Cluck, cluck?' Her tail turns bushy. Now, while sitting on my lap she is dreaming about them, I can feel little quivers moving through her body.

Puddie is very nice to them. Donsje, of course, has no problem with the new kids but Mickje is really very upset. I try to give her extra attention and extra cuddles but she is angry and tense and refuses to eat. Fortunately she leaves the kids alone. I understand Mickje's reaction very well. She is really afraid that she is going to lose my affection and her place in the house. Fortunately at noon she drank half a bowl of catmilk. Not eating is dangerous for cats, especially for such a well-rounded pussy like Mickje is now. They could get

Fat-Liver-Syndrome which is lethal. That's the reason cats should never be put on a strict diet like dogs. They should lose weight gradually by means of 'slim'- food and more exercise. (If ever they are not eating a few teaspoons of green tea will decrease the risk of Fat-Liver-Syndrome)

I found the results of Daimke's blood test in my mail. Indeed, there was some deviation from the average totals of eosinophils and platelets. The number of white blood cells was too high too. But nothing to worry about. She plays, she runs, she eats and she cuddles. Oh, may everything turn out well! We love her so! I try to see everyday that she spends with us as a present, which it is, of course. She was so, so ill!

Catje is becoming more 'cuddlable' and her confidence is growing. Our bond was strong from the very first moment. If there is one fluffy who selected her mama, it is Catje! She never left me when I was at Maria's place. She fixed her big beautiful eyes on me and pleaded: 'Take me with you, please, I long to be with you. Let me stay with you forever, together with Daimke. I love you so much, you are my mama!' She regularly comes to report how happy she feels here and jumps against my hand. Daimke and Catje sleep cosily together, their little paws intertwined. It really is an advantage to take two kittens at the same time. It is much more fun discovering new things together.

I love all five of my fluffies equally as much, but Maria is right when she says that Daimke is a dream of a fluffy. After two days she has learned to wear the harness without problems. Every morning we walk around the garden. Her diesel engine never stalls and she finds everything beautiful. The leaves, the acorns falling down and the exercise. She doesn't want to be carried at all! Running is so much more thrilling. But Catje is equally special. When I call her she comes flying out of the run, just like Luckje did! I'll never give up waiting for him, I keep on hoping that some blessed day he'll turn up.

Mickje does not seem so sad any more. She eats again but she still refuses chicken. Well, I give her dry food and fish instead. I eat fish every day and make some more for her. In spite of the cold weather the fluffies like to be outside. Maybe they don't feel the cold, like children when they are busy playing, but after four o'clock I keep the kids inside. At night, after office hours around nine o'clock, we play together before I start cooking. The others do not join in the fun yet, but they watch and observe. The biggest hits are cork sticks stuck on a wire, which sway up and down so nicely and also, of course, the always-thrilling feathers tied to a fishing rod.

Today I also took Catje for a walk. Maria had warned me that she might not like it as her life is already burdened by a bagload of horrible experiences. But when I took Daimke out, she watched us so forlornly from behind the wire-netting - her eyes almost filled with tears - that I decided on the spur of the moment: 'Okay girl, let's just try it.' I put the harness on and she loved it! I think it is mainly human to carry around the burden of the nasty things which they have experienced in their lives. Animals, cats in particular, are smarter when it comes to that. They stow their luggage in some dark place and only check on it when they need that experience to survive. Cats certainly don't cherish it or carry it around. 'A waste of energy', Catje wisely puts it, ' better hide those bad experiences in some far away place and lock them up, so that they are out-of-the-way and not in-the-way!

It is good if they get used to the garden, so that they won't get lost should they ever escape. I think I said before that according to me, Catje was a dog in one of her previous lives. She walks on a leash as good as a well-trained police dog. I am very proud of her. Sometimes she stops for a moment and looks at me with questioning eyes: 'Is everything all right, mama, is it not dangerous and am I doing well?' 'Sure, girl, you're a champion, you're super!' 'Purrr prrr prrr'.

They are having a super busy day flying through the living room. The big sunny room with its funny slippery floor is an inexhaustible source of delight. Everything they find on it must be kicked around. Mickje and Catje played ping-pong together. Suddenly Mickje remembers: **'Oh help, I was angry, wasn't I?** ' Quickly she leaves the game to start grooming herself as diversion. The wisest thing to do after a mistake! But I noticed it. Puddie didn't mind Catje playing with his tail. Sure, he swore at her, but he didn't lash out. Donsje behaves as if the kids have been around as long as she has, but I would love to see her join in with their fun and games. She's has not done that, so far.

We have a watercat! This morning the water bowl lay upside down. I thought it had been knocked over in the heat of their game, but just now Catje went to the water bowl and stirred the water first with her left and then with her right front paw. Donsje and Daimke watched her with dumbfounded faces. Puddie got up from his bed and couldn't believe his eyes. Mickje almost fell off the printer while craning her neck so she could follow Catje's actions. How funny! A real watercat! Maybe she's got Van Cat blood in her veins? Van Cats love swimming. Yes, they are very special fluffies indeed!

Doctor Jef and Filip, my friend and piano teacher dropped by. It was wonderful to see Catje and Daimke say hello without the least bit of fear. They were thrilled by this visit. Poor Jef, he is more for dogs. Wherever he looked he saw fluffies. Too bad for him! He and mama loved to tease me about my kitties.

There was rain for the first time in a long while. Daimke and Catje found the puddles very interesting. Later I noticed Daimke high up on the new climbing post, which Maria and I had bought at the show in Nijmegen. I called to her: 'Will you not come to me?' She came at once. 'Miewwwuuwie, I want to lay curled up in your lap, do you mind?' Should I mind? This night I'll try to let them free in the room. I can always put them in the indoor-kennel should they keep me awake. It would be so nice feeling them nuzzling close to me. And it worked! They don't need to stay in the indoor-kennel any more. A few nights later I was very proud of Puddie. In the dusk - there's always a small light on - Puddie and Daimke were sleeping on the bed back to back.

It was a full moon and the weather is often stormy then. Still, it was nice outside with lots of sunshine, but there was a strong wind. It was funny to see our reactions to the full moon. We were very restless. All five fluffies had been racing through the living room all morning. They had lots of fun and so did I. Puddie and Mickje mostly played together while Daimke played with Catje. Donsje lay down and watched, but just once in a while she joined in the game. I do hope she'll get more exercise that way. She only moves when we walk in the garden. She rarely has fits of wildness unlike Mickje and Pudje. Maybe the kids will stimulate her to become more active. She is always very hungry but she is really well rounded and I have to limit her food. It's unpleasant for her and so hard for me. She has such a cute way of begging for a titbit. She'll put her paws around my neck and rub her head against me and kiss me while purring in full gear. I always end up giving her something. She is just irresistible. Yet I have read warnings against overweight for cats in all the cat magazines I subscribe to. A dangerous lecture for me, considering that I am an ex-anorexia-patient.

Daimke now runs with me in her harness like a fullly fledged hiker. Everything arouses her interest and she wants to explore it all. Today again they had much fun chasing leaves floating in the wind. Catje races best but sometimes she suddenly gets into a panic when she hears a car. Now all five are resting exhausted on their cushions in the office, it was such a marvellous day!

But still it's hard to accept the loss of all those lovely Poezenbel-kittens. I think that Maria, Gé and I will never forget those horrible days. When I look at Catje and Daimke I realize how easily they too could have fallen victim to the Panleucopaenia and I shudder. I feel so very grateful indeed that they have been spared, but the sorrow over the lost kittens remains, of course.
Everything that happens to us in this life serves to make us grow stronger and more mature. Yet, it's hard to keep this wisdom in mind at the moment the very sad things actually happen. Still, it is very important to always keep thinking positively and to realise that things **will** get better after a while. They always do! Papa used to say:' My child, if there was no black, there would be no white.' The more sorrow you experience in your life, the more you value and enjoy the good things. Sometimes people are afraid to love another living being, for fear of the pain if they lose her or him. But then one is not really living any more. Sorrow and happiness alternate. Life and death belong together. Of course, all this wisdom doesn't mitigate the pain of your bereavement. I still miss Mama and Karma, my dear Collie, every day. It is a wonder though that Femke looks more and more like him. She cannot be Karma's reincarnation for Femke was alive at the time he died, but I am sure that Karma passed on his friendly habits to Femke. I can still picture Femke lying on the cold floor in the animal shelter. One bundle of canine misery. Dirty and scared. Yes, I could never have found a better mate. Mama was also very fond of her.

Daimke is so extremely cute when I - as is my habit before going to sleep - read for a while. She lays on her back in my arms and purrs all the time while 'reading' with me. Now and then she looks up to me and softly rubs one front paw over my face. When I then kiss her cute pink nose she'll look at me so infinitely lovely and wise. Catje then nuzzles against me while Donsje lies on my belly. She serves as bookend. How rich I feel then and how lovely to feel them!

I never fall asleep immediately so their playing around after the light is out makes bedtime all the more exciting. They use me as a springboard and I can tell from the pressure of the legs and the weight who's running over me. Regularly a small white (Catje) or a grey and white (Daimke) face comes looking to see if mama is really sleeping. Sometimes they tap their little paws on my cheek, so cute! Or I feel a wet nose. Afterwards they sleep all night long. Always in the same place. Donsje sleeps on a second pillow against my head. Daimke curls up against me under the covers. That's deliciously warm and purring is the best sleeping pill there is. After a while she usually feels too hot and then she moves on top of the covers. Catje sleeps either at the foot of the bed or on the climbing pole.She prefers a high and secure place. Puddie mostly sleeps at the foot of the bed.

He still doesn't really like the kids being around but he just endures it. Mickje is still unhappy with the new situation too. Of course, the bad weather doesn't help, she has to stay more indoors now. She likes being outdoors. Still, I am afraid there is something else bothering Mickje. But what? I should consult Puddie, he always knows what's going on.

CAT-ALPHABET

A is for "aw!" when I get a jab
B is for basking in the sun or on your lap
C is for cage, please never put me there
D is for dogs which sometimes are a scare
E is for eyes that see in the night
F is for fur to feel for mutual delight
G is for grooming so I look neat
H is for hairballs, with or without feet
I is for idea, for making a plan
J is for jumping, as high as I can
K is for kitchen, a favourite hunting ground
L is for love to keep me safe and sound
M is for Maurits, and also for mice
N is for Nepeta, a plant that makes me smell nice
O is for Obelix, my dear friend Daimke's "beau"
P is for purr, to let my engine go
Q is for quarrel, please never with me
R is for run to play in and feel free
S is for swear when you make me mad
T is for tail to fluff out when I feel bad
U is for unique, a feline always is
V is for vacation I never want to miss
W is for whiskers, long and white
X is for Xmas to enjoy at your side

Y is for yippee! Hey guys, I didn't goof
Z is for zippy, that 's very quick to move

© *Kater Maurits*
(With help from his mama Els Vossen and
translated and adapted by Jozef Gommeren)

The trees are splendid now. We have a red oak in the garden, really beautiful! The bright yellow leaves are just tiny suns. This morning Daimke and I have walked down the street in front of our house. She is fantastic, our little girl. Sitting in the pouch-bag she watches, with bright eyes and purring with joy, the leaves falling down. Cars driving by are very interesting for her. Cyclists too. She is a brave fluffy. Soon I'll take her for a ride in the car. I am still amazed that they adjusted so smoothly and quickly got to know our habits. When I call them they rush to me. It takes more time to train a young dog to be obedient, though I admit that Femke learned fast. Cats are more intelligent and they also smell better than dogs. Tomorrow Maria and her friend Kyra are coming. I am curious to hear their comments. Thrilling!

Maria and Kyra brought along fine weather. A real golden autumn day showing the leaves in full splendour. How nice to be able to talk about everything. It did her a lot of good, Maria faxed afterwards. I am so happy. Of course, they found Daimke and Catje gorgeous. Oh, what fun they had! Maria brought a lot of lovely toys. Kyra gave them a wonderful tunnel, which also can serve as basket and chair. The tunnel was a big success; they never tired playing in it. Even Donsje joined in.

The day after this visit, Maria unexpectedly received a friend for Cruimeltje, Fleurtje. Cruimeltje is a slightly backward British Shorthair kitten which Maria had rescued. The mother cat would not accept him so Maria, of course came to the rescue. According to Puddie, Cruimeltje is not stupid at all, but super smart. By pretending to be 'stupid' he doesn't have to do anything he doesn't want to do. As my father used to say: 'Just see, hear, and keep your mouth shut and you'll get far in life.' It is a fact that Cruimeltje does not really know how to climb, race and play, so he was rather lonely. Maria searched for a lovely girlfriend for him and found one now. It is a British Longhair. Cruimeltje is very happy with his new friend and follows her wherever she goes. She is gorgeous. I am very happy for Maria and Gé. At last the sun is piercing through the dark clouds.

Daimke has discovered the use of trees. They are living climbing poles, of course! She never received any training but like a fully-fledged fluffy she climbed high up along the trunk. There she hung for a while and then she neatly came down backwards and very carefully. Of course, there's no stopping her now and this morning she wanted to try every tree she passed. I don't want her to climb too high and she is only allowed to climb trees with straight and safe trunks. Trees with sharp side branches or treacherous protuberances which could hurt her are dangerous, especially because she is leashed. How clever cats are. She hardly saw trees before, but she instinctively knows what she can do and what she cannot. Probably her mother visits her every night in her dreams to give her sound advice.

Catje follows me all day long. She sits with me as much as possible and is fond of playing the piano too. When I have finished showering she'll calmly step in the wet shower tray. She treats all water bowls as if they were fishponds. She is not a lap cat but she demonstrates her love in another, equally intense way. Daimke still has that endearing questioning look in her face like before. Oh, she is so lovely! As soon as I am sitting down she jumps on my lap, throws herself on her back in my arms and shuts her eyes in a state of supreme euphoria. And than she purrs and purrs! Regularly she rubs her front paws over my face and tries to nuzzle even tighter against me. The happiness I feel then!

Mickje and also Puddie still feel like teasing Donsje now and then. Especially at night Puddie sometimes suddenly pounces on top of her. She is therefore afraid to really relax and sleep. Of course that makes her tense and is bad for her health too. The solution was obvious but I hesitated. So Puddie decided to take command since mama seemed too dumb to act. He had been asking it for some time, but I pretended not to hear it. Tonight, mewing loudly, he positioned himself in front of the door: 'Mieuaauuuwwww, I am too old now for all this bustle and my friend is sitting there all by her sad lonely self in the sitting room. No wonder she is sad! Please, mama, let me go and comfort her.' Yes, Puddie was right, this was the solution. Puddie and Mickje together in the living room, while Donsje, Daimke and Catje sleep with me. Donsje will feel very happy not to have to be afraid any more of a sudden attack out of the darkness. From that day on, Mickje was her lovely and happy old self again. She must have felt 'abandoned' after all. Poor dear Mickje, I guess she'll never get rid of that fear.

86

The clocks have to go back one hour today. We are back to wintertime. We just hate this summer time, wintertime stuff. Must be crazy people that concocted this, city-dwellers remote from nature. Naturally my fluffies don't accept this. They awoke as usual and equally as usual had fun. They jumped on my bed, rushed over my body and woke me up with soft caresses over my cheek and kisses. And, what a delight... I could stay in bed for one more hour and enjoy it to the full! Daimke is fond of disappearing under the covers now and then and to cuddle herself against my body. How I enjoy feeling her against me. Catje doesn't approve of this for some reason. She doesn't like to go under the covers herself, so she pounces on the moving bulge and tries to catch it. I make a tunnel then with my arms so that Catje can't actually jump on top of Daimke. But Daimke can't keep it up for long. She rushes from under the covers and starts a delightful romp. Yes, sleeping is out of the question then, but to watch them frolicking is more beautiful than the best dream.

In the newsletter from Poezenbel foundation Pudje wrote:

Dear Readers and Fluffies,

You will not believe this but it's the truth. I have been promoted to kitten-sitter. Yes, it's true and what's more, I am awfully good at it! Well, mama says so time and time again. You know when mama was a kid (kitten?) herself she had a nanny looking after her. Now, I look after our little fluffy girls Daimke and Catje. I already wrote you last time that I have to mind what I write. Hardly had I said how nice I found it that Mickje had joined us, than Marg started talking about little Daimke. At the end of September we all seemed wrapped in a dense dark cloud of gloom and doom. Marg told us about the horrible things that had happened to the poor kittens from Poezenbel, but we did not really understand. We did feel mama's sorrow and powerlessness, however, and it made us desperate. We tried anything to brighten up mama's days, but it was all in vain. Then Daimke and Catje arrived. At first mama disappeared upstairs for many hours. When she returned we could smell 'kittens' but also the nasty smell from 'disinfectants'. 'Guys', mama explained, 'we'll have to exercise some patience. Our kids can't come down yet but at least they are here and playing happily. That's what matters most now.'

Thrilled we awaited the moment we would meet the kids. At least mama was a bit happier again. Anything is better than sadness you can't do anything about.

Besides, we had become curious. Then, on a fine Sunday morning, mama introduced the kids to us. At first she kept them in the indoor-kennel so they could get used to us and, of course, we could get used to them. You can imagine that our tails swelled to twice their size and once in a while there was a hiss and a swear, what would you expect? It is not something simple, getting two new sisters, even though I must admit they're very cute! They smelt all right. They sat on their behinds and watched us calmly and in purrfect silence! After an hour mama released them, and they started exploring, for, of course, they were curious too! They hardly noticed us because they were thrilled by that big room full of new things and toys. I moved to the top of the climbing pole to follow their activities.

Mickje didn't like it. She swore and kept apart. Donsje was upset but curious at the same time. When the kids got tired and curled up in a chair, I went down to take a closer look. I sniffed at them and licked them. Then I went to Mickje who was watching us with a sad face. 'Come on, Mickje, it's not as bad as you'd expect it to be!' I comforted her. 'Don't worry, girl, they won't cause us any trouble. As long as Marg will be happy again and play with us like before, we'll all be happy!' Yes, Mickje had to admit I was right, but she couldn't help feeling afraid that she had to leave. Poor girl indeed, when will she have trust in people again?

A couple of weeks passed but she still felt sad. I took her aside and said: 'You know what, Mickje, I am going to ask mama's permission to sleep with you in the living room. How about that?' Mickje's eyes sparkled with joy. 'Oh yes, Puddie, we being together at night. How wonderful! Then we both can try to catch mice in the garden. Even when we are indoors, we'll just pretend and that's also fun!'

So that evening I positioned myself ostentatiously in front of the door. At first mama didn't take notice, but when she saw me she asked at once: 'Puddie, you want to leave? Is it too hectic for you now we have two kids around or do you want to go to Mickje?' 'Wraaaauuuuwww, the latter', I mewed and that's why I now sleep cosily with Mickje. Of course Donsje keeps me informed of everything going on with the kids and of the fun she is having with them. 'You should see us, Pud, we fly over the waterbed, up and down mama, who laughs and laughs. I feel young again, a kitten like Daimke and Catje.' ' Well, be careful though, they are still very small.' Surprised Donsje looked at me.

*'Funny that **you** tell me that! What about me? I am not so big either but you sometimes play so wild with me that it hurts!'*

Yes, she was right, but I couldn't explain why I sometimes behave like that. So I mumbled a bit ashamed: 'Ill weed grows apace!' Still, I must admit, I have changed. Of course I am older now. Besides it is fun to be the only male around and to be in supreme command. Although all that responsibility is quite exhausting, you can take my word for it. Lots of nuzzles and purrs from us all.

Your Puddie.'

Today is All Saints Day. This morning Daimke and I went to the cemetery to visit mama and papa's grave. It was the first time that Daimke 'got out and about'. I was curious to see how she would react. I had put her in the cat carrier though, while in the car. Both Maria and Kyra had warned me about the risks of letting a cat run around freely in the car. When Pudje was young, I took him everywhere with me in the car. I loved driving with Pudje sitting beside me. Often he put his front paw on my shoulder, watching the cars pass by. When the going got boring he curled up in my lap. But Maria is right. It's dangerous. There is always the risk of a door flying open in case of an accident. Daimke found it excellent anyway, and of course we could talk. We had a real conversation, as she is becoming more and more talkative. I told her about papa and mama. That I still miss them very much and how much mama loved Donsje and would certainly have loved Daimke and Catje also.

When mummy was still with us, on All Saints Day I always took pictures of the cemetery full of flowers and of daddy's grave for her. Such small memories hurt. But now there was Daimke to cheer me up. She threw herself on her back in the cat carrier and waved her front feet in the air. It was difficult to keep my concentration on the road. Once we arrived at the cemetery, I put her in the pouch bag and took her with me. She found it exciting. So cute, that curious little head jutting out of the bag. There was much activity, but Daimke calmly looked around. When we stepped into the car again, I thought I had forgotten to switch off the engine but no, it was Daimke, running 'her' engine at full speed. She was tired though. I left the cage open but she didn't leave it!

Brave Daimke and so full of confidence. I hope it will never be betrayed.

The kittens are growing well. I don't think they'll become really tall, but they are more compact. I don't give canned food any more. Their stools are better now that they get Hill's kitten dry food and some chicken bits. Dry food is also better for their teeth. They like it. The first day I gave it, Daimke did question me: 'I thought I was getting food, mama, what is this stuff then?' But now she is fond of it, especially when mixed with pieces of chicken.

Catje still likes to pretend she's a doggie. She runs around all day carrying things in her mouth. Ball pens, collars, handkerchiefs, she's a real retriever. Half of the bathroom is brought to my bed in the morning. It is always a surprise to discover what she has collected when I wake up. Last night she brought me something that I could not define. Something hard and small with a tag on it. I was too tired to switch on the light. It was a flea comb! Maybe she thinks I have fleas? Daimke runs around carrying big slippers. Very smart. In her basket I found the little bucket for body oil that I use when I take a shower. When I entered the

bathroom I saw her lying down amidst the shreds of a kitchen paper roll. How I laughed! It was so funny. She joins my laughing then, she throws herself on her back and moves all four legs in the air. She really has fun. Of course I took away the roll and told her that she shouldn't do that. But I do enjoy it so much, and she knows it! Kittenhood doesn't last long.

Rolls of toilet paper seem to have become ambulatory. I spot them in the most unlikely places. Socks seem to feel the cold. They hide themselves under the covers. I expect one of these days to find a little mouse in bed. Catje has already caught her first one. She was so proud of that! Fortunately I succeeded in snatching the mouse from my little tigress and released him far away in the garden. He was shivering but still very much alive. Boy! He will have a story to tell tonight! Catje still talks about her first 'live prey'!

As the weather was still fine, Catje and I went for a walk along the road. She doesn't like heavy trucks or noisy cars but she is not as scared of them as Donsje is. I fear we won't be able to keep up this good habit now that the weather has changed. It is stormy and the forecast says rain for tomorrow. It's better to stay in the garden then, where trees protect us from wind and rain. Besides it's getting colder.

Fluffies make excellent barometers. Storm! All five have been running and playing the whole morning. Mickje enjoyed the many leaves flying over the ground in the run in front of the bedroom. It looked like a black bulldozer tearing through the leaves. Donsje's tail became a 'live' toilet brush from excitement. The kids had a fantastic time. Donsje joins in the playing now. I am very glad about that. And Puddie has no problems with all the frolicking around him. It is very touching to watch mature cats play. Now they are tired. When Daimke is at ease, she lies down and crosses her forelegs.

At night before we go to sleep we have a real party. Catje starts it. She climbs up the curtains to the curtain rail. It's high up there and very narrow but she runs calmly over it, like I do over a forest trail. Daimke and Donsje were watching her acrobatics, looked at each other and then again at Catje. I was afraid to move but my worry was unfounded. One jump and she landed safely on the bed. Daimke was next but she didn't take any risk, she lowered herself down backwards. 'Tomorrow better!' I saw her thinking. Donsje looked at me: 'We would better not try any of this, mama, we're too old and wise for such antics, aren't we?' 'Indeed, Donsje, and besides, someone has to watch and applaud these entertainers.' 'Prrr prr' she nodded, ' That's it'. And she curled herself up against me. Like every new game, this one was the number one hit for a couple of weeks. It was fun to watch, I usually fell asleep chuckling. I hadn't slept so well and been so relaxed in weeks.
Today was a day full of adventures. Daimke and I have been to my dear
friend Doctor Wim. Readers who have read 'Miracles on little Feet' will wonder: 'Is this worth mentioning?' since Puddie and Donsje often went with me. But Doctor Wim now has a practice in the Klina-Hospital, our new district hospital that centralises three local hospitals. I agree with Doctor Smalhout - the author of interesting columns in the newspaper the Telegraaf - when he claims that a merger of hospitals does not necessarily benefit the patients. On the contrary! Usually the atmosphere changes and becomes more aloof. More laws and regulations and less compassion, that seems to be a growing

tendency.

A consequence of all this was that now I had to use the main entrance and not the terrace door as before when I visited him with my fluffies. Now, I had to pass through the entrance hall, walk up a flight of stairs, and then pass two more corridors. Thrilling! I had passed this way only once before and I hoped I would find the way. Daimke's conduct - it was the first time she came here - was really exemplary. I could not use my pouch bag so I used the cat carrier. In fact it was well suited for the purpose. Both sides have small 'windows' of thin dark wire netting so that Daimke could see everything and had fresh air. It has a cute plastic spy hole and it's easy to hang over my shoulder. And so, carrying the bag over my right shoulder and skimming the right wall, I hurried upstairs. I arrived unnoticed at Doctor Wims office, only, he was not in yet. Phew!

There is a 'beautiful' toilet opposite his room. We rushed into it. A safe place to hide while waiting for him! Daimke and I conversed in hushed voices. We had it cosy there. But there was a four-year-old boy walking around. I was afraid he might suddenly shout: **'Oh, look there, a PUSSY!'** Fortunately he didn't pay any attention to us. When Doctor Wim arrived we hurried into his office. I put Daimke on his desk and introduced them to each other. 'Oh, she is so pretty! So cute and soft!' Doctor Wim said delightedly. Daimke fully agreed and stood purring loudly before Doctor Wim, kicking with joy. I was amazed that she found everything thrilling and fun. She cuddled Doctor Wim again and again and looked intensely at the many interesting things around her - now and then consulting me like: 'Mama, what is this? Is it dangerous?' Then she crawled into my arms, turned on her back and began purring. She had shut her eyes from pleasure and caressed my face with her front paws now and then, while pressing herself still closer to me. Of course Doctor Wim was very moved. He has a lovely 'golden' Tommy now himself! Surely because he fell in love with Daimke!

The days became colder and darker. I dread the coming of winter. Just like the fluffies I hate the cold and my hands cause me a lot of trouble in winter. Indeed, you cannot live for thirty years in Anorexia land and get away with it unhurt.
My sweet dog, Horry, has gone to the Rainbow Bridge. Twenty years ago, Horry really 'rolled into' my life while I was driving on a Belgian motorway on my way to friends in the Ardennes. It was a day of freezing weather and snow

covered fields and hills. All of a sudden I noticed something rushing down a slope. Automatically I checked my rear-view mirror. By amazing good fortune there were no cars behind me. I slammed on the brakes. A kind of big Dachshund rushed onto the road, chased by a pack of barking dogs. I opened the door, called...and, oh wonder, it's really true, the dog jumped in. Quickly I accelerated as I saw cars approaching. There we were! Whining, the dog crawled against me, trembling and panicky. When I arrived at my friends' place I immediately phoned the police and the animal shelters but nobody had reported the loss of 'Horry'. So I had named my new friend after Captain Hornblower, Daddie's hero! I was happy for I was already fond of him.

When I returned home I had some explaining to do, but, of course, Horry could stay. He would be around twenty now. He was deaf and blind but still enjoyed life. I had to be careful when Femke was a puppy. When she felt like playing and jumped on top of him, he would bite. Horry didn't have any teeth left but still, I kept them separate when I was not there. This morning my dear friend Mariette heard a strange sound coming from the scullery. She went to have a look and found Horry lying on the floor, kicking wildly with his legs. She called me and we immediately phoned the veterinarian. It was clearly an epileptic fit. Doctor Liliane couldn't do anything for him any more, just put him out of his misery. And so my dear mate calmly passed away in my arms while I asked papa, mama, Karma and little Fern, mama's beloved dog who is certainly with her, to welcome him. I felt very sad. At such moments good and understanding friends like Mariette, Emmy and Maria, with whom I could talk about Horry are a godsend.

Raymonde, my dear French friend came to stay with us. She comes twice every year. She is a dear and she loves the kitties and dogs. Horry was her special friend and it was so sad for her to have to miss him. We had made her bed the week before her arrival. After having admired Daimke and Catje for a long time she went upstairs. Suddenly I heard her shout: 'Marg, viens vite voir!!' (Marg come here and look!!). When I entered her room I saw on the blanket on her bed a neat row of eight perfect little turds. We were overcome with laughter. One for every day, Femke must have thought. I still don't know why she did this, for she is house-trained and clean. Surely, her way of giving a present to Raymonde?
December came, the last month of a year in which so many things had happened. Many sad things but also many good things. The most important

lesson I learned this year was that the Lord will always give us just that extra power we need to cope with the many things that happen to us and which sometimes are very sad and difficult to accept. That's a secure and confidence-inspiring feeling. Of course I talked a lot with Raymonde about my parents. When we were living in France she took care of us. She knew my parents through and through. I consider Maria as my sister, but Raymonde is also a sister to me. She is such a dear and a very wise woman.

I had almost forgotten how difficult it often was. I took care of my parents twenty-four hours every day. I wonder whether I could do it again. In those days I didn't know life as I know it now. Now I know the happiness of going to bed accompanied by fluffies and having an undisturbed, delightfully warm, cosy fluffy night in prospect. It is a real luxury and I am very grateful for all the good things I have now. But I couldn't have this gratefulness if I hadn't experienced that other life first. I am indeed glad I was able to hang on. With the help of the power, the love and the support of the Almighty, the fluffies and the close friends I got to know these last years.
Donsje and Puddie were worried. They sat down on my desk, looked at each other and then at me. I sensed they had something on their minds. 'Mama', Puddie started, 'we've been talking about this some time ago but we're afraid you kind of forgot it. Do you remember promising us that you were going to write a book about us and...' 'Yes,' Donsje interrupted, 'about us and about your life before we were with you and how I was found in a wheat field. And how mama Maria rescued me and about Luckje and Mickje and...' 'But, Puddie interrupted her, 'now we are so afraid you will not have the time any more 'cause the kids are here.' Oh, how awful! Indeed that had been my plan but then I had somehow pushed it into the background because of Daimke and Catje and the pain I had when losing the kittens to that horrible illness.

'Guys, excellent idea! You are indeed excellent assistants! Our book! Yes, let's work on it during these long winter months! I promised you and I'll keep my promise. What a marvellous diversion. As you know I have already collected a lot of things that I can use for the book.' 'What's the title?' Donsje asked. I thought for a while. When did I first think about writing a book? When I heard that Donsje had been found in a wheat field. The connection with our big farm, on which I always worked in the summer, helping in the wheat harvest and the little kitten found in a wheat field. In a flash I realized that Donsje would be 'my' Donsje and also that I would write down her story. 'Puddie, what do you

94

think, how about titling our book provisionally ' The Donsbook', but it is also your book, don't worry about that. It's just such a cute nice title. Besides you as Number One Pussy-Kid will be the first of its heroes.' Slowly Puddie nodded his assent. But I could read his mind: 'Hey mama, what's wrong with Pudbook? But I don't mind Donsbook as long as I am the first one appearing in it...'
Donsje's nose turned red with joy. She licked Puddie in his neck. 'Thank you, dear Puddie, you're my swell big brother. ' 'Purr purr', loudly purring she raced away to tell everybody the big news. The cats were right. No better idea than this to make this first Christmas without mama easier to bear! And mama would have loved it too. She was so proud of me for the two books I've written about anorexia, 'Free at Last' and 'I have a Key'.

And thus we started 'Miracles on little Feet', as the official title of the book will be. 'Donsbook' was great as a working-title but we needed a more official title for the final book. Because we consider every cat as a little miracle we decided on Miracles on little Feet. For the time being the book had two titles. And why not?
T.S. Elliot says: 'Cats must have three names – an everyday name, such as Peter; a more particular, dignified name, such as Quaxo, Bombalurina, or Jellyorum; and thirdly, the name the cats thinks up for himself, his deep and inscrutable singular Name.' Why shouldn't cat-books have two names?

It was exciting to write down everything of the past. The memories of my youth. To tell about the cats living in our stables. The sheep, the horses, the dogs. The wonderful years on our agricultural business, my 1800 hectares vast playground. I enjoyed it so. And the book turned out to be a success, something I had never expected. Indeed, writing was my best therapy and a delight to do. In this book I will put some stories that belong to Miracles. Purring Angels will be 'two books in one'.

The French novelist Colette was a firm cat-lover. When she was in the U.S. she saw a cat sitting in the street. She went over to talk to it and the two of them mewed at each other for a friendly minute. Colette turned to her companion and exclaimed, "Enfin! Quelqu'un qui parle français." (At last! Someone who speaks French!)

Anonymous

Chapter 6

Ophelia and the Hereafter

Eyes so transparent that through them the soul is seen.

Theophile Gautier

It was Christmas. The first Christmas without mama. Of course I missed her and Daddy even more on those 'special' days, but I knew that she was happy now, not ill and tired like she was that last year. Anyway, I was never fond of 'special days'. Even as a child I hated to have to sit for long hours at the dinner table. I preferred being with my animal friends. Once I was a prisoner of Satano, the anorexia-devil those days were horrid. It was living on the 'edge'. I didn't want to hurt the feelings of my parents, but I knew that by not doing that I hurt myself even more. It's impossible to enjoy eating with people or any other festivities as an anorexic. I am healed now but the kitties and I still say: No better days than normal days. And aren't we happy souls? There are so many more 'normal' days in a year than special ones. Thankfully!

All of a sudden the snow had covered house and garden. 'Fortunately not so inside, mama!' Donsje remarked when I was complaining about the cold. Our central heating is excellent but my inner heating seems out of service. I shivered all day. I was so happy I had gained a kilo in weight but it won't last long, I'm afraid. Shivering consumes lots of energy.

WATCHING
(Dedicated to Astra)

I watched her on Christmas Day
sitting silently 'neath the fragrant pine needles,
gazing wide-eyed at the sparkling orbs
dangling on silver threads, from the boughs.
I watched as she gently touched her oval paw
to the delicate glass and set it swinging
to and fro, and I saw how it mesmerised her.
And oh, how she mesmerised me as I watched her
sitting there, absorbed in her play.

I watched her on Christmas Day
while she pounced among the wrappings,
scattering them hither and thither,
and crouching and springing on invisible prey.
I watched her climb into bags and boxes,
therein to hide, and peer discreetly out
at the chaos she'd created.
And oh, how she created chaos in my heart
as I watched her hiding there, blinking wise blue eyes.

I watched her then, on Christmas evening,
as she stretched herself and yawned,
drowsy from the heat of the crackling log fire,
and idly kneading the rug as she squinted
sleepily at the leaping flames.
I watched as she settled herself down to rest,
tucking her daintly paws neatly beneath her,
and I saw a dreamy smile of contentment lighting her face.
And oh, how her contentment enveloped me
as I watched her lying there, serenely purring.

©Sue Wingett

97

Donsje returned from the run. Her furry coat felt ice-cold but underneath it she was wonderfully warm. What an advantage to "wear" a coat like that. Of course, you can't take it off and that is a disadvantage. I thought she was sleeping on the windowsill together with the others, but she had been outside instead, exploring that new white world. Well, the run is a real delight for them. Even on this cold winter day Donsje and Catje played in it. Daimke, however, preferred to stay indoors.

We don't have real Christmas decorations, except for the lights on the tree in front of the house. Why should we want to put up a tree inside the house? Trees belong outside. Inside they shrink from sadness and pine needles are poisonous to cats. All the trees were white with hoarfrost and the sun was shining. The view from the office-window was like a beautiful Christmas card. The birds were enjoying their sunflower seeds in the birdfeeder in front of the window. Catje was playing in the snow. Donsje and Daimke were lying cosily warm on the windowsill, while Mickje and Puddie were enjoying a nap in the living room. We live in a real paradise here. Swiss music in the background. Winter sport indeed! For all this beauty and marvel I have to thank papa and mama. They found this place and made it possible for us to live here!

On Chrismas-Eve we were sitting cosily together. 'Please mama, do tell us that lovely story from Puss. We have heard it already but the young ones haven't. We love it sooooooo much! Please? Purrr purrr!' Donsje put her little head against mine.
'Oh yes, mama please do!' Pudje and Mickje purred, 'it's our favourite story too.'

A Kitty's Best Christmas

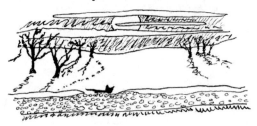

my Darlings,' sobbed Momma. 'I was trapped in a basement. I tried and tried to get out. I was so afraid.'
The happy family purred madly and licked and kissed each other again and again. Finally they looked up at a beaming Santa Claus. Momma stepped forward and bowed her head. 'I thank you, Dear Santa, for helping me and my children. But Sir, if I could be bold enough to ask, would you please take them to someplace safe and warm? I can get by, but my babies must have food, and warm shelter, and I cannot give them either in this cold winter.' 'Momma... NOOO!!', cried the three, 'we must stay with you, we love you!!'

Santa stooped low and gently spoke. 'Now hush Puss, Meme and Kiki. Your Momma is willing to sacrifice her heart's desire for you. This is the greatest gift that can be given, the true meaning of this Holy time of year. But the sacrifice need not be made, for I will bring you ALL home with me. Because of the love you have shown, you will stay in my magical kingdom. You will lead all those cats who leave their mortal lives to a  *wonderful garden called the Rainbow Bridge. And you will be warm, safe, and loved until our Father calls us all home to Heaven. And so it was, and still is.*

By Wayne Pond. Text and drawings © Wayne Pond, 2002 redrawn by Anne Versteyne to make them fit for printing.

Yes, it's is a lovely story. That night we all dreamed about the wonderful things little Puss did for his family.

Not just by coincidence (that is God Incognito) I had, shortly after mama's death, made the acquaintance of a very dear lady. Her name is Jos and she became such a dear friend of mine. We are so close that I consider her now as my 'spiritual mother'. Sometimes I can't help thinking that my parents must have sent her to me. I love her so much. I'm sure that we have lived several lives together on this earth. We felt so familiar from the very first minute we met. Jos lives with her son and daughter-in-law and she has three feline sweethearts. Maaike, a pitch-black she-cat, Olivier, a half-Persian with kidney problems and Basje, a very gorgeous tabby, very sweet and wise, who, like Donsje, is always being teased. I have his picture here on my cabinet. Then there is Inga, a very beautiful yellow Labrador.

Jos is fond of everything green: flowers, plants, trees. I am also fond of plants and flowers of course but mama only loved roses and didn't want any other flowers in the garden. That's why I had never considered planting other flowers. We had a swimming pool but we never used it - too wet and too cold as Puddie put it, but also too much maintenance - and so I had it converted into a rose garden. Jos taught me about other flowers and plants. A new world opened itself to me. It's a pity though that most plants and flowers are poisonous to cats. In Chapter 18 you can read all about 'good' or 'bad' plants for cats. The FAB, the Feline Advisery Bureau was so kind to give me permission to use their sheets.

I made several small cat gardens in the run close to the office. I planted red sage, curry plant, tarragon, thyme, mint and of course catnip (Nepeta) and Calamintha Nepeta in upended drainpipes and two large flower boxes. The last two plants flower, the other plants do not. That's why I selected them. Flowering plants attract wasps and bees, and these are naturally dangerous for the fluffies. If I trim the catnip before it flowers, there is no problem. How the kitties enjoy lying in it. Mickje especially loves it. Her cute black head just sticks out above the plants. She has a delicious fresh smell then. 'And', Mickje says wisely, 'it is so good to keep fleas away. Prrrrr!' What an excuse to lay in it all day!

Jos' daughter, Miguella, is a famous medium. I am very interested in anything related to the hereafter. I have read a lot about it. It's wonderful that I can discuss it now with Jos and she can advise me what books to read, for there is an awful lot of rubbish published about this subject! That's only logical, since faith and belief cannot be proved. Belief is the sure knowledge of things that one hopes for and evidence of things one cannot see. So anybody can claim anything but it cannot be verified or checked out. Except for your intuition.

Deep down inside you there is a very soft 'whisper', like papa said. That is your inner self. The direct link to the Lord, to the universal consciousness. It is your conscience or your intuition. When you listen to it you will know whether something is true or false. Our Dear Lord did not just give us brains, common sense and intuition for nothing. He wants us to make use of them. So, never just simply take something for granted, whether it comes from a human or from a spirit.

Anyway, we always have the possibility to change the course of our life. A medium sees what will happen to us if we continue on the course we have taken. But if we change that course, our life changes as well. There would be no sense in consulting a medium if that was not the case.

We often receive messages from the hereafter, by way of thought flashes or in a dream. Such a thought will suddenly occur to you. But we must open ourselves to it and listen attentively. Our own thinking often overwhelms those messages. When such a sudden idea makes you feel well and it is light and bright, it is often sent from the hereafter. Such an idea will always help you in solving a problem you are struggling with or deciding a choice you have to make. Our beloved, who crossed over before us, our guides and guardian angels converse with us in that way. The more we listen to those thoughts the better we will hear them.

Often such thoughts come to us when we are completely relaxed. Just before you fall asleep or in the morning just before fully waking up. I mainly receive them during my walks with the dogs in the garden, when I listen to the wind rustling in the trees and to the birds and my mind is completely blank. It is then that many counselling letters I write to anorexics, columns I publish and my books are 'conceived'. When I have a problem, I give it to the Lord at night before falling asleep, with a plea for His help. Very often I have a solution when waking up next morning.

Many people think they can't do this. 'You have to be trained well before you can do that,' they say to themselves. But that's plain nonsense. Everybody has helpers. When you open your mind and listen with your heart you will receive their messages. Only one thing stands in the way. Doubt! When you have doubts you cut yourself off from these thoughts. Your intuition equals that of any good medium. And only you can judge whether the advice you receive is correct and sound.

We live many lives here on this earth. After every life we return to the hereafter where our 'friends', the creatures with which we always remain connected, receive us with love. Often our reincarnation is simultaneous with theirs. Sometimes they return to the earth while we stay behind to rest and guide them from there. And next time it is the other way around. James Redfield, author of books like 'The Celestine Vision' and so on, is a famous medium who speaks of soul groups. It is so marvellous when we receive a message from them and learn that, after 'death', they keep on living happily in the hereafter. And how wonderful it is to notice they are still among us.

It is a secure feeling to know that we are protected by our beloved ones we have known on this earth. And that's how it is. I know for sure that papa is my guardian angel. I sense his presence close to me very clearly. Especially when I am doing something risky, like driving my car or cleaning the roof. Before doing these things I always ask for his assistance. When he was still on this earth he taught me everything I had to know. Often I can hear his voice warning me: 'Child, pay attention, the road is slippery.' Or he says: 'Watch that bend in the road.' Very reassuring. Mama always watches me, her hand on my shoulder, when I play the piano and softly hums the tune I'm playing.

We are surrounded by guardian angels. Sometimes they take the shape of a dog or a cat to help us and to protect us during our life on earth. I always say: 'Not all angels have wings.'

When we die our helpers always guide us. Often our animals who crossed before us welcome us. What a wonderful feeling to be able to embrace them then and to know they are with us forever. At first we are allowed to rest. We are received in some sort of hospital where our health is restored. All our deficiencies disappear and we will feel young and vital again. Then we just continue the work we did on earth.

In the hereafter you receive things by just thinking them. You can think yourself from one place to another. If you want to meet a certain person, you just think of that person and there he appears. You can build yourself a beautiful house simply by thinking of it. That's the reason why often animals are not mentioned in books about the other side. The authors had no pets when they were on the earth. They simply don't think of animals, so they don't see any. Probably, and that is my strongest wish, later in my next life I will be able to do a lot for cats. Shelter them and comfort them when they have crossed over. That's something I can't do now because of my health. Writing, of course, is another way of helping cats. That's the most important reason why I write this book.

It's easy to know if a medium is honest. If somebody charges a huge amount of money for a reading, you can be sure you are dealing with a wrong and unreliable person. It is a God-given talent to be able to do a reading and therefore it should not be a source of self-enrichment. Of course expenses and the time may be charged. But there is more. Even if a medium is good and reliable, 'bad' spirits may interfere, if he or she does not protect him or herself before starting a reading. There happen to be many wandering spirits which have lost all bearings because of a sudden 'death'. They wander around the earth. Eventually they are helped and sent to the light but in the meantime they can enter anybody who did not adequately shield him/herself against them. Hence the dangers involved with such games as ouija and questioning spirits. Lots of accidents have happened during such performances.

A fantastic book on this subject is: 'Char, the Medium.' Char is a famous American medium. In this book she explains in a clear way how everything fits together. I advise anybody who wants to know more about this subject to buy this book. It is so beautiful. She explains how our dearly beloved, humans and animals, live on spiritually after 'death' and watch over us.
Everything in the universe consists of energy. Matter is spirit in materialised form. Each form has its own vibration number and its own degree of consciousness. Energy can never be destroyed. Everybody, human and animal, each individual, has his own pattern, which is unique to that person. That is our spiritual body, which is disconnected from our physical body. When we die, our physical body is left behind while our spiritual body moves on to another dimension and continues to live there. We keep our identity in that new world. Animals too cross over spiritually and remain their unique self. When doing a reading Char often sees people together with their beloved animals. Sometimes they visit us and then we suddenly sense our beloved ones who 'had gone' close to us. Char gives so much comfort, support and love to the people in her work. She is doing a fantastic job. I have watched her performances on television. Rosemary Althea is also wonderful. She too has written some really great books about this subject. And the books of James van Praagh are also very interesting!

So we all have guides, guardian angels and beloved ones on the other side, who help and protect us. But they can make mistakes. They are not omniscient. They were not omniscient here on earth either. Therefore we must protect ourselves before trying to contact them. Then, when we proceed we can prevent any lower spirits from entering us. This is very important!

Place yourself in a radiating yellow-white light. Visualise a beautiful yellow-white cocoon around yourself. Then we must first and foremost ask The Lord for protection. Say for instance: 'I rely on the Lord and on everything that's good. His love is my shield everywhere and always.' That's my mantra. Check every message with your feeling, your heart. Ask your unconscious self, your intuition, whether it's right and use your common sense.

Placing yourself in a radiant yellow-white light also helps when people want to hurt you. The more you listen to your intuition, the sooner you will feel that. Cover yourself at once from head to toe in that blinding yellow-white light. Visualise that the negative energy is bounced off by this shield and returned to its source. You should do this also when you help people or animals that are ill, for the negative energies emanating from them may pass to us. We can then become ill as well. That's why there are so many burnt-out people in that sector. Prayer and yellow-white light will protect you.
To read bad books is a waste of time, but consulting a bad or a stupid medium without protecting yourself in the first place is extremely dangerous. The first thing Jos did was to warn me about that. Shortly after, I experienced two things that still make me tremble.

An acquaintance of mine had ordered a run for her cats. Sadly it was constructed without wire netting over the upper surface. Very silly, but the man making the run had told her that electric wire would suffice to keep her cats inside. That's nonsense, of course. A cat will always find a way out of a run that is not completely closed, especially when it's a half-wild stray rescuee as in this case. Desperately the girl looked everywhere for days but found nothing. When she was at her wits' end, she consulted a clairvoyant who she had found through an advertisement in the newspaper. A big man wearing a turban let her in. The place was full of burning candles and incense. All very impressive. He performed all kinds of bizarre rituals and promised her that he would send the cat back to her. But for that to happen she first had to buy a certain piece of wood which had the power to make the cat find his way back to her home.

Price: 700 euros! The girl hesitated for a moment, but then paid the price. I don't have to tell that she never saw her cat again. It's hard to believe that she fell for it, but I must admit that when my Luckje went I also tried everything to get him come back to me. Only, I would never have visited a clairvoyant I didn't know anything about. A friend of mine, Doctor Focco Huisman, a very well known medium advised me to put a candle on the windowsill and 'think' Luckje back. Of course I tried that and I am sure Luckje felt it too. For some reason he could not come back. But he is still with me somehow. I feel it!

I advised my acquaintance to have a reading by Miguella. Miguella saw that the little tomcat had been run over by a car, pretty soon after his escape. A very logical conclusion since she lived close to a busy road. What a revolting man that clairvoyant was! They exploit somebody else's misery and despair! They'll have a lot of explaining to do some day!

The second case is even more tragic and I still feel so sad about it. This case is also a proof that thoughts are really things. Thoughts create situations and by thinking something you give power to it. To send negative thoughts to somebody might boomerang, they always return double as powerful to you. When our thoughts are positive, they will attract the positive and then we can heal and help others. If we think negative, however, and give power to evil, we create evil. When you are bothered by negative thoughts, you'll be surrounded by a negative field of energy and many things will go wrong. You'll attract the negative. Of course, positive thoughts don't guarantee happiness in your life. Still, they do brighten up your life a lot.

When you are not in control of your thoughts and allow those bad fantasies to live a life of their own, horrible things may happen. The self-fulfilling prophecy!

There was a woman who lived with her three cats. She wrote me long letters about her 'childern'. She had a run but the cats were often running around free. She lived at odds with her neighbour, who, according to her, disliked not only her but hated her cats. They hurled recriminations at each other. Things went from bad to worse. I tried to make her understand that anger is always wrong and that action gives reaction. Why not just talk it out and then simply try to ignore each other? Cats would do that. So, why not take a cue from them? It was no use.

She consulted a medium. This woman predicted that her cats would die a most horrible death. Her neighbour would 'destroy' them and they would suffer agony. How stupid and dangerous of that woman to say so! I had misgivings about the whole situation. Suddenly I heard nothing about the neighbour any more. Weird! When I asked her about this she gave me evasive answers. Then I received a letter: ' My cats are safe now. They are somewhere where that terrible scumbag can't hurt them any more. Never ever! They are safe!'

This made my hair stand on end. I phoned her and kept questioning her until, at last she told me everything. After the visit to the medium she had panicked and taken her cats to the veterinarian to have them put to sleep. I was shocked and very sad. I could feel the desperate fluffies, knowing they were about to die. For they knew! Of course they felt what's going on. Animals know so much. So you see it is really very dangerous to consult a medium who does not shield herself first so as to prevent any misreading of someone's fantasies as an advice of her spiritual helpers. Because this is what had happened. She 'caught' the thoughts of the woman instead of a message from above.
Yes, I was really shocked! My pussy-children sensed my sorrow and tried to comfort me by snuggling up very close to me and by lying in my lap. Wisely Puddie advised me:' Mama forget it, there is no purpose in thinking about it. They are now in the light and play happily on the Rainbow Bridge.' He was right, still...

What interests me most is the fact that our pets will wait for us later. The beautiful poem about the Rainbow Bridge is so comforting. Many people have stated that during a Near-Death-Experience they also met their deceased pets. The books written by James van Praagh and Doctor Focco Huisman contain very moving stories in this regard. I have listed the titles in the bibliography.

When on earth you have a strong bond with an animal, then this bond is so strong that it will never be broken. When your pet dies, it doesn't return to its 'group' as animals without a bond with humans do, but it will wait for you on the 'Rainbow Bridge'. Until we join her or him, our pet is cared for with love. It's heavenly there. The animals play together, there is never a fight and they are extremely happy. There are gorgeous flowers and colourful birds and a brightly shining warm golden yellow light.

Sometimes people ask me: 'How can you be so sure that our deceased cat or dog is now on the Rainbow Bridge and that we'll meet again later?' Indeed, to believe is just that: to believe. There is no real scientific evidence for it (as yet). Still, keep in mind that our knowledge hasn't reached so far yet. If we had told our ancestors about computers and television, they would have considered us out of our minds. Television is a fitting example, by the way. When the television set is on, the screen 'lives'. We cannot see those waves, but we know they are there. When the set is old and defective, we discard it. Yet we don't think that those waves are gone too. As soon as we plug in a new set and switch it on we can see those waves again. You can't catch them, you can't see them, but they are there!

To believe is precisely that inner certainty that you can't buy anywhere, that you can't find in books, although reading about it is very inspiring. It is a certainty you can only acquire by conversing much with Our Dear Lord and by opening your mind to all 'so called' coincidences and nature. It is literally a blessing! And very rarely, but it does happen - like a ray of bright light in the darkness - a message comes through from that 'other world'. A real proof of its existence! Just read the following story.

Jos phoned me and told me the following: That afternoon Miguella, her daughter and medium, had done a reading for an elderly woman who was brought to her by her psychic guide. Miguella always proceeds as follows. When someone wants a consultation, she asks for her name and where she lives. Then she arranges an appointment. Miguella doesn't want to know any other details, for any further knowledge might cloud the message from Miguella's guide. One of the main dangers of a reading is that the one giving the reading puts his or her own interpretation on the message coming through.

Miguella prefers to work by means of a picture only, also in the case of animals. She holds the picture in her left hand. Then she gets a 'far away look' and she comes into contact with her guide. With her right hand she writes down the message she receives. She doesn't know what she has written. She has done that a couple of times for me, among other things for my hands. Since I followed her advice to warm my hands in camomile tea and rub them with Calendula cream, my chapped fingers are much better.

So, this afternoon those two people visited Miguella. She gave the reading. The boy - a very tender and sweet person according to Jos - looked around him after the consultation and noticed Boris, Miguella's black Labrador. 'Hey,' he suddenly said, 'there is another dog like this sitting there, only it's yellow' 'Oh,'

109

Miguella says, 'that must be Inga, my mother's Labrador.' 'No,' the boy replied, 'this dog has died and he is accompanied by a young man whose hair is cut very short!' Miguella was amazed. Jos had a favourite dog, Aisa, which had died young and which she had loved immensely. She still missed him very much. He was yellow. Harold, her son, died of cancer and had very short hair as a result of chemotherapy. Jos phoned me about this immediately. Isn't it wonderful? This comes really very close to a proof. Even though I don't need a proof, this story makes me very happy, it is so magnificent! I can sense daily papa and mama and all the animals that 'have crossed over' around me.

Miguella also saw Cartouche, Jos' cat. Cartouche had died in 1996 in Jos' arms. She missed him terribly of course. One day Miguella got a message from Harold. He was carrying Cartouche, now healthy again, in his arms and smilingly teased Jos through Miguella: 'Fear not, ye men of little faith, Cartouche really is with me here.'

Miguella has told me that she has seen many animals in the hereafter. People who loved animals here on earth are appointed in the hereafter to take care of animals who need lots of love and cuddles. Domestic animals like horses, cats and dogs are sometimes cruelly treated and abused by people. When they have crossed over they are tenderly comforted and nursed by animal lovers. They are also helped by animals that have been treated well and are full of confidence. This calms them down. Even animals living in the wild are welcomed with love. When they have been injured, they are nursed back to health before being taken to their group.

Miguella told me that Horry, my dog who had recently died, had been welcomed by his dog friends and by papa and mama. It might very well be possible that my parents now also look after other dogs and horses that never had good owners. My parents were very fond of horses. Daddy participated in the Olympic games in Berlin just before the war. Show jumping! He was really good. And he was a wonderful cavalry-officer. He fought in the battle of Arnhem in the war with his horses, who saved him many times.

Once Miguella wrote me:

' I am sure that Juulke, my parakeet, will fly with me later. Guinea pigs don't have many brains, they 'sense' something and their intuition is limited. Dogs are 'followers', very much pack-and-leader-oriented. Cats are very special creatures. They are very intelligent and have a strong intuition. They are real

110

solitaries but if they give their heart to someone it's with real deep love and the bond they then have with their people is so strong! That love will never 'die'.

There are many people on the Rainbow Bridge who want to be with their animals. When you are cat-minded, so that you feel at one with your cats, you will go later to the place where they are. But there are people who do not care at all about animals and just take my word for it, they will go to another place. That is, they will go to the place their mind is focused on. Life after this life is much better and easier than this one. Everybody - human and animal – will cross over. Once arrived, it is always a feast, a joyful recognition with lots of surprise, acceptance and happiness. There is only one big sorrow: departing from that which you love. But someday everything will be one again!! You will meet everybody you love, if you want to.
The Rainbow Bridge is a fact!
Love
Miguella...'

Beatrice Lydecker, a well-known animal therapist was very sad because she had not been with her little dog when he died. Later, in a dream, the dog visited her to tell her he had understood it all. 'We will meet again,' he told her. Some time after that she saw him playing on the Rainbow Bridge. She was so happy.

Yes indeed, it is very nice to know we'll see our animals again later, but this knowledge does not alter the fact that it is terribly sad to miss them while we are still here on this earth. Yet, time is the great healer. You will never forget your beloved cat or dog, but after some time you will be able to come to terms with your loss and move on with your life. Usually people outlive their pets. But what if you are the first one to go? That is also possible! In that case your animals cannot just live on without you. That's why you should make a will in which you clearly stipulate what is to become of your animals if... This is very important! If you don't do this a tragic situation may arise.

Suddenly your beloved cat or dog has to leave its familiar surroundings. Their world literally turns upside down. They are desperately sad. If at such a crucial time there is no one who can shelter them with love and affection, the animal may get ill and even die. I had never really considered this until I read the beautiful book 'Ophelia's Winter' written by (Marilyn a.k.a) Sarah Ann Hill. My dear American friend Marilyn relates the moving story of her cat Ophelia in this book. I was so shocked and moved that I immediately made the necessary arrangements to prevent this from happening to my pussy- children and dogs. Marilyn has given me her permission to render this tragic but wonderful story here in my own words.

'Ophelia's Winter'

'Mow, mow, mow,'Ophelia sobbed desperately, sitting on a huge stack of books. 'Mow, mow, mama Janet, where are you now? I am so scared and so lonely! Mow!' But mama Janet could not come any more.

Miss Janet was a highly intelligent woman who had specialised in anesthesiology. In 1955, she had founded the 'Medical Center School of Anesthesiology' in West Virginia. She taught doctors, students and assisted in operations. Her job was her life. Her youth had been lonely. Her father, an engineer, had been killed in an accident. Her mother had remarried. Although Miss Janet hadn't related well to her stepfather, she had been able to finish her studies. Something not to be taken for granted in a time of crisis. She had inherited her Irish temper from her father and that would come in very handy in her later years. She had never been very social, because she worked long hours and had no time left to meet people. She only felt relaxed and at ease when she was alone with her beloved cat Macbeth. Her father had left her the complete works of William Shakespeare, hence she had chosen the name Macbeth for her constant companion. How they loved one another, the gorgeous Abyssinian and Miss Janet! When she arrived home from work exhausted every day, Macbeth welcomed her. Then all the hard and sad experiences of her time spent at the hospital vanished. They would prepare their evening meal together and watch television afterwards. People gossiped that Miss Janet was a real old spinster, so 'pathetically alone'. Miss Janet felt far from lonely. She just preferred to live 'guest-free', free of people but never felt alone. Macbeth was always there to keep her company.

She had one close friend though, at least before her retirement: Sue, a nurse, who assisted her in the medical center. She sometimes visited Miss Janet and also took care of Macbeth when Miss Janet had to go on a trip for her work. When Miss Janet retired, she decided to move to Florida and to live close to her only niece, Annie. Annie had said that she would love her aunt to come. She probably hoped to inherit everything should her aunt die. Miss Janet had accumulated some savings and Annie would inherit. Life in Florida turned out to be even 'lonelier' than before for Miss Janet. Annie and her husband had no time for her and found family just extra obligations. Of course Annie visited her but never without all kinds of comments on everything Miss Janet did. Moreover Annie found the mutual love and affection between Miss Janet and Macbeth strange. 'Oh, don't mind Annie,' Miss Janet explained to Macbeth, 'she doesn't understand anyway.' For a couple of years both lived reasonably happy. Macbeth grew old and tired and one night he just lay down and waited for the end. Of course, Miss Janet was very sad but she realized that nature had to have its way and she knew that Macbeth would wait for her on the Rainbow Bridge.

Some weeks after the sad event Miss Janet felt the longing for a fresh companion. She told Annie about it. Stupid Annie commented: 'Aunt Janet, you're not planning to take another cat at your age, are you?' That did it! Miss Janet stepped into her car and drove to an animal shelter. That Irish temper, remember! Sadly Miss Janet walked past cages full of disconsolate kittens. Suddenly she felt something rubbing her arm. She looked up and saw a gorgeous little brown tabby with a beautiful M on its forehead and cute big eyes with a white rim. Her front paw was on her arm and her eyes begged: 'Oh, please, take me with you, I am so sad and scared!' The kitten's guardian angel had done a good job. Then and there Miss Janet decided to take her. Ophelia, as Miss Janet named her, had found a new mama.

When you consider the fact that, in most animal shelters more than sixty percent of the cats end up being euthanized, you may say that Ophelia had a very lucky day. 'Who could dump such a cute cat?' Miss Janet thought while driving home. Ophelia was an American Shorthair. That breed looks very much like the British Shorthair, like my Chummy. They are fantastically quiet and lovely cats which can live very long. If Ophelia would be twenty, Miss Janet would be ninety-six. But now she was still strong and healthy. It's absurd not to adopt animals any more when you are older, just because you fear they'll outlive you. Even if a shelter-pussy has only one happy year with her new mama, that's still preferable to staying in the shelter or being euthanized. In that single year she will receive more love and care than many a cat will receive in a whole life.

Ophelia was very talkative. She didn't say 'miauw', she always said 'mow, mowmow.' Those three words were enough for her to clearly express what she wanted. Soon she felt at home and, as often happens, she showed some specific habits from Macbeth, who, of course was in touch with Ophelia. So she could let Miss Janet know that he was still around, for Miss Janet still mourned Macbeth's sudden death. Naturally, Ophelia was not a substitute for Macbeth, that's impossible, but she was a big comfort. Miss Janet had saved Ophelia but Ophelia had not come in Miss Janet's life just for nothing. She, in her turn was going to 'rescue' her mama and that not only once but many times. For some time now, Miss Janet didn't feel well. Being an anesthesiologist herself, she knew the meaning of the symptoms. She underwent an examination and yes, she appeared to have cancer. In her case it was even worse as she realized that the prognosis for the kind of cancer she had was bad. But she was going to put up a fight nevertheless. Again her Irish temper was a great help. She decided to undergo chemotherapy.

That meant Miss Janet had to stay in the hospital for some days. Niece Annie would take care of Ophelia during her absence. Her eyes filled with tears, Miss Janet said good-bye to Ophelia and promised to be back as soon as possible. Two days later, exhausted and still sick from the chemo, she was brought home. While still on the driveway, she heard Ophelia 'mow, mow mow' from the top of the little cabinet in the hall. How happy they were to be together again! Ophelia cried real tears from joy, 'but what kind of horrible, nasty smell was that hanging around mama?' Something was wrong. Very worried Ophelia nestled close to her on the couch, purring loudly to calm both of them down. Miss Janet still had to undergo some chemotherapy sessions. And every time Ophelia purred her back to health. Ophelia was the only reason Miss Janet fought for her life. She knew many people who had been healed by chemo but it is a very exhausting treatment. In fact there should be people around to help the patient recover. But Miss Janet only had her niece to rely on and she was not much help. The chemo seemed to work, she really got better, only she still got tired very quickly. But then she was not young any more.

It came as a big shock when one year later she learned that the cancer had returned. She cried desperately and took Ophelia in her arms. 'What is going to happen to you, little one, when your mama is not there any more?' she said. Indeed, this was a problem because 'Dear Annie' couldn't care less about Ophelia. Moreover Miss Janet had come to the conclusion that she could not get any further help in her present location. She decided to return to West

114

Virginia. Sue, her friend, lived there, as well as many doctors she knew from the time when she was still working at the center. Of course, niece Annie objected but Miss Janet couldn't care less about that. She phoned the hospital and fortunately there was a flat available which she reserved. It was a thirteen hours' drive but Miss Janet and Ophelia took five days for it. Ophelia enjoyed the trip tremendously and proudly sat in her harness next to her mama on the front seat. Everything was fine for Ophelia as long as her mama was not sad.

When she drove into her town and showed everything to Ophelia, Miss Janet felt back to normal again. Deep down she had been very unhappy in Florida with her niece. Now she was home again and everything would be fine. Amazed, Ophelia watched Sue and her mama embracing, tears of joy running freely. The flat was small and the movers hadn't arrived yet. But there was a bed, a television and an easy chair. They didn't need anything else. They could see the mountains, 'her' beautiful mountains. Oh, how Miss Janet had missed this view! That night they slept close together. Ophelia did have to get used to all those strange noises and she did miss the salty sea air but she was happy because her mama was happy. Two days later Miss Janet had herself examined. This time the doctors wanted to try a very different approach, a rather more aggressive one, but also one with more chance of success. Sue took care of Ophelia while her mama was in hospital. Sue had three cats and was fond of Ophelia. Miss Janet also met Sue's neighbour, an elegant lady, professor in literature, who taught at the university. She was also fond of Shakespeare. This could have developed into a friendship but unfortunately Miss Brown only had time for an informal chat now and then. Her agenda was full and planned down to the minute. Still, she promised to care for Ophelia when Sue couldn't. Miss Brown also loved cats and the name Ophelia had made her very enthusiastic when she met her for the first time.

How nice it was to be back home! The new approach seemed to work. This time for real and Miss Janet was profoundly happy. Together they celebrated Christmas. Miss Janet was not really hungry but she prepared turkey nevertheless and Ophelia enjoyed the meal. They watched television at Christmas. They showed a beautiful Christmas movie. The hospital was decorated with beautiful Christmas lights. When the curtains were left open the whole room was bathed in light. Miss Janet told some Christmas stories to Ophelia and both felt immensely happy being together. Nothing indicated that within a month Ophelia's life would be hell.

'Mow, mow, mow,' Ophelia desperately cried. She was sitting next to Miss Janet who was lying on the floor. She couldn't get out to fetch help and didn't know what to do. She nearly panicked! 'Mow, mow, mama, please wake up, what's the matter with you? Why don't you listen to me?' That night she tried to warm up her mama's cold body by crawling on top of it. Ophelia sensed that something was awfully amiss but there was nothing she could do about it. The next day, late in the afternoon, someone knocked at the door. Ophelia now was weak from hunger and could hardly mew. The person at the door knocked again and then left to return after a while with the caretaker who had a master key. When he found the body he was shocked and called for an ambulance and a doctor. When the paramedics came in Ophelia was sitting terrified next to Miss Janet, ready to attack in defence of her mama. The paramedics, however, were kind to her. They understood what Ophelia was going through. Slowly they transferred Miss Janet from the floor to a stretcher. They finished the paperwork. Suddenly Ophelia jumped onto the body of her mama, sniffed under her nose and uttered a loud desperate cry. 'Mowwwieeee Moowwww moouwww!!!!' Genuine tears rolled down her cheeks. The paramedics were deeply touched and cried as well. But they couldn't do anything to comfort the little cat.

Oh, how terrible that Miss Janet had not left any instructions about what should be done with her pussy-child! Miss Brown, the neighbour, had promised to look after Ophelia but she had gone to her old mother. Sue was not available either, she had left with her family for the South where she had a house. She was away for months, so the paramedics decided to take Ophelia to an animal shelter. Fortunately the caretaker had said that probably someone would get the cat later. So Ophelia was put in a separate cage but still she could hear the desperate mewing and barking of the other animals. She was really scared and sad. 'Mow, mow,' she softly sobbed, 'mama, where are you then?' And so Ophelia's icy winter of discontent started. It would last three long months. Terrible months which she would remember for the rest of her life.

Some days later Miss Brown returned. She kept her promise and fetched Ophelia. Ophelia was overjoyed to see someone she knew and to be able to use her basket and blanket again. Miss Brown put her in a room, quickly opened a can, put out the litter tray as well as a bowl of water before disappearing again. No time! That evening Ophelia tried to resume her old life and habits. She challenged Miss Brown with a ball of paper. Throwing balls of paper was *her favourite game with Miss Janet. But Miss Brown picked up the ball and threw it in the waste-paper basket. When Ophelia tried to fish it out, she yelled: 'No, naughty cat, that's not allowed here!' Ophelia wasn't allowed on her lap either and sadly she hid in her basket, feeling lonelier than ever. Miss Janet and Ophelia used to rise early. So, next morning, Ophelia woke up at five and went begging for food. 'Mow, mow, mow, I am hungry, can I have something to eat?' Miss Brown opened one eye, saw Ophelia's worried face and angrily turned her back to the cat. Ophelia decided to play a bit to pass the time. As Miss Brown loathed to discard anything, her room was filled with stacks of books. Funny mountains to climb and jump on! 'Pop, pop,' the sound of her little feet. Then all of a sudden there was a little earthquake when a stack of books collapsed. Angrily Miss Brown got up. She scolded Ophelia and locked her outside, in the hallway. Miss Brown now regretted the promise she had made. What should she do with Ophelia?*

Next week she found the solution. She read a note in the supermarket saying 'I want to buy a cat.' Miss Brown dialled the telephone number written on the notice and was answered by a man. They arranged when and where he could get the cat and so it happened that poor Ophelia changed hands without a cuddle or a kind word on some cold parking lot. Her new owner would prove to be a real devil. 'You will take good care of her?' With this question, asked while transferring the cat carrier to the new owner, Miss Brown felt she had done her duty.

The man who had bought Ophelia was mentally ill. He lived with his old mother and a giant snake. He found it 'fun' to have a cat. Ophelia was put in an almost empty, dark room smelling strangely. There was also a very big glass tank. Her fur bristled out. With all her might she wanted to escape but where to? When the man left she dared to move. She jumped on a cabinet and huddled up there, feeling lost and forlorn.

Some time later the mother brought food and water. She was kind and talked to the poor cat. She explained that her son sometimes behaved a bit weirdly and promised her that she would take care of her when he was away. She herself was scared of him as well. And rightly so. It is known that serial killers often abuse animals in their childhood. He had often done so. Now he was 25 and his mother feared the worst. He had been behind bars for some cases of battery and one time for a sexual offence. What was he up to now?

117

During the day he worked and then Ophelia was allowed to run freely through the house. It was safe then, the mother looked after her well. To her horror Ophelia found out what the big glass tank in her room was: a terrarium containing a huge python. In America these snakes are called "balls" because they roll themselves into a big ball when they are afraid. Pythons are in fact rather gentle animals, curious but not really dangerous. At night the man released the snake. Following her instinct Ophelia then raced away and climbed onto a cabinet, her tail as big as a brush from fear. She couldn't know that the snake was harmless. The man apparently got a kick out of this.

Ophelia lived like this for three months. Fortunately, as often is the case with disturbed persons, all of a sudden he had enough of this 'entertainment'. He instructed his mother to find another home for Ophelia. He put an advertisement in the local paper: 'Cat! Willing to trade for snake or cash. Tel...'

Deep down inside, Ophelia sensed Miss Janet's protection. That had been the only reason she had put up with this and hadn't lost heart.

So far this was Ophelia's story as far as my friend Marilyn was able to reconstruct it.

It was Sunday morning and Marilyn was casually reading her morning paper. Her eyes caught the strange advertisement. First she burst out laughing. 'What a funny ad, Schnookie, just listen!' Schnookie was her dear pussy always present on the breakfast table. Suddenly she understood the meaning of the ad!! 'Oh, how terrible! How unhappy this little cat must be!' She went to the telephone and dialled the number. Fortunately the mother picked up the receiver. She quickly explained what was going on. They agreed an immediate pick up so that the deal was finished before her son arrived home from work. Marilyn would get the cat in exchange for some money. And so it happened that Ophelia was again put in a cat-carrier and handed over to someone totally unknown to her. But, she felt it clearly, this person could be trusted. She looked like her Miss Janet. This person spoke to her and radiated love. Still, Ophelia didn't have much hope and was far too afraid to talk. Hadn't Miss Brown been so angry any time Ophelia had said something? But Ophelia's fear subsided. After half an hour she arrived at her new home. Marilyn decided to put her in a little study for a while so she could adjust in peace and undergo an examination by Marilyn's veterinarian. After that Ophelia would be introduced to Schnookie.

When Marilyn opened the cat-carrier, Ophelia hardly dared to move. For three months she had been locked up in that terrible room where she had faced the python every day. She was traumatized, but she would never scratch or bite. Marilyn noticed the deep despair and the fear but also the awakening hope in Ophelia's gorgeous big eyes. 'Please, please, take care of me, help me! Please, I am so afraid!' Very carefully Marilyn took her into her arms and tenderly stroked her till she relaxed. She got some food and prepared a cosy warm spot for her close to the radiator. Ophelia's fur was dirty and infested with fleas. Marilyn had no choice. Ophelia had to take a bath. Very carefully Marilyn washed her. It took more than an hour to catch most of the fleas. How wonderful of Ophelia to allow Marilyn to wash and groom her! She really had a golden character.

The next day Marilyn took Ophelia to her veterinarian. He was shocked when he saw the condition of the cat. American Shorthairs have compact bodies but Ophelia was just skin and bone. Tufts of hair fell out and her body was full of scabs from scratching, yet the tests were negative. She had no fungal infection and her health was all right. She received a vaccination, a de-wormer and a spray against fleas. 'Lots of rest and tasty food and soon she'll be her old self', the veterinarian said. 'Another ten days and Ophelia may meet Schnookie.' When Marilyn turned into the drive, Ophelia already recognized her new home and this time she walked purring out of the cat-carrier. 'Mow, mow, mow?' These were her first words to Marilyn. And indeed, she recovered. She groomed herself again, a sure sign that things were better. She ate well and most important, her confidence grew, but there was still a long way to go. While sleeping she sometimes woke up with a start and cried for her new mama, 'Mow, mow, mow, where am I? I had a bad dream again, oh, please help me! Mow, mow.' When Marilyn caressed her she then crawled towards her and put her head against her. She was not yet willing to sit on Marilyn's lap. When she heard something she jumped up and hissed, while all her hairs bristled out. Big eyes full of fear looked everywhere then. It was heart-rending to see her panic like that.

Of course Schnookie had quickly realized that a new friend had entered her world. So, when the ten days were past, Marilyn opened the door of her room and prayed that there would be no fighting. This would be a terrible setback for

Ophelia. But luckily there was only some swearing. During the first days the pussies avoided each other but after a week Marilyn caught them lying together on the bed. Not yet touching, but it was a good sign. They were becoming buddies.

It took some months before Ophelia really had confidence in Marilyn. One night Marylin sat in her chair, half asleep but watching television. Suddenly she felt a leg on her lap. Marilyn didn't move. Then Ophelia jumped softly on her lap and, oh, so sweet, smelled her nostrils to verify whether her mama was still breathing! Tears sprang into Marilyns eyes, that's how it happened. Ophelia's previous mama had died and that's why she had ended up in the animal shelter.

'All this misery, Marilyn thought, 'could have been prevented if only Miss Janet had made a will in which she clearly had written down what was to happen to Ophelia in the event of her dying. You should never count on some lightly given promise from a neighbour or friend, but you should write down your last instructions in your will. Isn't that the least you owe your pussy-child?' 'However, now, you're really home, Ophelia,' she said to the cat, 'Once and for all!' I have made all the necessary arrangements for you and Schnookie in case I unexpectedly have to go. You're safe this time.' Purring loudly Ophelia snuggled up to Marilyn. Yes, she had found her new mother at last.

Marilyn has reconstructed Ophelia's life to write a book about it. She wanted to remind people how important it is to put down in writing and in a will what is to happen to your pets. To get more information she and a friend visited the shelter where Ophelia had been. Suddenly her friend said: 'Oh, Marilyn, look at the despair and sorrow burning in the eyes of that cat there in the corner! He has given up hope.' Marilyn looked and indeed she saw a gorgeous Siamese crouched in the corner of his cage. The sadness he radiated! Marilyn went to the counter to find out how come that such a splendid tomcat ended up in the shelter. It was almost the same story.

For years, Simon, this little boy, had been the help and love of some old lady. They lived peacefully and happily together. For hours the lady played with Simon who never got bored retrieving things. They watched television and sat for long hours on the balcony enjoying the sun. And then the lady died. Her grandson, who had often visited her and enjoyed playing with Simon, had promised his grandma to look after Simon in case of her death.

Indeed, he did take him to his house after his grandma had died. But he hadn't thought of the wonderful temperament of a Siamese. Since he worked during the day, Simon was alone all the time. So when, at last there was someone around, he insisted on playing and getting attention. And rightly so. He missed his mama terribly and tried by means of the old rituals to get some order in his life again. Those delightful games he and the lady used to play, those brushing sessions which both of them enjoyed. The grandson had other things on his mind. He liked to spend his time behind the computer and got more and more irritated by Simon who walked over the keyboard or sat down on his papers. After a couple of weeks he took Simon to the animal shelter.

What a sad story! Marilyn decided to take him home. Where there are two cats, there is room for one more. And so it happened. First she had her veterinarian examine him. A good idea as Simon had very serious cat flu that almost caused his death. For two weeks Marilyn forced him to eat little bits. Every day he had to receive fluid injections to prevent dehydration. Thanks to Marilyn's tremendous devotion and love Simon made it. For a couple of years he had a lovely time, until last year he died of a tumour in his ear which could not be removed by operation.

*Marilyn always signed her mails with Marilyn and SOS: Schnookie, Ophelia and Simon! She had fortunately received the SOS-signals from her 'cat-children' in time. Two years ago Marilyn herself had to undergo a serious heart-operation. When she returned home afterwards, her three little angels purred her to recovery. She wrote me: 'Thank you very much for your support and friendship. Doctors can do an awful lot but as important is the knowledge that there is love and warmth for you from other creatures. My pussy-children have been a great help. The three of them sensed there was something wrong with me and tried to heal me in every possible way. My friend, who looked after them and after my house, told me that Ophelia refused to eat two days before my return. She just sat at the window and waited for me. When I came in she rushed into my arms: 'Mow, mow, mow!!! You're home, oh mama, I was so afraid you would abandon me **as well**! Mow, mow, mow!!!'*

I am so grateful Marilyn allowed me to put this extract from her wonderful book 'Ophelia's Winter' in this book. Marilyn is a fantastic woman and

Ophelia's story has touched me deeply. What can be done to make sure that your pets are safe and sound once you suddenly are gone?

There is a choice of possible solutions.

In England it is possible to bequeath money to your animals. Unfortunately this is not possible in Belgium. Still, it is not always the best solution. Just think of the beautiful movie: 'The Aristocats.'

Another possibility is to set up, together with a few really true cat-friends who know what they are doing, a non-profit making foundation. Each member agrees to bequeath all or part of his money to the foundation when he dies. The advantage of this is that death duties are considerably lower. The members also agree to look after the pets of the deceased members. Together they look for a good solution. With money lots of things are possible. Of course, setting up a foundation without lucrative objectives costs money.

It is also possible to add a codicil to your will in which you leave some money to a friend of whom you are very sure that he/she will indeed take care of your cat. If this friend has cats of her own, they must of course be willing to accept the newcomer. A problem is that your friend, in her turn may fall sick. It is next to impossible to plan everything ahead, but it makes a lot of sense to think deeply about such matters.

You can also leave money behind to a cat shelter on the condition that your cat will be sheltered and looked after for there, as long as you make clear and solid arrangements in writing and are sure that the shelter will keep its promise.

For the pussy-child, your passing away is an enormous change indeed. Not only does she suddenly lose her mama or papa, but also her home and habits are gone. Everything has changed.

In the beginning the cat will have problems in adjusting. Maybe she'll forget she's house-trained for a while or she will become ill from sorrow and stress.

So it is important that money is available to help her, as medical expenses are high. A promise is quickly made and often really meant but sometimes people don't really understand what they are undertaking. Therefore, it is important to put it all down in a last will. It's the last thing you can do for your dear cat or dog child. She has devoted all of her life to you!

MESSAGE FROM A KITTY ANGEL

I look down upon you.
I see you crying on your pillow,
holding my favorite toy.
Oh my friend...

Please don't grieve so.
I'm not gone,
You just can't see me any more.
I'll always be near you,
follow your footsteps,
sleep cozy in your heart.
Oh my friend...

You loved me so,
you spared me the pain,
Your kindest act let me rest.
Now I'll watch you
and my brothers and sisters to come.
Till we can all play together,
in these rainbow fields forever.
Oh my friend...

I'll always be here,
and I'll ALWAYS love you.
Oh my friend...

© *Wayne Pond*

123

Chapter

The turn of the Century and Neutering

A cat's got her own opinion of human beings. She doesn't say much, but you can tell enough to be anxious not to hear the whole of it.

Jerome K.Jerome

It is the turn of the century. We are now 2-1-2000. What a funny date! I keep on thinking: 'Hey, something is wrong here, this is not possible!' My PC has the same opinion and asks me: '2-1-00? What de hell do you mean?' 'Well, I mean New Year!' 'Oh!' Let it be a good, happy, cat-friendly, wonderful year. Especially a peaceful year. Inner peace for all creatures. Peace is, next to health, the most important thing. And they go together.

Old and New passed rather calmly. I had to laugh about all the fuss that is made about these days. There was no other news. ' I bet that 2000 will just come by itself', Donsje said wisely, while we were watching the crowds of perspiring and dancing people on television. I had prepared a tasty fish-dish for dinner and we were relaxing and reading in bed when midnight came. It seemed like war had broken out! Maybe it wasn't too bad here, but we found the noise terrible. What terrified me most was the shouting of the crowds. It made me think of a riot. The dogs were afraid but didn't bark too much, they had heard this before.

Puddie and Mickje were in the living room. I was not at ease, so I checked up on them. They were sleeping peacefully. 'What's the matter?' they asked surprised. 'Happy New Year, guys, may 2000 bring us many purring hot days full of sunshine,' I wished them. 'And lots of that delicious fish we

124

tasted tonight', Mickje added sleepily. Puddie was purring, he agreed though he is more fond of meat, but he was too sleepy to argue. I was so proud of them.

When the explosions and bangings started, Daimke and Catje sprang to their feet with big bushy tails. 'Come on, guys, don't mind it,' Donsje comforted, 'people are firing off their foolishness. Just let them do it, they can't help behaving like fools.' She put her paw over her ear and continued sleeping. Daimke expanded her body, looking like a real Siamese queen, which of course she is. Rigidly sitting she listened to the noise. She really resembled an oriental cat-figurine. Catje, very brave, jumped onto the windowsill to look at the fireworks exploding high up in the sky. I was happy my cats were not too afraid. Firework mean hell to animals. I hate it! When I switched off the light, Daimke slipped under the covers and snuggled up against me. God, I felt so grateful, happy and rich. To celebrate Old and New in this way, together with my five super lovely fluffies, is heavenly. Daimke, so healthy now, purring the New Year in. How relaxing this purring is!

In 'Poezenpraatjes' (Cat-talk), the magazine of the Association 'Kattenzorg Dordrecht '(Cat-care Dordrecht), I found the following piece and got permission to include it in my book:

Purring heals felines

London, American scientists have found out that the purring of cats has a healing effect on their health. Injured felines, both domestic cats and wild cats, purr because their bones and organs then regain their strength and they recover faster. The saying ' A cat has nine lives' is herewith for a considerable part scientifically substantiated according to the Sunday Telegraph. Researchers at an institute for animal communication in North Carolina, America, listened carefully to several felines. They say that the healing power of purring lies in the low-frequency tones which the animals produce. Besides, sound waves also have a demonstrable positive effect on human bones. They can strengthen bones.

Purring is a wonderful phenomenon. It is indeed true that the pain in my neck disappears when Donsje lays herself on my shoulder to purr. She senses immediately when I have pain. She then jumps onto my shoulder and curls herself around my neck as if she were a scarf. A real little nurse. All small-sized cats, among which also the puma, my totem-animal, purr, both when breathing in and when breathing out. Big cats like tigers and lions don't purr, but sometimes they make an almost similar sound when breathing out. They can roar, however. I find pumas gorgeous cats, that's why I am so fond of Abyssinians. Some day...but well, our little family is indeed complete now, isn't it, Puddie? (Puddie's face was on "Rain Coming", he knows his mama).

We fell asleep around three in the morning. The explosions kept us awake. Next morning - I went outside at around eight - it was very quiet. The curtains were still closed at the neighbours', no cars on the road. Most weird. Well, the 'morning after' is not so easy. I guess everybody was happy these hectic days were over. I was grateful that there had been no power failure and that the lights kept on burning, unlike in France where a terrible storm had caused power failures, resulting in thousands of people spending a dark New Year. What a horror! Our central heating has the idiosyncrasy to stop working preferably on Christmas Day, but this year it has done its duty so far.

I gave Daimke a very beautiful domed cat-carrier for when she accompanies me in the car. It looks like a birdcage and just fits on the front seat. It is high enough for Daimke to see out of the window. She puts her front feet cheerfully against the wire netting and talks all the time. When I point out the things we come across, say a dog or another cat, or more thrilling a little bird, she notices them at once and grows very tall. It's great to have her with me in the car. But I only take her on short trips. It must remain fun.

All of a sudden I was bothered by a sudden itch under my beautiful cat-watch. Tension? Puddie suggested I try Frontline. He regretted his words immediately, for I found his idea super and started at once 'Frontlining' all fluffies and dogs. It was time anyway. 'Look Puddie,' I said cheerfully, 'then I will get enough 'Frontline fall-out' from you all to become flea-free as well, in case it 's fleas causing my itch.' Donsje advised Puddie diplomatically to think twice next time before voicing such suggestions. 'Look at us now, smelling horribly!' Yes, according to Puddie, Donsje is putting on airs. She feels so sure and strong, now that she has two sisters to back her up when Puddie or Mickje feel like teasing her. It works both ways because when Puddie or Mickje are playing too roughly with Daimke or Catje, Donsje will interfere. ' Come on, you two big clodhoppers, try to get me!'

To be sure I went to the dermatologist. Doctor Jan is a friend of mine. He loves cats(of course). It was some kind of contact allergy for certain metals (cobalt and chrome) and their alloys. In future I had to avoid contact with everything containing nickel and chrome. The hunt for nickel was on. What a sport! You cannot believe how much nickel you'll find in your home. For starters: coins. Yippee, at last a valid excuse for spending them. At once I phoned my friend and agent, Kees. The door handles were metal, I replaced them with plastic ones but these kept on breaking loose. Regularly we were holding door handles in our hands. I wrapped the water taps with tape. I made it into a game. Humour is a terrific help.

I had taken a lot of things with me to the dermatologist to ask him whether they were 'safe'. I have Chinese health balls from the World Wildlife Fund which I always use on my walks. You have to roll them in your hands. They stimulate the blood circulation and they make a funny jingling noise. They are 'safe', Doctor Jan said. I also showed him Daimke's new cat-carrier. When the Doctor saw it, he burst out laughing and shouted: 'Help, a hold-up! Are you gonna put me inside? Help police!' Well, I could have done. He would just fit in. It was really funny. I could just see him inside there! Fortunately the cat-carrier was also safe. After some time I had the house pretty free from nickel, but the itch didn't go away. On the contrary, it became worse. I wasn't happy about it.

Puddie got fed up with it. He came to sit in front of me and yawned deeply and heartily. 'You've had it also, little guy?' I sighed. 'Oh, look at your beautiful white teeth, if only mine were so complete and shiny!' Err...teeth? Cavities? Fillings! Bingo, I knew all of a sudden. Of course, that was it: the amalgam fillings in my teeth! The main culprit was inside me. I checked a medical reference work and, indeed, it was true. I knew already that they are very bad for your health. But for me, with the allergy, they were pure poison. They had to go, and now! I had plenty of them and often visited the dentist. 'There, you see,' Puddie proudly told Mickje, 'if we weren't around, what would mama do!' Daimke, Catje, and the other fluffies helped tremendously to fight the exhaustion and pain. It is a rather drastic measure to have all one's fillings removed and replaced. As a matter of fact that should have taken more time but I wanted them out as soon as possible. When I arrived home and the fluffies raced to me, all pain was gone.

Both girls have grown into gorgeous teenagers and they enjoy life. My dream has come true, I wanted two girlfriends for Donsje and so it happened. Donsje feels young again. No, I should say, she feels young for the first time. I knew she had humour inside her and could be very elated but I could never have expected that she would play so delightfully with Daimke and Catje. And Donsje is the one who often starts the game. She will jump at the kids sideways, her tail enormously big and all the hairs on her back on end to feint an attack and the kids react with pleasure. How nice it will be when we all can stay outside again!

SUGAR PLUM

"You've done it again mum, missed the fun,
And the bravery of your smallest son,
We were all busy playing, hurtling round the floor,
When Sugar Plum strayed through the kitchen door,
(That's 'other mum's' name for him, - not ours,
She's nick-named us after fruit and flowers!)
Anyway let's get back to the tale,
He shot through the door and went quite pale,
There was a creature in the kitchen that gave him a scare,
Not very tall, but it had a lot of hair,
We all cleared off, and watched from the table,
But Sugar Plum made himself as big as he was able,
He hop-skipped forward and gave it a bite,
And we all cheered him on cos he'd given it a fright,
Now, get this mum, you'd have been so proud,
'Other mum' came in - well we'd been a bit loud!!
"MY BRAVE BOY" she said as she walked across the room,
You've really seen off that sweeping broom!

© *Maureen Eadon-Mills*

Daimke is very special to me and our bond is firm and unique. She has a mission here and she knows it. She is mama's fluffy! A golden fluffy with a super soft fur coat. Now she is running around with a white mouse trying to challenge Catje. Catje has been chasing a yellow ping-pong ball for about an hour now. How delightful. Ping-pong balls are excellent playthings on the slippery floor in the living room. What fun they have! Outside in the garden Daimke has fun as well. She asks me about the danger factor of anything she comes across. 'Can it hurt? Is she not a very brave kitten? Prr prrr.' Everything is fine as long as mama is around. The beauty of it is that the bond with the fluffies grows stronger with the time. Puddie and I are so close, so trusting of each other, just like happens in a good marriage.

March came. Slowly, very slowly nature revived. SPRING! At last. Oh, how we longed for sun and warmth! Yes, I didn't mind mosquitoes as long as spring arrived. But it was still pretty cold. Some brave crocuses did appear in the garden, though.

I am very proud and happy that Maria and Gé have invited me to be a member of the board of directors of the Poezenbel Foundation. Two members had to resign because of circumstances. It gave me great joy to have this chance to be a member of the board. I want to devote my heart and soul to Poezenbel and anything connected to it. I only hope I will meet the challenge. Thanks very much, dear Maria and Gé! The new season is coming. Oh, let everything work out well this year, so that the sorrow and sadness of last year fades away. It still hurts and we'll probably never forget it altogether. But a bunch of little kittens asking for love, warmth and attention will be a great help to Maria and Gé.

Papa and I used to take long walks in the mudflats of the Hollands Diep. A

129

world apart. So many different kinds of birds were there, especially owls. I was very intrigued by this beautiful and wise bird. Sometimes we could approach them almost within touching distance. I spent my whole youth there. When I dream I almost always find myself back in the manor. No matter how much I love living where I live now, part of me will always remain a Numansdorper. Around this time Papa and I collected bunches of willow catkins for mama, who was fond of them. 'They were allowed inside the house', I often thought sadly. With all my heart I longed to have a little cat friend, but mama refused. I was allowed to have cats in the stables, but the house was definitely off limits to cats. In those days children still obeyed their parents. Certainly children like me, who did anything to avoid a quarrel. But the willow catkins were beautiful.

There is a fine legend about willow catkins:

'All night long the mother cat had been sleeping restlessly, her kittens closely nuzzled up to her body, as if she sensed...This year she had made her litter even deeper in the hay barn, far at the back, under a wood partition. It was safe there but her kittens were starting to move around. Four splendid grey kittens. Oh, how she loved them! Quick, quick, off she went to the stable before they woke up so she could drink some milk the farmer's wife had put there for her. Later she'd catch some mice to feed to her kittens, but first she had to regain her own strength.
Indeed, the farmer's wife was a kind woman. The farmer however, he was the terror of all animals. A real brute! Woe to the poor kittens he found on his way, they all ended up in the deep ditch running behind the barn.

The previous year...but mother cat tried not to think of it. Quickly she hurried back. To her great horror she found one big chaos there. Bales of hay in all directions but...no kittens...Desperately she fled away, away from that cursed spot. Her kittens were calling for her! Following her intuition she sensed where they were. She ran to the deep ditch. She heard them thrashing about in the water desperately crying for help. Without hesitation she flung herself into the ice-cold water and grasped the kitten closest to her. But what about the others? She'd never succeed in saving all four. She cried wildly.

Her desperate cry awoke the wise old willow tree, growing along the ditch for more than a century. He understood at once what had happened. 'Not again! Oh, that miserable wretch of a man, but this time he won't have it his way!!!' Quickly the tree stretched its thin but very strong twigs to the kittens so that they could grip them and managed to climb out of the water onto the bank. Overjoyed the mother gathered her family and guided them hurriedly to a dry, warm burrow a rabbit had once dug close to the willow. There she licked her children clean and dry while they drank themselves warm with her deliciously sweet milk. 'Never again will I have kittens in that barn', she firmly decided. 'This hole is much safer. Sure, her big strong friend Mister Willow would guard them, wouldn't he?' And so it happened.

Ever since that time each willow wears grey buds in spring. They are as soft and sleek as the fur of newly born kittens.'

March came. Daimke and Catje grew up. A bit too fast for my liking, but of course I was happy about it. Their fur shone like mirrors. Daimke was growing faster than Catje. She had long legs and was very slender and slim. She looked like a figurine depicting Bastet, the Egyptian Cat Goddess. Catje had expanded more in width. Her head had become cutely round and her body beautifully compact. I was proud of them, but I'd have preferred them to stay small for at least one more year, if I had had any choice, because it wouldn't be long before they would be on heat.

Puddie's behaviour betrayed to me that Daimke's body was changing. He became restless. Daimke herself didn't understand what was happening to her. She asked Donsje why she didn't have fun like before. 'I don't get it', she said sadly, 'normally Catje and I are overjoyed in everything we do. We play joyfully together, the five of us and mama. We can go outside in the run, we cuddle a lot with mama, for short we have a wonderful life. But now, I have a tingle in my tummy and always want something else. I am so restless, as if I have forgotten to enjoy life. Do you understand?' Donsje looked at her. 'Yes, girl. I understand, I think you have grown up. Nice in a way, but in another way, I don't know...' Daimke couldn't get more out of her.

Daatje and Dotje, Daimke's sisters, who live together with my dear friends Diny, Hans and Marielle, wrote to their little sister that they had been 'helped'. *'We were so scared and we didn't like it at all. When will you and Catje get your zipper?'*

131

Daimke didn't understand a word about it and asked me what they meant by 'helped'. Helped with what? And 'zipper'? Where were they talking about? I explained it to her and told her to quickly write a reply to her sisters to comfort them.

'Dear Daatje and Dotje,

Oh, dear sisters, you must have had a strange adventure. I didn't understand everything mama said when she told us about it. 'Your sisters, dear Daimke,' she said, 'have been to uncle Doctor to get a zipper.' I think I looked like one big question mark. Marg says that I look so cute when I don't understand something. Indeed, I must have looked really stupid! 'A zipper? What's that again? Is it tasty? Can you play with it?' The three of us were sitting in the office. Puddie and Mickje were in the living room. I asked Catje whether she understood what mama was talking about. 'Well, I'm not so sure, but I guess it is something that means that you cannot have babies any more. Isn't it, Donsje?' But Donsje had gone, she was invisible and also untraceable. Mama went away to look for her. She couldn't be far, she had been sitting on the desk just before. In the end we spotted her, hidden on the climbing pole. 'Why are you hiding there and why are you shivering?' we called to her in unison. But mama understood. 'Yes, my dear little girl, we'll never forget your operation. Oh, how frightened we were and how grateful we where afterwards that everything turned out well.' She put Donsje on her lap and cuddled her till she stopped shivering and could talk again.

We didn't understand any of it, of course. 'But what do you mean when you talk about a zipper?' I asked again, 'I want to know'. 'Donsje', Marg said, 'could you explain it to the kids? Talking about it will make you feel better but just don't scare them. Remember that Mickje hardly noticed it happening to her. You just had bad luck. And then, the following day, just when you felt a bit better Puddie played too roughly with you. You jumped away and got a long splinter in your front paw. Of course, that made matters so much worse for you.'

Donsje looked somewhat uncertain and started her story. And then we began to understand it. It was something that the veterinarian removed in our belly so that we could not have kittens. We didn't like the idea and even when Donsje said that Mickje had forgotten all about it, we were not put at ease.

132

What about you, dear sisters, did you find it nasty and are you all right now? I will think a lot of you and send you many purrings. They will help, for sure! Do you two also enjoy playing together like Catje and I do? I was so very grateful she could come with me. Fortunately mama understood when I begged for that. I was still so ill and weak and tired at that time. So many sad things had happened around me. I didn't exactly know what, but I felt a black cloud hanging above us. And then, suddenly, you two were gone. Oh, how I missed you! I looked everywhere and called your names. In the attic, in the kitchen, in the hall, but no sisters! I really cried. Fortunately Catje noticed my sadness. She cheered me up by pushing her head against me and jumping on me so that I rolled over the floor: 'come on, little girl, we're still together, we can also play!' And yes! We could indeed and we did! To our great joy we became true buddies. We could romp together and had much fun. But more importantly... we could comfort each other when so many of our other playmates left for the Rainbow Bridge.

Suddenly I learned that I could go to my mama in Belgium. I was so happy because I loved her already very much. But then I thought about Catje. Oh no, if Catje had to stay behind, then I would stay behind! But Marg received my desperate message and asked mama Maria to bring Catje also. And mama Maria agreed. It was so marvellous, also because we had to live, all by ourselves, upstairs for two weeks. You two are also together. I am so happy for you.

Lots of love from your sister Daimke.'

Fortunately Daatje and Dotje immediately replied to Daimke and told her that they were better and that it was not so bad as it had seemed. *'Afterwards, we got so many delicious titbits that we almost found it worth the trouble.'*

Indeed, it is not so bad, but I shrank from it nevertheless. But of course I wanted to have it done. Poezenbel-cats have to be neutered anyway – all new 'mamas or papas have to sign a contract stipulating this - and, besides, I am all for it because too many cats end up in shelters as a result of people's irresponsibility regarding neutering. But that doesn't mean I don't feel bad about it, especially since Daimke had already had such a bad start.

133

Many people speak about sterilisation when in fact they mean spaying. Sterilisation means that the Fallopian tubes are tied off. The she-cats cannot have kittens any more, but they still will be on heat. Then they will desperately call for a tomcat. They will get very nervous and upset, often stop eating and lose much weight. For their health that's very bad, of course. Spaying involves removal of the ovaries and then she-cats will not come on heat any more.

I decided to wait till the cats had been on heat for the first time. And so it happened that after one week Daimke became very agitated. She mewed a lot and kept on begging for cuddles. Then she rushed off to look for something, but what precisely she didn't know. Of course she didn't find it. Yes, clear signs that she was on heat.

Her oriental nature got the better of her. Everything in the extreme. Love, play, fear, heat. Of course she didn't understand herself and kept on asking me to 'please stroke her back'. Catje became tense from it as well. One time - we were lying on the bed, playing and reading - Daimke flew desperately at Catje and begged: 'Catje, Catje, please, help me! Mama doesn't understand me and there is something I need, I must do, please help me. Mieeuwwweee, mieeuwwii!' And Catje, so cute, gripped her with both her front paws and started washing her. When that didn't help she climbed on Daimke's back and tried to cover her. She got very near Daimke's wish! Daimke enjoyed it but there was still something lacking, for she rushed off and raced around the room, shouting loudly and looking for 'it'. All my doubts about neutering dissolved into thin air. This was no life for her. Moreover, she was visibly losing weight. As soon as she was not on heat any more - it is better not to operate when the animal is on heat as the risk of a bleeding is higher then - I made an appointment with Doctor Liliane. A couple of days before the operation I started giving Bach flower remedies, Rescue and Crab-apple against stress. It is always effective.

The spaying

This morning at 9 a.m. we were in Doctor Liliane's office. I have full confidence in her; she is very able and also very fond of cats. She preferred that I went home and returned to pick up the girls at twelve noon. I would have preferred to stay with them but I understood, of course. Anyway I had seen the operation when Mickje had had her turn. Oh, how slow the time passed. So slow, I wanted to push the hands of the clock to twelve. I had prepared hot-water bottles and put the baskets in the warm bathroom. There they could not climb on things and fall off while they were still groggy. When I entered Doctor Liliane's consulting room and saw both of them wide awake, I was filled with joy. Anaesthetic is always a risk. Two pairs of sad eyes looked up at me and softly they mewed: 'Mama, mama, where **have** you been? We're so scared and lonely, please help us! We want to be with you, we want to go home! Oh, we have so much pain and feel so ill, mieeuww, mieeuw!' I carefully cuddled them and assured them that everything was fine now and that we were going home. The operation had gone smoothly, Doctor Liliane said. She had taken a sample of Daimke's blood, just to be sure, as her previous blood test had shown some deviation from the average blood count.

How happy we were to be home again. Once in my room I carefully took the kids out of their carrier cages. Catje was still rather sleepy but she walked a bit and tried to jump on the climbing pole. She is a real rascal. Daimke however had much pain. Softly she cried and crouched down with her behind up in the air. She felt rotten and lousy. I had made delicious chicken broth and gave them some drops every half hour, so their mouths would not be too dry and they would get some liquid and warmth inside.

Donsje was so kind. I had left her in the office, but when we were going to eat, I took her with me to the kids. I left Puddie and Mickje in the living room with lots of excuses, but it was safer so. At first Donsje's tail grew very big. Were those two kitties in the bathroom her little friends? They smelled so differently. They smelled of fear, pain and dirty vet stuff! Still, they did act like Daimke and Catje! 'Prrr prr,' she softly asked, 'is it really you?' Slowly she approached them, rubbed her head against Catje and licked her comfortly over her face. Next she went to Daimke but from her she received a hiss. Daimke was too ill to be bothered with politeness now. Donsje understood and looked sadly at me. Yes, neutering is not a simple matter.

Catje revived visibly and calmly went to sleep, a healing sleep. But, a couple of hours later Daimke still seemed in shock. Worried, I phoned Doctor

Liliane who reassured me there was nothing wrong. 'Daimke is a true Oriental, they are more sensitive.' Maybe she had to pee? I put her on the litter tray, but she was to afraid to move. Quickly I lifted her out. I didn't want her to lie down there. Catje, however, had already peed twice.

Tenderly, I put Daimke in her basket in the bathroom and went outside for an hour. When I returned there was not much improvement. I couldn't comfort her. She had completely cut herself off from the outside world. I felt so helpless! I phoned my dear friend Jos and explained my worries to her. She calmed me down and told me that her cats had also been very ill after their operation. She promised me to send healing rays to Daimke by means of her picture. Jos is terrific and really can take pain away. I took Daimke into my arms and tried to warm her up. She felt so cold. Suddenly she crawled under the climbing pole and started shivering. I was startled, but maybe she'd get warmer that way? After a while I thought it better to take her back to the bathroom and put her on the hot-water bottle. Maybe she'd sleep a bit then. And indeed, when I returned half an hour later I found her asleep.

For at least three hours she was on the hot-water bottle. She felt more relaxed. Thanks to the Lord, she was feeling better! I had been so scared. I phoned Jos to tell her. 'What time did she go to sleep?' she asked. 'Around five p.m.', I replied. Exactly the time when Jos had sent the rays. She had felt the pain and the cold through the picture and had been able to remove them. She does that by moving her hand counter clockwise in many concentric and smaller growing circles upwards over the pain zone. Then she pulls the pain out of this zone. It is a kind of corkscrew movement. She allows the pain to travel through her body to her feet and into the earth. After that she shakes her hands off and washes them. This is very important, otherwise she could take the pain over. It really happened this way and it is a proof of Jos' great power and also of the fact that magnetising and telepathy are not mere suggestions, but are really effective.

Catje was running around again and rolled over on her back to be cuddled. In the evening she was even hungry enough to eat some titbits of chicken with broth. Daimke had no appetite. But she slept and sleep is the best medicine. All night she wanted to remain in the bathroom. I checked her a couple of times, but she slept soundly.

The day after...

In the morning two pussy paws playing with my toes woke me up. So cute! Catje was awake! Suddenly Daimke, more or less groggy still, stood in the middle of the bedroom. She was very thin but she was back 'home' again. She looked at me intently and when I happily shouted: 'Daimke, there you are! Girl, how happy I am! Come here quick, ' she came to me, stepped on the bed - the waterbed is low - and snuggled herself up against me. I was so happy. This morning both of them ate. It will still take some time before they are back to normal, but everything will be all right. Tomorrow the sun will shine according to the weatherman, but for us, she is shining already in our heart.

'Yes, now and then this mama of ours can be mean,' Catje mused this morning when I plucked her out of the run. The clever girl had found out that she could escape through the cat flap. To my great surprise I found her parading outside. Super smart she is, but in view of her condition I prefer to postpone outside expeditions for at least one more hour. It will be warmer then. Daimke and Catje are almost back to normal. Certainly Catje, who's playing her old rough games again. Daimke is a bit more careful. She is not as hungry as usual. I gave her some extra vitamins. How great it was, last night, to feel her warm little body close to me again. Both fluffies felt colder than usual and slept, cosy and warm with me under the covers. Even Catje did so for a while. It was nice to observe also that Donsje and Catje are growing closer and closer to one another and play with each other. Mickje and Puddie looked puzzled for a while when they saw the kids and there was some extensive sniffing. Mickje got it at once and told about her own 'being helped' adventure, Puddie jumped on my lap. 'Women-talk again!', he sighed resignedly.

Daimke wrote to her sisters:

'Dear Daatje and Dotje,

Only now Catje and I fully understand the meaning of your letter. No, it was no fun, it was horrible! But your letter was a great support. A trouble shared is a trouble halved. I kept on reminding myself: Daatje and Dotje have been through this as well! It's Sunday morning. I lie cosily on mama's lap, rub my

137

front paw over her face and give her little kisses. I think she was even sadder than we were. We missed mama very much when she left us behind with Doctor Liliane, but for her it was even worse. She was wide-awake all that time! But first things first. We feel better even though still tired. So don't you two worry about us any more! Let's start at the beginning.

Friday morning both of us were put in a separate carrier cage and then in the car. Usually, when I accompany mama in her car, I stay in the front seat in the big cat-carrier so I can help her check the road and traffic. Traffic has become so hectic, that she really needs my assistance. I can warn her for example, when there is suddenly a car coming from the right. But this time Catje and I landed on the backseat and there was no fun on this trip. There was only fear! We sensed it very well! When we arrived at Doctor Liliane's place - I know her already and I find her rather kind - mama just left us behind. 'I will get you at twelve noon, girls, just be strong, I will think of you!' Mama tried to cheer us up but I sensed tears behind her words. Then we got a small jab and then...all black and nothingness.

Slowly we started to realise again what was going on. Our cage was covered with a cloth, we were standing against something warm, but we didn't hear anything. 'Mama, mama,' we softly cried, 'where are you? We feel very ill and everything seems to spin around us. Where are you, for heaven's sake? Wieeewwwwaiuwww'. Suddenly we heard her voice and her hands were cuddling us. Oh, such a lovely reassuring feeling! Now everything would be all right. But we cried victory too soon. We thought that we would feel well again, as soon as we were back in our familiar room. But that was not so. The pain, the dizziness and the sickness remained. Sure, we found everywhere hot- water bottles and cosy pillows but we were still too groggy and scared to use them.

Catje, who has more fat than I, felt better sooner. I, on the contrary, felt even more miserable when the anaesthesia wore off. I couldn't find a comfortable position in which to lie down or to sit, so I just stood upright with my behind high in the air. Fortunately we were regularly given drops of broth, as our throats were very dry. So, out of despair, I just crouched down at the foot of the climbing pole. There I suddenly felt icy cold and started shivering. Mama was very startled. Carefully she picked me up and laid me in the bathroom against a hot-water bottle. At once I became calm and better. I fell into a deep, healing sleep. Later, mama told me that I fell asleep exactly at the moment aunt Jos from Sittard was sending me rays of love. I guess they must have lifted the blockades so that my innate 'healing power' worked again.

However, I slept...and slept and slept. I did hear the usual noises coming from the kitchen. I felt Catje who often came to lick me and Donsje, who also was very compassionate. It was good. Everything was good! That night I slept practically without interruption. Next morning I kind of felt lost in my surroundings. I sat somewhat groggy in the middle of the room. Catje was playing on the bed. Donsje was still asleep and so was mama. 'Miaaauwwwieee', I complained, 'where am I, what happened to me?' 'Daimke, there you are', mama shouted with joy,' girl, how happy I am! Come here quick. I will tell you everything.' Still unsteady I climbed on the bed and snuggled firmly up against mama.

She told me about the operation. The fact that we could never have kittens. 'Small pussy-kittens are so cute', she explained, 'but the animal shelters are full of sad lonely cats and kittens waiting for some sweet man or woman to take them into their home. When kittens are born they take the place of the cats sitting in such shelters. Often they are just sent to the Rainbow Bridge.' We, for Catje was all ears too, didn't mind as long as we got better. We didn't want babies anyway! We wanted food, we were hungry! Mieeww! Donsje nodded wisely. 'Indeed, that's it. I have had the same experience and I can assure you it's really great to be able to live after the operation without the restlessness like Daimke felt when she was on heat. You two have a beauty of a small cut. My cut is much bigger'. We compared and indeed, ours was a small cut with two very tiny stitches. Rather beautiful if you ask me! Strange we were not allowed to eat anything the night before. We always eat together with mama and find that really cosy. We didn't understand. But now everything is back to normal. I lie on my back on mama's lap, so my zipper is showing while I dictate this letter. The sun is shining and mama has promised we can go outside in a while. So, I have to end my letter now. We are going to eat deliciously and play much in the sunshine, so we'll soon forget this zipper-business. Purrr prrr.

We do hope you two have fully recovered as well. Listen, mama says that we'll have our birthday soon! What's that again? Puddie had his birthday last twenty-fifth of March and he received so many packets and lots of tasty titbits. Seems purr purrfect fun to us! Lots of lovely purrings and love from your sister,

Daimke-with-zipper and from all of us.'

When I play with my cat, who knows whether she isn't amusing herself with me more than I am with her?

Montaigne

Chapter 8

The Painting, Miracles and Christmas Eve

If animals could speak, the dog would be a blundering outspoken fellow, but the cat would have the grace of never saying a word too much.

Mark Twain

At last the weather improved. Oh, what a delight! I was devising ways to extend the run close to the living room. It would be great to have additional run-space. The garden is big enough for it. Only, it was not simple because the new run had to be connected to the existing run.

Puddie had received a beautiful tunnel from Maria and me for his birthday. The fluffies played in it for hours. It is a big and sturdy tunnel and the game 'Catch-me-in-the-tunnel' is still number one on the hit parade. There are many holes in it and it's fun to see their heads sticking out.

Then May 24 came. Exactly one year ago Renate had found Daimke and her siblings. I often remember that time. How fortunate that Rob had just happened to pass that way! How would the mother be now? Would she still be running free? I do hope so and I often send her purring thoughts. Daimke had her birthday! The sisters had exchanged beautiful cards and I had bought some fine toys for the three of them. I hate my birthday, I don't celebrate it. What fun is there in getting older? But of course we do enjoy celebrating the birthdays of the fluffies. Besides, our Feline Scribes Club has declared April 4 to be a General Cat Birthday. Very handy, because we are plenty. To remember all those birthdays separately would fill almost half a birthday calendar. Daimke was elated! All that attention. All those tasty titbits and rustling packets! She told Catje that she wouldn't mind having birthdays every day. 'Well,' Catje replied cleverly, 'isn't that a bit too much? Don't you forget that, in that case, you would grow one year older every day too? Still, I don't object, because we share in the fun.' Some time later she sadly asked me if there was a chance of her having a birthday of her own also.

Poor Catje, since she is so brave and hardly had trouble with her spaying, I had given more attention to Daimke, these last weeks. I took her in my arms and cuddled her tightly. My strong brave fluffy, playing the piano so well. Yes, she does! She really walks deliberately over the keys while looking at me to see if I hear it. 'Yes, dear Catje, sure! You can count on it! June 17 is your birthday, in about three weeks. I will select something very beautiful for you.' Happily she bounced off. Catje is quickly contented. I do love her so! She has a very special sense of humour. While showing a real poker face she can do the craziest things, such as suddenly, without any reason, jumping straight up into the air and whooping an Indian war cry. Very useful when you spot some tasty titbit you want to snatch away from a competitor. It always works!

Renate had invited me to visit her. I was looking forward to it. She and her husband Rob live together with twelve gorgeous Norwegian Forest Cats and two Norwegian Elkhounds. The name of her Cattery is Zihuatanejo. I have listed her address at the end of my book. Norwegian Forest Cats are beautiful, tall, robust cats that make you think of Norway's vast forests. They are also very lovely and cuddly. Puddy sensed something in the air and tactfully reminded me that I had promised not to add any more pussy-kittens. 'Don't forget, mama, you promised!!!' he sternly said when I took my leave and asked him to keep an eye on everything during my absence.

Renate has made a beautiful stud house. It is downright horrible to see the conditions under which studs are sometimes forced to live. People intending to breed, sometimes prefer to keep their own stud, but it is next to impossible to keep a full tomcat in your house, because he will spray. That's the normal behaviour of a tomcat outdoors. He stakes out his territory, so that other tomcats know they have to stay away while she-cats on heat can 'read', that a possible marriage-mate is around. A tomcat sprays by directing a jet of urine on a vertical surface while kicking with his hind legs and vibrating his tail. The odour is very penetrating, so that usually the poor macho cat is banished to a separate pen outside the house. Just imagine being locked up for life, only to receive a visit once in a while from a she-cat on heat to cover. Life imprisonment without having committed any crime, except for having behaved like Our Dear Lord intended you to behave! What an injustice! Strays may have a tough life, but their life is still much better than the life of a 'banished stud'.

142

Renate is of the same opinion and therefore she has made splendid accommodation for her studs in the garage. A really cosy room with attractive colours. Of course, cats don't see colours very well, but it has a positive effect on them. Renate also has an enclosed garden. Half the day the she-cats can play in it and the other half of the day it's for the tomcats. The stud house has a run connected to it, in which there are tree trunks and little shelves. Her garden, fenced in by a wall, is full of marvellous plants under which her felines can hide and play. There is also a pond with real fish in it. Indeed, cats feel fine in Renate's place. Entire she-cats on heat also spray sometimes. That's why it is better to have your cat spayed if you are not going to use her for breeding purposes, even if she is alone and always inside. It is so unfair towards her when every couple of weeks she is on heat and has to call desperately for a tomcat. Nature is so prevalent that she gets exhausted, eats less and suffers from the restlessness in her body. To give her the 'pill' for cats is a bad option as it may cause mammary tumours. (And often does!)

© Renate Leijen

When I came in I was welcomed by a couple of gorgeous Norwegian Forest Cats. How beautiful they are! There were also four kittens running around. Ohhh! Good thing that Puddie had warned me, because I was very tempted. Renate has made a painting of Daimke. It was so beautiful! Just purrfect! Daimke has a special way of lifting her leg when she is watching something with interest or is listening to some sound that puts her on alert. It looks like the poise of a pointer dog. Renate has captured this precisely in her painting. Daimke stands close to a tree on a splendid carpet of golden brown autumn leaves, lifting her front leg in surprise. 'What is that sound I hear?' The frame also is in autumn colours. Renate allowed me to buy it. Puddie wouldn't object to my bringing it inside our home, even though it was, indeed, a kitty again. Happily I drove home.

First I took a quick shower and cuddled everybody abundantly. Then it was time for the big moment. I put the painting on the bed against the wall. 'Guys, come and see what I have brought home with me!' Full of interest the fluffies rushed to the picture and started smelling. 'Smells like a Norwegian

Forest', they concluded. Maybe they discovered some thrilling Norwegian saga in the painting. I am sure that they are able to receive messages from the Norwegian Forest Cats that way. Cats have a sense of smell that is immensely better than ours. And they communicate by telepathy.

It was funny to watch Daimke sitting for a long time in front of the painting, thinking deeply. 'How come, there is a gorgeous pussy there, but she doesn't move! Donsje, Catje, come and see, wraauuuuweeeeiiieeee, what is it?' She went behind the frame and smelled. I explained that Aunt Renate had made this beautiful painting for us and that it was her, Daimke, she saw. 'Oh, am I sooooo beautiful?' It took some time before she accepted the fact, but then she walked tall on her cute white paws.

I am so grateful to Renate! First she rescued Daimke and her sisters and now she has immortalised our little girl in such a unique way. Dear Renate, in the name of the six of us, a thousand thanks! Your paintings really live. They are something very special! I hung the painting above my bed and went to my room now and then just to admire it. In Maria's place there are paintings of Fleurtje and Cruimeltje which have also been done by Renate. They are (almost) as beautiful.

Just on Catje's birthday my friend Greet, who like Maria shelters small kittens, sent a beautiful drawing of Catje. I was very happy with it. Puddie also, because he was getting fed up with Daimke who was 'bragging' all day about 'her' portrait. Now, Catje also had something to be proud of. And proud she was!

Meanwhile I continued working on our book. Writing is a rewarding job, but it also consumes lots of energy. It is more like 'feeling' in the first place. You have a vague idea about what you want to write down, but you can't really catch it in words yet. It's like trying to relate last night's dream. You remember what you felt but what the dream was about, you can't recall. In the beginning I forced myself to put the ideas, however vague, on paper, but that didn't work. Now I let my ideas develop and mature by themselves and then suddenly, like a flash, they are there! Than I know exactly what I want to write down. I 'write' mostly when I walk in the garden. There the ideas are born, or better, sent through, because I feel more like a channel of my guardian angel who dictates to me. A cat-guardian angel he is, because I

144

write to point out to people how wonderful cats are! My mission in life is to help cats.

Jos and family came on a visit. They brought some beautiful plants. Together we searched for the best spots for them, so that they would be happy. It was a cosy time and we had a lively conversation. Miguella, the medium, explained to me how she intercepted the feelings and thoughts of a lost cat she was trying to trace. She really experienced everything from that cat's point of view. How she crossed the road and recoiled from the exhaust fumes thinking: ' Boo, what a stench!' When entering an area of tall grass, she thought: ' Oops, how high, but then I can hide in it. I have to lie down for a while, I am so tired and scared.'

'Cats are very sensitive to voices,' Miguella said. ' and they have a very accurate sense of smell.' She is more of a dog person but she says that cats are more interesting, more 'profound' and more intuitive. When cats are staring intensely or full of interest at something we don't see, for instance a speck on the ceiling, they see it like a gigantic bubble. That's how sharp they see. For them it is something like a kaleidoscope of light, a beautiful movie. They can also see in other dimensions. For instance they see and feel spirits of deceased beings appearing for a short visit. That's why cats sometimes may suddenly look up and stare at something we don't see. Dogs also have that ability.

Cats immediately notice stress, sorrow and happiness in their people. Also in strangers. People radiate their feelings through their skin and a cat knows perfectly how to interpret them. There is no way kidding them. Cats are curious and notice everything. Even blind cats are happy and 'see' the radiation and smell of their people. Objects also radiate smells and cats concentrate on them. The funny thing is that Miguella herself has many abandoned guinea pigs she is very fond of and a Labrador, but no cats and she doesn't know much about kitties, but she gets all this information from intercepting their messages.

Puddie was listening while lying high up on the climbing pole. Later he confirmed everything Miguella had told me. 'We cats feel immediately whether people are genuine or not. Haven't I warned you many times before? Beware of such and such straightup-walker, I told you ever so often! He says

'Yes' but means 'No'. Now, Jos and her family are all right, I was not so afraid as usual. They felt good and they love you very much. You know, my dear pussy-mother has warned me sternly about strange straightup-walkers. That's why I always select a high vantage point. I want to have a commanding view, you see. We cats don't communicate with words. We use body language to express how we feel. We communicate with our eyes, our posture and by telepathy. Straightup-walkers talk too much. That's why they forget to observe body language. The speaker wraps his words in glossy paper and sends them to you with a smile. And so he can tell you whatever he wants without really meaning anything of it. That's the horrible thing about people. They say something but do something else.' Indeed, Puddie had a good point there. I have often experienced such behaviour. Mostly though, I am able to pretty well 'read' the truth, probably because I am thinking like a cat. I often intercept thoughts and watch out for body language.

I love to divide people into dog- and cat persons. I don't mean people loving dogs or people loving cats, but how they look like them. Cat people are calm, often spiritual and tender. They don't make noise. They think before speaking and don't get on your nerves. Dog people are livelier. They make a lot of noise and their presence is very noticeable. They talk loudly and sometimes seem to jump at you. They get on your nerves after a while. Nevertheless I also love dogs very much.

A dear friend of Maria and me, Chantal, also from Sittard like Jos, offered to make a website for us. How great! I did not yet know much about the Internet and had started emailing only recently. But the idea seemed wonderful. I shall regularly write an update as it is called and Chantal will put it on our site. Now my dear friend Paul does it for me, but in the beginning it was Chantal. www.rietkat.be is our website. Tedje, a Poezenbel-kitten and one of Puddie's pen pals lives with Chantal. He is very good at the internet too.

It is such a marvel, The World-Wide 'Waiting' Web. Papa was delighted when we - one of the first in the village - had a telephone installed. I remember how we organized dyke watches. A dyke watch had been set up after the terrible flood in 1953 which had killed so many people and animals. Papa was 'dyke-count' and co-ordinated everything. He allowed me to help him during the night by recording the water levels which were subsequently passed on by phone. It was a beautiful old-fashioned telephone-set with a handle.

Now life without computer and email seems unimaginable. I don't know though, if I really feel good about it. Often I feel rather a slave to the incoming emails. The fluffies say: 'Yep, Mama proposes, the Mail disposes!' And they are right, if I don't watch out. If you ask me, I much prefer the good old days when the mail came by the postman only and I found everything neatly deposited in my letterbox. I just collected my mail, made a plan for the day and had finished everything by evening. Now it's the other way around. Mails mostly arrive at the end of the day. True, with a nice "mew". My computer mews when a new message enters my in-box, and that does have a soothing effect. Still, emails mean more work and less sleep. 'Slave drivers' they are!' Donsje says and she, being my secretary, knows all that happens in the office.

Since they have been spayed, Daimke and Catje are very afraid of strangers. Donsje reacted in exactly the same way. She loved people but after the operation she became scared of everybody. Such a pity! I do understand them though! Daimke really panics. If an unknown upright-walker enters the garden, she will rush off and hide behind the curtain, rigidly shivering with fright. I feel so sorry for her. There is not much I can do to comfort her. Slowly she has to gain confidence again. Donsje is beginning to lose her fears now. Fortunately Daimke and Catje still enjoy running in the garden. I carry them when we start our walks. Daimke then rolls over on her back and starts purring in my arms. When traffic passes on the road or - as happened today – a pony cart with bells, she'll look amazed at me and than at the noise. (Can one 'look' at noise? No, only in the direction where that noise comes from.) Often she will stretch her front paws one by one, while pulling her claws in and out. It looks like kneading, like a kitten does when trying to start her mother's milk yield, but then in the air. I had to think of mama. When she let her nails dry in the sun after painting them, she did the same. Daimke does a lot of talking by way of her front paws. Catje sometimes jumps through the tall grass like a young lamb. She keeps her four legs tight and hops forward with skips.
Yes, we do enjoy the summer immensely.

Daimke has appointed herself policewoman and feels responsible for keeping the peace in the family. I had a hearty laugh this afternoon. We were sitting in the run. I have put little shelves everywhere so the kitties can lie down, but every shelf was occupied. They like resting on them. Mickje lay on the topmost shelf. Donsje, laying on the shelf immediately below was studying Mickje. Slowly she crawled to the shelf above her and suddenly bellowed in Mickje's ear: 'Miiiaaaauuuuuwuwwwiiieeeee'! Poor Mickje, she almost fell down from terror into the catmint below. I was in stitches. Suddenly a very angry Daimke flew at Donsje and boxed her ears. Everything happened in a flash, so that Puddie and I looked at each other: 'Are we dreaming or is this real?' Daimke chased Donsje into the house and then jumped on the table next to me and started washing herself nervously. 'Right, girl,' I said, 'The evils we bring on ourselves are the hardest to bear.' Daimke had grown up and she knew it. 'Oops, I hope this will not trouble Puddie,' I suddenly thought, 'two captains on one ship!'

Kirby, mama's dog, acts the same. When Femke, who was starved as a puppy, tries to steal food from the kitchen table, Kirby will attack her. I don't know the real reason. Maybe Kirby really thinks it is not allowed and wants to punish Femke, or maybe she just is angry because she is too small to reach the top herself. For me it is very easy. But I understand Femke's behaviour. When she was two months old she was found, totally starved somewhere in a street. Fortunately she ended up in the animal shelter in Schoten. Some days after Karma's death I felt a strong urge to go there. I really had to go! I am sure that it was Karma who sent me. He wanted me to adopt Femke, because he knew how sad I was about his crossing over to the Rainbow Bridge. I still find it very special that I found Femke that way. But Femke knows what it is to be hungry and therefore steals anything she can eat. Otherwise she is very obedient and a wonderful friend. I love her so.

Every day, if the weather is good, Puddie likes to lay on the lawn in front of the house. I tie him to a long rope so he really can walk around. He, and he alone is allowed to do that! And rightly so, he is the pacha! He enjoys it tremendously. He had caught a little mouse and proudly showed it to me. I find it rather pitiful and always try to quickly snatch it away, to release it in some safe spot far from the run. Of course I give some chicken instead: you scratch my back and I'll scratch yours, isn't it, Puddie!

'That mama takes my little mouse away,' Puddie irritatedly commented to Mickje, 'I can understand. As you know, straightup-walkers are too clumsy and too slow to catch anything, let alone mice. What I don't get at all, is that she'll release it afterwards! But, you know, I won't mind too much. I get chicken and the chance to catch that pathetic little mouse again, which means more chicken! Chicken is classier than mouse anyway. Too bad it doesn't run off too. That really would be fun!' Smart, Puddie!

When I was a teenager my parents made a deal: if I didn't smoke before I was eighteen, I would receive one hundred Dutch florins. A big amount in those days and, anyway, I only wanted to smoke because my cowboy-heroes smoked. I didn't like the taste. But then, when I had received the money, I lit my first cigarette. Ugh. But it was 'macho' and for a couple of years I rolled cigarettes like my friends the farmhands, with whom I often worked the fields. Then I tried to make a new bet with my parents. If I promise not to smoke for another year…I thought it an easy way to get a hundred guilders every year! But Papa said: 'No way! You are old enough to know the dangers of smoking!' And he was right. Puddie seems to be using the same system with mice.

Slowly the weather became colder. Mama found autumn the most beautiful season, but I prefer spring. After spring comes summer, while after autumn comes winter. Our book 'Miracles on little Feet' was at the printers'. Full of expectation I awaited its arrival. It is fantastic to write a book about your own life and your pussy-children. It's a wonderful job but it does consume lots of energy. When at last the book is finished and you're satisfied with it - otherwise you'd change it anyway - you take it to the printers. And then it's waiting and waiting! Waiting lasts long. Suddenly it's 'D-day.' My friend Rudi had collected a couple of boxes. Thrilled I opened a box -assisted by my fluffies who crawled helpfully in my way - and…**Oh, how beautiful!** It was splendid! The magnificent drawing of Donsje, who cheers you up whatever mood you are in, smiled at me. 'Hi, here I am', she seemed to say. 'Pick me up, read me, love me! Spoil me! I love you!' Oh, I felt so proud. Donsje must have sensed that it was kind of hers too. I couldn't get her away from the boxes.

Half an hour later I was in my car with a box full of 'Miracles'. Sure, the first copy was for Maria and Gé. It is their- and Poezenbels- book as well. A big part of the proceeds will go to our foundation. The fluffies sensed it this morning already: mama is going somewhere. Puddie sat sad-eyed in the run. I know he will wait for me there till I return. I always find it hard to go. Of course I had told them that I was going to Aunt Maria and Uncle Gé to take them our book and that they were to guard the house very well during my absence. But Puddie didn't like it. He suffers the most when I am not there, so I think of him a lot when I am driving and he feels it.

On entering Maria's house I was immediately surrounded, or better still lifted upon a cloud full of kitty-love. They cuddled me, even before I could embrace Maria. Every one of them has a past, mostly too horrible to talk about. As kittens they were found in dustbins or glass containers. They were thrown in the bushes along the highways and so on. But all are tremendous cuddlers. The champion is Asselijntje, Puddie's fiancée. Hardly had I taken a seat before she clung to me. So cute! She is a rare beauty with red flames in her fur. She was a kitten the farmer, thanks to the Lord, couldn't catch to drown! So Maria saved her. She is one of the so many cats that Maria has saved!

Maria too found 'Miracles' a beauty. Suddenly I became conscious of the fact that I was sending my book into the big, wide world. How would it be received? Would reading it bring the people as much pleasure as writing it, together with my fluffies, had brought me? Or would there be people who wouldn't understand any of it? I looked at Donsje on the cover, smiling at me full of confidence. My doubts melted like snow in the sun. It was all right.

When, very tired I arrived home - it is a four-hour drive there and back - I was so happy. When I pass through the gate I always feel a wonderful relief. We made it again! Driving is so dangerous these days. It is a delight to leave the road full of traffic and exhaust fumes behind me and to enter my tree-park with its invigorating air and serene silence. And then, most of all, to be able to embrace my fluffies and find everything fine and in order. To leave home is a drag but to return is a delight!

Since her youth Donsje has problems with a runny eye. Reddish brown tears sometimes run down her cheek. Whatever I do – treat the eye with Geomycine, clean the eye with eufrasia or just let it be - there is no change. In agreement with doctor Liliane, I consulted a veterinarian who specialised in eyes. She was a very kind woman who calmly talked to Donsje while examining the eye. Nothing wrong with the eye itself, she said, but the tear duct was clogged. She would try to puncture it. Too bad she had to sedate Donsje first.

I had to wait in the waiting room while holding Donsje on my lap. Slowly she fell asleep. Suddenly she stopped breathing. She stopped!!! I was terrified and rushed to the doctor's office. The door was locked! 'Doctor, help, help! Donsje has stopped breathing!' I was about to kick the door in. Luckily she heard me and opened the door. 'Oh,' the doctor reacted matter-of-factly, 'that's normal. Just wait here a moment.' My legs trembled. The thought that I was about to lose Donsje! Fortunately our turn came soon. The doctor tried to puncture the tear duct but it had completely closed. Inserting a synthetic tear duct was not an option according to the doctor because the body often rejects it. The best solution was to let it be. It doesn't really trouble Donsje anyway. At least I knew now that it was not an infection and that her eye was all right. I just had to clean her cheek a couple of times every day.

Donsje was still unsteady when we arrived home. I let her quietly regain her strength in the warm bathroom. I shall never forget the anxiety I experienced in the waiting room. I had been present during Donsje's and Mickje's neutering and so I was aware of the fact that a cat under sedation will breathe slower, but Donsje had stopped breathing completely. I am sure the anaesthetic was too strong. But everything was fine again and next day my little girl was playing like before and had a ravenous appetite.

Raymonde, my French friend had been on a visit. She had helped me with the Christmas cards. A very welcome help, as I was very busy with the orders for Miracles. I was proud and happy. It was good that the fluffies were there to assist me. Their specialty: clearing my desk and sorting the mail. 'Letters smelling of cats are Priority Number One!' Puddie said, while snatching them out of the piles. A pity emails don't smell.

There were so many beautiful reactions to Miracles. Often people wrote to me about their cats. Of the love and support they got from them. It was a relief to read such letters for it is sometimes hard to believe that there is still goodness in humans. Those letters were like Christmas presents to me. I have filed them all in a big document file to read them again later when I am old and walking with a stick. In the meantime, I cherish them deep in my heart.

Christmas Eve was comfortably quiet. I had prepared extra tasty food for the dogs and they slept in their baskets. The pussy-children and I were in the office. I had finished my work and was reading an interesting book. Reading is a delight but usually I don't give myself the time for it. Sometimes I read aloud to the fluffies and they do listen! Just like Qwill does to his beautiful detective cats Koko and Yum Yum. I adore those books: The Cat who... series. I have them all.

One of the most beautiful stories, I think, is the story of the St Elisabeth's flood and the rescue of the little child Beatrix. A friend of mine, Arie, who made the wonderful CD-ROM 'Animals in the Bible' and who gave me the beautiful proverbs about animals in the Bible (see Chapter 16 Miscellaneous), was born in Kinderdijk (Children's Dyke), the village that owns its name to this story. Arie sent me the following story:

In 1421 a terrible storm was raging during the night of 18 to 19 November. The wind raised the waters into the storm flood that will go down in history as the St. Elisabeth's flood. This flood swept away vast stretches of land all over Holland. It created among others the Biesbosch. About 2.000 people drowned and 28 villages were destroyed. (During the war Daddy lived in the Biesbosch, a sparsely populated and 'wild' part of the Netherlands. He was commander of a resistance group which had its headquarters there.)

The story about Beatrix, the child in the cradle, dates back to this night. The cradle with the child in it was drifting on the swirling water while a cat kept it balanced. Whenever a wave tried to upset the cradle the cat jumped to the highest point to bring the vessel with its precious cargo back into balance. On the dykes the people who escaped the flood were watching with bated breath. Would the cradle make it? Would the cat succeed in keeping the cradle balanced? She was getting tired and the water was icy...
But it ended well! The cradle drifted ashore and child and cat were rescued. The spot where the child drifted ashore is close to Alblasserdam and later the dyke was called the Kinderdijk and the village that sprang up there is also called Kinderdijk. This village is known all over the world for its windmills which attract thousands and thousands of tourists every year.

Later it was claimed that the cradle drifted ashore at Dordrecht but I stick to the original version, since my birthplace owes its name to it. The people named the child Beatrix, Latin for the Happy One. Later she married Jakob Roerom and moved to Dordrecht.

On the spot where the cradle drifted ashore there is now a house with the name House at Kinderdijk. The front of this house depicts the cradle, the girl and the cat.

My thanks to Arie for giving me the permission to use this story in my book.

There is a very similar story that happened in February 1953 when a terrible flood made many victims in Numansdorp, my native village.

Leen, the husband of my dear friend Nel, was swept out of his house with his old mother and the sheepdog on a mattress. For long hours they floated in that terrible night on the ice-cold water. Suddenly Leen's mother slipped off the mattress. Desperately Leen tried to hold on to her but in the end he had to let her go. He was emaciated and collapsed down on the mattress, numbed by the cold and the misery. There was only the sheepdog now to watch that the mattress remained balanced. He kept on moving to the higher part so that Leen could not slip off the mattress. At last the mattress collided with a haystack and Leen transferred to it. Next day the rescue teams were alarmed by the sheepdog who was desperately barking and circling the haystack. They found Leen, totally numb with cold.

I looked at my five kitties and recalled all the moving stories I had read about people who were rescued by their pets. There are so many beautiful stories about the unique bond between cats and their owners. Dear friends of mine, Allen and Linda Anderson from America wrote wonderful books about Angelanimals. They are noted in chapter 22. You can subscribe to their weekly Newsletter in which you can read the loveliest stories. www.angelanimals.net

It's rightly so that ages ago, in Ancient Egypt, cats were adored and considered the most cherished domestic animals. They were not only real friends to their people; they were also very useful. They caught mice, rats and even snakes. If only the Church Fathers in the Middle Ages had considered those facts before ordering all cats, especially black ones, killed, the plague wouldn't have taken so many victims!

Daimke intercepted my thoughts. 'When we were still inside mama's belly', she said, 'she used to tell us about The Great Goddess Bastet. My mama was a princess and she had heard those stories from her mother, who had heard them from her mother and so on. Bastet had the appearance of a magnificent cat. She was the daughter of Ra, the sun god and Isis, the mother goddess. She represented the loving and protective part of her mother. Quite logical: are there better mothers than cat-mothers?

Indeed, my cat-mother could not really take care of us, but that was not her fault. Quite the contrary, she would have given her life to save us, if necessary. Bastet is often depicted with a rattler and kittens at her feet. Women prayed to her for fertility and for successful delivery. She protected man and animal against evil spirits and gods and killed the snake that menaced the sun. She was the goddess of fertility and of the joys of life, for example music and dance. That's why we enjoy everything so immensely. Bastet is a very kind and gentle goddess. She makes everybody happy. It is said: 'Friendly as Bastet.'

The Greeks named her Artemis (Diana), also called the 'Mother of the cats.' The Egyptians even built a splendid temple for her in Bubastis. Cats were also kept in temples. They were worshipped and treated with respect. In Ancient Egypt the cat was a holy animal. Killing a cat was punishable by death. Tomcats were the reincarnation of Ra, the sun god and pussies were the sun's eye. Lots of cat figurines from those days wear a scarab, the symbol of the rising sun. In those days every family in Egypt had one or more cats. When a cat died the whole family shaved their eyebrows as a sign of mourning. The cat was embalmed and put in a wooden coffin that was decorated with precious stones. The family carried the coffin to the cemetery where the cat was buried. People really grieved and mourned for their lost cat-friend. A cemetery with more than 300,000 cat-mummies was discovered in the city of Beni Hasan.

The Persian king Cambyses skilfully turned the Egyptians' worship of cats to his advantage. He wanted to invade Egypt but the Egyptians defended the port of Pelusium very well. So what did King Cambyses do? He ordered his soldiers in the front rows to carry cats. When the Egyptians saw this they surrendered without putting up a fight. They didn't want to kill even a single cat.'

Full of admiration, Mickje looked at Daimke. 'You know so much, Daimke girl, you're very smart! But you're right; we are connected to the hereafter and with the Great Bastet. That's why we can often foresee happenings. Take earthquakes, we sense days in advance when one is coming. During the war, cats warned when air raids were about to happen. They knew to within a minute when their owners were in trouble or had died. There is much evidence of that. What about Luckje? Did he not bring me to you?' Quickly she jumped on my lap and hid her head under my arm. She still can't talk about what she experienced before she came to us. Oh, I am so thankful that she is with us.

'Do you know why some Siamese cats have a kink in their tail?' Daimke said, 'That is because they guarded the rings of the princess when she took a bath. The princess pushed her ring over the Siamese's tail and the cat twisted the end of its tail so the ring could not fall off.' 'Gosh, Daimke', Catje said while eyeing her full of admiration, 'I thought you had made up all that, but now I'm convinced your mother was a princess.' Puddie cast a furtive glance at his tail, but he didn't see any kink. Too bad, but maybe it was invisible?

'How about the book you're reading, mama? Is there no story in it about a Siamese who ordered a bird via the Internet? Come on, tell us all about it.' 'You mean "Feline Online"?' I asked, 'yes, it's a lovely little book, written by my friend Elyse Cregar.'

Emily is a young girl fond of cats. Her neighbour Amanda is deaf and lives with two gorgeous Siamese cats, Foo Foo and Tarzan. Tarzan is extraordinarily clever. When he was still a kitten he used to swing from curtain to curtain like a feline 'Tarzan'. Hence his name. Emily is not allowed to have cats, so she often visits Amanda so she can play with them. One day she had to write a composition about Ancient Egypt for school. While Emily was working on her computer there suddenly appeared a big eye on the screen. It said: 'I am Bastet, daughter of Isis. I am the Cat Goddess of Ancient Egypt. I have an important mission for you. I will show you the Eye of Horus so that you will know everything. You must tell the people about the wisdom and power of us cats, so that they will worship us again as they did in the old times. Pay attention to Tarzan. He has great power. You will see, he will learn to read and to write and to surf on the Internet. Through him I will reach the whole world. I, Bastet, taught him, others will follow after him.' Slowly the eye faded away. Emily didn't understand any of it and found it rather horrible. But it fascinated her. 'Was it a dream?' she wondered. But more and more the eye appeared on the screen and it followed her even when she moved around her room. She decided to be careful and to say nothing to anyone. She was very intrigued.

Tarzan is so smart that Bastet selected him to learn to read and to write. She has visited him many times in his dreams and so he is well prepared. Amanda bought a new computer. Suddenly Bastet's eye also appeared on her screen. Astonished, she called Tarzan who recognized Bastet immediately. Tarzan had taken an interest in computering. From now on he tried to sit before the screen as much as possible. The Goddess told him: **'Mau is our name in old Egypt. We all are named Mau. Mau means 'see'. We can see things that people cannot, especially during the night. The wise Egyptians worshipped us because of that power as well as for all other powers we have. You will see, Tarzan, just wait, you will see. You also descend from old Egypt's great cats. Some day, when you will be able to read, you will have it all. Food, affection and lots of attention. People will worship you. You will always have fresh fish and lots of tasty titbits and even your own bird to play with.'** *That was one of Tarzan's wishes: to have a bird. He spent hours and hours sitting on his footstool watching birds. He didn't want to do them any harm, he just wanted to have his own bird to play with and to chase for fun. Fortunately Amanda didn't switch off her computer during the night so he could practice. Pretty soon he knew how to read. Every night easy-to-read texts appeared in large and clear letters on the screen:* **'the old Egyptians worshipped Cats as Gods. The eye of Horus knows everything. We Maus know everything!!'** *Tarzan was a quick learner and he also learned how to surf on the Internet. When Amanda had to leave her house for a couple of days for her job, Tarzan decided to order a bird for him and Foo Foo. He preferred a parakeet. It was so quiet in the house because Amanda was deaf. But, oh help, his paw slipped and instead of a cute parakeet he ordered a big parrot. It arrived next day in a box that was put in the hall. Tarzan had made sure the door was not locked when Emily had left after playing with him and*
Foo Foo the night before.

156

Together with Foo Foo Tarzan managed to chew a big hole in the box. To their horror an enormous beak suddenly appeared in the hole. Scared, they hid under the bed. In a jiffy the bird freed himself. He was overjoyed to move again and flew through the house. Soon everything was a mess. Curtains were torn to shreds; dishes were shattered on the floor and plant pots turned over. Tarzan had the bright idea to lock the bird in the greenhouse behind the kitchen. Amanda grew magnificent ferns there. Tarzan lured the bird in there and together the cats pushed the door shut.

When Emily arrived that night and saw the havoc, she was flabbergasted. She had noticed that the computer was still on, but she didn't have the faintest idea that Tarzan knew how to use the computer, let alone order a parrot. Quickly she tried to tidy up the mess. When Amanda came home she noticed that things had changed places. Amanda thought her cats had turned the place upside down out of sheer boredom. She went to the greenhouse. She was surprised to see a very big parrot that flew at her, deliriously happy to see someone who could feed him. He had only eaten a few bananas before arriving here. Emily explained to her now about the eye always appearing on the computer screen. Together they checked the computer to find out what had happened and found Tarzan's order in the emails outbox. Full of admiration they looked at him. How was it possible! 'Better switch off the computer before leaving', Emily chuckled when she left. 'You never can tell!'

All this had made Tarzan very tired. 'Indeed, to work on the computer is fun,' he thought, 'but in future I'll just keep my knowledge to myself. I can read and write now. That's very comfortable and also useful, but I'll leave ordering things and birds to Amanda and Emily. Come on, Foo Foo, let's find us some tasty titbits. Purr prrr.'

'Oh mama,' Puddie shouted, 'do you think I will ever learn to use the computer? Now, I need you to write to my feline pen friends. I wish I could do it myself.' 'No problem, Puddie,' I replied, 'sure you could learn it. But this is a laptop. The keys are very close to each other, too close for your paws. You know, you already tried the computer by walking over the keys. The result was Chinese.' 'Oh, that's it, then,' Puddie said relieved, 'I thought I was too stupid to learn. '

I am happy to have laptops only. Imagine suddenly an elephant appearing on my lawn. I love elephants, they are intelligent and beautiful animals but I reckon that they are a bit costly to keep. What about our computer-pussy, so obediently carrying out all assignments and mewing so pathetically whenever too many emails come in...would she also work under Bastets orders?

Donsje reflected about the fate of felines in the Middle Ages. 'Horrible, all those cats who were killed. Why mama, why?' Indeed, why? Church orders! Personally, I am sure that the Lord condemned this meaningless killing of cats. The Lord loves cats very much. 'Just forget about it, dear Donsje. It's Christmas now and it won't happen again. You know what I'm going to do? I'll look up beautiful proverbs in the Bible which prove that the Lord loves His animals very much. We'll include them in chapter sixteen. Anyway, Buddhism and Islam are other, beautiful manifestations of religion, which teach compassion for all living creatures. All religions are basically earth- and animal-friendly. Only evil persons find some excuse in them to commit cruel acts against animals.

Actually, there were priests who loved animals and even kept cats. Pope Leo XII, for instance, had a beautifully black striped greyish-red tomcat with the name Micetto. He was born in the Vatican and often visitors saw him sleeping cosily in the wide folds of the papal garments. Cardinal Richelieu, Prime Minister in Louis XIII's government, was known for his love of cats. He had a black Angora cat, Lucifer, which he loved very much.

And do you know that our New Pope Benedict XVI loves cats? Cardinal Tarcisio Bertone said that the Pope is fond of the stray cats who roam near the Vatican. Often the cats follow him when he walks to his office. He has, of course, cats of his own, which he loves very much. To his great sorrow he was not allowed to take them with him when he had to move to the Vatican. What a terrible thing to forbid! Now he has to go to his apartment outside Roma to see them and look after them. Most of the time the poor cats are alone. I really hope he will tell the people of the Vatican who's the boss. I am really glad he loves animals and cats especially. Probably he will make some special laws to protect them better.

My favourite saint is Francis of Assisi. He considered all living creatures as his brothers and sisters. Their source and creator was the same as his source and creator. When he preached to the birds, they stopped singing to listen

158

intently to his prayers. Beautiful stories tell how wild birds sat on his shoulders and how wild animals had complete trust in him and calmly lay down at his feet

Here is such a story. This beautiful story about the birds is by Thomas of Celano. He was the first to record Francis' adventures. He met Francis in person and has spoken to his companions, so this story is really true.

ST FRANCIS AND THE BIRDS

Francis lived around the year 1200 in Assisi, a small town in Northern Italy. He was born into a wealthy family and lived well. According to a then prevailing custom, big feasts were regularly organised. There was much drinking and merry making and everybody tried to outshine the other. Francis also took part. When he was a child, he had been fond of animals and nature and spent most of his time outside. When he grew up he didn't find time for nature any more.

One day his city was attacked and Francis was one of the first to report for the battle. He didn't want to be inferior to his friends and wanted to become famous, but he was soon taken prisoner. He spent one year in prison. When he returned home, he was ill for a long time. This was an opportunity for him to think about his life. He realised he didn't want to continue living as he did. He decided to devote his life to the Lord. He gave all his possessions away and moved into the mountains. A couple of years later, he returned to the ' living' world and started preaching to the people. He told them about the Lord's great love and about His creation. Some people thought him a funny fellow but others became his followers. Francis decided not to isolate himself but rather to go into the wide world to reach more and more people. He told them how to live according to the Gospel. How to find happiness, like he had found it.

In the first place Francis wanted to help people, but his heart went out especially to animals. Together with his followers, the brothers, he made long journeys. How they enjoyed God's creation. The sun, the moon, the stars, the wind, the water. The magnificent flowers they saw everywhere and the birds that sang so melodiously. Oh, how Francis had longed for all this in the days he had allowed himself to be carried away by his friends and went to all those feasts. 'Yes, this is real life', he happily thought. Every plant, every animal told him something about God's greatness, about His wisdom and His beauty.

One day Francis and his companions passed through the majestic Spoleto Valley. Many birds were eating fresh seeds and young plants. Spontaneous as he was, Francis left his companions and walked over to the birds. 'May the Lord give you peace', he greeted them. Those were the very words he used to greet people. Instead of flying away as birds usually do when people approach them, they remained calmly where they were.

It was as if a wonderful peace had come over the valley. The peace of the Lord. 'Paradise must be as beautiful and as peaceful as this,' Francis remarked to himself. 'So this is what happens when you live according to the gospel. Even the animals lose their fears. How beautiful!' And he thanked the Lord from the bottom of his heart for this wonderful experience. Amazed, the brothers watched the birds and Francis. They had never seen this before!

Humbly Francis asked the birds if they were willing to listen to the word of God. And they were. They stopped singing and waited in complete silence. Francis told them the same things he told to the humans. He talked about the Lord's immense love for all creatures. He ended like this:

'My bird-brothers and bird-sisters, you must always give high praise to the Lord and love Him always with all your heart. For He gave you feathers to dress you in, and wings to fly with. And everything else you need to live. He gave you a place of honour among all creatures and assigned the free, pure sky as your residence. You do not sow nor mow, but there is no need to. The Lord takes care of you and protects you.'

To Francis' and his brothers' great surprise the birds uttered their joy in their own way. They stretched their bodies and fluttered their wings, opened their little beaks and looked at him. Francis walked among them, his habit touching their heads and bodies. At the end he blessed them, making the sign of the cross and then the birds resumed their life.
Happily Francis and the brothers continued on their way. They discussed this remarkable meeting with the birds. There, in the orchard close to Cannara, Francis realised that birds and other animals, by simply 'being', serve, acknowledge and obey the Lord better than most people do. From then on he treated all creatures like brothers and sisters.

ST FRANCIS AND THE WOLF

Francis and his brothers were in Gubbio, a small town where they liked to stay. They were always cordially received there. But this time the townspeople were not happy. For some time a big, cruel wolf had prowled around the town. Not only had he killed their cattle, he had also attacked and killed people and nobody ventured outside the town's walls any more.

Francis listened to their stories and decided to go and talk to the wolf. 'He must be very desperate,' Francis concluded, 'to attack animals and people.' The people advised against it, but Francis didn't mind and wanted to find the wolf. He prayed to the Lord for protection and left without carrying any weapon. Full of fear and curiosity the people watched him from the walls. As they expected, the big, angry wolf flew at Francis. But Francis crossed himself and called: 'Come to me, brother wolf. In the name of Jesus, I command you not to hurt me or anyone!' The people watched with bated breath. A miracle! The dangerous animal wagged his tail and threw himself on his back at the feet of Francis.

Francis talked to him: 'Brother wolf, you have done much harm and caused much grief. Not only have you killed animals, you have also killed people. You deserve to be put to death. Everybody, indeed, the whole region is against you. But, brother wolf, I want to make peace between you and the town of Gubbio, under the following conditions: you will harm them no more and they will forgive you your crimes. They will also stop hunting you and sending their dogs after you.' The wolf promised he would observe this pact. He did so in a way befitting a true wolf: he bowed his head and extended his front paw to Francis.

'Brother wolf,' Francis went on, ' as you are willing to make peace, I promise you to make sure that the people will always feed you, as long as you live, so that you will not starve any more. I do realise very well that you committed all those crimes because you were hungry. But you must promise that you will never again harm man or animal.' Again the wolf bowed his head and placed his right front paw into the hands of Francis.

Francis invited the wolf to accompany him to the square of Gubbio to confirm the pact. A huge crowd had assembled there. 'Listen, sisters and brothers, brother wolf here has promised to make peace with you if you promise to give him the food he needs every day. I will personally guarantee that the wolf will strictly observe this pact.' Unanimously the people promised to feed the wolf. Before the eyes of the people, the wolf bowed his head for the third time and extended his right front paw to Francis.

How happy the people were! After that day the wolf lived for more than two years in peace and love in the neighbourhood of Gubbio. The people loved him and fed him well. His presence reminded them of Francis, whom they cherished. When the wolf died, the people were very sad.

Just outside Gubbio there is a small church dedicated to St Francis and the wolf. It has a beautiful bronze commemorative plaque that glitters splendidly in the sunlight between ten and twelve a.m. And so this moving story lives on.

(With many thanks to Hans Sevenhoven, who adapted these stories. I included his site in my list of addresses at the end of this book.)

The fluffies had listened carefully and even Puddie was impressed by the brave Francis who was not afraid to approach the wolf. 'I would not dare to do that,' he honestly admitted. 'He is our patron saint, guys!' I said. 'Do you know that the day he died, October the fourth, is World Animal Day?' Donsje chuckled. 'Here every day is animal day, fortunately. Purr prrrr!' And she was right. I quickly gave her some treats. It was Christmas, after all!

St Francis is the patron saint of all animals, but cats have their own patron saint. Her name is **St Agatha** and she lived during the third century after Christ. Her name day falls on February sixth. Let's celebrate it from now on! Good intentions for the New Year! At least one already!

Real love stories don't have happy endings, because real love stories never end.

Source unknown.

163

Chapter 9

Strays, Catje's Disease and the Run

To gain the friendship of a cat is a difficult thing. The cat is a philosophical, methodical, quiet animal. Tenacious of its own habits, fond of order and cleanliness, and does not lightly confer its friendship. If you are worthy of its affection, a cat will be your friend but never your slave. He keeps his free will, though he loves you, and he will not do for you what he thinks is unreasonable. But, once he gives himself to you, it is with such absolute confidence, such fidelity of affection.

Theophile Gautier

It was New Year's Eve. The fluffies and I were reading and playing on the bed. Next to me I had a pile of interesting cat-magazines and a cup of lovely warm tea. The radio was broadcasting some good country music. Not a bad setting to celebrate Old and New. Some time before midnight the banging broke loose. The Old-into-New-Lunacy! As usual, Daimke lay in my arms, her head on my shoulder. I felt her body going rigid. She got up. A beauty to see, all tenseness but tender and slender. Slowly she moved to the window. More banging! She jumped back to me: **'Mama, mama, listen, they're firing out there! Don't you hear? What shall we do? What is that racket out there? I don't like it!! It is hurting my ears. Mama, do something! Weeeiiieehh!'** But mama didn't move. She only assured Daimke that everything was all right. **'No, it's not all right!!'** Daimke replied and crawled again to the window. Catje concluded that, since Donsje and I didn't react to the noise, she shouldn't either. She just calmly moved to the foot of the bed. Yes, Donsje had heard the racket before, but for the kids it was something new. They were still very small last year.

Soon the noise stopped. But I guess that the fluffies, with their very sharp ears, must have heard the fireworks in the port of Antwerp for quite some time. In bird-flight, Brasschaat is not far from the port of Antwerp. Next morning, sitting behind my desk with a delicious cup of coffee to start working, I felt so thankful that we could begin the New Year in this way. I'm such a lucky dog!

To be able to work at home with in front of me the view of a beautiful white lawn and frost-covered trees, each of which has its own story. I love trees. They have been through a lot, because we live close to a military zone. Papa pointed out to me the many pieces of shrapnel that had hit them. They are full of holes. Sometimes they tell me about it, mostly when the wind rustles through them. I love wind. I grew up in the wind. I am a polder landscape-child! Birds fly on and off to get sunflower seeds from the birdhouse. It's like live television for the fluffies. What a comfort not to have to be stuck in a traffic-jam. Not to have to leave my pussy-children because I have to go out to work. No, the fluffies are always with me and they assist me in the office. One he-secretary and four she-secretaries! What a staff! As I said, I am a very lucky so-and-so! If I had to make one single wish I'd choose 'being satisfied'. Immediately followed by 'being thankful'. You're always happy then. And yes I am.

My heart feels for all the animals and the people who have it difficult in life. How is it possible that thousands of euros are wasted on fireworks? While everybody knows that lots of poor unwanted animals are killed because there's no place to shelter them. While there are so many old and ill people who hardly can make both ends meet. People for whom a small Christmas parcel would mean heaven on earth. As long as even one single animal or human lacks food or shelter, how is it possible that money is wasted on that stupid banging? Moreover, fireworks cause a lot of stress in animals and it also pollutes the air. 'Well, there are people and pencils, and both can write!' This is an old saying from Numansdorp, my native village.

What will the year 2001 bring us? Again the abandonment and dumping of numerous poor and helpless kittens? Or, some improvement, even if only slight? Oh, let us hope for that, for precisely cats, such wonderful sensitive and spiritual creatures, suffer so intensely. Maybe they can survive for a while when they are abandoned, if it's not too cold. But especially the knowledge that 'they are not wanted any more' makes them depressed and ill. It is simply not true that cats prefer to be alone and care more for their home than for their people. Quite the contrary, they have a deep affection for their people, only they don't show it so exuberantly as dogs do.

A pet-shop allowed me to display a box to collect money for the strays my dear friend Gerda Thys looks after. I pasted following text on the box:

Please, dear, dear people,
Help us. We feel very, very cold.
We are wet, sad and very hungry.

Any small gift will make us happy.
We'll have a real Christmas then!

Thank you very much in advance and many
Lovely purring greetings from us, poor dumped
stray cats.

There must still be kind people around for the box slowly filled with money. But there is such immense suffering and so much money needed to help the poor strays. If only local authorities would finally assume responsibility. Fortunately they do that more and more. Gaia, our animal rights organisation tries to persuade the local authorities to organise actions for neutering. There is our 'green' minister Tavernier who has a big heart for animals. But it is mostly private people who are concerned about the fate of stray cats, like my two dear friends Gerda and her husband José. They are about seventy years 'young' but devoted in many ways to the cause of the strays. Every stray in need they happen to meet gets help. It is indeed unbelievable what they achieve. Not only the work but also the love they give the cats is so beautiful. They are magnificent people.

They collect food by placing boxes in shops in which customers can deposit food. Too bad fewer and fewer shops are willing to cooperate in this. Every day they feed about thirty-five strays. Another group numbering about forty stray cats gets feed twice a week. Further, Gerda has a stand at jumble sales where she sells things. The money she earns that way is used to buy food for the strays.

She serves fifteen feeding spots. The cats which visit these are or have been neutered. Gerda captures them and takes them to the vet. They are first examined there. If they look ill, they are tested for FeLV and FIV. When they are negative, they are 'neutered' and, after a couple of days, wormed and deflead before Gerda returns them to the feeding spot. Should one of those cats fall ill, Gerda will take her or him back to the vet.Gerda is also an inspector for the Animal Protection Society. She partially works for Apma, a Foundation

166

fighting vivisection. This revolting animal abuse, allegedly legitimate because it is 'in the interest of science', is in fact outmoded and nothing more than a false alibi. Apma has achieved a lot already! The law against tests on animals for cosmetics especially is a great leap forward. We owe this law to Minister Tavernier. Gerda's husband, José, has a pair of golden hands. He makes feed-cages, warm sleep-cages and lots of other things. Gerda and José also volunteer to take sick animals, belonging to people without their own transport, to the vet.

DEAR JUUL,

For months you stalked the street
Eyes looking for love, body in pain
Longing for someone to meet
Hoping it was not in vain
But everybody turned you away
Something I cannot understand
Until on a wonderful day
A lady lent you a helping hand

She found you at a thoroughfare
Trapped by cars, trembling in the roar
Now people gave you their best care
Didn't leave you alone any more
Dear Juul, you were so eager to live
With your last strength and lots of pluck
Did people their utmost give
But you just had run out of luck

You were surrounded with love
A week with intensive care filled
Then you left for the heavenly Above
Yet remain forever in our heart instilled
You are now happy in heaven and play
Far from loneliness and pain
For me it's a fact when I say
Man and animal will meet there again

So, rest now in peace
You have touched us deeply
Out of powerlessness and unease
I made this poem to express me

Dear Juul
I'm so happy your last days
Were filled with love and kindness
Non-profit Association Care for Strays
To you, a thousand thanks and God bless!
Love, Nicolet

© *Nicolet*
(With many thanks to Jef who translated this wonderful poem)

Resi Packolet of Poezennestje (Pussy-nest), also linked to Apma, is doing a good job as well. She takes care of the Antwerp port cats. These are often very sociable and beautiful cats which are simply dropped out of the car in some lonely port area. Even Persians who cannot miss their daily brushing are dumped there. Dazed, they run around. 'Where are our people? When do we get our tasty titbits? We are so afraid, cold and hungry! Miaauwww?' When they arrive at Resi's place, they often look miserable, their fur in tangles. They are undernourished and sometimes hurting from abuse. First they are put in quarantine, and then they are placed in a beautiful cathouse with a run. They can recover there. Then Resi tries to find good homes for them. She doesn't just confine her activities to the docks only, but also tries to - if money is available - alleviate the suffering of cats north of Antwerp and its districts. Quite some organising.

In the province of Belgian Limburg, two persons, Els and André, have founded the association non-profit making 'The Felix Project'. During the five years of its existence, this association has helped 5000 cats. I got permission to include the following text, which very well sums up the problem of stray cats.

The greatness of a nation and their moral progress can be judged by the way their animals are treated.

Gandhi

Man seems superior to the animal but his behaviour often proves the opposite. The true human being can be recognised by the way he treats the animals.

More and more people now realise that every animal with feelings, wishes and pains of its own, also has rights.

The only way to reduce the suffering of cats is by having them neutered. Many people let nature, an unrelenting force, just go its way. With terrible consequences: 1 + 1 = 6 and this up to three times every year. Soon one runs out of places to shelter all those kittens. The 'surplus' of cats thus ends up in some overcrowded animal shelter. The shelters cannot cope with the inflow of cats. So they are forced to have more than half of the mostly young and perfectly healthy cats put to sleep. This means thousands and thousands of cats every year (for example: in 1999: 24,897 cats in 55 animal shelters) are killed unnecessarily.

Other cats are left to fend for themselves under the pretext that a cat is a resourceful animal. This is sheer narrow-mindedness and shows lack of insight and sensitivity that condemns cats to a life of wandering and straying from place to place. Another 'solution', equally showing lack of understanding and feeling, is to kill cats instead of neutering them. Regrettably, many local authorities prefer this 'solution'. It is animal-unfriendly and solves nothing. It goes without saying that this killing greatly upsets true friends of felines. It causes sorrow and powerlessness. For years these people devote themselves to the cause of the well being of 'their strays'. What a pain for them when they learn that again cats were captured and killed. And all this because some people have something against stray cats, especially cat-haters and animal abusers.

And the problem won't go away! Other strays will fill the gaps left by old strays and have kittens in their turn. It is a vicious circle. However, if the cats were neutered, new births on the grounds would become rare and so both the number of cats and the number of mice would remain in balance. And volunteers would see to it that the animals would not die from hunger or thirst.

Impact of neutering on the behaviour of stray cats:
- *Less straying, hence less spread of infectious diseases and parasites.*
- *No more matings, hence a reduction in sexually transmitted diseases and consequently healthier cats.*
- *No more nocturnal noise nuisance.*
- *More stable groups, hence less spraying by tomcats to mark territory.*
- *Increase in life expectancy and life quality.*

Positive effects in the area:

- *For people: satisfaction and pleasure as a result of their caring for the cats. This is a very important social benefit.*
- *People becoming socially isolated, converse with 'their' animals, feed them and so improve their quality of life. Animals keep humans away from depression.*
- *Stronger, healthier animals keep weaker wild animals away and markedly reduce the stock of rodents.*

What to do if your local authority doesn't have a neutering policy?

Your local authority doesn't do anything with regard to your local stray cat problem. Often all that is done is catching and killing the strays. Or they are taken to an overcrowded animal shelter. Almost all stray cats, unless they are still very young, cannot be placed somewhere because they have gone wild, so they are simply killed. The assignment of an animal shelter is to receive abused, neglected and lost animals, and to find a new home for them later. Consequently sheltering stray cats is not part of an animal shelter's assignment.

Politicians who claim that animal welfare is not on people's mind, don't know their electorate.

So stand up for the strays and voice your concerns for them!!!

An official in charge of the environment, supported by local citizens, is sometimes willing to concern himself with the problem. Write letters and send emails to local newspapers, weeklies and the local bulletin of your town. Get in touch with environment-friendly politicians. Often it's the citizens with a heart for animals who win over their local authorities by simply stubbornly persisting.

Begin, if possible in cooperation with your local authority an action to make cat owners aware of their responsibilities and convince them of having their cats neutered.

See GAIA's website, under 'Strays' (address included in the list at the end of this book) for a text to sensitise the population. This text may be reproduced freely and adapted to your local situation.

So much for the text on the Felix-Project. The relevant address is included in the list at the end of this book. They are doing a splendid job. So, it is clear that there are only advantages connected to having strays neutered. It is absolutely not true that cats should have kittens first before being 'helped'. Quite the contrary, the risks of uterine problems and mammary tumours decrease when she-cats get a 'zipper' at the age of six or seven months. Neutering prevents lots of problems. Cats become more affectionate and more cuddly. When running around free they will stay closer to their home and so run less risk of being injured or killed by a car, though every cat running around free remains at risk. Traffic is a big cat-killer. Neutered cats fight less and search less for company so the risk of contracting lethal diseases like FeLV (leukaemia), FIV (cat aids) and FIP (peritonitis) is reduced. You will find more information about these diseases in Chapter 17, Feline Disorders.

Slowly, people's minds are changing. This is also due to organisations like GAIA and other animal protection societies. Very slowly they succeed in instilling awareness that animals have the same feelings as humans; feelings of pain and sorrow and even mourning when their children die or when they lose their companion. I'm so happy about this change!

I always tend to tidy away "rubbish" on the first day of the New Year. **'Something to make good use of'** according to my fluffies because it doesn't happen often. So lots of things move from file to refuse bag, under the enthusiastic eyes of my pussy-children. What a thrill to move all that trash into refuse bags! Especially the double-check to make sure mama didn't throw away something she might need again. And the best way to check? Very simple: turn over the bag and dig yourself a way through all that rustling paper, purr prrr! I still don't understand why I feel obliged to copy everything, just to put it away in space-occupying and dust-gathering document files. Isn't everything neatly stored away in my PC? Obviously I consider computer files not yet solid and really-available-at-the-moment-I-need-them. Well, it's common in people of my age, Daimke says.

Sun! It is still around! How blissful that first sunny day of the New Year. A faint sun, maybe, but giving lust for life and hope. Spring is coming and then a long delightful summer.

Catje, Daimke, Donsje and I enjoy our circuits through the garden. Too bad Puddie has out-lived this fun while Mickje never learned it. I think she would panic if I fastened on the harness. But they have their run where they spend lots of time. Puddie longs to be able to sit on 'his' lawn and so do I. Oh, how we enjoy that! But it's too cold and wet for that now. I take turns with the three girls. Catje is the best co-runner. Part of the garden borders the road. Catje doesn't mind people, dogs and cyclists, but those horrible, nasty, huge trucks that **hiss** when they pass speed ramps, they make your tail bristle out from fear. 'Tssjiiieeee tssjjiii,' they curse. What a horrible noise. Her tail grows bushy and round then and she shifts to her lowest stalking-position. Sometimes Catje will stand stock-still and looks up at me with her loyal eyes: 'Everything all right, mama?' So cute! Of course, she wants a cuddle too and I readily oblige. Then we continue our walk: 'Catje, raise your aerial!' I ask and woops, her beautiful thick tail goes up in the air.

When we return we find Daimke waiting for us behind the door, calling: 'Weeehhh wheeewwww, whiiwweee, mama, now it's my turn!!' As soon as I put her down on the path, she starts exploring. She must see and smell everything. I hold my fluffies tied to a very long retractable line, so that in fact they feel free. When I ask: 'Daimke, roll over, she immediately rolls on her back. Funny and lovely to see. She adores it. The funniest thing to do is to move a twig alongside the trunk of a tree. She will chase it and fly high up the tree. It is fantastic to see her hanging there. One fur-ball of muscles and alertness.

Donsje likes to hitchhike part of the walk on my shoulder. She has done so since she was a little kitten. I enjoy feeling her cute soft head next to mine, bobbing up and down with every step. When I speak to her she rubs her cheek against mine. But she also is a good walker, my dear little Donsje-girl.

She also is the one who always lies on my shoulder when I am cooking. Without ever using her claws, she floats from the kitchen table on to my shoulder. Before take-off she always warns me softly: 'Prrr...wieeraaauwww, I'm coming.'

Today all my cats have taken Milbemax, a wormer also effective against tapeworm. As they sometimes catch mice, it is better to worm them twice yearly. How special these fluffies are! Without making any trouble they swallow the pill. I take their head, hold it slightly backwards, open the mouth, and put the pill at the back of their tongue. I wait till I feel them swallowing and let go. Immediately afterwards I give them some water with a needle without syringe, so I make sure that the pill does not stay blocked in the oesophagus, which can cause serious problems. To give butter afterwards is more effective than coating the pill with butter. Then it will slither out of my hands. And a reward afterwards is justified. Imagine having a pill pushed down your throat!

'Miracles' is doing fine. We receive many reactions from people who read the book. Many lovely emails, letters and yes, also orders. We are happy and proud. It's a lot of work, but wonderful work. The fluffies are doing overtime for they assist me in this job. Donsje usually sits on my desk, very close to me. Sometimes she'll nestle her head against my arm or put her paws around my neck and say: 'Miiuueewweee, great isn't it? I love you mama, but can I have a titbit now?' I always have a box with titbits in the drawer next to me. He who works deserves food. I join her with a Grether's Pastille.

The living room is really an ideal place for my pussy-children. I enjoy it tremendously when they fly through the room like little balls of fur. Catje first, over the chairs, onto the climbing pole, back over the chairs. Then they race to

173

the run, up the wire-netting, hang there for a while to look at me: 'Miieeuuuuwwww, mama, mama, just watch me! I am an acrobat!' One week later I often thought back to Catje's circus-acts.

There is a small shelf just below the ceiling in our living room. Just wide enough for a cat to 'catwalk' on. Donsje used to entertain my mother by 'cat walking' there. Mama almost lost her breath watching Donsje perform from her sickbed that stood in the living room, during the last years of her life. Mama was full of admiration then! And so am I. Turning was not possible but I caught her when she reached the point of no return. Donsje never did her 'catwalk' if I was not there. Now the tall 'wander lusty' climbing pole stands there for them to jump on. When Daimke walked the shelf for the first time, she ran past the pole till the 'terminal', the wall. It was impossible to return and also to turn. 'Mama, help!!!! I am stuck up here, wiieeheii wheeiiieee!' Fortunately I heard her cries. I went to a spot below her and called:' Just drop yourself, Daimke, into my arms!' Without hesitation she jumped into my arms. Catje never makes that mistake, maybe Daimke has warned her?

It's a fact that cats warn each other of dangers. Last summer Catje was stung on her front paw by a mean wasp. How that hurt! Her paw swelled. I immediately put sugar water on the wound and gave her Ledum, a homeopathic remedy. There was no angel. It was some hours before the pain stopped. Since then she has never tried to catch a wasp again. And Daimke, who saw it, won't either.

Catje is lither than Daimke, but Daimke is a real ballerina. She dances through life like an elf. Catje is everybody's dear. Puddie and Catje play like hell and are very wild. Daimke and Catje are inseparable and perform several wrestling matches daily. And Donsje acts, to my great pleasure, more and more the pacifist. It's impossible to make her angry. I have never heard her swear or snarl. When there is something she really doesn't like she will just mew plaintively. But that is very rare because she finds fun in almost everything.

It started on Saturday night. I had the impression that Catje was a bit unsteady on her legs. She stumbled a couple of times. I thought she had miscalculated one of her jumps. She does play rather wildly. Sunday morning it was even clearer. She stumbled over her legs in the living room and at one time she landed with a thud on the floor when she miscalculated her jump from the desk. I still hoped it would pass, but I was worried nevertheless. It became even worse. But she ate well and that's a good sign. She tilted her head, the right ear downwards. Maybe her ear was hurting? That night she slept calmly on the bed, but I was very worried by now. Why do these things always happen during the weekend? Doctor Liliane was away. Catje can't fall off anything in my bedroom, except from the low climbing pole, but I had removed it to be on the safe side. Being a mother of cats, one remains alert.

On Monday she was even dizzier and refused to eat. She felt sick surely, as if she was seasick. It was typical that her eyes flickered very quickly for left to right. Also she couldn't stand the light. I called Doctor Liliane as soon as she was in her office. We could come immediately. Catje did not have a fever but Doctor Liliane noticed that her right ear was somewhat red. She was dizzy and that's why she was also sick. Doctor Liliane is very good. She made a diagnosis at once:

Catje had Feline Vestibular Syndrome. It would take some weeks to pass.
The term vestibular refers to the vestibule of the ear.

Symptoms:

Sudden disturbances of equilibrium with abnormal eye movements. The animal cannot stand light. When only one ear is affected, the cat often shows it by tilting the head. The affected side is held low. Sometimes the cats prefer not to move, but if they move they do so unco-ordinatedly. When both sides are affected, the cat sometimes exhibits creeping or staggering movements.

Causes:

The Feline Vestibular Syndrome may be caused by pressure in the ear as a result of an ear infection, e.g. after a cold. This is the main cause of Feline Vestibular. The condition will disappear by itself within three weeks, if necessary with the help of antibiotics. Recovery is slow. There is a 15 per cent possibility of a slight handicap remaining.

There were other more serious causes mentioned too, but I refused to think of them. Doctor Liliane gave her an injection of antibiotic. I had to complete the treatment with tablets. Catje also had to take 0,5 cc Primperan three times daily against the sickness. It worked excellently. As soon as I had given it to her she wanted to eat. She spent the rest of the morning on the windowsill, curled up, unhappy, sad and with a tilted head. Fortunately she ate the chicken with broth very well, a positive sign. She slept quietly and that was the best thing for her to do. She was still quite dizzy but when I cuddled her she rolled over on her back and stretched her legs out to me as she usually does. She purred and kneaded her front paws then. Oh, please let she get better soon. An earache is terrible. I had it often when I was a child and had to go swimming with my class. I feel calmer now. The disease has a name and that takes away some bite out of its threat.

Four days later our girl felt much better. I was so happy. She was still unsteady and fell off things if I was not alert, but she was very smart and learnt quickly. I felt confident that this condition would pass and if that 15 per cent handicap remained, well, it's not that bad. What mattered most was that she felt well and got pleasure out of life again. The past days she watched her world with a frowning face: 'Good heavens, what's happening? The world is tilting and turning. Wiiieeehhh mama, help me!!! I am so afraid and unsure.' But now she seemed to adjust to her tilted world or maybe it was going back to normal?

She found swallowing a pill every day too much of a good thing and sometimes succeeded in moving her head in my hand in such a way that the pill didn't get where I wanted it to be. Well, it was also a sign of her recovery. Of course the highest places attracted her most now, especially since I stayed around to see if things worked out. Great all that attention from mama! She took up playing again. Not really wildly yet, but playing anyway.

Daimke is delirious with joy for she was completely at a loss. She felt very down when her friend suddenly stopped playing. She followed me everywhere and looked with her beautiful golden-green eyes at me and at Catje and at me again. I explained to her that Catje was a bit ill and that she should be very careful with her. And, oh how cute, Daimke understood. Very softly she started grooming Catje while she lay on the bed. Hide-and-seek is the favourite game of Catje and me. I have a large bed where she can find many hiding-places. When I lose her, I have to touch all the bulges to find out whether it is Catje or just air. How happy we will be when our little clown is back to normal!

Hide-and-seek! Yes, it's fun indeed. But this afternoon it was not so funny for a while. I had just brought Catje to the office. The screen was in the window so the fluffies couldn't get out. I returned to find four fluffies waiting for me on my desk, but Catje was not there. I called. No reply! I searched...nothing. 'Where is Catje?' I asked Puddie. Usually he answers by looking in the direction of the spot where Catje is sitting, but not this time. I checked behind all cabinets, in all drawers. Impossible yet a fact: **Catje was gone!** I have a kind of toy animal that mews like a kitten in distress when I squeeze it. The fluffies come racing to this sound if they hear it. I very rarely use this toy, as I find it rather mean, but this was an emergency. Probably a way to call Catje. 'Wwwiieeeheh' it sounded. The fluffies flew at me except...Catje. Now I became scared! Maybe she was lying somewhere? And then I looked up...there she sat, on top of the window! **Laughing!!!** It's true, she laughed! My funny little girl! Still, it was a good thing that she stayed put and didn't jump down by herself. Our little clown has returned. And mama also could laugh again.

Indeed, she is better. Only she still tilts her head and when we are walking in the garden, she sometimes still stumbles when looking over her shoulder. She has resigned herself to the inevitable, she has to take a pill every morning and gets homeopathy. Today she opened her mouth as soon as she saw me coming with the pipette. So good of her. She has realised that it helps her. I do always explain to the fluffies first why I do something and why it is necessary. They understand, I am sure.

'Mama, mama, come and see, wake up!! Come on, miaaauwww raauw wieeh, purr pr!' I sprang to my feet, was there something wrong with Catje? No, it was Daimke's excited face I saw above me. Loudly mewing she jumped from the bed and raced under the curtain onto the windowsill. It was already light outside, although it was still early in the morning. Strange! Quickly I looked outside and, oh, what beauty! Everything white!! Not just a bit of snow, but a thick layer indeed! Gorgeous. I hurriedly put on my clothes to take the dogs for a walk. The fluffies had to remain inside for a while. Especially Catje.

It was really too cold still. How nice to step on virgin, crunching snow. Like mini-snowmobiles the dogs ploughed through the garden, barking loudly. I felt five years old again and saw myself, papa and the dogs walking through the fields and over the dykes. Winters full of snow were common then. Oh, what a lovely youth I had! It was a special thrill to see everything covered by a thick layer of snow again. There had been no snow for years. When it was a bit warmer I took the pussy-children out. Donsje found it rather a wet mess, but played for a while in the snow. Her head and tail rose just above it. Catje was thrilled and amused. I just let her run around for a short while. Daimke enjoyed it to the full. Like an elf she danced over the thousands and thousands glittering diamonds. The sun was shining, everything literally glittered. As she threw up snow in front of her, it looked like she was throwing little snowballs. She tried to catch them when they came down. So cute to watch. I joined in and also threw mini-snowballs. Woops, she jumped on them immediately. Puddie found the weather too cold and too wet for a tomcat of his rank, but Mickje amused herself by rolling in the snow. I enjoyed myself tremendously and my camera loved it too. I shot more than six rolls of pictures. A unique opportunity!

And then, it was bound to happen. Of course, and as usual, on a Sunday! On mama's birthday at that! We had a power failure. All at once all machines stopped and a deadly silence came over our house. In no time it was ice-cold. So, what is one to do then? Well, go and find the cause. First, I checked the fuses. These were all intact, so the cause was outside. Then I tried to phone the Electricity Company. Of course they had put tapes on with annoying music (why don't they give country music?) and with a teasing voice that said: 'please wait a moment!' Five times I was put through to some other number and I gave up. In the meantime the house had turned very cold and we were becoming very hungry too. I fetched the camping gas stores and heated some food. That helped a lot! A few hours later there was power again. But I still shivered.

That evening I lay stretched out on the bed and tried to read. We were all still numb with cold. Puddie was getting very worried about his shivering mama. So what did my dear fluffy-angel do? He stretched himself out on top of me to warm me up. Yes, a real nice, warm, purring cover he made that way! It really helped. I was reading a lovely book about a tomcat Mefisto, who explains in great detail to his human how a cat is to be taken care of. I read some pieces to Puddie. He agreed wholehearted with the contents. He half-shut his eyes and said: 'Right you are, mama.' So, all in all, it was still a beautiful albeit somewhat boisterous Sunday.

Did I tell that Puddie once saved mama? My mother was more than eighty years old then. She was invalid and her bed stood in the living room, so she could always be with us. One night she fell out of her bed. It should never have happened! At night we always put a screen around the bed, just to prevent that. But it did! Every night I checked up on her at five in the morning. That

178

particular night I was woken up at three by Puddie growling loudly, while pulling my covers. I thought he had heard a fox or stray cat prowling in the surroundings and I wanted to turn back to sleep, but he didn't stop. Then I got the point and rushed to mama's room. She was lying unconscious on the cold floor...I phoned for the ambulance at once and an hour later mama was safe in the hospital. She had many bruises and was in shock, but she was not seriously hurt. Only thanks to Puddie it all turned out well....If not for him, mama would have died on that cold floor.

Indeed, cats are small wonders. Bob, a friend of mine, has diabetes. When he gets into a fit of hypo - and often you don't feel that coming when you are asleep - Pio, his wonderful Siamese, wakes him up. She won't calm down until her papa has gone downstairs and has taken some sugar. It's a fact that dogs specially trained for that purpose can anticipate an epileptic attack. I am sure cats would even do better.

My dear friend Mariette, who lives upstairs, has a brother, Eddie, who can create and repair everything. I hadn't abandoned my dream to add another run to the existing one. Eddie came and promised to help me. He devised a beautiful construction. It looks somewhat like the roof of a Chinese pagoda. And so the terrace in front of the living room was converted into one big run. This way I can still add another long run, which will skirt the rose garden, later on. I am sure Papa sent Eddie to help me. He is such a fantastic friend. He is fond of animals and the fluffies trust him completely. He really can construct everything. We watched with admiration when he and his son Roland built a beautiful play area for the fluffies. A dream come true!

March came and Catje played piano again! When she was ill she didn't even come close to it. Maybe the tones hurt her ear. It is moving to watch her playing piano. When I am playing she will first sit next to me and look at me with those gorgeous golden green eyes: 'Mama, may I...?' When I wink or smile, she will jump on top of the keys and carefully walks back and forth over them. I try to continue playing, that's the game, of course! Sometimes I succeed, sometimes not. Then she sits down and puts her forehead between her front paws on the keys, as if she is standing on her head and looking at me upside down. So cute. Of course, she receives some titbits then, and the others know. They share in the reward and are waiting nearby. I am sure that they ask Catje: 'Come on, girl, showtime!' And yes! I have pictures to prove that I'm telling the truth.

One time Catje was very worried when she learned that I had made an appointment with a 'piano tamer'. 'Puddie,' she told her big friend,' I find that very unfair! The piano is kind and calm. It doesn't mind me walking on the keys. In fact, it likes it. It told me so! So why should it be 'tamed'? Is that like I saw on TV? Some big man in a leather suit with a whip that cracks so cruelly? Don't let him hurt the piano. Please, then you must defend him. You're such a strong tiger!' Puddie didn't understand either why the piano should need 'taming'. He rushed onto the high climbing pole to observe the situation, when a man with a briefcase entered the house. Well, it was not that bad. He only tried different tones and listened. The piano didn't complain and there was no whip that cracked. Puddie smiled, 'Now I understand'. Quickly he raced to Catje: 'You Catje, you got me worried there! That man is a piano tuner, not a tamer! He tunes the keys so the sounds will be clear'. 'And you, mama', he added in my direction, 'don't use difficult words when the kids are around! A good thing that I am here to explain and advise!' And that's true!

It is great that, when I play, all the pussy-children come and sit around me. They really love music. It is very moving and an extra motivation for me to play. I always feel mama's presence then. She didn't allow Puddie and Donsje to walk over the keys, but I think that now she likes them doing that as much as I like it. That I started playing the piano, made mama very happy. She enjoyed it immensely even though I am not at all good at it. But when I played to her, she relived her youth, when she played the piano with skill and beauty. She had studied at the Academy of Music and loved music. She had even played concerts. I was glad though, she did not like classic music so much, but preferred French chansons and even enjoyed my favourite country music.

Sometimes people ask me: 'You live in the middle of a forest, why don't you just release your cats, so they can enjoy running around free?' Indeed, why not? Well, there are many reasons for me not to do that. In the first place, I never want to experience the sorrows again that I felt (and still feel) when Luckje suddenly disappeared. It is terrible not to know what happened to your pussy-child. Where is he? Is he lying somewhere? Is he hurt or ...? Is he calling desperately for his mama, who does not come? Even now tears come into my eyes when I think of it.

One dismally wet and cold day in March I experienced how 'safe and secure' living in a wood is. My French friend Raymonde was staying with me. She had gone to feed the chickens and I was in the office. Suddenly she rushed inside, her face deadly pale. 'Viens vite, vite, les poules...' (Come quickly, the chickens...). I rushed out behind her and the scene I saw was beyond all description. My twelve chickens lay in a row in pools of rainwater. Headless! The heads had been removed and had vanished. I was petrified. Just a nightmare or one of those horror movies on television, which I always quickly switch off. But I couldn't switch off this one. It was a bloodthirsty sight! Malicious intent or...? I didn't know, but Raymonde and I were shocked. I called the police who came immediately. Even on Saturday. Wonderful and very friendly people! They were not sure but they thought that a fox had killed the chickens. That night their inspector and animal expert came to take a look and he confirmed the police's suspicion. Foxes! I felt horrible. I should have protected my chickens better!

Many foxes have been released in the neighbourhood. This has led to a surplus of foxes. They are beautiful and smart animals but they can do a lot of harm. Everywhere chickens lost their lives and, yes, foxes also attack cats. I felt very guilty. The wire netting of my chicken run was higher than two metres, yet still not high enough keep out foxes, so Eddie and I closed the upper surface with strong wire netting. Since then we had no more visits from foxes. They are one reason to keep your cats inside! Another reason: poisoning. Regularly the newspapers report about poisoned cats. Just recently there was a story about owners who found their cat lying dead on the lawn. They found it strange as a cat usually hides when he feels ill. An autopsy was performed at the University of Ghent. It was established that the cat had been poisoned by Temik-poison-pellets. One can buy this strong poison in many shops. Just like that. Cats or dogs will not easily eat it, that's true, unless it is coated with meat or fish. So this was malicious intent! Maybe the cat looked too keenly at someone's birds?

Francien van Westering, the well known cat-painter held an enquiry in the weekly *'Margriet'* about keeping cats inside or letting them run around loose and free. She got many reactions. Some people found it an injustice to keep cats inside. A cat being the outstanding freedom-loving animal. 'Every animal should be free', was their opinion. Others found it completely irresponsible to let cats run around free. A third group made a compromise by building runs for their pets. And so have we! But we understand that many people have no space to build a run. Even though one can often make some kind of place, with a bit of wood, some wire netting and 'plenty' of skill. A cat doesn't need so much space, as long as he can feel the sun shining on his fur and he can hear and smell nature. It is indeed terrible to have to stay indoors for the whole of life, even though cats especially know how to adjust to any situation. Provided they get enough love, attention and warmth. But it's better to be always inside, than to be run over by a car. As the saying goes: *'Better inside and fat, than outside and flat.'*

I have read in an English magazine that people living in flats sometimes fix something like a small cage in wire netting to the window. A teensy-weensy balcony for their cats, so that they can look from high up down on the traffic far below. They enjoy sun and fresh air, even though they are "apartment-dwellers". Cats need sunlight for the production of taurine. Maria and Gé have made themselves a dream of a run, in spite of their lack of space. On our site you can see some runs. (rennen) www.rietkat.be

If it is not possible to install a run, then one should get the cat used to a leash. Lots of people can be seen walking with their animals on a leash in England - the country for pets, indeed. In the Chapter 'Training', I explain how to train your cat to walk on a leash.

There are so many reasons why one should not let cats run around free. Puddie's mother several times had a litter of five kittens. Only Puddie and his brother survived. All the others perished in the traffic, even though the owners lived quietly in a remote place. That's a great danger. Busy motorways will put cats on alert but a quiet country-road with just that single speed merchant...Those cats are not trained to watch out for traffic and so that isolated car proves fatal.

Then, what about feline diseases? There are more and more cases of Feline Aids (FIV). Even when the cats have been vaccinated against Panleucopenia and against Leukaemia (FeLV), they are not protected against AIDS. There is no vaccine against that horrible illness yet. Cats transmit AIDS to each other through fighting and mating. It is a contagious and lethal disease. (Not transmittable to humans). The vaccination against Leukaemia is controversial as it sometimes causes tumours on the vaccination-site.

A cat can perfectly hold its own in nature. He is still the animal he was ages ago. Only, his environment has changed. Man has polluted the environment. Traffic is the biggest culprit. Cats just can't correctly judge the speed of an approaching car. Certainly not in the dark when the headlights blind him. And it is not so that they are killed outright after being run over. Often they die a slow and agonizing death, desperately crying for their owners who don't come. Would you allow a four-year old child to run around on the street?

This beautiful poem my friend Heleen wrote when her cat Marius was lost.

FOR MARIUS

Suddenly you went away
Haven't seen you since that day
Still feel the warmth of your fur
Still hear the hum of your purr
Ah, the touch of your little paw
Marius, my dear, where are you now?

I search yet I do not find
But you're always on my mind
Are you lonely, feeling the pain
Of hunger and cold out there in the rain?
Let me help you, set you free
Release us both from this misery

Where are you then? Marius, my dear
In vain I search for you, far and near
'Cause wherever you are, missing you
Is something I will never get used to
Are you hiding behind the Rainbow
Safe and sound in the eternal Sunglow?

I'm all tears, I'm so sad
I miss you so much, Marius, my cherished cat!

Your buddy, Heleen

© Heleen van Duyvenbode (January, 2003)
(With many thanks to Jef for the translation)

Your pets should not bother other people. Pigeon fanciers or owners of aviaries with song birds don't like a cat prowling around making their birds restless. Further, there are cat-haters, they are more numerous than we think!

And then, it happens more and more, cats are in danger of being shot at with airguns. It seems to have become a real 'sport'. What kind of horrible hairballs do things like that? Don't they know how that hurts, an airgun pellet? Or do they just do it on purpose, because they 'enjoy' watching animals in pain? Probably they hate cats! Anyway, it has become a real danger for cats that roam outdoors. Airgun pellets cause nasty deep wounds, that are hardly visible. But even if you see them, the pellets can lodge in the spine or in other vital organs, where they can't be removed. Often they cause a lethal infection. Eyes especially are at risk. Even dogs and horses can get seriously wounded by the pellets or even die. Sometimes they have to be put down because of airgun wounds. Hopefully there will soon be new laws which will ban airguns altogether or at least will forbid the free use of these horrible weapons.

It's sometimes hard to keep a cat, who is used to running around free, inside. But often he will get used to it. Just make sure that there is plenty of diversion like scratching posts, toys and of course, lots of cuddling. Then your cat will be happy even if he has to live indoors. Statistically speaking, on average the life expectancy of a free cat is three years. A cat who stays indoors or has a run lives about fifteen years. That says enough.

Thanks to Eddie my pussy-children now have a splendid, three-star, all-in playground. I don't know what made me decide to install a door between the runs, so that I can use them separately. Premonition surely!

Puddie had turned six. 'A very important milestone in the life of a tomcat', he said, 'the birthday-gift should be commensurate with it!' And yes, he got a special present! He was the first of all the kitties to take possession of the run. How great that it was ready exactly on his birthday. A very thrilling event! I opened the door and proudly Puddie stepped into the run. Slowly and calmly he walked around and inspected everything. He checked the wire netting for strength and holes. Next came Donsje who let Puddie do his job and 'woops', immediately jumped high up in the wire netting. Mickje stalked low over the ground along the wire netting and inspected everything carefully. All of a sudden she started rolling from joy. She was very happy. Catje and Daimke were overjoyed. Now they could really race outdoors. And I could sit with my laptop in the shade of the majestic Catalpa.

There was another reason why I was so happy with this expanded run. As there are more people in the house now, I am afraid to let the cats use all the rooms and the hallway. What if somebody left a window or door open? They would be outside in a jiffy. So, I limit their range to three rooms. That's not much for five cats. Now, at least there is added space. Puddie, always alert, told Mickje: 'I hope this won't mean another addition to our family, I have my suspicions, you know...' Indeed, I am not the only one having premonitions.

Mickje is such a cutie. She is a real tortoiseshell kitty. They nearly always have a well-developed will. They know what they want! And that's true for Mickje too! In the evening about seven o'clock she wants to go to the living room. She is sleepy then and wants to rest. All those young fluffies around her, that's ok for a while but not too long. Of course I prefer her being around. Because she loves me so much, she will stay on, but not too long. If she is really fed up with it, she will start clearing the drawers of my desk. The drawers are open so she can easily jump into them. The contents then land in neat piles on the floor. When one drawer is finished she moves to the next one. She knows very well that than I will give in and bring my cute Garfield-shaped fluffy - she has grown beautifully round - to the living room. It's funny to see her thinking: 'Marg doesn't want to mix the contents of one drawer with the contents of the other, so if I start re-arranging the next drawer, I'm pretty sure I'll get where I want to be. In the living room.' As Pudje will join her later, this also has the advantage that she can eat in peace. Sometimes Puddie can't help showing that he is the pasha and then he drives her away from her dish full of delicious titbits.

Again my dear friends Jos and Miguella with her husband and children came to see us. Oh, I was so proud to show them my new run. They were full of admiration. Such a pity we couldn't sit outside. It was much too cold. We had a lot to discuss. Some time during our conversation I asked Miguella to try and contact mama. She cut herself off and said after a while:

'I am told that your mother is satisfied. She feels better and has found real inner peace. She has joined her loved ones, who crossed over before her. Of course now her body does not impede her any more and she can move around freely. When I ask I don't get in direct contact with her, but I do receive messages. She has lived a complete life on earth and she arrived full of expectations in the hereafter. She is a well-prepared soul who adjusted without problems to her new situation. She was received into eternity with her natural grace and courtesy. Her mission and lives on earth have been accomplished and her successes balance her mistakes. She will regularly return to see how

you are doing and to help you with love.'

Miguella had not known mama but she drew a correct picture of her! Behind a facade of standard formulas like 'That's how it should be' and 'Child, that is not done' - a formula I came to hate when I was a child as it inevitably meant the end of something I was enjoying – hid a kind, intelligent and sensitive woman. Not for nothing she had been a concert pianist. Oh, how grateful I am that I discovered the real 'mama' she was in those last years! Elly, Maria's friend, had said almost the same things. Yes, mama is happy now and has reached her final destination.

Too bad my fluffies are so afraid of strangers. Puddie and Daimke especially are very panic-stricken. As soon as Puddie hears the sound of a motorcar he doesn't recognise, he rushes to a high place and remains there until the coast is clear. (When I arrive he welcomes me happily in the run. He knows the noise of my car so well). Daimke starts shivering and hides behind a curtain. When I pick her up, her body is stiff as a board, so I let her stay in the bedroom when I have visitors. Stress is not good for her.

I have thought long and much about the causes of Daimke's fears. Maybe it is in her genes. Daatje and Dotje are also scared. Yet they were with Maria since their birth and they have never experienced anything nasty in their lives. Only the neutering of course. I guess their ancestors must have had very bad experiences with humans. In any case their mother, a stray, must have had them. Probably she passed on the fears to her unborn kittens. Or maybe Daimke must have been through some terrible experience in one of her previous lives. Naomi, also a medium says that in her previous life, Daimke was always chased away when she asked for a cuddle. One time she was put in a bag filled with stones and thrown into the water. That would explain her fear of dark closets, cabinets and so on. Puddie has been with me since he was five weeks old. But before that time he must have been very frightened by something. And he must have learned the lessons from his mother who was also afraid. According to my friend Rudi, Puddie's father was a big wild tramp. 'Chief of a gang of desperadoes!' Puddie claims.

I very well understand that Mickje, Donsje and Catje are scared. Yet Mickje, who has been terribly abused, is not so much afraid as suspicious. As soon as the visitors are seated, she comes to ask for cuddles or to get some cake.

187

Donsje has a trauma as a result of the high-pressure baler which destroyed her litter and also her bad experience when she was neutered. When she received her anaesthetic, she struggled free and fell off the table. She also had a small accident when she was sitting on mama's bed and was frightened by something. Mama tried to hold on to her collar while she panicked. Donsje bumped her head on a metal pillar and hurt her neck quite badly. Poor Donsje, when I came back she was traumatised. So, she has her reasons to be afraid, yet she won't hesitate to get a piece of cake when there is an opportunity and gladly comes to beg for it. Catje has been through a lot as well when she was still a kitten but she is not too afraid to roam around.

I think that Puddie and Daimke will never get rid of their fears, they are rooted too deeply. Mickje, Catje and Donsje have learned by experience to be afraid but are gaining confidence now. They notice that most people who come here are kind and that visitors mean tasty pieces of cake. And...Donsje is now a Fabulous Feline and she knows it. She dances real well. She can make three or four turns on her hind legs, without touching the ground with her front feet. It's so cute! I move my hand above her head with a piece of chicken in it and say: 'Donsje make a little dance', and woops...there she goes! She is a real ballerina, our little Donsje. Oh, I love her so!

The Animal which the Egyptians worshipped as divine,
which the Romans venerated as a symbol of liberty...
has displayed to all ages two closely blended characteristics
courage and self-respect.

Saki 1870-1916

Chapter

Donsje's Prize and Chum

He loved books, and when he found one open on the table he would lie down on it, turn over the edges of the leaves with his paw, and after a while, fall asleep, for all the world as if he had been reading a fashionable novel.

Theofile Gautier

I had registered Donsje for Belgacom's photo-competition, which was organized by my friends Freya and Leo Decap. Everybody was invited to mail a picture of their cat. The best photos were shown on the website. The winner was selected by tele-voting. In the beginning it was just fun to keep the score, but when Donsje and another cat got into a neck-and-neck race, things got really thrilling.

I got to know Leo years ago when he installed my new telephone exchange. Puddie just walked up to him, something he seldom does when a stranger comes into the house. I understood when I learned that Leo and his wife Freya live with more than a dozen cats, Somali, Burmese and Maine Coons. Leo smelled "safe". We became friends. Puddie is a good judge of human character. They are just swell people! They are also members of Poezenbel.

For weeks Donsje's only topic of conversation was the photo competition. At last the day came to ask Freya and Leo the result. I had promised Donsje to ask the 'score' from Freya and Leo. So, that morning Donsje jumped on my desk and asked: 'Mama, mama, is it true? Have I won? I am number one? What do you think? Please, ask Uncle Leo and Aunt Freya, will you? I am sooo curious. Please, dear mama, just ask them now! I do hope to win so I have something to tease Puddie with. He 's always bragging about his American Prizes, but I find a Belgian contest much more important. Yes! Puh! Prrrr purrr purr.' Every year we send in photos to the contest of the Traditional and Classic Cat International. Puddie especially, with his beautiful green eyes, has won many prizes. Of course he is very proud of that. It's fun to join in. The kitties don't have to sit all day in a cage, which they would hate and we get many lovely prizes.

I let Donsje mail to Freya and Leo and the reply came quickly:

'Hi, Donsje and Marguerite,

Donsje is indeed the winner in the class for domestic pets. We'll pop in in the next few days to bring the prizes.

Love,
Leo & Freya'

We were proud and dying to see the prizes. Freya had told us the prizes were very beautiful.

The singer Jan de Wilde has a unique song: 'I love to wake up next to you!' He sings about his beloved kitty. He enjoys her company very much, especially when he wakes up in the morning and sees her lying next to him *'with her cute sleepy face.'* I experience the same every morning, when I open my eyes and discover Donsje's lovely face on the pillow next to mine. I woke up early that Saturday morning. 'Donsje, wake up, little one! It 's your day, our day, celebration day today!' 'Whiiiieeee', was the sleepy answer, 'What's the matter, mama? Can't I just sleep some more?' Well, getting up isn't easy for cats either. At exactly 11.30 a.m. Freya and Leo came into the living room with a beautiful carrier cage. We had a cup of coffee with some delicious cake first. Keenly interested, Donsje observed everything from the piano. No hiding this time! She knew she was the VIP today! And the prizes! The cat-carrier was beautiful, big and high. When I opened it, I saw a cute grey cat with a red bow tie around its neck and a Tyrolean hat on its head. It was a teensy-weensy toilet brush holder. Gorgeous! I immediately put it on my desk. There was also a big packet of delicious titbits. So Donsje could treat the others too! Without being asked she did some pirouettes out of pure joy.

A welcome balm for Puddie. After all, winning photo contests is his speciality. The whole chimney is hanging full of his ribbons! This time however, it was Donsje who carried off the first prize. I cuddled him and explained that we all had won, not just Donsje alone, and that we would select the photos for the American competition the next day. It's a fact, since then Donsje is not afraid of visitors any more. Quite the contrary, now she is the first one to come and check whether she has won a competition again. She has experienced that Visitors equal tasty pieces of cake which she licks graciously from my fork, and titbits afterwards. One year later she appeared twice on a television show. Once on the regional station ATV and once in 'Afrit Negen' (Exit Nine), a regular show broadcast by the Belgian Company TV1 which is also watched in the Netherlands and other countries. Yes, Donsje was an FF now, a Famous Feline. She hasn't changed, however, she's still my dear cute Donsje and hasn't put on any star-like airs.

At last the weather cleared up so Puddie and I could sit on the lawn. 'Quality time' for my dear little man. I should do that more frequently. I often have a feeling of guilt towards Puddie, who, in fact would have preferred to have just me for company. If only I could spend more time with him on the lawn, that would make up for a lot, yet, the orders and the emails make this almost impossible. But now we were enjoying the healing, heavenly and golden yellow rays of the sun on our skins. Sun is so heavenly. I had noticed that Puddie sometimes got angry with Daimke, who never runs away like the others do. Instead she challenges Puddie when he teases Donsje or Catje. Puddie, being Cat Numero Uno, feels he has the privilege to act the boss. Daimke, however, doesn't feel inferior to Puddie and hates any injustice. She is 'The Keeper of the Peace' and takes her task seriously! Hopefully this will not lead to war between those two. So, I try to pass more time with him. If he is happy he will not be so irritating to Daimke. The joy is mutual of course. I love him so much!

The Foot-and-Mouth Disease Crisis had put me in a sad mood. I couldn't understand it. Every day countless beautiful, healthy and totally innocent animals were 'cleared away'. Mother cows who had licked their calves dry and reared them with love. Ewes who love their lambs like human mothers love their babies. Gorgeous and proud fathers, they all had to go. Not because they actually suffered from foot-and-mouth disease, but because they might get it. Foot-and-mouth disease had been found on some farms and out of 'prevention', many farms in the neighbourhood were 'cleared'.

Did Hitler also not act like this to keep his people free from foreign blemishes? Thousands and thousands of animals were outright killed. Yet, there is a vaccine against this disease. But vaccination was not permitted, vaccinated animals cannot be exported, because there is no reliable test to see if the animals actually have foot-and-mouth disease or whether they test positive because they are vaccinated. What then about the vaccination certificate? Doesn't it prove they can't have the disease? Well, it's all a matter of money. The government doesn't see animals, it sees only euros-on-legs. Terrible! I was especially shocked by the complete disregard for the feelings of the animals and the owners who really loved them. Not all farmers and ranchers are cruel to their animals. I saw on television the wife of a farmer clutching her pussycat while she related with tears in her eyes that her cattle had been cleared away that morning.

Maybe the time isn't here yet for some people to live without eating meat, though there are meat substitutes now. But at least let us take care of the animals during their short period here on earth. Let's give them the pleasure of running outside and let's handle them with care. And especially, don't move or ship them around. The transportation of animals causes such a lot of unnecessary suffering. Why not kill the animals on the spot and freeze the meat, then it can be transported all over the world without provoking any suffering. It is said that the civilisation of a people can be inferred from the way it treats its animals. If that is so then we are in a sorry state of affairs. I comfort myself with the thought that the animals are much better off on the Rainbow Bridge than on this earth. A good thing I did not know then that the Bird Flu would enter Europe and would cause many more deaths. The flu itself claimed lives, but so many more animals were cruelly and unnecessary killed because of the government's outdated rules and regulations.

Puddie observes that people can't help it. 'They don't know better because they have lost their tail. That's why, in our feline opinion, they act bizarre, incomprehensible and especially downright stupid.' I think he is right. It must be a huge convenience having such a beautiful long bushy tail. Very handy in winter to cover your nose with at night when it's so cold. Deep down I already felt more cat than human. Now I feel ashamed to be 'partly' human. All those horrible news bulletins on the radio and the television had put me in a depressive mood.

So, I took a day off and went to Maria and Gé. Maria had a cute small kitten, Pipeloentje, and she allowed me to give her the bottle. There is nothing more endearing than such a tiny ball of fluff in your hands. My motherhood was aroused. As a matter of fact I'd like to add another cute kitty. We would be seven then. Of course, I love Kirby and Femke with all my heart, they are real Buddies. The geese and chickens also count, but my bond with my fluffies is much stronger. Maria also sheltered four beautiful, shaded silver British Shorthair kittens. They were simply gorgeous. British Shorthair cats are wonderful round fluffies with a thick fur, just little bears. But the best part is their character. They are usually very calm and easy cats who seldom quarrel.

Chantal, who takes care of the Poezenbel- and our site, breeds British Shorthair cats. The name of her Cattery is 'Easy Blues'. A cattery name is a must when breeding cats. She has 'Blue and Lilac' British. Of course, 'blue' is not really blue but marvellous dark grey and Lilac is very light grey. I find Lilac very beautiful.

While driving home I reflected on it. It is a very important decision. My heart said 'Yes' but my mind hesitated. Another kitten would take away my sadness but what about my pussy-children? Most of all, what would my dear Puddie think of it?

Always, when I approach Brasschaat and I sense the nearness of my fluffies, I can hardly wait to cuddle them. To return home is heaven! When I opened the gate I could hear Puddie welcoming me. He really waits for me in the run all day, as Emmy, who housesits, told me. I never leave my place without someone attending it. I am sure Puddie feels it, when I leave Maria. Daimke did a headstand when I entered. That's her way of expressing her elation. And Donsje...she was so happy! Emmy said that she had been sitting sadly in front of the window, awaiting my return. Indeed,
if I am at home, she is always with me. I had also missed her terribly! Catje kept on talking though normally she is rather taciturn. She had so much to report. Puddie and Mickje literally flew in my arms from happiness.
'Oh mama, there you are! So nice that you're back!' Puddie shouted. 'Did you see Asselijntje and did you give her my compliments and purrrrs and er...I hope

you didn't bring a stowaway-kitten with you...some of your thoughts I received contained pictures of a 'kitten...???' My wise boy, he knows things even before I do. Of course he had sensed I wanted one more (last?) kitten. I told them in detail about Pipeloentje and the British cats I had met. How I had enjoyed their company, how gorgeous they are. Pudje and Mickje looked at each other and said simultaneously: 'Oh-ho here we go again!

Quickly I said: 'Come, let's unwrap Maria's presents for you. Purr prrr!' No more discussions for the moment about it! Maria always prepares a pamper-package for us, she is such a dear. 'You Mickje,' I said, 'You must have British Shorthair blood in your veins. You have just the same cute round head as Maria's little British kittens. How beautiful you are!' Mickje was overjoyed.

Puddie heaved a sigh of relief when I told him that Pipeloentje already had a home to go to. But my little man wasn't born yesterday, I heard him say to Mickje: 'Mark my words, there is something going on. Mama has spring fever or motherhood-fever and I wouldn't be surprised if there is another kitten around here soon. I feel it in my whiskers. My inner voice advises me to refresh my English. My English has become very rusty. We might need it these coming months...' 'English?' Mickje was amazed. 'Well, British then, I have caught mama admiring pictures of British Shorthairs in her cat-books. I must admit, not a bad choice if she has 'expanditis' again. They are er...really jolly and smashing and things like that. Yes, if she has put her mind on a cute British Shorthair tomcat...'

I listened full of astonishment. Puddie liking the arrival of another fluffy? A tomcat at that! I had always thought he preferred ladies. 'Guys, let's forge the iron while it's hot!' I said to Donsje, Catje and Daimke which raised questioning eyebrows in my direction.

But I was not yet sure. Deep down in my heart I would prefer to give a home to a pitiful unwanted kitten. I had always wanted to be a veterinarian, specialising in cats. Because I looked after my parents this was not possible. When they had crossed over I was too old. I am glad I can still help cats through the Poezenbel Foundation. If I were young and healthy, I'd start a rescue centre for unwanted cats. But I am too old now, hampered by osteoporosis and my hands don't function very well during winter. Fortunately I can help by imparting love and facts about cats through my books like 'Miracles on little Feet' and this one.

Further I write articles about cats for several magazines and also I advise people who have problems with their cats.

In that way I am also helping cats. I still very much regret that I was not able to realise my dream. I would then shelter ill and old cats or cats with FIV and FeLV, which have no place to go to, something that Sabine van der Meer is doing with her foundation Zwerfkat in Nood (stray in distress). *www.zwerfkat.com.* She is a wonderful woman doing a tremendous job for cats. Well, that will be my intention in my next life.

Hence my hesitation. A purebred gets a good home anyway, though I find the living conditions of some studs abominable. Compared to them, the life of a stray is paradise. On the other hand, it would be easier for Puddie if I adopted a calm British Shorthair kitten, instead of an abandoned kitten with an unpredictable character.

There are solid reasons why purebreds are bred. In general their character is predictable. Siamese and Abyssinian cats are very cute, I am fond of them, but they demand lots of attention. I sensed I had to be careful now. Puddie had almost reached his limit and he feels threatened because Daimke tells him once in a while: 'Up to here and no further!' Maybe a calm and quiet pussy-child would bring peace? I couldn't make up my mind and decided to wrap all my doubts in a prayer and send them to the Lord. I firmly believed that 'so-called coincidences' would come my way. They would point out the direction I had to take. Deep down however, we all knew: another kitten was about to join us!

I had prayed for signs and I got them. But I got so many that my confusion grew. I certainly didn't come closer to a decision. A couple of things happened simultaneously. Aukje, my friend from Rotterdam, came to see us on a Saturday morning. She was accompanied by Joepje, a blue British Shorthair tom kitten, who was on his way to his new home in Belgium. Aukje also breeds British Shorthair cats. That same morning Chantal and Ron with their baby Yorian also visited us. Joepje was allowed to keep us company. Small though he was, he jauntily paraded around the room. He explored everything and later on, exhausted, he fell asleep in my lap. Puddie watched everything from outside in the run. He sat on the windowsill with a big frown on his forehead. He had fled the bustle and to prevent Joepje going outside, I had closed the door. He was quite irritated. I explained to him that I was not keeping him locked outside, but just closed the door to keep Joepje inside. 'Oh, I see.' His expression changed and he followed Joepje's exploits with interest. 'Well, Joepje seems a kind and cute kitten, I must admit,' he commented later.

I fell in love with Joepje. How beautiful and lovely and most of all, how calm those British Shorthair cats are! Chantal told me that her British Shorthair queen, Kaya was to have kittens soon. She would like to give both Maria and me a kitten from her litter. I couldn't believe my ears. Fantastic! What a marvellous present! Meanwhile Maria had received four little kittens from Rotterdam. Black and whites and one of them, Katouche, looked very much like Luckje. I fell for her immediately. And that made my confusion complete!

Puddie told me he wouldn't mind having a British Shorthair kitten in the house. 'Especially a tomcat', he added. 'So I will have a companion and then we will be two to maintain order in the house.' Didn't I say that Puddie is a very smart cat?

We were enjoying a 'Happy Hour' on the lawn. 'Oh, Puddie, it is so hard to decide.' I said. 'On the one hand my wish is to give a home to a rescuee, on the other hand I fell in love with Joepje. British shorthair cats are so kind and calm. But, you know Puddie, I still miss Luckje and Katouche looks so much like him. What do you think?'

Puddie nestled himself close to me and brushed away a tear. 'I know, mama, I know! You still miss Luckje. But I think it would be unfair to Katouche if you take her because she resembles Luckje on the outside. In the first place: she is NOT Luckje. She has a right to her own life and her own character. She also has the right to be loved for herself! In the second place: it is never good to take a substitute for someone you have loved very dearly. Nobody can replace Luckje. Luckje appeared here just at a time you needed him. A time when aggression from the outside was trying to get control of your mind and body. He was the perfect shield. I realised that, even though you know there was not much love lost between Luckje and me. He brightened you up with his funny antics and the way he walked with you through the garden. He stayed here for a while and then moved on, to some new mission. I know that and I think it is better to close that period now. Anyway Luckje remains in your heart forever. You will love him forever, but don't try to find a substitute for him. He'd be the first to advise against that.'

196

Surprised, I looked at Puddie. 'Puddie, dear, where do you get your wisdom?' I cuddled him tightly. 'If I didn't have you, my dear Puddie, whatever should I do?' 'You have me, mama', he replied sweetly, 'you have me, forever and ever!' I phoned Maria and she told me briefly and to the point: 'Each kitten that comes to me will not leave unless I have found it an excellent new home. You know that very well! Hence the argument: 'I want to give a home to some pitiful rescuee', does not apply to Katouche.' Those words did it! The newcomer would be British! I phoned Chantal immediately.

And then things got thrilling. On 13 May 2001, Mother's Day (mama used to say: 'Nonsense, every day is Mother's Day!)' Kaya delivered her kittens in the sock drawer in Ron and Chantal's wardrobe. Kaya of the Kraayenberg is a gorgeous blue British Shorthair. The father of the litter is Ikula of the Safraenberg, a Belgian! He is a Lilac tomcat with a marvellous bold head and a terrific, lovely presence. It was a radiant and warm day. The fluffies and I were sitting in the run in front of the office. Next to me the laptop rested in a cardboard box to screen it from the blinding sun. I kept a constant eye on my mailbox. Ron and Chantal emailed me every time a kitten saw the light. All in all five kittens were born:

At 13.58 Easy Blues' Choco Paws was born, Lilac tomcat 110 grams
At 14.12 Easy Blues' Comedian was born, Lilac tomcat 108 grams
At 14.45 Easy Blues' China Girl was born, Lilac she-cat 102 grams
At 16.20 Easy Blues' Cyrano was born, Lilac tomcat 110 grams
At 18.22 Easy Blues' Calot was born, Blue tomcat 108 grams

At least that's what Chantal and Ron first thought. Later little Calot turned out to be a girl. That can happen in the best of families and we had a good laugh.

That evening we received pictures by email. Oh, how lovely! Now, we had to make our choice! Cyrano flashed through my mind. Papa had often told me about Cyrano de Bergerac, the man with his long nose. Was he the one? I spread the pictures all over the floor and tried to listen to my feelings. Which kitten was going to be our new companion? Of course the fluffies surrounded me and keenly followed the doings of mama. 'Guys, take a look, these are Kaya's kittens. Which kitten is the loveliest one?' They sniffed at the pictures, licked them and – it's really true - Puddie suddenly sat down on the picture of Cyrano. Wonderful. 'So, Puddie, he is the one? Cyrano will be our new pussy-child?' Indeed, Puddie being the oldest one has the biggest say, but the others all agreed without hesitation. Unanimously we made a fair and honest decision. Maria wanted a blue kitten and selected little Calot, later renamed Cadootje, which means present or gift.

Although Cyrano is a cute name, it is not a good name to call. I was allowed to rename him, but his new name should also begin with the letter C. So, what was it all of us longed for? A real friend, a mate, a...'chummy.'

The English dictionary says:
Chum: close friend, mate
To Chum up: to form a friendship
Chummy: friendly, intimate

That was it. Chummy! A kind friend for each and every one of us.

Chummy wouldn't arrive before early August. Fortunately, Chantal and Ron regularly emailed pictures. Also, I could contact them by phone to find out how the kittens were doing. Waiting takes so long! Two weeks later Sanna, another of Chantal's British Shorthair cats, delivered her kittens. Both mothers reared their children together. So cosily! When the kittens were four weeks old I drove to Sittard. Chantal had given me very clear directions, but there was a diversion, I couldn't take the exit she had told me to take and so I lost my way. But after asking around and having been misdirected many times - there is left and there is another left - I arrived at the correct address.

When I went in I saw many teensy-weensy kittens walking through the room. Oh, how cute! They had just been released. Everything was new, big and thrilling to them. Their aerials stood up from excitement. Suddenly one of those cute fur-balls rushed at me, his tail vibrating. It's incredible, but when I carefully picked him up and looked at Chantal, she said: 'Yes, that is your Chummy!' She was surprised as well. He knew it! He sensed that I was the one thinking of him so much and talking about him to my five kids. Chummy clearly chose me for his mama and our love was very spontaneous and mutual. It was very special! Just like Puddie, who also chose me when he was five weeks old. How is it possible? Yet Chummy was only four weeks old.

It is unbelievable how wise and cute these, oh so small kittens are. When I sat down, Chum nestled himself against me and purred so loudly that I could hear it during my conversation with Chantal. The other kittens also climbed on my lap. I felt so happy. I told little Chummy about Puddy, his 'chum-to-be', about Donsje and the prize she had won. About Mickje, Daimke and Catje. He looked at me so intensely wise and lovingly, with his gorgeous, then still blue, eyes that I am sure he understood it all. That intense look of Chummy, it is something very special. He still has it but his eyes are gorgeously orange now.

Of course, Cadootje is just as lovely. I explained to her that her mama-to-be shelters many poor abandoned kittens and that she might help rearing them, when she grew big. Naturally I recorded everything on video and took pictures. Sanna's children were also very beautiful. Kaya came first to check me out. She wanted to be sure that I was looking after her children well. When she noticed how calm and happy her little kittens were, she felt reassured. She is a really super mother whose priority number one is her children. It was good to see Tedje again. He'd grown into a gorgeous cat! Yes, we are relatives now!

Of course I also spent some time with Jos. She lives in the same town. It was nice to get to know her son and her daughter-in-law and, most of all the pussy-children and Inga. Yes, Jos is right. Basje is as sweet as Donsje is. He has the same 'knowing' look in his eyes. Oliver is half Persian, he came to me for cuddles and that's not his habit with strangers. I felt proud! Maaike is a gorgeous black lady, with beautiful green eyes. They were not afraid at all. But of course they see many people. I mostly prefer to be 'guest-free'.

I was so thankful that Chantal had given Chummy to us! From all the kittens, he is really the one who loves cuddling the most. When Chummeke came to us, he brought a beautiful kittenbook with him 'When our cat was a kitten'. Chantal had noted in it: 'And so Marg (Chummy's new maidservant) came last weekend for an interview. Those two have found each other and have become inseparable!' And that's the truth! I intensely hoped that he would be happy with us. And... that my pussy-children wouldn't have any trouble accepting him. Catje and Daimke are still young enough to play with him, though playing is something for all ages. Donsje turns younger and more playful by the day. The prizes have given her self-confidence. That's a fact, she is simply proud now. It was fun to show the video to the fluffies, especially as the sound is also rendered and so they could hear the kittens mew and squeak. Chantal and Ron had given me a beautiful children's bath and I put it in the run next morning.

Great fun! Most of all when I filled it up with water and floated some plastic ducks in it. 'From our Chummy, guys,' I said, 'his first present for you.'

Puddie wrote in Poezenbelletje, number 25:

Dear Readers,

Yes, we are really expecting a new kitten to join us and the best part of it: we are all very enthusiastic. I think this is because of Joepje, a small Brittie which visited us recently: Joepje is an ambassador for his breed indeed. He smelled so nice. Britties are mostly very calm fluffies and make excellent companions. At least, that's what mama told us. Of course, let's wait and see how Chummy will be, but his name already offers one big positive clue: a real chum!

*One big advantage for me: at last **assistance in keeping the girls under control!** Sometimes I am downright burned-out! I have to arrange everything here and maintain order. And, after all, I am getting on in years and need more time for myself. Time to meditate and to write. Things I hardly find the time for now with five girls to watch! And what about mama? She is the biggest problem! Working as she does till she almost collapses from fatigue. We get headaches from racking our brains about her. I 've been thinking of sabotaging that computer by, say, squatting on the keyboard. It is my hope that Chummy's coming will keep Marg away from the computer, so she will have more time and attention for her fluffies. A baby may be the solution to this problem!*

Donsje, Catje and Daimke are very excited: 'Look how handsome Chum is, gorgeous grey and a beauty of a round head!' Mickje also finds him a dear. She told me about the kittens she had before she came here. 'And now I can't have kittens any more,' she ended sadly. Well, we all can't. 'But dear Mickje,' I comforted her, 'maybe you can mother Chum a bit'. She felt better at once. Yes, our Mickje went through hard times when she was young. It 's great to have her in the gang.

Many many greetings, shoves-with-the-head and
cuddles from yours truly, Puddy.'

I wrote to Chum some days later:

'Dear, dear Chummy,

I don't know if Chantal and Ron let you type on the computer already, but I will send you a short mail anyway. Oh, how I love you...and so wonderful that our love is completely mutual. Jauntily you stepped towards me when I came in, something I'll never forget. You picked me! My dear little fellow!!! I am so proud of you! Please grow up quickly so you can come to us. Puddie, Donsje, Mickje, Catje and Daimke were very curious to hear about their new 'chum'. Daimke and Catje especially look forward to your coming. 'It's going to be fun playing with him, isn't it, mama?', they keep asking. 'We will play hide and seek in the tunnel and climb in the wire-netting of the run and get into a lot of mischief!' 'Indeed, I'm sure you will,' Puddie chuckled, 'take my word for it! Tedje will teach him a thing or two..!'

We've watched the video so many times that my pussy-children already know you very well. 'Is Cadootje also coming?' Donsje asked. No, I don't think so, because she will go to Aunt Maria. Oh, Chummy, what a thrill! The pictures will be ready on Thursday. If they're good I'll mail them to you.
Today I've prepared a document file for all the letters to and from Daimke.
Yes, Daimke had written to us already when she was as old as you are now. I am curious to know if you are allowed to learn it. Asje taught Daimke. She knows all about computers. Maybe you could ask Tedje to show you but I'm afraid he is too busy right now. You already have your own document file. Some day there will be a sequel to Miracles on little Feet. A book especially about Daimke, Catje and you. It was such a delight cuddling you.

Lots of hugs and cuddles and much love from us six but most of all from your mama Marg, I love you! Many purrs... Pudje, Mickje, Donsje, Daimke, Catje and Marg.'

The weather was heavenly. I often took Donsje with me to the glasshouse. Carefully she walked in between the rows of lettuce-plants, never stepping on one of them. 'Lettuce-plants,' she says, 'also feel pain. They have feelings too! I don't want them to get a bushy tail out of fright from me.' Donsje is very compassionate. I, of course, eat lettuce! But I do talk to them and can feel their radiation. Plants and flowers grow better when you talk to them. Prince Charles of England also converses with his plants.

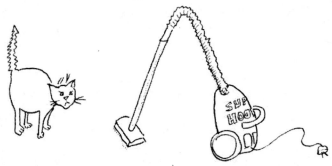

Yes, my Donsje-girl is very special. When I prepare breakfast in the morning, Catje, Daimke and Donsje, of course, are present. Catje and Daimke receive their breakfast in the bedroom, but Donsje gets hers in the office. When I carry the tray with Donsje's and my breakfast on it to the office, Donsje is waiting for me on the high windowsill, which I have to pass. She then jumps on my shoulder for a free ride. But this morning she didn't want to jump on my shoulder. I didn't understand and asked her: 'Donsje, why don't you join me? Look here, delicious chicken for you! Come, giddy-up' 'Mieeuuwwww, mieeeuwuwaauuuuwww' she said and ran to the sliding door. She can also enter the office through the run, so I opened the door and she went outside. When I came in the kitchen, I understood why she refused to come with me. Emmy was vacuuming in front of the office and Donsje hates vacuuming. Smart, our Donsje. I hadn't heard it.

SCAREDY KIDS

'Hi there mum, where have you been?'
Something happened today, you should have seen!
A great growly creature came heading our way,
Well, we arched our backs and hissed 'make our day'.

But in the end we abandoned pride,
And all as one decided to hide,
While we tried to recall your three basic laws,
'Hiss', then Spit', then 'Use the claws'.

We made our plans to pounce, then maul,
But when we looked up it was ever so tall'.
'Don't worry gang', our other mum said,
Then made it quiet with a smack on the head.

She wound its tail around its back.
Honestly, mum, we thought it would attack.
It was fun to watch, you should have seen her,
Oh Yes – She said it was a vacuum cleaner!'

© *Maureen Eadon-Mills*

Daatje's and Dotje's papa Hans and mama Diny and Mariëlle, their daughter, came on a visit. They are such dears and they are very fond of their pussy-children, Daimke's sisters. That made their visit a double delight for me. Instead of hiding, the fluffies joined us. Diny said that Daimke has exactly the same habits as Daatje and Dotje. She utters the same high mews. Daimke doesn't say 'miaauwuwue', but 'wieeh, wiiheeee', very short mews. Daatje also lifts her front leg as if she were a pointer dog smelling game. They talk all the time, just like Daimke. When Mickje chased after Donsje in the run and Donsje rushed inside screaming, Daimke jumped down from the climbing pole and raced outside to give Mickje a big box on the ear. 'Watch out, you! Stay away from Donsje! If punishment is required, I am the one to mete it out, do you hear?'

That's exactly what Daatje does also. When there is a strange cat outside, Daatje will stride up to it. Dotje says: 'You go first, I will follow.' It's really nice that we became friends and that we can talk about our kids.

Daimke has learned something funny. When we play on the bed at night, she brings a coloured soft ball. Time after time I throw it away. I make feints, to the left or to the right. She really jumps up into the air to follow the course of the ball and races behind it. Mewing loudly with her mouth full of plush, so that the tone of her mew is muffled, she returns the ball to me. Even more fun is jumping right in the middle of the newspaper while I'am reading it. To play tunnel with the newspaper is also great fun. It rustles so thrillingly. Oh, she is such a dear. When she is exhausted she flops flat out on the floor. It's funny, but Catje, though she likes to play dog - running after me, looking at me for confirmation when we are walking through the garden and immediately coming to me when I call her – she doesn't want to retrieve anything at all. Retrieving is her absolute 'no-no'! Yes, racing after the ball, no problem, but bringing it to mama? That's out of the question! 'I leave that to Daimke', she says, 'everyone has his speciality.'

It was almost August. Donsje was engrossed in her study of 'blackbird-ology'. A blackbird has built its nest just below the gutter in front of the living room window, fortunately on the other side of the wire netting. Papa and mama Blackbird rear their babies together and keep on - what a hunger those birdies have - bringing beaks full of worms to the nest. Each in turn. So funny, both provide food. I thought papa Blackbird would give the worms to mama Blackbird and that she would feed the children, but not so, papa Blackbird is a modern papa. How nice to be able to see all this from nearby. Naturally my fluffies keep their eyes glued on them. Catje has already tried many times to reach the nest. Fortunately her legs are a bit too short. Donsje and Puddie content themselves with just watching for long hours. They know they can't reach there. Daimke prefers to play with a rustling ball and Mickje has lost interest. Wise, she can't jump very well since she received that sharp kick. She is still a bit lame and sometimes falls off something. We just look the other way then. She has her pride too, you see! When the blackbirdies flew out, I kept the run off-limits for a while. 'Very mean of you, mama,' they protested, but I considered it better for the sake of birdies' health. One flying lesson did it anyway. Next day they sat high and dry in the Catalpa.

Daimke, so cute, lay on her back on the bed, just out of reach, so I asked her if she would not like to come in my arms. She showed interest, her head tilted backwards, two eyes glittering with pleasure: 'Wheeeeee, wheeee, I feel delightfully lazy, but indeed, resting close to you is not bad either.' She stretched her front legs out to me. Still flat out on her back, so that I hardly could reach her. But she wanted to be tickled under her chin and that meant getting up. She dropped herself in my arms and caressed my face with her paws. Quickly I kissed her cute pink nose.

Chummy and his sisters and brothers had received their first vaccination. I immediately wrote a letter to tell him how proud I was of him:

'Dear, dear Chummy,
Oh, how brave you were when you got your shot yesterday! You all stood quietly on the doctor's table and thought: 'We don't know what is going on here, but it can't be bad for us!' When the doctor gave the injection, there wasn't a sound from you. So plucky and oh, so British! That famous 'stiff upper lip'! Another seven days and you will be home. If only you knew how happy we are! I have just spoken to Ron on the phone. Everything is fine, you haven't had a reaction to the 'jab'. Marvellous, now we will count days.
Lots of purrs from us seven here'

At last it was 12th of August. Chummy and Cadootje had packed their bags and were ready for the trip. Cadootje came along, as she would go on to Maria's afterwards. How nice for the two of them that they could travel part of the journey together! As the waiting took so long, I had started writing short letters to Chummy. I knew he would receive them by telepathy and so I didn't actually mail them. I would read them to him once he was here with me. I continued this tradition for a while, even when he was already here with me.

12-8 'Dear Chummy,
*It is almost 12.30. Now you and Cadootje must be somewhere between Sittard and Brasschaat. They say: 'The last mile is the longest one.' How true! But soon you will be here. We've been walking in the garden already. The coffee is ready and Donsje lies cosily on my lap. The others are playing in the run. Of course, they all know you are coming and they promised me to be very kind to you. It will be hard for you when Cadootje leaves you and you remain here without your mama and your brothers and sisters. We'll do everything to make sure you won't miss them too much. What is that sound? An engine???? Yes, yippee, **You have arrived. I see the lights of the car!** You're home now. At last!*

How thrilling! I took the cat-carrier out of the car and peered into it through a crack. I immediately looked into your eyes. You had the same intense and loving look that I remembered you had that first moment we met and you so jauntily stepped up to me. And you recognised me also! I sensed it very clearly. Cadootje was sitting next to you. As soon as we were in the living room, you

205

were released. With genuine British phlegm you came out of the cat-carrier and started to inspect the room and the run. You had been outdoors already, but you had never seen grass. Blimey! What a tricky plant and so tickling to the tummy! With wide jumps you flew over it. Great fun!

*Side by side, step by step, together you went. You and your sister explored every nook and cranny of the run. Very slowly the other pussy-children came to take a look. Quite a sight: two strange fluffies walking around in their run. 'Whieeee mama, help, **what is this? Who are they???'** You also felt somewhat afraid and therefore now and then you let out a low but impressive growl. My fluffies understood what you said even though you have a Sittards accent. Anyway, it wasn't so bad. You loved playing with the feather fixed to a fishing rod! Chantal moved it up and down in front of your nose so that I could film you and take pictures. It was the last chance to film you two together. I must have undone all the good manners Chantal and Ron had taught you, because I gave you little bits of cake. Although, it must be admitted, you ate neatly from the fork. Very politely! At 15.30 Chantal, Ron and Yorian left, taking your dear sister with them. The good-bye was nasty, good-byes always are, but Cadootje remains in the family.*
I took you to my office, to the run, the kitchen and the bedroom to show you everything. The trays are there, here is the waterbed, there your water bowl. Oh, my little man, so much to remember! In the bedroom we took half an hour off, just to sit cosily together enjoying each other's company. Suddenly you purred, came to me for a cuddle and rolled full of joy on your back. You were happy! You drank some water and then did a neat pee-pee in the box. Good! How brave you are! And soooooo cute, with your Lilac coat.

I put you in the indoor kennel when it was cooking-time. It's better to be careful. When I returned and sat down with the laptop next to you, I opened the door. Slowly you came out and sat under my chair. One by one the fluffies came to see. Mickje found it a bit creepy and nasty, but she reacted the same way when Daimke and Catje were still new to her. Puddie understood and found it more or less normal. Donsje carefully smelled you. Catje did the same. Daimke was still pretty tense, but she will learn to love you too. And then you gave me a beautiful present. Slowly you climbed up the chair and now you sit purring on my lap. Oh, how nice! Now and then you look up with your gorgeous great orange eyes, full of trust and intense love. And your purring, just a small diesel engine.

206

Yes, I will be very happy when my other fluffies have accepted you as their real 'Chum'. I am sure that will happen, only they first have to adjust to your being around. So, I cuddle them all very much and assure them I love them as much as before. They feel kind of threatened. Of course they do! I have brushed you with the brush I also brush them with, so they will get used to your smell. We have been awaiting your arrival for more than three months. In our minds, you were already here, of course, but now you are indeed here. A delight, you're purring here on my lap. Welcome home, dear Chummy, we love you!

During the meal you were on the table all the time, a grey ball of fur. Now and then you looked at me as if to check: 'Everything all right?' And when I winked at you, you let your engine purr. Daimke still found it creepy and watched you from the other side of the window. The table on which I take my meals stands in front of the window. You immediately picked the right spot when you lay down there. Cosily warm, close to me and with a fine view. Now we are in the office and you are exploring my desk. Puddie sits on the television set. Mickje lies on the table behind me and the kids are outside. Donsje is already completely used to your presence. But then she is Donsje. Now you're washing yourself next to me, one paw on the pc. You're learning to use the computer already. Your calm, little man, is a beauty. I should use you as my model!
How we played this morning! All of us, even Puddie and Mickje joined in. We played with the feather fixed to a fishing rod. At one time you jumped high up in the air and collided with Daimke who jumped at the same time from the other side. Fortunately both of you had to laugh. Great, this means you have been accepted as a member of the family now. Dear little man, how did you manage to do this so quickly? You have only been here for two days! I am very proud of you and of the other fluffies.

Last night was so funny. I was eating and you and Donsje were sitting on the table. You sat behind the bookend against which I put my book when I eat and read. You're not very big yet, so you couldn't see me. 'Boo, how lousy', you must have thought and you put both of your front paws on the book. So cute. But it was getting late and you felt tired. You became sleepy and your head sank lower and lower. Your eyes shut and you slept. I took pictures for this was a very cute thing to see.

Last night we all slept wonderfully. You curled cosily against me and after a quick wash you fell purringly asleep. You lay next to my pillow on the left side. That was your place since the first night. Donsje slept, as usual, to the right of me. Daimke and Catje slept, completely at ease, as usual at the foot. When I got up and went to the bathroom, you awoke of course, but after playing a while you fell asleep again. This morning you lay behind the pillow. Sometimes I wake up in the middle of the night feeling somewhat short of breath and tickly. How come? Not hard to guess, my nose touches your beautiful fur. Because I have to move then, I set off your diesel purring. What a nice sound to hear! People may consider themselves smart and think themselves way above animals, but I have never heard a human being purring, or maybe they purr only when purrrchasing something.

Purr purrrr purrrrr.'

I intended to take Chummy with me in the garden and also I wanted him to get used to the car. But the outdoors was off-limits until he had had his second vaccination. Sometimes cats from neighbours come into the garden, so I didn't want to take any chances. Inside, I had put the harness on already. He didn't object. When he was used to that, I took him outside in the pouch-bag. It was so cute, those two beautiful eyes, turning more and more orange, watching everything with amazement. I showed him the birds, the chickens, the geese. There was even a squirrel rushing up a tree while swearing loudly. Oh, they are such funny animals! Mariette and I love them. Chummy was very thrilled.

One week later he was given his final vaccination by Doctor Liliane. She found him gorgeous and very cute! Chum was not so impressed, but that is logical. He had already received his first shot and knew what was coming, but he didn't let out a sound. Fortunately the vaccination did not cause any trouble and in the afternoon he was playing with the others again. Now it was safe to take him outside!

I have studied many philosophers and many cats.
The wisdom of cats is infinitely superior.

(Hyppolyte Taine)

Chapter 🐾🐾

Autumn, Angels and a Christmas Message

It is hard to believe, but some people claim their cats are almost human...and they mean it as a compliment!!!!

Source unknown

A lady phoned me. 'I've just been to the doctor,' she said, 'and he told me that my child is allergic to cats, so I have to get rid of my cat! If you don't take her I'll take her to the animal shelter!' I asked her how the doctor came to that conclusion. 'My child has red blotches on his skin and he says that's from the cat.' 'Did he do scratch-tests on the skin or any other tests?' I asked. 'No, of course he didn't. He simply told me: 'Get rid of your cat and the allergy will go away. Now, will you take her?' I felt terrible but I had, of course, to say no. I gave her some addresses of no-kill cat rescue shelters and could only hope she would contact them.

I receive many of this kind of blackmail-calls. This was an extreme case. Mostly I can persuade the caller to think things over. Of course, it **is** possible that someone is allergic to cats. But even then, in many cases, the cat doesn't necessarily have to go. First it's important to have the allergy thoroughly examined and to get a second opinion. There are so many things that can cause an allergy. Some doctors just hate cats or pets in general, so they quickly jump to conclusions and order the cat or dog out. They don't care about the despair and the pain resulting from such a peremptory decision. There are effective medicines to treat allergy. Giving your cat a weekly bath will certainly help too, if the allergy is caused by the skin flakes and the protein she gives off. A bath will almost completely remove them. Your cat won't like it at first but she'll quickly get used to it. It's important to dry her very well afterwards, to prevent her catching a cold.

In 'Your Cat', a much-read English cat-magazine I read there is now a remedy for cat-allergy. The name is Petal Cleanse. It prevents the spreading of the allergens given off by the cat's skin. The address is listed in the address-list at the end of this book. Further, there's a vaccine against asthma coming, which also will work against allergy caused by pets. Also, some people are allergic to cat litter dust, not to their cat. Simply changing the litter will solve this problem.

The mother I talked about found a good excuse in the allergy to get rid of her 'unruly' cat. Oh, it's horrible but it happens so often! Allergy is the most used excuse to dump the animals people want to get rid of! I found comfort in the Dordrecht-based association 'Kattenzorg's magazine 'Poezenpraatjes', which published a scientific article that said that a cat in the house reduces the incidence of asthma:

The presence of a cat in the house may reduce the risk of people developing asthma. This is so because the human immunity system reacts protectively to the allergy-inducing substances spread around by the cat. Up to now it was always assumed that domestic pets could cause allergies and asthma. This is true in the case of the common house mite. But exposure to a cat is different, as a study by a centre for asthma and allergy at the University of Virginia, USA, shows. There children were examined for the number of antibodies they had against the cat's allergy-inducing substances. It appeared that children will develop asthma and allergies especially when there is only a small amount of allergy-inducing substances in the house. A large quantity of such substances, for instance when there is a cat in the house, caused asthma in fewer cases.'

Great! But it won't help much. Once people have decided to get rid of their cat, the poor animal has to go. They'll find a reason anyway. But I am happy that scientists at last found out that cats are good for our health. I already knew this for a long time!

MAEVE

The cute head of a feline
Two eyes used to sunshine
Now staring full of disbelief
Wondering why you caused her this grief.
You caged her, put her in a bind
And walked away, left her coldly behind.
What kind of person is he or she

211

Who treats animals so cruelly?

Poor cat, no room to even stretch a paw
But all that is history now.
A kind heart stopped to see,
Opened your prison to let you free.

Now you can romp around and race,
Play with delight, you have the space.
Now you are cherished, cared for in everything
Until the time someone invites you to his dwelling.

Dear Maeve, dear pussy black as soot
Believe my words, now everything will be good.

Cuddles from Nicolet and the Seven Angels

© *Nicolet*
(With many thanks to Jef for the translation)

When I wake up in the morning and look at the intensely lovely face of my Donsjegirl - a grey ball of Fur - then I feel so deeply happy. Then there is Chummy, a beautiful grey cloud on the other side of the pillow, and Daimke who crawls under the covers to escape the early-morning cold. It is a delight to feel that purring little body close to mine. Indeed, purring heals and is good when you suffer from osteoporosis. Yes, they are and they remain miracles on little feet, my fluffies. Catje stretches her arms towards me when I get up. A real loving embrace! If I suffered from early-morning bad moods, they would melt away like snow in the sun.

Speaking of 'Miracles on little Feet'. 'They' are doing fine. We are very happy and proud. I ordered a reprint two weeks ago, as my stock is dwindling fast. It is wonderful to read the reactions from readers telling me about their cats. About the strong bonds they have with them, or how they miss them, now that they have left for the Rainbow Bridge. I do hope my book brings comfort and hope. It's a certainty that their beloved cat will wait for them. But, oh, missing them here on earth... what a pain!
While I 'm writing all this Puddie is lying on my lap. Daimke and Catje are, what a thrill, hunting for mice. They are all so special to me. Often Donsje

leans her head on me or puts a paw on my arm. In any case she's always sitting very close to me. Catje comes in every fifteen minutes to tell me she loves me and ... could she have another one of those titbits, please? She is so beautiful, with her big, round yellow-green eyes. And Daimke? Well, Daimke is just Daimke. Talking with me all day long and performing some funny antics in between those conversations. She is so elegant, an elf dancing in front of me or jumping up and down my desk. And Mickje? She gets lovelier, calmer, happier (and more Garfield-like) by the day. Of all my fluffies she is the one who least fears strangers, unless they are men.

The kids enjoy the tunnel very much. Sometimes I move it to another corner. I make a bend in it or put some obstacles in it. Catje especially flies from one room-corner in and out of the tunnel and than on the castle, on a chair and back. All I have to do is wave the feather-on-the-fishing-rod. Daimke joins the dance while on the climbing pole and Donsje while on the chair. Chummy is growing fast, he is not so fond of the tunnel but all the fonder of the feather-on-the-fishing-rod. Mickje and Puddie also play in the tunnel but they are more careful. Of course they are a bit older now and afraid to get stuck in the tunnel.

The sale of Miracles made the days very hectic. I sensed I had to watch out for a burn-out. But there was more. The terrorist attacks in America on 11 September had deeply affected me. That people could commit such horrible crimes! They must really be demons! And what would be the consequences? What had happened to all those poor animals present on that fateful spot? I tried not to think of it. There is a very moving story that came out of this terrible event:

A blind computer operator related how his guide dog guided him down seventy stories in the burning WTC-building.

'Eduardo Rivera had been trapped by the fire after the terrorist-attack on the northern tower on 11 September. He ordered Dorado, his Labrador, to leave him behind and run for safety. But the dedicated dog fought his way through the flames to be at the side of his boss. And then, Dorado, through all the panic and fleeing persons, guided his boss down hundreds of flights of stairs to ground level and managed to get him out of the collapsing building just in time.
Eduardo, 42 years old, said during an interview with the Daily Record: 'I

thought I couldn't make it through all the obstacles and down all those stairs and I found it unfair that both of us would die in that hell. I had given up. The heat and the noise were overwhelming. I felt I had to give Dorado the chance to get out. But he was obviously prepared to risk his life to save mine.'

What a brave dog! Animals are so wonderful. There are so many stories about animals saving people.

At last Puddie found the time to email his friends.

'Dear Asselijntje, Esje, Stappertje, Tedje and Slaapmuts,

At last I have found the time to drop you a line! I was beginning to feel so guilty that sometimes I hid my eyes behind my paws so as to forget it for a while. You know that helps. You pretend it's not there, so it's not there. But then, mama sometimes seems glued to the computer. Downright horrible, so I didn't get a chance to write you sooner.

Well, lots of things have happened here. The biggest event is Chummy. We all enjoy his company tremendously. He is such a kind, sociable 'chum', that we have to stand in line so each of us gets a chance to play with him. Me as well and I find it a privilege to teach such a cute tomcat some lessons of life. He isn't pushy at all and won't interfere to get mama's attention, when I am enjoying a rest on her lap. A couple of times each day he gets his crazy half-hour and then it's best to run for cover. He jumps on the desktop and tidies it up in one swoop. Yes, dear Tedje, you taught him well, congratulations! I must admit Chummy has even taught me a thing or two.

We are very worried about our mama. She is too tired because she works relentlessly till deep into the night. We have come to the conclusion that working is good for your health, but stopping in time is even better! So we held a powwow and decided to get into action around nine p.m. I usually give the go-ahead. Than we start with 'Operation-Shut-Down-the-Office'. There are different ways to bring that about. If the weather is dry and warm, Daimke goes outside to lie down on a piece of wire-netting that serves as hammock. It is just above the door between our two runs, so she lies quite high above the ground. After a while she starts wailing: 'Mama, mama, please help me. I am

214

afraid to move, it's so cold and dark up here! Help, mieeewuuwuwuw mieuuwwweeeeeeeiiii, wheeee!' That does the trick, almost always, if the television doesn't make too much noise. But we are there to show mama the way to her child in distress.

Then it's Catje's turn. She tries to park herself on the computer or on the papers next to it. Now and then she does a headstand, very funny to see. Marg can't help cuddling her then. Donsje approaches from the other side and swings her paws around Marg's neck. If there is no reaction she will lick Marg's face and softly bite her nose. Computering is next to impossible then.

Mickje's job is to jump into the drawer of the cabinet and start 'cleaning up' ostentatiously by throwing envelopes around. I watch it all from my command post on top of the television set. I fix my gaze on mama while keeping an eye on my soldiers, as befits a good commander. But the real champion in getting mama away from her pc is our Chummy. Sure, he is a real cat but he can wreak havoc like an elephant.

Like yesterday. I saw it happen. It was just a fly buzzing around...Of course, Chummy got interested. So when the fly landed on the table, Chum went for it like a tiger. But our Chum, I must admit, is not very flexible as he is sturdy. He miscalculated the distance and got caught in the tablecloth. Can you imagine what happened? Clatter-clatter-dash-smash!!! Everything fell down, including the vase of roses. Marg had just left for a while. To be on the safe side, we all hid under the cabinet. The devastation was huge, but the fun we all shared was even bigger. When Marg returned and saw nobody around she concluded that our poltergeist had been at it again. Yes, we have our own poltergeist. We also have dwarves here, but they are kind. They help cats in distress, you know, just ask Asje. One by one we left our hiding place to be cuddled and comforted by Marg. A pity there hasn't been a cloth on the table any more since then, so we cannot perform this act again.

'Yes, in the evening, Chum has his 'happy hour' and then he swings through the office,' that's what mama tells everybody. 'And he never breaks anything!' Hi, if only she knew. But it works! Now mama stops working almost at a decent time!!

What about you? Also very busy helping your papas and mamas? What would they be without us? Prr, purrr. Lots of loving purrings for you all and I wish

215

you lots of tasty fresh fish and cuddles. Your friend, Puddie.'

I had got the joke, really, but I let them have their fun and just enjoyed it. When Chum starts his thing, it's as if a herd of elephants stampedes through the office. It's so funny. Usually, the first one to join in is Catje. They all fly into the run, come back inside through the window, race around the room, pass under the desk and then rush outside again. Sometimes Chum takes an enormous leap "forward" on to an empty office desk chair, which starts spinning around like mad from the impact. He puts his claws in the cloth and he flattens out to keep hold. He does it on purpose. At nine p.m. he as well as the rest of the gang have enough of their antics and mama should call it a day! I won't listen? OK, Chum knows what to do: tearing up things or throwing picture frames off the cabinet. Daimke and Catje join in this fun. Donsje positions herself in front of the door. She knows I am about to surrender and that her cat milk is coming.

Indeed, we are never bored. Some days ago Chum jumped and landed with one leg in a jug of water. Good thing that I lost the habit of putting my drinks close to my computer. Once the mug fell over and the computer got a complete foot-bath. It didn't like it and broke down. This time the jug was at a safe distance, but it hit the floor so hard that spatters of water reached the screen. Surprised, Chum licked his paw. 'So, something fell down? And er...why is my paw wet? 'Gravity, my dear fellow', Puddie explained, 'just gravity! Too bad things never fall upwards. That would be an interesting change, we could catch them then.'

Kitten time is fun, yet, the bond with the older cats is very dear to me. It grows stronger with the years and it is so marvellously reliable. Puddie is my friend Numero Uno, he is so special and kind and wise. Only, he sometimes gives the others a hard time. I found a big beetle, a kind of May bug (December bug) on the floor. Donsje paw-dribbled it through the office. Fun to see but not so funny for the beetle. It was so happy when I put it outside so it could fly off. Quickly I gave Donsje some tasty titbits. 'I know I did not behave like a lady should,' she sadly said. What they also like are 'teeth-chunks' from Hills. Big chunks that need chewing. I throw them one by one on the floor, while calling the name of the pussy that may pick it up. The game is, of course, to throw it in such a way that the cat I call is also the one which gets it. A marvellous game which never ends in trouble. The doggies would fight if I should do it with them. Donsje often snatches titbits away right before the nose of the others. She is the best chunk-catcher. No wonder, Dons is a real "sponge", she eats anything even cucumber, chicory and fennel. Chum is the champion chunk-breaker.

When I am under the 'inside-rain', as Donsje calls the shower, my fluffies are either in the office, or in my room or outside in the run. When I take longer than usual, for instance because I'm washing my hair, Puddie is the first to come and see what's keeping me. He has a very special Siamese 'miauwww', very loud and clear. What he says leaves nothing to be desired: 'Mama, what's keeping you? I want to be with you!' Daimke comes later to peek around the corner: 'Whiiiieeeheeh, weeieieiiheeee why are you not coming?' Mickje takes a quick look but returns immediately to the office. She prefers that place to the bedroom.

Then Catje appears in front of the bathroom: 'Rruauawwe, are you coming or...'. Chum marches purring into the bathroom. 'Purr purr purr' and flops down in the middle of the mat. My bathroom is small so when I step out of the shower cubicle I stand in between two lilac paws. Just enough space! Donsje is then usually sleeping on the cabinet in the bathroom. It is a plastic stand with shelves. The topmost shelf is hers. There's a warm towel so she takes her afternoon nap there. She 'inside rains' on the dry. When I've finished, she jumps on my shoulder for her free ride to the office, my dear fluffy girl.

But my fluffies are right, these are very hectic days. Some reviews about Miracles were published in the Belgian newspapers. A very nice one in 'Blik' and one in 'Gazet van Antwerpen'. They were really very beautiful, with cute pictures of my fluffies. The weekly 'Zondagsblad' also published a wonderful story about Miracles. The newspaper 'Belang van Limburg' published an article about us. Limburgers are warm and spontaneous people. We received many orders from them. It is all very nice and really a writer's dream come true. Still, it also involves much work.

Tomcat Slaapmuts, wise as he is, wrote the following nice poem especially for me:

'Thank you so much for your letters and emails
With your personal stories and moving details
It's just – no offence - that there are so many!
And I long for a break without any
Now if there were only two or three
That would not bother me
But their number is getting on top of me
I need to stop, I want to be FREE
Free to sleep for a long, long time
After all, I'm not exactly in my prime!

It's getting too much
I'm losing my tuch-
See there's another mistake
I really, really need a break

I'm losing sleep and in my nightmares
The letters are now arriving in pairs.
I feel I am in deep trouble
I'm beginning to see all things double

A blissfully mail-free holiday
To chase my nightmares all away
Now that would really make my day
There, that's that, I've had my say

© *Tomcat Slaapmuts*
(With many thanks to Slaapmuts who wrote this wonderful poem and to
Alicia Koster who translated it.)

When I was overwhelmed by not really necessary tattle-mails, I included this poem in my reply and, oh miracle, it really worked! (Sometimes).

Pussy-children are just like human children. You may plan and plan and hope they will accept your plans. But if they won't, you have to change your plans anyway. If you don't, everybody will be unhappy. I really hoped that Chummy would like to accompany me on my garden-walks and also join me, without fear on car-trips. I looked forward to going places with him at my side. Well, when Chummy was still small, he accepted everything and showed no fear. But

218

as he grew older - and that happened in no time - he started developing fears during our garden-walks. He was not just afraid, he was really seized by panic. It was so pathetic. When a car or a motorcycle passed on the road bordering our garden, he shot away. Of course, he was suddenly pulled to a stop when the retractable line reached its end. I couldn't prevent it. I persisted for a while and brought him with me, hoping his fears would wear off - all strange things provoke uneasiness - but it just got worse. One morning he just hid himself when he saw me coming with the leash. Then I got the message!

I took him in my arms, looked him seriously in the eyes and asked:' Dear Chummy, do you really feel so bad about walking with me through the garden? Isn't it fun to watch the birds and the leaves fly away? You found it such a thrill before, didn't you? Don't worry about those cars, they can't cross the ditch and the people and the horses can't either. It's too wide and deep for them.' Chummy looked shyly away, and suddenly I saw tears rolling down his cheeks. He sighed and hid in my arms.' Oh, dear mama, 'he softly sobbed, 'I want so very much to do you a favour and accompany you everywhere you go. I have discussed it with Puddie yesterday. He understands how I feel. But I just can't help it. Whenever there's a vroom-vroom thing or a noisy two-wheeler coming, I can hear my mama's voice warning me: 'Son, watch out, please be on guard for vroom-vrooms, those metal things that make a lot of noise and move very fast. They are a mortal danger to us, cats. Make sure you are far away, whenever you hear a vroom-vroom coming.' I know, mama, you will never expose me to danger, but I just can't help to run for cover whenever I hear such a thing approaching. Puddie told me he experiences the same fear and that's the reason he doesn't accompany you. So, please mama just let me stay inside? I really want to do everything to make you happy, but this...I am soooo afraid.'
Oh, my dear little man! I comforted him and assured him that I would never again force him to do a thing he didn't really like. 'Never mind, dear Chummy, you don't have to come with me any more. I am so sorry I didn't realized at once how bad you felt. From now on you just watch from the window when Daimke, Catje and Donsje walk with me through the garden. And you know what? I'll just make two rounds with Donsje. Anyway, she sits half of the time on my shoulder, so she will not get tired from that! She enjoys our hikes. In the beginning Donsje was also very afraid of cars, but now she couldn't care less. Your mother was right in warning you, cars are indeed a mortal danger.

Overjoyed, Chummy got up and rushed off to tell Puddie the big news. Puddie is becoming Chummy's confidant and I think he told Chum to tell me frankly what was bothering him. Well, that's Chum's 'Britishness' for you. If there's something he really doesn't want, he'll show it. And he is right! Of course my fluffies don't have to do anything if they feel bad about it, unless it's necessary for their health. Especially with Chum, I do everything by mutual agreement. Yes, he's received a good education and he knows how to behave. 'Never belie your nature, son!' Kaya taught him well.

It's autumn now. Beautiful golden-yellow leaves are fluttering down. The fluffies enjoy all those funny things floating past them. They try to intercept them. If they're successful, they proudly parade with their 'prey' in the mouth. Daimke makes long stories, rather hard to understand. 'Don't talk with your mouth full, Daimke, that's not allowed!' Puddie scolds her while looking at me. Yes, the first child always gets the strictest education! And than there are the acorns! I like so much to kick them around while we're walking. (Acorns in Dutch also mean 'very annoying', bad people or bastards). 'Just admit it, there is no greater fun than kicking acorns away!' 'Right so!' Daimke agrees while chasing after them.

I have at last bought a digital camera. I love to photograph Donsje or Daimke when they're hanging in a tree. They always oblige, except when I have my digital camera with me. It makes photographing very thrilling.

Chummy has wound us all around his gorgeous grey paws. He is every inch a gentleman, gallant, kind and lovely towards the others. He divides his attention fairly among us all. In turns, we're all in for a cuddle-session. Very self-confidently and loudly purring he approaches his 'victim', his gorgeous long tail straight up or curled over his back. 'Here I am, let's have a cosy chat, shall we?' he asks politely. Daimke's turn means that Chummy gets a good grooming. Donsje's turn means rubbing noses and then lying down against each other. Catje, who doesn't like 'sticking', nods curtly and then starts some wild game. I love it so much when Puddy and Chummy run through the room. The two tomcats playing together! Nothing can move me more deeply, especially because I know how hard it is for Puddie to share his life with other fluffies. 'But mama,' he says, ' it's only logical, Chum sees me as his wise uncle whom he can ask everything: 'Puddy, what's an airplane? Puddy, why do I have to go to the doctor? Why are she-cats different from us, tomcats? And what about those dogs? They won't hurt us, will they?' Of course, I feel very honoured that

I may teach him all that. After all, we're both tomcats, and there are things women don't understand! Especially cheeky girls like our Daimke.' Puddy trains Chummy to open drawers and doors. Twice a demonstration and Chum has the knack of it.

Now that the evenings are still warm enough, they often sit close together to observe the birds and the mice searching for food in the leaves. So cosy. The birdhouse in front of the office window serves as a supermarket again. Fortunately the birds are back. We had almost no birds left this summer. They all went away. It is a delight to watch them relishing sunflower seeds. Chummy hadn't seen it before and for a couple of days he sat like glued to the window. With his big, round, golden eyes he gazed to those flying things outside and then looked at me. One big question mark. 'Whhhhatttt isssss thaaatttt?

How beautiful Lilac is! Chummy is just a little teddy bear. He has an elastic trot, very funny. And how big he is now!!! He is six months old and weighs almost five kilos! More than Catje and Daimke. What will he become? A giant?Thanks to this heavenly weather, I can leave the office window wide open in the evening. Of course that's an invitation to moths. They usually make for the neon light hanging above the cabinet. This causes my cats to jump to the top of the cabinet which - big surprise - is littered with framed pictures and drawings of cats. The cabinet remains on its feet, but the pictures and drawings hit the floor. If there are no moths around, my kitties walk calmly in between the pictures without overturning even one. But when they are in the middle of a moth-chase, well, they mean business, so everything that stands in the way has to get out of the way.

I feel sorry for those little moths and try to catch them for their own safety. Usually I have no success. I can't get onto the top of that cabinet. Humans are simply too clumsy for that. Although I must admit, Chummy isn't exactly very lithe either. No, the real ballerina among the fluffies is Daimke. She has natural grace and dances through her feline life like an elf. Catje is the best gymnast and she knows perfectly how to balance herself on the small shelf alongside the wall, even though she still slightly cocks her head to one side. It's a marvel to see.

December came and suddenly the temperature dropped. We really felt the difference. As happens every year around this time the central heating failed just when we needed it, so I wrapped a tartan rug around my legs and sat down with Puddie on my lap in our 'new' old rocking chair. Sure, we have come by a new old-fashioned but delightfully, second hand rocking chair. It's made of reed and in perfect condition. I had the intention of using it every night but... so far have sat down only twice in it. Immensely happy, Puddie looked up at me:' Lovely, mama, the two of us here in the rocking chair, now we're really getting on in years, aren't we?' He is right! The only thing lacking are geraniums, for the rest all ingredients are there: rocking chair, Puddie, rug and electric heater. Well, **getting** old is not such bad thing, as long as we **are** not old! I always take care that the paws of my pussy-children are out of the way when I'm rocking though. They are alert, but you never know...

It was new moon. 'Does she also get the bottle and does she also have to be stimulated afterwards, like I was by Aunt Maria?' Daimke asked while playing with a ball on my desk. It reminded me of the splendid job Maria and Gé did and are doing for the little abandoned kittens. They have rescued countless little ones. With endless patience, love and know-how Maria nearly always succeeds in saving any rescued kitten she takes in her house. I am so proud of her! I looked at Daimke, who had been very ill but had grown into a gorgeous and healthy cat. A furry ball full of the joy of living. It must be terrible for a kitten to miss its mother. It is also very difficult to substitute a mother cat. Yet Maria always succeeds. Pussy-mothers are real super mothers. It was wonderful to observe Kaya, Chummy's mother's concern about her kittens when I had them on my lap. That look in her eyes, so intense and clear: 'You will be careful, won't you? My kittens are still so small.' She remained watchful all the time.

I am still deeply moved by the story of Scarlett, a mother cat who rescued her kittens from a building on fire and was seriously injured in the process.

Scarlett
Pussy-mothers are prepared to go to any length to rescue their children. Some years ago, March 1996 actually, Scarlett, a mother cat rescued her kittens in a very special way. The New York firemen had finished extinguishing a fire in an

222

abandoned building in Brooklyn, when they suddenly heard a chorus of kittens crying. Surprised they checked it out and found three very scared kittens desperately crying for their mother, in the middle of the street. Pretty soon afterwards the firemen spotted the mother cat on the other side of the street where she had already taken two of her kittens to safety. She was seriously burned and exhausted, but she had managed to pull all her kittens out of the fire. First she had dragged them out of the building. One by one she had carried them some metres into the street before returning into the inferno to get the rest of her litter. Then she had tried to carry all five to some bushes, where they would be better hidden.

But after two trips she had collapsed. When the firemen picked up the three kittens and brought them to their mother, she nudged them with her nose to assure herself they were by her side. Her eyes had swollen because of the burns and she had become totally blind. The whole family was sheltered in the North Shore Animal League in Washington. Scarlett and four of her kittens recovered, one died. More than seven hundred letters were addressed to Scarlett and her children. Twelve hundred persons volunteered to adopt them. Scarlett became a symbol of abandoned animals and she got her own website. Of course, good homes were found for the kittens.

There are more stories about pussy-mothers which literally did everything to save their kittens. *There was, for instance, a very special tabby mother, Kitty, who protected her kittens with her body during the Blitz in London, when the building in which she had hidden her kittens collapsed during a bombardment.*

She had really thought that she had found a safe shelter for them, when she had carried them to an outbuilding of the church. But it wasn't to be. During the all-devastating bombardments the roof and walls collapsed completely. Everywhere around her was fire, water and destruction. Kitty though posted herself calmly and quietly over her kittens and hid them in her warm fur while absorbing the shocks. She was found by accident the next morning by people searching for victims in the rubble. The building was still smouldering. It was a wonder that mother and kids had not been seriously wounded. It was a true blessing. The Animal Protection Society awarded Kitty a silver medal and a certificate. Her picture is still hanging in the church with below the story of her wonderful mother love and dedication.

The following story fits in very well with the season of Christmas.

Molly

Jenny, an old Dutch lady, sat sadly in front of the stove staring into the fire. It was almost Christmas but she was in no mood to celebrate. One month ago her husband had died. She felt deeply sad and lonely. What was the meaning of her life now that her beloved had gone? She had nothing more to live for. Suddenly she heard a noise coming from the front door. 'Oh, that must be the wind', she thought, but when she heard it again she went to check it out. Slowly she opened the door. Nothing but darkness. 'Miaauw', a soft sound, 'miaauwww?'' She looked down and saw a soaked little black cat, scared and huddled on the doorstep. 'Oh, dear,' Jenny said, 'look how wet and cold you are. Come on in and sit close to the stove. I'll get you something to eat.' But the cat could hardly move. Carefully, Jenny picked her up and carried her inside. She tried to wipe her dry and noticed that her nipples were swollen. Maybe she had kittens? Now? In these cold and wet days? Than she must have been dumped! Jenny lived in a very isolated place.
Fortunately the little black cat drank some milk and ate some food. Jenny fetched a basket, spread a warm cloth in it and put it close to the stove. 'I will call you Molly, like my cat before', she said while putting her softly into the basket. Molly tried to lick herself dry, but she fell asleep from exhaustion. Jenny suddenly felt less sad: she was not alone now.

Next morning Molly waited at the door to get outside. 'You be careful and come back soon!' Jenny said. 'You can stay here with me. Forever, if you want to. You know that, don't you? I would love you to'. The cat walked down the path without looking back. She looked very tired and ill! 'Maybe I should follow her,' Jenny thought. 'But if she has kittens she must go to them. She will be scared if I do that. Late in the afternoon - Jenny had left the front door ajar - she saw Molly approaching the house carrying something. When she realised what it was, her eyes filled with tears. It was a beautiful black-white kitten about four weeks old. Molly had gone to fetch her child and to bring it to the only place she knew to be safe: Jenny's.

Together they took it to her basket. It was very moving to see how happy they were. For the first time Jenny heard Molly purr. But she refused to eat and that night Molly quietly passed away. She knew she could go now. Her child was in good hands. 'And I have again something to live for,' Jenny thought, sad and happy at the same time, while softly pressing the kitten against her body. 'You are the most beautiful Christmas gift I have ever received. I will name you Faith.'

Mother love is the best love there is. It has also been proved that mothers can feel from a distance of thousands of kilometres away that their children are in danger. How terrible then for a mother when her kittens are taken away from her, because her owners didn't want kittens. Yet, they were too (damn) lazy to have her neutered in time. She must feel desperate. She will look everywhere for her kittens. Besides, a mother cat's body is all geared up for the suckling and rearing of the kittens. Suddenly they are gone. It is not only a big blow mentally, it also upsets her body completely.

Cats don't only save their own kittens. There are also stories about cats saving human children. That's why it is such a shame when women get rid of their cat when they are pregnant. They have heard something about the risks of contracting toxoplasmosis, but don't know anything precise about this matter. It is true that toxoplasmosis can be dangerous for the foetus. Indeed, this disease can be transmitted through cat faeces more than two days old, so it is better that a pregnant woman wears gloves when cleaning her cat's litter tray or has someone else do the job. But infection occurs **in the first place** by eating partly cooked or raw meat and/or insufficiently washed raw vegetables. I include info about toxoplasmosis in Chapter Fifteen. Children growing up with animals are much healthier and more balanced than children who are not allowed to have animals.

Here below is the story of Tommy, Hannie's tomcat. When her son Bob was born, Hannie had been persuaded to get rid of Tommy. She didn't want to, because she loved him, but her mother in law kept on nagging about it. Finally she gave in. Fortunately she hadn't carried out her decision yet.

One morning she was drinking a cup of coffee downstairs while Bobbie was sleeping in his bed upstairs. Suddenly she heard Tommy mewing very loudly. He must have gone upstairs. Hannie was angry and called him to stop making a noise, but Tommy mewed even louder. She was afraid Bobbie would wake up, so she rushed upstairs. 'I'll teach him a lesson or two, she shouted!' When she arrived upstairs she saw Tommy desperately jumping against the door of

Bobbie's room. Something bad was going on there. Hannie rushed into the room to find her son entangled in the phone cord. He was already blue in the face. With a desperate effort Hannie succeeded in cutting the cord and took her half-strangled and desperately crying baby into her arms. Tommy jumped onto the bed and rubbed his head over and over against mother and son. He shared in their happiness. Needless to say that 'getting rid of Tommy' was something totally out of the question after that. He was their hero and Bob and Tommy became friends for life.

Doctor Allen Schoen has written two magnificent books about the strong bond between human beings and their pets. 'Love, Miracles and Animal Healing', and 'Kindred Spirits.' He talks about the profound love that people and pets feel for each other. Also he tells about the significance of animals for their sometimes terminally ill people and the other way around. Very moving and beautiful stories!
I remember very well, how my dear Daddy, who had had his first heart attack, sat night after night with his beloved Golden Retriever Echo on the sofa. He could not sleep and it was only Echo who kept him from giving up on life. He was such a strong man, my Daddy. A real commander. And then, from one day to the other, he was not even allowed to walk in the garden. In 1960 it was like that. He felt so useless and afraid, but Echo needed him and Echo was there for him. Day and night. All those long months he felt like an invalid! I was a child then. When I saw the light burning in the sitting room I always went to talk with them. The love they had for each other brought tears into my eyes.

I am convinced of the fact that our pussy-children are angels in disguise. I can hear Catje laughing now, she is hanging from the curtains. She tries to cheer me up. I have a nasty cold (a 'snot-fall' as we say here). How such a half-flu can make your life miserable! My throat is sore and very itchy. Daimke thought I had fleas in my throat and suggested Frontline...but Catje said it would not help. Well, it'll go away some day soon, I hope! Anyway I feel better already, now that Catje has made me laugh. It is good that my germs can't harm my fluffies. Donsje draped herself around my neck like a warm scarf during our morning walk. 'Keep yourself warm, mama, so your sore throat will get better,' she assured me.

Raymonde had been on a visit and together we made our Christmas cards-homework again. Every year I get the Christmas-cards-itis. I don't want to hurt anybody, but I've been brooding over just how to tell everyone that I will send no more Christmas cards. It's difficult, because I feel obliged to reply to the cards I receive. Secondly, rituals do matter, they are like anchors in your life. I would feel a void if I stopped receiving and sending Christmas cards. The pussy-cards that I receive are so beautiful. I keep them in a couple of special document files. My friend Anne Versteyne, who drew the wonderful cat-pictures in Miracles, made such a cute Christmas card for us. Really wonderful. It's Donsje eating cream out of a jug.

But we have to do something. The post is getting more and more expensive too. Every year I write a Christmas Letter. This year I wrote:

*It's very hard to change habits, but it **can** be done. For centuries it has been the habit to exchange expensive gifts when it's Christmas. People eat and drink till they feel like bursting. And then there are those horrible loud noisy fireworks. A real horror for most animals and many 'peace loving' people! It costs a fortune too, all that noise! Would it not be more in line with our Lord Jesus' teachings if all that money were to be used to help as many animals and people in need as possible?*

And, you know, that would be possible! What if we used that money to help strays, which are now so cold and hungry and long for a full tummy? What if we were to give that money for the cats who are now sitting lonely in rescue shelters waiting for an owner? What if we were to donate it towards animal shelters and to the authorities devoting themselves to the cause of animals? How much happiness you could spread that way! And would it not give a much more 'real' Christmas-feeling, just a simple meal with your beloved, surrounded by your kitties and other animals? Isn't that much more cosy and warm?

227

'Especially on Christmas Days,
Let's think first of the hungry strays.'

Isn't that a great Christmas wish? Of course, it's a utopian dream, but a bit less celebration and a bit more concern for the strays, that must be possible!!! I know these few lines won't make much difference, but if they make even one person think of the idea, I will be the happier for it!

Sure, there are people who don't care about animals, well, they could help other people who are in need: the poor, the sick, the lonely, the poor children, the aged.

Getting into a real Christmas mood is rather difficult this year. But I have my pussy-children. Pure love, warmth and humour tied up in balls of fur. And I have my doggies happily running in front of me through the garden. The geese, chickens and birds. The big tree in front of my house twinkles full of lights.

Why is there no Good-News-Show on television which only reports the good things happening around the globe? Because they **do** happen! I think it's wrong to broadcast too much negative news. You get the feeling that the world is going to 'pieces'! It makes you 'loose your purrr!' Whereas there is also so much 'peace' on earth. Many good things are happening too! Also, we can be sure that there are extraterrestrial beings around us, which will always protect us and won't allow our planet to be destroyed, even though the reports are sometimes very disturbing. It says so in the book 'The Only Planet of Choice' by Phillis Schlemmer. A beautiful book and recommended reading for the Christmas days (after Purring Angels that is).

This lovely story is from my friend Wayne. I am so glad he allowed us to use it. It really makes you purr!

In The Beginning

Chapter 1

Hello, my name is Angel. I'm a two-year-old white Angora cat. I have a wonderful family that I'm very happy to be a part of. There's Momma Barb, Daddy Jake and my dear Traveller, whom you surely know.

I don't remember much of my kittenhood. It always seemed that I was cold and hungry and I don't really remember a lot of my own mother; except I know she loved me. One day she just didn't come back and I was alone for a long time. Life is very hard for a young kitten all alone and many times I was so lonely and afraid.

Then one day when I was shivering and wet my life was changed forever. 'Hello', said a gentle voice, 'are you alright' I looked up into a grey face with the most beautiful amber eyes. It was my Traveller, although he didn't get that name until later. Something about him just made me trust him and before I knew it I was telling him how unhappy I was. 'I'll be right back, don't leave', he said and in a few minutes he was back with food. 'Eat this please', he told me, 'I have a place nearby where I can get more. When you've eaten I'll take you to a place where you can be warm.' I'm afraid I wasn't very ladylike as I gulped it down but I was soooo hungry. 'Now come along', he whispered, 'you need shelter'. He led me along and stayed close beside me even though I couldn't go very fast because I was weak from not eating. He led me through a hole in the wall of a building and into a snug corner where he had a comfy nest. 'Rest now', he mewed, 'I'll stay right here with you and watch.' With that I curled down and snuggled in. He sat beside me and gently smoothed my fur with his tongue. It felt sooo good, I'd not been groomed since my mommy disappeared. As he worked a throaty purr bubbled up within me and I drifted off to sleep happier than I've ever been.

The next morning I woke with him lying beside me and more delicious food at my bedside. I looked at him and asked, 'For me?' He smiled and slowly blinked those wonderful eyes. 'Of course', he purred, 'I have human friends at a place where other humans gather to eat. They leave tasty bits every day. I'll take you there when you're stronger.' As I washed my paws and face he looked at me very seriously. 'You know, you're really very young to be out on your own. If you would like to we could sort of team up. You could stay here with me and we could kind of look out for each other. This can be a dangerous neighborhood for a cat alone and it sure would be nice to have someone to talk to.' I looked up at him, such a handsome tom, all grey and sleek with a beautiful white patch on his throat and sparkling white paws. 'Do you really want me to stay?' I asked softly. 'Oh yes, I...I...I sometimes get very lonely here and it would be very nice to have you here. I mean, if you wouldn't mind? You can trust me, really you can, and... would you? Please?' He ducked his grey head down and his whiskers drooped, a single kitty tear dropped on the ground.

'I'd like that very much', I whispered and put my paw on his. He looked deeply into my eyes and touched me with his nose. 'Thank you', he purred. We snuggled down together and I've never felt safer.

Chapter 2

As the days passed I regained my strength bit by bit until I could venture out with him. All through this time he stayed close and watched over me. It was so wonderful to have him there. In my heart of hearts I loved him so deeply and began calling him My Grey. He smiled when I called him that; 'My Angel', he purred and kissed my ear. Oh how happy I was. Then one day I was strong enough to go wander with him. He took me to the place where he had found food. 'We must be careful here', he whispered, 'we're not the only ones who know of this place.' 'What do you mean?' I softly asked, 'are we in danger?' 'Always here', he replied as he looked carefully about, 'there are several large feral dogs running loose and they are very dangerous. We must always watch and never give them a chance. I'm afraid they've harmed other animals who have come for the food. Please just stay here and watch, I'll show you what you must do.'

With that he scooted like a shadow to the place where the food was put. He stood listening and sniffing the air before he climbed into the can. I sat there in the shadow of the boxes and crates, extending my senses to their fullest. My heart was pounding with worry for Grey. 'Hurry my Grey, oh please hurry', I whispered under my breath. 'OH, I hear something, oh hurry Grey please.' Then, just as he popped out of the can, there they were. DOGS!!! Huge shaggy evil looking monsters! And they SEE him. Grey leaped across

230

the alley screaming at me 'RUN, run fast my Angel. GO, GO!!!' The pack howled and came after us.

Faster and faster we ran! Grey right behind me urging me on. I ran as hard as I could, but I was still weak. My breath came in great sobs and my legs began to wobble. Then I fell, and I could not rise! Grey tried to push me on but I was totally spent. 'Go my Grey! Run my love, save yourself please', I cried. 'NO', he moaned, 'I must save you whatever the cost.' Then the dogs were there. Grey leaped and knocked over a box, hiding me from their sight. Then he spun to meet them. 'GREY', I screamed, 'Noooooo Grey!!!!'

Then the terrible snarls and screams drowned out all else. I tried to climb out of the box so I could die at the side of my Grey, but I could not. I fell back and lay there unable to move. Oh my Grey, my beautiul Grey.

Chapter 3

Then I heard a human's shout and howls and yelps from the dogs. Then all went silent. I lay there shivering. I prayed that I would die so I could be with my Grey. The human's voice was talking but I wasn't listening. But...a scratching at the box and...Grey's voice! How can this be? The box opened and.... 'GREY, oh my dear Grey, you're alive! 'This human saved us', Grey cried, 'he beat the dogs away just in time.' The man bent down and touched us both with his hands, talking softly. Then he lifted us both up in his arms. I mewed in fright but Grey calmed me. 'He's going to help us, don't be afraid.' Grey knew the human language much better than I, so I relaxed.
The man placed us into a big red truck nearby. He laid me on a warm soft bed; ahhh so soft. I sniffed at my surroundings as Grey murmured softly over me. I could smell love here, a gentle love, but sadness too. I was tired, so very tired, and as the warmth spread over me I drifted into sleep. I could feel the truck moving and the man talking softly to Grey. I slept. After awhile Grey slipped back beside me and told me the man's sad story. 'He's taking us home Angel, can you imagine?', said Grey with a touch of awe in his voice. 'A home Angel, I've never even dreamed of a home! But see, we can also help them! We can be a family, think of that. Oh Angel, this will be so wonderful.' I smiled at my Grey's happiness and fell asleep again with a warm feeling in my heart.
Finally, I felt the truck come to a halt and the man lifted me back up in his

arms. *As we stepped down my eyes fell on a sweetly smiling woman. My heart leaped in my breast, so great was the feeling of love that poured from her. Immediately I leaped from the man's arms and flew to her. She scooped me up and held me close. Oh my, the love just poured from her heart and I fairly vibrated with joy. My Grey was prancing around her feet like a silly kitten. Ah, what a wonderful day.*

In the next few days we all settled into our new family. Momma Barb and Daddy Jake were very happy and I like to think we had a little bit to do with that. Our new home fairly shone with joy. Momma Barb was very smart, she knew the name that Grey gave me. He smiled at me when I told him and said that Angel was my natural name. He's so sweet. He travels with Daddy Jake in the red truck so naturally Daddy Jake calls him Traveller. But to me he will always be My Grey; my first and only true love. I know that somewhere my mother is purring and very happy for me.

By: Wayne Pond Copyright © 4-20-2003

It often happens that a man is more humanely related to a cat or dog than to a human being.

Henry David Thoreau

Chapter 22

Adult Chummy and Mausie

They come and sit close to the author on his desk. They think with him and watch him with understanding and tenderness. It seems that cats surmise the thoughts flowing from the mind into the pen and try to catch these while they are on their way.

Theofile Gautier

It feels great when the days are growing longer. Up to January nature seems to be waning and the days are dark and gloomy. Suddenly there is a turning point. We all wake up and start living again. Hibernating is not such a bad idea. I am susceptible to the 'Winter Blues', S.A.D. Fortunately the kitties and I have our own private 'indoor-sunshines'. They save us during those long, dark winter days. A light-therapy device is so wonderful! We all need bright light. It elevates the body's natural 'feel good' chemicals during the day. Bright light also suppresses melatonin, so you feel less tired. The great advantage of those lamps is too that they don't send the dangerous UV rays. You can use them as long as you like.

I put one on the piano so that I can play at the same time. I must admit however that I am mostly in the shade, as pasha Puddie spreads himself flat out in the light. He knows what's good for him! Light-therapy really works. On the site Site: www.medilux.com you can read all about it.

Chummy had a big problem. As usual he consulted his big pal Puddie about it. Just read what Puddie wrote about it to his pen friends:

Dear pen pals,

I've got some news about my new friend Chummy. Oh, he was so down last night. With tears in his eyes he came to me. 'Puddie,' he stammered, 'Puddie, listen what they're saying about me. **They say...ttthatttt I donnn ttt'havvvvve balls...auuuww mieeauuuuutttwwww!***'Poor Chum, it made him stutter. 'So, why do you think that?' I asked surprised, because they are very visible. As a matter of fact I am very jealous of you, I haven't any, you see.' 'Well, Chantal and Ron, remember I was born in the sock drawer in their wardrobe, asked mama to check whether my equipment was complete. Of course, mama knows I have two splendid balls, still she checked me out. And so I learned what they're thinking of me, sniff, sniff, but why should Chantal have doubts? I am a real super-duper tomcat, aren't I? Anyway, you all keep on complimenting me and mama tells it to every person she meets.'*

Well, I didn't get it either and I felt awfully sorry for my new friend. You see, us tomcats are a proud lot and this was a downright insult. Something like asking a Scottish nobleman whether he is learning to be a woman because he wears a skirt. Besides, Chum is going through his adolescence and so is rather self-conscious at the moment. Indeed, you'd start stammering for less. To know the ins and outs of this matter I went to Marg. She told me it was just a routine question, for the file or something that is kept for any purebred cat. And in it everything from his head down to his claws is recorded.

So I returned to my pal who was impatiently waiting to hear what I had to say. I explained to him how important it is for a tomcat to have two descended testicles. That this sometimes is not the case and then a real operation is required to remove both balls. I told him that such a tomcat shouldn't be used for breeding, because his kids could get the same problem. 'Well, Chum, just be happy that everything is in order with your equipment. You won't have much trouble when you come to be neutered. And, pal, don't ask me why you have to be neutered. It's all part of the game. Anyway I've had it performed on me as well. Fortunately, it's not so bad for us as it is for the girls. Just ask Donsje and Daimke, they were very ill afterwards. And, just relax! It has nothing to do with our inner beings. We are who we are, just a little bit less than before, you got it?' 'Weeeeelll,' Chum replied softly, 'I don't know whether I really **want** *to understand all that. But I am very thankful to you, Puddie, you have helped me a lot. It's nice to have such an all-knowing tomcat like you for a friend. Purrr* *purrrr.' He licked me over the head. I felt good about it. I had explained it all to him. I don't always understand the bizarre behaviour of straightup-walkers myself. They do whatever they want to do and expect us to understand and accept it, 'because it is for our own good.' On the other hand, I must admit we could be worse off with our mamas and papas! Even though they don't have tails, or maybe their tails are just invisible?*

Many nice preeetings from yours purrly Puddie'

Indeed I had noticed that Chum started playing rather 'tomcattish-ly' with the girls. It was wonderful to see how he approached them. So gallantly and high on his legs. His head a bit tilted and his tail straight up in the air like the banner of a knight. But then came the action: he tried to take them by the scruff of the neck and to cover them, which they naturally didn't appreciate. 'Are you out of your mind?' Catje angrily shouted, for she is Chum's exercise-victim number one. So I made an appointment with Doctor Liliane. I was glad that it's a much simpler operation than it is with the girls. Still, I felt sort of a traitor when I put my dear little knight in the cat-carrier. Once on the examination table, he made himself very small. He flattened his ears and begged with his gorgeous eyes: 'Please, don't hurt me. I am so afraid, mieuwwwiieee! Oh please, put me back in the carrier.' He clung to me when he received his anaesthetic.

I was allowed to stay at his side during the operation. It is indeed a small operation. Doctor Liliane prefers the animals to wake up under her supervision. That's safer anyway, in case something happens. I returned home but felt very lonely without my Chum. The girls looked everywhere for him. 'Where's our Chum, mama?' I was very happy when it was all over and I could return to get him. Fortunately he didn't have much pain and a couple of hours later he came to me asking for food. Only sitting was still some problem. 'Well, you'd feel bad for less,' remarked a compassionate Puddie. Since the operation Chum has become even more affectionate. He kept on coming to ask if everything was all right and if I would kindly tell him how muuuuuch I loved him!

235

VET

I think that fellow's low and mean
and therefore I am not so keen
on going there once more
I wouldn't even know what for!

So I want to state quite clear:
I'm just not going, sorry dear!

© *Slaapmuts*

Doctor Liliane told me that a couple of weeks ago a cat had escaped from the arms of his owner when they brought him in for his vaccination. Absolutely terrified he had crossed the big and busy road in front of her door. Up to now he hasn't been found. Terrible! It is impossible to understand why people just carry their pet in their arms when going to the veterinarian. Doctor Liliane keeps on telling everybody how dangerous that is. She sells very comfortable cat-carriers to put cats in, but still there are people thinking: 'Oh, my cat will stay in my arms. But that's rubbish! Any cat can suddenly get frightened and then, believe me, you can't hold her. A cat in panic is very strong. She should always be transported in a carrier cage. Not in a cardboard box, because she can tear that open in a jiffy. The best cat-carriers are those made of plasticised wire. While the cat is in it, she is secure and she can see everything. Those carriers can be opened from the top and that's very convenient for putting your cat in or taking her out.

February came. The days were longer already but it was still very cold. We'd had a nice layer of snow again. Chum found the stuff rather odd. 'Wet and cold to the feet', he observed, 'nothing for a tomcat of my status. When the sun shines on it, it is as if the ground is covered by thousands of glittering diamonds. But then, when I try to pick them up to exchange them for tasty titbits, 'peng', they're gone! Just like happiness. When you hunt for it, you can't catch it. But if you let it come to you, suddenly it's there.' Yes, our Chum gets wiser by the day, according to Pudje. 'His wisdom grows proportional to his weight.'

For a change the central heating had been functioning well these Christmas days but then it had had enough of it and broke down. An icy cold set in. It was frosty weather outside. Fortunately the serviceman came at once. He repaired the whole system, including the office heating, which didn't work very well. The following day, we experienced a real adventure. It was a very hectic morning. Still, mothers have that special sense that warns them when something is not all right with their children. All of a sudden, I thought: 'Where is Daimke?' Of course, she had accompanied me to the office, but since then I neither saw nor felt her presence.

I ran through the house, rattling the can filled with titbits. I inspected the run. I didn't see her anywhere. Now, the other fluffies got nervous. They sensed my fear, for I started getting worried. I know the location of all the hiding places she has. The fluffies had been in the run that morning, watching the birds. Amazed I saw a wren on the stairs in front of the window. There is a little staircase to make it possible to go to the bedroom. Not a very smart move by the birdie, as Chum was watching it, full of interest. Maybe Daimke had gone hunting? To be on the safe side I checked the run's wire netting. I do this on a regular basis. I am a real inspection-freak on that point. A couple of days ago everything was still firmly fixed. I felt with my hand along the wire netting until I came to the corner and pushed against it with my foot. There the netting simply opened. Heaven forbid! **She was gone!!!!**

I stood there shaking all over. Where to start looking for her? We live in the middle of a wood. I walked through the garden, called...nothing! Mickje sat mewing in the big run. 'Did you see something, Mickje? Oh, do you know where Daimke is?' 'Miauw, miaauwww, rraauuu', she replied with urgency. Did she sense my anxiousness or did she know something? I walked in the direction she looked to but found nothing. Daimke is rather white so I should easily spot her if she was moving around in the dark wood. I went back inside the house. I felt lost and prayed to the Lord for advice, help and wisdom. Daimke, with her super thin fur, Daimke who has to take enzymes every time she eats. She is the one that should not get lost! She can't survive on her own.

I took a couple of deep breaths and tried to listen to my feelings. I went back to the office and looked at the window. I sensed something…Below it there is the built-in radiator which the serviceman had repaired the day before. I had a board nailed in front of it so that the fluffies could not get under it. I tried the board. It moved! It was not fixed very well! Quickly I removed the gratings and, yes, there, under the radiator I found Daimke, cosily warm and chortling with glee! She was enjoying herself very much and looked downright mischievous. 'Here mama, I've taken you for a ride, haven't I, wieeehhh wieewe!' I could hardly believe my eyes, but there she was! Gosh, I was happy!!!

A good thing it had happened, because it made me discover the hole in the netting. We fixed that immediately. Eddie and I made another inspection-round. This was the oldest part of the run, installed some years ago. I think the sharp frost had shrunk the netting, so that it had worked itself loose from a clamp. The run installed by Eddie is stronger and better. Now everything was fine, but I kept a special eye on Daimke on the following days. Sure, she would never just run away and she would be careful, because Daimke is very wise. But with this icy cold! Imagine her forced to stay outdoors for one night. I can't bear the thought of it!

Fortunately the temperature started to rise. Oh, spring! What a wonderful season! Every year it's a marvel again to see and hear nature waking up. What a difference sunshine makes. You feel elated and full of energy. The fluffies race around and play all day. Only Puddie had his itch again. Maybe that made him so edgy towards the other fluffies? Regularly, he chased Donsje so she had to hide under the cabinet. True, she's used to that kind of thing, but I didn't like it. Still, they are merely moods linked to the moon, stress and now, of course, to his itch. I can understand that it all gets on his nerves.

In March Raymonde came again. And then, with the help of Eddie and his son Roland, we painted the whole house. The weather was delightfully dry and warm and so the job was finished in two weeks. But oh, what a horror for the fluffies! My dear little girl Daimke especially was terrified. Rigidly she hid behind the curtain in the bedroom. That's her hiding place. In spite of the Bach flower remedies I gave her, she was terrified. I couldn't comfort her. She cut herself off. I must say, it was something to be afraid of! We were all in a dither. Wherever they looked, the fluffies saw ladders. Because the old paint had to be removed first, Eddie and Roland used blowlamps to burn it off. 'Not only were straightup-walkers constantly peering inside our house,' the fluffies said - who couldn't smell through the closed window who those straightup-walkers were - 'but also they kept on hissing their fiery tongues at us!' Puddie moved to the top of the climbing pole to watch everything from there with big, green eyes. He too was more than afraid!

This was the first time I found little spots of pee in the cabinet where I store envelopes. A sure sign that my fluffies were very upset, because normally they are absolutely clean. They seemed to do it especially there where the rubbish was. I got a fit of spring cleaning and started tidying away. That helped. Suddenly I thought of something else. I had just bought a 'moving' painting for my dear friend Leen Belder who was seriously ill. As I couldn't go to Numansdorp to give it to him, I had hung it in my office for the time being. It was a beautiful rendering of a splashing waterfall. Maybe the sound and the sight of falling water had induced my fluffies to urinate? I know that horses can be made to pee by turning on the tap and letting the water run. People too, by the way. Anyway, it betrayed that they felt insecure. I'll include information about urinating outside the litter tray and spraying in chapter 14. I felt terrible about it, but there was nothing I could do. The house had to be painted. Fortunately the job was soon finished and everything went back to normal. They were perfectly housetrained again. I had removed the painting, just to be sure, although I don't know if it really caused the problem.

But a much bigger problem arose. Even before the painting had started, I had noticed that Puddie was getting more and more annoyed at Daimke. Daimke is our elf. She just dances through the day. When she plays, she does it with total abandon. When she sleeps, she really sleeps. Everything in the extreme. I should use her as a model! 'Present Moment, Wonderful Moment!' Daimke also has a strong feeling for justice. She can't bear injustice and interferes immediately. Catje especially, her special friend, should at least be treated with politeness. And so she got into trouble with Puddie. In the beginning Daimke was full of awe for Puddie. Both are very Oriental and speak the same language. But I think Daimke loathes cursing and Puddie sometimes curses. The painting of the house had created much unrest. Daimke was very afraid of the ladders, the blowlamps and the people popping up everywhere, but so was Puddie. So, one morning, to work off tensions, Puddie chased Catje. Catje called in Daimke: 'Help, help, wiaawwwu, help!' Raving mad Daimke attacked Puddie and dealt him some resounding blows. Puddie resented Daimke's action very much **indeed**. Puddie is the king or the Pasha. This was sacrilege! Moreover he has his 'special' moods. He can't help it, but for the others it's not always easy to live together with him. I know that his aggression is, in fact, fear. Sort of 'the first blow is half the battle.' That's why he regularly feels like driving off the others. It's his way of stressing that he is the boss and always will be the boss. Only so he feels secure. The others seem to understand that. They accept it and just get out of his way.

But not Daimke! She has her pride and has learned from her mother, Little Princess that a kitty of Royal Blood never runs away! When Puddie is angry, he has the killer-look in his eyes. His tail gets three times as bushy as normal and he attacks to hurt. As Daimke is a tender cat with a thin fur-coat, I did not like it at all. I sometimes heard a dispute when I was in the garden, but in the beginning I preferred to stay out of it. We all have our differences of opinion and the arguments they entail. I did not want to make things worse by intervening.

Then, one day, I found my little Daimke hidden under a chair with a scratch on her little nose. She was really shocked and so were the others. Things could not go on like this! I had had enough of it. I felt so sorry for my brave little pussy-girl. I took her in my arms and promised her that I would make sure this would not happen again. It was no use being angry with Puddie. He acts like this precisely because he resents the fact that he has to share his life with other cats. All he wants is just to be alone with me. Period!!! He'll only accept other felines on the condition that they will be his subjects. Felines willing to kow-tow to him like Mickje, Donsje and Catje. So by being angry with Puddie, I would just make matters worse. He would say: 'Yes! I thought so! Mama is angry with me because the others came into my life. She never scolded me when we were together!'

It's a real miracle that things work out very well with Chummy, he being a tomcat! I had been so afraid Pudje would hate to have competition. Now, I must say you have to be very clever indeed to get into trouble with Chum. He is Mister Amiability in person and just leaves the scene if he is sworn at. He shrugs his shoulders, looks back and says to himself: 'What's all the fuss about?' Oh, I was so happy I had chosen a Britty. They are so full of inner peace! I tried to cuddle Puddie as much as I could, for love conquers all. When Puddie is lying on my lap - precious moments for both of us - he feels intensely happy and looks up at me with his eyes filled with love. Puddie is such a lovely boy. But he finds life very difficult, and makes it even much harder for himself than it is in reality.

Yes, I had to face the problem. I couldn't let Daimke and Puddie stay together in the room any more. I had to insert a 'time-out'. After that I could slowly let them get used to each other again. In the approved manner. I first put Daimke in an indoor kennel to respect Puddie's feelings. According to human logic I should lock Puddie in the kennel whenever he bothered Daimke, but that would make him even angrier with her. 'He is behind bars while Daimke runs around free in **his** room! What an injustice!' I am going to brush both of them with the same brush and also I will exchange their baskets so they take over each other's body smell. And then, when they don't hiss or hurl killer-looks at each other any more, I will try to let them be together again. They'll never be real pals, but a truce might be possible. And who knows, what if there were to be more space for them? A very good excuse to expand the run. So Eddie and I drew up a plan. It was going to be a beauty!

And Puddie wrote to his pen pals:

Er...ok, I'll just write it down, though I am not so proud about it. Again, my little fury-devil got the better of me and I attacked Daimke. Mama doesn't get it, but Daimke is always challenging me. I try to ignore that, but a couple of weeks ago I lost control of myself. Suddenly I got up and grabbed Daimke. We had a real fight. Marg was frightened and rushed after us. She missed a couple of times, but then got hold of me and put me outside in the run. Only then did I realise that I had been very wrong, but it was too late. Sad, sick at heart, I reclined in front of the window. Fortunately, Daimke was not hurt. Logical: ill weed grows apace. But I had to go outside, banished to the run! Later, mama put me on her lap and had a serious talk with me. She understood what I am going through and so we had it all out. I told her I was terribly sorry for what I had done and that I had not intended to react that way. It was something stronger than me that had taken hold of me.

'You know what, dear Puddie?' she said, 'Let's consult Carina about what we should do. Maybe she can give you some homeopathy so you will remain in control of yourself. Until that time I will not let you and Daimke be together.' Oh, I was so happy. Although I felt very much ashamed, I **had** succeeded in getting rid of Daimke's presence. 'Yes, Puddie, I do understand you. I also hated it when, as a child I had to share the room with other people who were real hairballs. Days before and after their presence I felt upset. Sometimes we meet creatures we can't socialise with. It's in their auras or it has to do with our previous lives. Still, I will keep on trying that you and Daimke, at least will tolerate each other.' Mama said and then cuddled me. I snuggled up to her while on her lap. Indeed, that is true love! Love one another in spite of our weaker spots, which we all have when all's said and done.

What about Daimke? Well, she told Donsje that she feels much better now as a matter of fact. After the walk she goes into the bedroom and Marg gives her some toys. That's much nicer for her than sitting full of tension in the living room. Admit it! The only one who doesn't like this arrangement is Marg, but she'll learn to live with it.

And than there is Chum, I don't know what I am to do with him. Just listen to this:
I am sitting next to mama, who is playing the piano. It is a privilege, to which I, being the oldest tomcat around here, am entitled. I am assisting Marg with turning the pages of the score, and so on. Suddenly that Brit brat popped up next to me. So I gave him a 'gentle' push and frightened, he jumped from the table. 'Puddie!!' mama said sternly. So I just jumped down as well. And then, Chum came to me, his head 'tomcattish-ly' up and tilted and...started nuzzling! **Nuzzling!** While just before I had him...I didn't get it. 'Well, Puddie, that's how a real English gentleman behaves,' Marg explained. 'This is an example of how to 'render good for evil', and, believe me, that really works!' Well, I didn't know what to think of it, so I just raced around the run a couple of times and then hid my frustration in a nice little hole. Admit it, this is not much fun! Now I can't chase Daimke any more and so I tried to take it out on my chum and what does he do? He starts nuzzling me! The life of a tomcat isn't easy, you know! Fortunately, I have read that you, Stapje, also have trouble with your co-fluffies. Sometimes you have to take action too. Well, that was just what I had expected from you. As you put it, someone has to keep order. You are a Tomcat or you are not!

242

Many purrings from your pen pal Puddie.'

Catje is such a special cat. She has a new habit of coming to ask for a titbit when I am playing the piano. She puts her paw in the palm of my hand. In fact she pushes up my hand from below as I am working the keys. It's such a terrific, lovely gesture that I am overwhelmed by it and of course give her some titbits. She is so smart. Chum has grown big and beautiful. When he enters the room and I greet him 'Hello, Chummy,' then, 'woops' his gorgeous long tail goes straight up into the air. So funny. Very cutely he approaches me to tell me that he loves me and then continues with what he was doing. At the moment mainly catching moths. I've seen a bumblebee fly past me, and there are ladybugs around now as well.

Mickje also is such a dear. She is so cute with her very high voice. When I give her her food she will never start eating before having thanked me by many 'thank-you'-mewings and a couple of firm butts of the head. She doesn't give shoves but butts. She loves to cuddle and tells me complete stories. She assists me when I'm working out on my home trainer in the morning. We tell each other about the dreams we had and philosophise about their meaning. She says that dreams are very instructive. I think she has a point there, as I mostly dream about my fluffies and about cats in general. Indeed, what the heart thinks... And there are no better teachers than cats.

Chum has found himself a new job: master-mosquito-catcher. It is a marvel how he goes about it. True, he has large paws so it would be difficult for him not to hit them. My bedroom has white walls and, of course, there are many mosquitoes around now, screens or no screens. When I'm reading at night, they usually sit on the wall behind my bed. Slowly Chum will get up - he's always on my side - and step by step crawl up towards them. When he is sure he can reach them, he'll lash out at them with both paws. Always bingo! It is marvellous to watch my little indoor-elephant, who can be as quick as lightning if necessary.

Since I had discovered the beginnings of tartar on Donsje's teeth, I decided to brush the teeth of my fluffies every day. I rub their teeth with special toothpaste for felines, which tastes of game. I use a child's toothbrush. But what matters most is that the toothpaste, which contains an enzyme that removes dental plaque, gets into their mouths. It's hard to really brush cat-teeth. It also has the advantage of them getting used to my touching their mouths, so it's easier to give them pills, if necessary. They queue up in the morning for this treatment. They love it.

Puddie still felt somewhat down. He didn't come to sit on my lap, as he used to do and he just looked sad, even though the living room was now off-limits to Daimke. I had noticed his sadness, of course, but instead of taking time out to sit down with him and find out what was wrong, I just continued my paper chase in the office. Believe me, paper runs quickly, so I had quite a lot of chasing to do! If only it would just run away and get lost! But it just makes rounds and so I always come across it again. I tried to give him extra attention, but that which we both love so much, writing together while he sits on my lap, just didn't happen.

Something was bothering him, but what? Suddenly - I was half-asleep and that's the best moment for telepathic conversations with Puddie - I knew what it was. Of course! Oh, how stupid! Poor Puddie! The other years, as soon as winter was over, he had been allowed to go to the lawn in front of the house. Sitting there was his delight. **He** was the **only** one allowed to move around there. That gave him special status. Eating fresh grass, catching butterflies and now and then some stupid mouse which crossed into his territory. Five pairs of eyes, belonging to five spectators in the run watched everything with fascination. If I saw him catching a mouse I immediately ran to him to negotiate its release with some chicken meat. Would he barter his poor prey for some delicious chicken? Proudly, the Pasha agreed. Right so, Puddie!

For some reason - probably due to the work-pressure - I had forgotten all about it this year. How stupid of me! So, I quickly turned the corkscrew-like spiral with the long line into the soil. I fetched the sunshade, a chair, a table and his little shelter against the rain and voilà, we had our Gold Coast in Brasschaat!

I went inside with his leash and yes, Puddie met me purring loudly: 'Purr purr, oh, mama, how wonderful! Can I really go? Oh, I am so happy, I found it terrible not to be allowed to sit outside. I thought you were still angry with me. Purr purr.' I had a lump in my throat. My dear little man! How discriminated he

244

must have felt when I took the others with me and he was not allowed to go to his special place on the lawn. I am glad he is not a human being. That kind of creature doesn't forgive so quickly. Soon everything was back to normal. Puddie took up his delightful habit of reclining in my lap. Oh, how both of us enjoy those delightful moments! And it was a fact that Daimke preferred to stay quietly in the bedroom. 'You will come especially to me to cuddle then and we will have time for us alone. We will play with the little ball and I will have you cosily for me alone,' she said purring loudly. ' And er, no, I am not jealous at all!'
…'Ehhh…is that so my little elf?'

To be honest… she is! Very much though. I am sure that's the main problem between Pudje and Daimke. They are so alike! It's a kind of projection. Daimke often teases Donsje a bit too much too. She does not want to hurt her really, but still, Donsje is certainly not amused. Luckily, I can prevent an escalation with the Bach Flower Remedies. It might be true what Pudje writes to his pals, that Daimke torments him too. It often irritates if you see your dark sides in somebody you meet! Daimke is a miraculous pussy-child. She can be scared to death by simple, totally harmless things and yet just remain sitting calmly when Puddie is about to attack her. And that is really dangerous! She does not mind the heavy equipment passing on the road. She jumps from tree to tree and rushes after flying leaves and the acorns I kick away. When the beautiful run was installed she hung on the netting wire to watch with keen interest Eddie and Roland lifting up and plopping down the heavy sleepers. What fear? But snow falling from the trees on the flat roof in the sleeping room makes her terrified. If somebody walks on the roof, she hides for hours behind the toilet bowl.

It is very important to realise that it doesn't take much to disturb the harmony in a feline household. Cats are very sensitive and take on immediately any stress their beloved people experience. The only way to find out what's wrong with your kitty is to talk with her. But feel **her** feelings! So change yourself into a cat and try to see and feel the world through her senses. Ask yourself in the first place: did I change? Am I too engrossed in my work and everyday life? Am I tired or ill? Am I feeling down or do I have problems with something? Because if you have, your cat will also have them! Have there been any changes inside the house or in the surroundings? Discuss it with her. Assure her that you are back to normal again and that you will listen to her. You'll get an answer. And

245

if you are honest with yourself, you'll have to conclude that it's mostly your behaviour that causes the troubles. It was great to see that my pussy-children were happy again. Thanks to the Lord, the house doesn't need repainting for some years to come. I am half a cat myself and hate pressure and change. The wonderful book Minoes by Annie M.G. Schmidt seems very familiar to me. The movie based on that book is very beautiful too.

The run was finished. It really was purrrfect! A dream came true! We were over the moon. It is seven metres long, four metres wide and two metres high. It is an extension to the living room run and there is that door between the two runs, which I had already asked to have made when the first run was constructed, so I that I could keep Pudje and Daimke separated. I have put tree stumps in it. They serve as chairs and I will also construct a real tree there, with side branches. I am very thankful to Eddie and his son Ronald for having constructed this run. They are real artists! It is a delight for Mickje and Puddie especially as those two spend most of the time in the living room. Along the sides we have put railway-sleepers, good for the fluffies to lie on and to sharpen their claws, and to keep their paws dry when it rains. It's fun to watch them trotting over the sleepers. Mickje lies in the grass for hours. Only her cute head with the golden flames sticks out. She enjoys it immensely. The girls fly through the run. Donsje rushes behind her tail, jumps into the air, races inside and then outside again.

Now Catje and Daimke can play delightfully in the new run when I take the dogs out for a walk. When it rains or it is too cold and Puddie can't be on the lawn, I bring Daimke for a while to the bedroom where she has her own run. When the weather is fine, Puddie can sit on the lawn and then Daimke can be released in the living room and run. And so everybody is happy.

To prevent my fluffies from sneaking out when somebody passes through the door, I have trained them never to pass the threshold on their own. I always carry them from one room to the other. Chum is a genuine British Shorthair. Every inch a gentleman with strong views. By mutual agreement he'll do everything for me, but he hates to be forced. He does not like to being picked up, but knows that there is no other way to get from one room to the other. Of course he likes to come with me to the living room. To the super-turbo-delightfully-large-run and so, he allows me to carry him. 'May I please, dear Chum?' I ask him politely…As soon as he has been lifted over the doorstep, he jumps out of my arms and proudly runs, his tail almost curled over his back from pleasure, in front of me to the living room. He will never go up the stairs or run into the kitchen. No, the living room is the destination and so he makes a beeline for it. Without looking to the left or to the right. Oh, he is such a dear funny big fluffy! I call him little Gold eye because he has big gorgeous golden eyes. He can look at me so cutely and wisely, with the same look he already had when he was a four week old kitten. Our Chum is a golden fluffy. I never hear him hiss or swear.

There are many dragonflies now. They are just tiny helicopters. They are a source of delight. Fortunately not one has been caught so far, they're so beautiful! Chum is very cautious in all his actions, but he can be as quick as lightning. Sometimes he turns real somersaults while trying to catch a dragonfly.

Just a moment ago, while walking through the garden with Donsje around my neck like fur, I heard the sound of squirrel paws. I stopped. Donsje got tense. About half a metre away from us a baby squirrel spiralled down the trunk of a tree. It was followed by another and then still another. Three babies so lost in their activities that they didn't notice us at all. They zigzagged up and down the trunk. I held Donsje tightly. Imagine if she caught one. She told me later she would never ever do such a thing. What a thought! 'No, mama, they are much too lovely for that. I'd never hurt them!' 'So, what was that low-pitched whining for?' I asked. 'Just like that, mama, 'she replied, 'the babies were chatting also!' Indeed, they were! So cute, just like little toddlers. Simply running behind each other mumbling sounds. Quickly I returned home. I put Donsje together with the others, fetched my camera and rushed out again to the tree, but the squirrels had vanished. What a pity! Still, an unique experience. We often see them in my little forest. Nature is at its best here! A little Garden of Eden, really.

Puddie amused himself very well on the lawn. Often I just went outside to sit with him. He then looked arrogantly at the others, who were confined to the run. 'Hey, look here! I am cosily alone with mama here while the rest of you have to stay in the run! Prrrr! Prrr!'

Puddie wrote in Poezenbelletje number 30:

'Hello, dear readers,

Wrrauuwee, how I'm doing? Er... I'm doing very well, thank you! And, ok, I really try not to be angry any more with Daimke, but sometimes that little teaser inside me gets the upper hand and then I feel like chasing her away. So, Marg has decided to keep us separate. 'But, I do love you, dear Puddie,' she assures me, 'I know what you feel. I've been under the spell of this ugly ano-devil Satano. So I understand there's some little devil inside you that sometimes gets the better of you. Let's fight those devils together. United we stand!' Aunt Carina Smeets, a friend of Marg and Aunt Maria and a homeopath, has prescribed some droplets which I really swallow. So you see, I'm doing my best. And now the big news. We have a marvellous new run, an extension of our living room run. Oh, it is such a delight of a run with real grass, moths, flies, beetles and lots of other thrilling creepy-crawlies. Wonderful, isn't it? Now we are looking for some tree trunks to make us a fine climbing pole. Purr purrr. We are very lucky fluffies. I wish you all had such a run. If I were a magician I'd conjure it for you before you could count to two!! Purr, prrr. Lots of purring prrreetings from yours truly, Puddie.'

It's the holiday season again, meaning dumping time for cats. It's horrible that so many cats are simply thrown away like trash! It depresses me. What kind of being acts like this? Usually those cats haven't been neutered and they have litters of course. Maybe an additional motivation to just get rid of the poor things? 'Dumping is easy and free!' Poezenbel has a special fund for neutering strays, but Poezenbel is a Dutch foundation and so it can't do much for the strays in Belgium. Fortunately I have permission to use the subscription fees paid by the Belgian subscribers for neutering Belgian cats. And we have quite a lot Belgian members now!

A woman I know, Marleen lives in a big town near a park where cats are regularly dumped. The poor animals roam around there, desperately afraid, disorientated and hungry. Some end up in an animal shelter and may find a new owner, but often they just are killed. That town is not known for its civilisation! The strong strays learn to survive and go wild. Marleen feeds those strays. Some are quite wild but others are rather tame and can be caught. With the consent of Maria we had them all neutered last year. I bought a few cat traps. Marleen captured them and took them to her nearby veterinarian. He checked them, examined their condition and - in case they looked unhealthy - tested them for FeLV and FIV. Fortunately nearly all cats tested were negative. He wormed and neutered them and clipped their ears to mark those that had been neutered. Afterwards Marleen returned the animals to the park where they now live free and happy and keep the area free from vermin. There were also kittens, but all have been re-homed.

Marleen adopted a cute white-and-black kitten, Felixje. Another dumped kitten, a lovely tortoiseshell found a golden home in the house of Marije, a friend of mine. It feels wonderful to be able to do something to reduce the suffering of strays.

In the week before Mother's Day, Marleen, on her way to Doctor Marc, was overtaken by another car. Nothing special, except that the car suddenly slowed down. The door was opened and something fell onto the road. Marleen looked back. 'What was it? A little ball?' But…it moved! The little ball moved! It was alive! It was a small cat! In a reflex Marleen rushed towards it and managed to pick up the poor fluffy, just before it was run over by another car. The road there is very busy.

Once safe on the pavement the two strangers looked at each other. The cute small black-and-white kitten and Marleen, her lifesaver. Both had had a terrible fright, but the kitten looked full of confidence to Marleen. 'I trust you, I'm sure I'm in good hands now!' Because of her own cats, Marleen was afraid to take her home and so she went first to Doctor Marc. Thanks to The Lord, the kitten had suffered no ill effects from her adventure. Not even a fear of people. You'd get scared to death of straightup-walkers for lesser evils! But not Mausie, as Marleen baptized her new friend. Mausie just purred when the doctor examined her. Doctor Marc is a kind veterinarian with a heart that goes out to animals. He didn't mind Mausie staying with him for a couple of days. In consultation with me Marleen had Mausie - when she had calmed down after a couple of days - neutered and vaccinated.

How does something awful like this happen? Probably it went like this:

A sweet little girl of about six years old nagged and nagged and kept on nagging for a cat. Her parents didn't want to hear about it, but when the cat of the woman next door had a litter, the mother gave in. The father, however, still loathed the idea of having a cat in the house. He kept birds and hated cats. But out of love for his daughter and out of consideration for his wife, he reluctantly agreed to put up with a cat in the house. And so Mausie came and grew up into a very lovely pussy. She made sure she stayed away from the father. Then the holiday time approached and the problem arose what to do with Mausie during their holiday-away-from-home. The woman next door was away as well and nobody could be found to take care of Mausie while they were away. The little girl cried and said she would stay behind to take care of her kitty but that was out of the question. 'Then she comes with me!' she sobbed desperately.

'Ok, have it your way!' the father snapped. An idea was developing in his mind. 'But I don't want any trouble, otherwise I will throw her out of my car!' Happily, the little girl selected a strong box for her cat and the following morning the family drove off. Mausie felt afraid and mewed all the way. Suddenly the father stopped the car and said to his wife: 'Mama, you drive, I am tired, let me take a nap.' So mama and her little girl moved to the front seat. Father moved to the backseat next to the box with Mausie in. The kid hesitated at first, 'Papa won't harm Mausie?' But the box was too big for the front seat.

For a while everything went fine. Suddenly the father took Mausie out of the box, opened the door and flung the poor kitty onto the road. 'That's it! Good riddance!' he thought with satisfaction, 'one problem less to worry about.'

Of course, you can make up lots of similar stories, but I think it's not far away from the truth. It's a miracle that Mausie didn't change for the worse. Her guardian angel must have been doing overtime!

I started thinking about finding a magnificent home for her. She really deserves the best basket there is. Maybe I could…? But no, I should not ask more pussy-children to live with us. That would not be fair towards my Magnificent Six. 'You have reached our limit, mama!' Puddie says and I know he is right.

A lucky coincidence (The Lord incognito), had made me visit Numansdorp, with friends a week before. We had been to my beloved manor, the Ambachtsheerlijkheid Cromstrijen, the 1800 ha enclosed agricultural area, which is almost completely car-free. It's a true paradise for the animals living there. Oh, the blessed years of my childhood! Well, in the middle of this vast farmland there stands a cute little house on top of a dyke. It overlooks the Hollands Diep, that majestic river along which many wild geese and ducks live. The little house is located in the little port where previously the sugar beets were loaded into barges. It's a dream to live there! It had been papa's and my wish to buy this house. Only, it was a bit too close to the industrial zone of Moerdijk with its stench and danger of explosion. So, in the end we decided not to buy it.

Soon afterwards the ABH was sold to an insurance company, the Amev. The estate was founded in 1492. Most of the time my family had run it and now, now it was sold. We were, of course very sad about it. But that did not help. Donsje says: 'It's wise to accept the things you can't change. Otherwise you make yourself ill for nothing!' Yes, she is wise our Donsje. At least, the activities went on as before. The farmhands, my friends should not lose their jobs! And the ABH was still the biggest manor in Holland. That was good. But still…

Jan and Corrie van Rij live in that little house. Jan was supervisor at the manor. At the beginning of this year I heard that Amev had sold the manor in its turn. This time the ABH ceased to exist. Half of the manor will remain farmland. The other half will be given back to nature. It will be a place to live for the geese, birds and other wildlife. Just like they did in our time! So why sell? In a way, that is a consolation. It could have been so much worse. There will be no factories or flats. 'Nature gives and nature takes', the saying goes. Now man gives… back to nature, the land he took first. That's good. But the farmhands have lost their jobs. Daddy lived for his work. The ABH was the most important reason for him to live. Just like it was for the other people who worked for him. They were one big family and loved the work. Suddenly all that they did for the manor did not seem important any more. They felt hurt and dumped, of course. But, from 'above', Daddy knows all now. All the whys and the wherefores. And as Donsje says:' It's no use crying over spilt milk.'

The couple always had cats and they loved animals. When we returned from France and were searching for a place to live in Belgium, Corrie and Jan were kind enough to provide a golden basket for Skippie, my dear red pussy, who had lived with us in the stables. He was so used to his freedom that it wouldn't have been fair on him to keep him in. Skippie had a delightful time with them and he was overjoyed. So, last week I visited them and learned that they didn't have a cat in the house. Skippie had died a couple of years before. 'Maybe you'd like to have another pussy?' I inquired carefully, 'I know you can't live without one. 'Weeeelll,' Corrie hesitated, 'But we are old! Jan is ninety. I don't know.'

I phoned Corrie and talked about Mausie. They wanted to think it over for a while. When I phoned again, she said: 'Why not, Mausie is welcome!' Oh, we were so happy! I found somebody who wanted to take Mausie to Numansdorp. When I called Corrie to inquire about Mausie, she was wildly enthusiastic:

'Such a dear of a cat! Full of love and trust and not afraid at all. She has explored everything and is now happily sleeping on the table.' Corrie still had Skippy's basket and toys. They stood ready for her when she arrived. When I went on a visit one month later, Mausie had grown from a puny she-cat into a gorgeous black panther. She and Jan hold real boxing matches. Every night is a party. Mausie had not been used to the outdoors, but now she enjoys her freedom to the full. I think that her place is the only place I know of where a cat can still roam around, without risking being hit by a car. It's off-limits to cars and strangers.

'All's well that ends well', for Mausie. I heartily wish that the monsters that dumped her have had a horrible holiday. What !@#$%^&* hair balls! But even out of such a low and mean deed something good may come. Not only Mausie is happy, Corrie and Jan enjoy her presence immensely. 'A life without a cat is no life at all,' Corrie said when I left. How true!

This beautiful poem seems specially made for Mausie:

AN ABANDONED KITTEN

How can I say no to an abandoned kitten?
I welcome it and warm and feed it
I'm moved by its sorrowful crying
Love always prevails and ties me
How sweet the magic of this dismayed creature;
How deep the pity that pervades me.
I stand moved and happy
And, as if by magic, I get lost.
Little tiny creature: as a vision you stand by me
You don't have your mother's tender care any more.
I can hug you; wipe your tears away
I can feed you and comfort you.
Later we'll be friends in perfect affinity
Now take a rest; good night and sweet dreams.
I'm close to you; you are alone no more.

© *Torre Argentina Van Leopoldo Di Persio (Un Gattino Abbandonato)*

Indeed my heart always beats faster when I drive into Numansdorp. I can see 'our' beautiful white house, on top of the dyke, overlooking the whole

252

Voorstraat. The cosy port with the Schippershuis (Captain's house) where such delicious food is served. So many memories of the golden days of my childhood. The beautiful river, the geese, the wind rustling in the reed. Not without reason did we christen our foundation: De Rietkat (The Reedcat)! The vast fields, the smell of mud in the air, especially during the sugar beet-harvest. But the sun-ripened wheat also has a delicious 'Welcome-Home-Aroma' for me. The office of the manor was situated on the ground floor of our house. When the workers waded into the meeting room with their dirty boots and made everything muddy, the cleaning women grumbled. Papa always replied: 'Never mind the mess. It's mud and mud we 'eat'! It is the source of our livelihood!' A variant on the title of a book by my dear friend Toon Kortooms: 'My kids eat peat' We ate mud!

Numansdorpers have a very special sense of humour. Everything has changed of course in the Equipment-shed. The small handy tractors we worked with are now replaced by enormous monsters with computers and air conditioning. But my two old friends were still there. Mud and Sludge they were called. The two old tractors I used to work with! In 2003, the commemoration day for the flood disaster in 1953, I went to say hello to them. It is great to think that Mausie is living there now.

It was Daimke's discovery and oh, how I loved it! The wastepaper basket next to my desk is usually filled with envelopes and papers. When Daimke feels bored she picks up her toy-mouse and throws it into the basket. And, of course, she must catch it then. But she can only catch it by sticking her head into the basket. So, it's not her fault when the basket turns over. The next problem: she can't find the mouse. So, she has to transfer every bit of paper to some other place. That's only logical, isn't it? The first time I fell for it and said to her: 'Oh, poor Daimke, just wait, I'll get the mouse for you.' So I picked up the mouse and threw it out. Big fun! She flew after it. I put the wastepaper basket up again, gathered up the papers and stuffed them back into it. As soon as I sat down again, bingo! There's the darned mouse again diving or better flung into the basket. 'Wiieehh, mama, help, my mousie 's gone again! Purr prrr.'

Another 'workhorse' doing overtime in the office is Catje. Frequently she acts as a hostess. Usually those are hired, but Catje works as a volunteer. She has taken it upon herself to make sure mama doesn't work herself into a burnout, so she tries in every possible way to make me stop working. For example by catching my fingers when they are clattering away on the keyboard. Just like

when I play the piano, she puts her little paw, with the pads upwards under my hand. It 's a funny kind of itch that makes me stop hitting the keys. Another very efficient Catje-trick is doing a headstand. Then she looks at me through her front legs with a wide grin on her face. Who can remain serious then? Anyway, she is our family's little jester and has the perfect poker face for it. Without giving the slightest hint of what she's up to, she sometimes just 'explodes', shoots straight up into the air and lands pretending to hit a ball with her paws. I can only see air but maybe she has seen some mouse coming down from the Rainbow Bridge for a short visit to the earth? In any case, cats do perceive more than we do and so they sometimes see beings from the hereafter. Sometimes cats fix their gaze on 'something' that's still hidden to me. How come straight upwalkers think themselves more intelligent than animals? What a nonsense! It's a sheer sign of ignorance that three quarters of humankind still believe that.

CAT

I'm really very proud to say
I am a cat in ev'ry way
from head to tail you'll clearly see
the sublimity of all of me

Yes
it's good to be such a perfect cat
except the loss for which
I blame the vet!

© *Slaapmuts*

As Daimke must have enzymes added to her meals, she gets her meals separate from the others. She can choose: either in the bathroom or outside in the run, and in that case I shut the sliding door for a while. But it's a hard choice for my girl. When it rains, it's easy, she goes in the bathroom. But when the weather is fine? Well, then she does a lot of pacing back and forth. I know the feeling. When I am too tired or have too much work to do, I can't make choices either.

Catje likes to play hide-and-seek. Of course she waits until I want to take her to the other room or take her out in the garden. That's more fun! For example, she vanishes under the cabinet. The last thing disappearing before my eyes is the tip of her tail. To 'catch' her, I have to lie down flat on the floor. Of course that's the funniest part of it. Two twinkling eyes watching me. 'Great, isn't it, mama?' Indeed, great! But to get her from under the cabinet I have to slowly roll her on her side, otherwise she can't get out. Recently I haven't had to roll her any more, she does it by herself. As soon as our eyes are in line, she rolls over. Some more exercise and we're going to perform in a circus-show!

'Miaauww miiwaauuwww, wheiieeee, raauww!' The fluffies gave a concert during our ride to Doctor Liliane for the vaccinations. You can take my word for it, it's a big job shuttling six pussy-children back and forth. Puddie behaves like a model ever since we just let him stand upright against me while he is on the examination table, his paws on my shoulder. If I hold him he will fight like a lion, but in this way he is calm. Daimke starts to shiver as soon as she smells 'doctor'. The whole cat-carrier shakes. Chum knows how to triple his weight, and he already weighs quite a lot. About six kilos! Would his weight then actually increase? They don't feel the little prick, but the fear hurts. How happy we were to arrive home!

Doctor Liliane vaccinates the dogs in my house. Cats are easier to treat when they are on the examination table, Doctor Liliane says. That's why she prefers us to go to her place. I was profusely complimented on their healthy looks. But then I brush them nearly every day and I give them plenty of cuddles and love. That's the best medicine there is.

In 'Miracles on little Feet', I said in the last chapter that there might be a sequel. And so we are very happy and proud that we have finished writing the first half of Purring Angels. Daimke, Catje and Chummy now also have 'their' book and they were entitled to their own book. The following chapters do not specifically deal with us, so this chapter concludes the story of our adventures.

The fluffies and I very much hope that 'Purring Angels' will be as well received as 'Miracles' was. Most of all we hope that this book will help many cats. We wrote it for that target and we have written it with so much pleasure.
Who knows some day this sequel will have its sequel...

But before going to chapter 13 I will tell about my lovely big Belgian Forest Cat Tommeke and about Karma. I am sure you will love them!

You will always be lucky if you know how to make friends with strange cats.
Colonial American proverb

TOMMEKE, OUR BEAUTIFUL BLACK BELGIAN FOREST-CAT

It was a cloudy, wet and cold day in November of the year 2004. My six kitties and I were sitting, warm and cosy around the fire. I looked at the rain which was pouring down. Suddenly I saw a black spot that I had never noticed before. It was nearly invisible, sitting in front of the small swimming-pool house, not far from the house. "Pudje, what is that?' I asked. We went to the window and suddenly 'the

spot' moved... 'Oh, look! Oh the poor cat!' I said to Donsje who had jumped on my shoulder. His long black fur was wet and he really looked miserable and thin. 'Mieewuww, that's our new friend. Didn't you know that he lives here too?' she asked. We are friends now.' 'No, I did not!' Quickly I went outside with some food and cat-milk. Of course he was gone as soon as he heard the door. I put the food inside the small house and left the door open. "Poor, poor cat", I thought; "what weather to be outside and lonely!"

The next morning the food was gone. So, at least he had a full tummy and a warm place to sleep. The small house is heated. Little by little we saw more of him. I called him Tommeke. The kitties told me that they often talked to him. He had had a rough life. As a kitten he was dumped in the forest. Just thrown away by a bad man, who did not want any more cats. 'One was enough and 'no' he did not bother to have the mother neutered. She would become a bad mouser!' That's what Tommeke had heard him say to his wife. He tried to survive on mice and other small animals. In the summer it was not too bad to be roaming, but now he was cold and lonely. Part of him longed to join us. But he had never learned to trust people. The ones he knew had treated him badly. Still... he came nearer and nearer. Did he feel our love for him? I am sure he did!

He looked like a big black Norwegian Forest Cat. 'Our Belgian Forest Cat', I told my kitties. He had the most wonderful green eyes I had ever seen. It took me a whole year to gain his trust. Finally I could get near enough to talk to him. Of course he had to be castrated and later vaccinated. That meant I had to trap him twice. He was not really amused. But he was such a sweet boy that he did not even hiss when he was caught.

All animals talk by means of telepathy to each other. They send thoughts in pictures. The wonderful thing about that is, that distance doesn't matter. Already as a kid, I had learned to talk that way to them. It really works and all animal communicators do so. What really amazed me was that Tommeke caught my thoughts so

clearly. I only had to think 'where is Tommeke?' when I was walking with the dogs and there he was, proudly sitting in front of 'his' house and looking straight at me. I had a health problem that winter. I often was in pain and - as I had not found the right cure yet - I felt lost and sometimes I was really sad. Somehow Tommeke always knew that and immediately he would come to my rescue. He would be there and would look straight at me with his beautiful green eyes saying: 'It will be OK, mummy! Don't worry, you will get rid of the pain and soon be well again!' In fact, only by looking at him I felt better already! I felt his love radiating straight through me. It was a wonderful feeling. It was so noticeable that, on bad days, I would say to the kitties. 'Tommeke will be there to take the pain away!' And when I opened the front door, there he was! It really was wonderful. Mariette noticed it too.

New year 2005 came and Spring arrived. Tommeke still had his long winter fur and he was not comfortable in it any more. I longed to brush him, but of course that was impossible. He didn't let me touch him yet. To my regret, I had to catch him again. He had lost his fur around his neck and I wanted to be sure it was not a fungal infection. Poor Tom, he is clever and it took more than a week before I could tempt him in the trap. I felt horrible when he looked at me with his beautiful green eyes, now so sad. 'I trusted you, I gave you all my love, and now, now... you trapped me! Why? What did I do to you? I was there when you needed me and now? Now you betray me! Mieewwwu!' But I had to take him to the vet.

Luckily, he did not suffer from a fungus but he had fourteen ticks! We have far too many of those horrible animals here in the forest. We took them off, put Frontline on and he got his second vaccination. Of course he had to be slightly anaesthetised. When we got home again, Tommeke was still half asleep. I took him to his little warm house and I sat by his side. I told him that I loved him dearly and that I wanted him to trust us. I promised him that I would never, ever hurt him and that he belonged here now. It was wonderful to be able to touch his silky long black hair and brush him. He looked at me with eyes full of love and he **did** like it!

Since that time he has trusted me. He came nearer and nearer and suddenly, on a lovely morning, he let me caress him. Oh, I had tears in my eyes. What a wonderful present I got from my big Belgian Forest Cat! Now, every morning he waits for me at the front door. We cuddle for a while and he tells me loud and clearly how much he loves me. Together we walk through the garden and it's great to see how sweet he and the girls are together. He is really polite to them and stops playing immediately if they tell him so! Even Pudje seems to respect him. Mickje is fascinated by him! They look a bit alike too. She is very proud at that! Often I see the kitties talking and playing with him from the inside of the run.

Of course I cannot restrict Tommeke. That wouldn't be fair to him. But if I don't see him, I am very worried. He is streetwise. That's a great advantage. I am so glad he does not wander so much any more. Still, I tell him every evening to be careful and I pray to St Francis to watch over him.

I am sure Tommeke is the reincarnation of one of my former cats, Ginger, who went to the Rainbow Bridge a long time ago. He was a wonderful soul and so sweet. Just like Tommeke. He has healing power. 'Not all angels have wings' and Tom surely is an angel. Cats are such lovely sensitive and faithful souls. If only people behaved more like cats, the world would be a much better place.

KARMA, MY FOREVER-DOG

'Please Mama, I am so tired. I will try to fight so that I can stay with you for a few more days but then... Please mama, may I go then? I am so, so tired. I don't want to go! I honestly wish I could stay with you and with Luckje and Pudje. You know how much I love you. But ...

Those words I read in the eyes of my beloved Shorthair Collie, Karma. All night I had stayed with him. He was so ill. With his head on my knees we talked. 'Do you remember all the wonderful things we did together, dear Karma?' The long walks in the forest. How you loved running around in the garden with Horry, your little friend? How you helped me to overcome the anorexia I had for thirty-five years? How we stayed at Daddy's bedside when he had to cross over to the Light nearly ten years ago? You knew then, didn't you that he would die? You tried to comfort me. How you helped me and urged me to eat more, to start fighting to get well again. I was extremely thin by then and nearly dying from starvation and now, now ... I looked in your eyes and saw your plea. Luckje, my wonderful black and white cat was lying at your side and looked at me with big worried eyes. 'Please mummy help Karma to go to the Rainbow Bridge. Please, he needs to go!' Yes, Luckje was your great friend.

 I had to make the decision soon. But also I felt that Karma hated to leave me. He felt my immense sadness. 'It's OK Mummy, I feel the warm loving Light already. I will be happy there and I will feel no pain any more', he said. Don't be sad. I promise you that I will sent you another dog, so you won't have to take your walks alone'. You will see! Please don't cry!' I wanted to say that I only wanted him, no other doggie!

But instead I told him that he was free to go to that wonderful place, The Rainbow Bridge, where Fern, Mummy's Cardigan Corgi, who died two years before, would await him. 'And we will never really part, dear Karma. Love never dies! You will come and visit us. And later we will meet again!'

Yes, it was a wonderful day when my dear friend entered my life. I had always longed to have a Shorthair Collie. But Daddy only wanted shooting dogs, Labrador- and Golden Retrievers. Of course I loved them too. I knew that it was just a question of time before ... I would find my collie-friend. Then I heard about a breeder whose lovely Shorthair Collie was about to have little ones. When I telephoned, he told me I could have number six. The others were already reserved. Anxiously I waited for the phone call. There were five doggies born, so no puppy for me. A few weeks later he telephoned me that he had heard of a poor four-year-old Shorthair collie, who lived in a dark barn. He had been the 'beloved' dog of a young couple, but they had divorced and the dog just stayed behind. 'Will you not give him a good home?", the breeder asked hesitantly. 'I have seen him and he is a sweet dog. But also he is in a pitiful state.' Of course I said yes. To put a shorthair collie in a barn is a horrible thing to do. They are such sweet natured dogs. They ought to be a real member of the family. They live only to please their people. They are also very sensitive dogs. He must be terribly hurt, being dumped like that! What a shame! I loved him already.

A woman brought him to us. When he came out of the car I couldn't believe my eyes. He could hardly walk. Oh, the poor boy, he was so thin and dirty. But the most horrible thing was the empty look in his eyes. He had given up. He just did not mind any more what happened to him. It took the girl exactly five minutes to clear out the car and she was gone. 'Good riddance too!' I thought. What a way to treat your dog! My parents were shocked too and very glad Karma was one of us now. He was safe. As soon as we were alone I washed him. Under his dirty grey-yellow colour a beautiful black and white coat was hidden. But oh, how thin he was.
Next morning I asked my vet to come and he said that Karma had a very weak bowel. A kind of IBS and also he had an autoimmune problem. His nose had eczema that never really got better. The IBS we got under control with a special diet and natural remedies. Very slowly, with the right medicines and much love and cuddling Karma gained weight. He taught me the importance of eating good healthy food and for the first time since I had had anorexia, I realised the importance of gaining weight. And to be thankful if that was still possible!

When Karma got stronger I started training him. Obedience and agility. We both loved it. But it took half a year before he really dared to start loving me. One morning, when we were walking in the garden, he suddenly jumped high in the air and started to run in small circles around me. He smiled and was so happy. I had tears in my eyes. Finally Karma took the risk of being happy again. He wanted to live, he was saved.

When Daddy, and shortly afterwards Beltza, his beloved Labrador had crossed over, my mother fell and broke her knee. She became totally immobile. I was very thin by that time and felt that I had to make a decision. Either I started eating now or I would join Daddy! That's what Daddy told me, one morning while I was walking in the garden. I clearly heard his voice: "Do you really want to die, Marg? Do you want to leave mummy and Karma behind? Or are you going to fight as I taught you to, years ago? I taught you never to give up, didn't I? Now, don't let me down! Don't let them down! Go to a dietician today! Promise!' It was then, that I realised how far gone I was. I looked in the beautiful eyes of Karma and saw his worry and sadness. 'No, please, please, Marg, don't leave me. I don't want to be abandoned again. Please! We have so many wonderful things to do. You begged me to live when I was so ill. Well, you saved me and I showed you the importance of eating. Now I beg you to start eating and get strong and healthy again yourself!' I hugged him and promised both Daddy and Karma I would fight. And so I did. But without Karma and Pudje, who joined us later and of course Luckje, I would never have made it. Satano, the anorexia devil is a very smart adversary.

And now I had to let Karma go. It was the last thing I could do for him. I called my dear Vet friend Liliane and he went to sleep peacefully in my arms. I felt lost of course. I missed him terribly but … I had to accept it.

A few nights later I dreamed about him. He was running in an enormous green field with the other dogs and was healthier than he ever had been on earth. It felt so good! But the empty place in the house…the lonely walks in the garden, they were reality too! Then Karma sent Femke to us. Of course I loved her from the first moment I saw her, but I still miss Karma.

But he is not really gone. Sometimes I feel Karma's head under my hand, when I am walking in the garden. He had that special, sweet gesture of putting his head under my hand, we often walked like that for hours. Just happy to be together. A few weeks after he had gone and Femke was still too small to go walking with me, I felt Karma's head for the first time. No, I did not imagine it. I really felt it! I often felt him around too. And still now, nearly ten years after he had to go, he comes and visits us. I wonder if he ever will come back as a reincarnation. But I am absolutely sure that we will never be separated. Real love never ever gets lost. Karma My Forever dog, we will meet again.

Chapter

Angels and Anorexia

Cats never say unkind things. They never tell us of our faults, "merely for our own good." They do not at inconvenient moments mildly remind us of our past follies and mistakes. They do not say, "Oh, yes a lot of use you are if you are ever really wanted" - sarcastic like. They never inform us, like our inamoratas sometimes do, that we are not nearly so nice as we used to be. We are always the same to them.

Jerome K. Jerome 1859-1927

On a sunny morning in January I got a phone call from the television company TV1. They asked if they could come and take some shots of my cats for their much-watched television programme Afrit 9 (Exit 9). Of course they could. 'Purr, prr', how thrilling! It's a fact that television reaches more people than books or newspapers. I wrote 'Miracles on Little Feet' to tell people what lovely, sensitive beings cats are. They are old souls, knowing so much more than we do. They have access to other dimensions. If reading my book could encourage people to love their cats even a tiny bit more, then I would be extremely thankful. Television has the extra advantage of showing the message in pictures.

Three very friendly men, lugging heavy cameras, entered my house. They stayed all day. It was interesting to observe their professional handling of the matter. Of course my kitties were not too keen on this in the beginning. But my Donsje-girl has gradually developed into a real starlet. She knows now that people always mean tasty titbits and sweets. 'You have to be prepared to suffer some hustle and bustle in return!' she told Puddie, who had retired to the highest place possible.'Well, you just bring me some titbits,' he

answered, 'I don't move from here!'
The topic was: How animals in general and cats in particular can help people that are ill or disabled. Especially in the case of anorexia.

TV1 knew that I have had anorexia for thirty years and that I managed to escape from that desolate and cold Anorexia-land. I had told them that I owed my healing for a considerable part to my dear Karma and Pudje. They motivated me to eat more and to enjoy life again. They were my reason to live. And I am not the only one! I often got letters from girls who told me that they had experienced exactly the same. 'Do you know I also had anorexia or bulimia and got tremendous support from a pussy-child?' The TV-people wanted my story. They wanted to know how a dog or cat could help to defeat Satano.

'Well', I told them, 'in fact it's only logical. Generally, anorexics are hypersensitive, intelligent and spiritual beings, just like cats. They love order and a well-regulated life. They hate the unexpected. Precisely to avoid that, they moved to Anorexia-land! Many Anorexics prefer to be on their own, that's true. Often they have had bad experiences in their youth. But, deep inside they long for love and tenderness. Every living being does. Still, it's impossible to live with another human being. But a kitty can give even more love than most people can. And that love is unconditional! As an anorexic, you look desperately for security. That's why you have made for yourself many rules. They give you the feeling that you have everything under control. You need them to be able to survive. But the 'others' think you are nuts. A person who has not had that horrible illness can't understand the fears you have. It's not his or her fault. They just don't have a ticket to live in anorexia-land. Well, cats have! They too are fond of love, peace and quietness. Cats and anorexics are companions, soul sisters and brothers. They understand each other!

But there is more. When as an anorexia-patient you start really eating, you expect to become as round as a barrel in no time. One sandwich and you are 'Garfield'! You are convinced that then the few persons who still love you will turn away from you and consider you a failure. That's why the step to start eating again is so hard to take. Don't forget there is this demon inside you, Satano (Satan and ano) who took control of your life. He brainwashed you. 'Hey?' your kitty asks you, 'Do you really believe I'll stop loving you when you eat well? Quite the contrary, I'll have more 'you' to love. Why, a cosy warm and well-filled tummy is a delight to lie and purr on, purr purr.' That's called unconditional love. Something extremely rare in the world of humans. Your cat regularly comes to remind you that it's time to eat and she enjoys her meal so much that, in spite of yourself, you feel like eating too. Her subtle humour and her crazy antics will pull you out of your gloomy moods time and again. Really, she knows very well when you are down.

Nothing is more delightful, when you lie exhausted, sad and hungry under the covers - shivering with cold in spite of the heating - than a warm purring cat-body snuggling up against you. At last you calm down after a long day of battle with Satano. And such a model she is! No animal knows better than a cat how to enjoy and to relax. For hours she can meditate on her back on the windowsill, her paw over her nose. That inspires peace, even though your ever present arch-enemy forces you to keep exercising. Cats are first-rate pleasure-lovers and the shining example which anorexics badly need.

You can't have ano for thirty years and get away with it. So, I often have pain as a result of osteoporosis. Mostly in my neck and shoulders. Donsje senses it immediately and then drapes herself around my shoulders like a warm (and purring) scarf. Bye-bye pain! That's why I say: Cats are just little anti-depressiva on feet. They're better than whatever therapy! 'Not all angels have wings.' No doubt about it! Cats are Angels sent by Our Dear Lord to help us in difficult times. Of course dogs are equal givers of support and love. Indeed, Karma and my pussy-children have rescued me.

I received many reactions to the broadcast. They were all very positive and oh, we were so happy about that. 'It should have lasted thrice as long!' I heard many times. I received a very moving letter from a very special woman who lives together with her two angels, Loesje and Dias, two gorgeous Siamese. She's had anorexia for ten years now. She gave me permission to publish her letter:

'Dear Marg,

*I am so happy I saw you in Afrit 9 (Exit 9). **Finally** another person talking with so much love about her cats. I am often afraid to tell others how much they matter to me. How they snuggle up to my cold body in bed at night. I feel safer with cats around me than amidst people, certainly when I am with men! I have two cats at the moment, but I hope that, in the future a third gift will come out of heaven. Yes, for me they are angels, disguised in the body of a cat, who came to me to help me.*

But I still have such a hard time and I am still very much a prisoner of Satano! Your strength and joy of living touched me. In you I perceived the freedom I so fervently long for, apart from whatever the outside world thinks or expects. I have suffered from anorexia for more than ten years now. Also, traumas from my childhood have distorted my soul. It is as if I couldn't continue living in my body.

But I don't want to pity myself. I am someone who, in spite of everything, keeps on believing in the great power of Love. And every moment in which I can open up for a while is a blessing. The love of my felines, the sun shining today, the crocuses now brightly blooming! But the physical and mental exhaustion are often too much to bear. Then I am powerless when the destructive force gets the better of me.

In your eyes, however, I perceived new hope and a voice telling me not to give up. If it's possible for you, I'd like to get in touch with you and I would love to read your book. Can I order it?

Warm greetings H...and pussy-children'

I answered her the same day.

'Dear H...and fluffies,

Oh, what a moving and beautiful letter you wrote! Many, many thanks. The pictures are wonderful! How beautiful they are, your kitties! Siamese are so special. My Puddie is half-Siamese and I love him so much. Because he was my only pussy-child for the first years, we have a strong bond. Indeed, since I was a little child I have only felt one hundred percent at ease with my animals.

266

People can hurt so much, often at the moments you don't suspect it. As a matter of fact I feel more 'feline' than human. I am extremely grateful you have your two guardian angels. They will help you more than any human being could do! Because of them you will defeat Satano!

How terrible for you that you had so many bad experiences in your childhood! It a shame! No wonder you took refuge in Anorexia-land. You know, things don't just happen. Everything in life has a reason. Also, this life here on earth is only one of the many lives we have to pass through on our way to a higher dimension. And you may be sure, our beloved cat- and dog-children will be waiting for us there in the case that they left before us. Our bond with them is eternal. When we come back to earth - and we have chosen to do that - we have lost our memories about what happened in our previous lives. That's why it is possible that somebody who has had a delightful childhood still ends up in Ano-land. It could be that she has to redeem a karma from a previous life. In your case it is pretty clear why you have an eating disorder, but that's not much help to you. More important is that you should be aware of the fact that you really can heal!

Maybe, from now on, you should ask yourself the following question anytime something happens: 'Why does this happen to me? Can I learn something from it and how can I change this negative thing into something positive?'

My karma was that I had to learn to conquer my fear of failure. Also I had to learn to say 'no'. When I was young, I was not allowed to have my own borders. I didn't even know I could have them. Now that I can say 'no', everything goes smoother. Your karma might be the same. People have intruded upon you so much that it is as if you have to learn to live all over again. Anorexia is an escape. We feel relatively secure in Ano-land. We **think** we are in safety there, but in reality the anorexia-devil has taken over the command of our life. He is The Big Negativist. And believe me, he is the meanest rapist there is. That horrible creature deep inside you, that forbids you to eat, to relax and to enjoy. In short, he forbids you to live. And you give in, because you never learned to say 'NO!' Fear is his comrade-in-arms.

Yet, you prefer that kind of life - no matter how cold and sad you may feel - to the big insecurity any change may bring. You know what you have, but you don't know what you'll get! Moreover, the leap from Ano-land to 'normal' land is too big. That's one of the reasons why many girls even won't start trying. The 'normal' life seems so unattainable to them. Besides, they don't **want** to join in the rat race.

Professor Myriam Vervaet wrote a wonderful book about anorexia, 'The secure Hell'. She is a very competent and compassionate doctor. And that is so important. As she puts it: 'To flee from emotions is a strategy of survival. Addicts or persons with eating disorders are fleeing from themselves and their problems. They want to be away from the world for a while. They prefer being 'dead' for some time. Because being 'dead for a while' is less hurting than having to face the chaos in your mind. The problem is that this solution works only in the short term. In the long run it mostly proves destructive.'

Before, doctors used the carrot-and-the-stick approach. If the patient added the required kilos within the required period, she got permission to, for instance, go out or to receive visitors. If she failed, she was punished! She got room confinement, without books or television. But why would punishment work? If your kitty pees on the sofa out of fear and you punish her, she will get much more frightened and will certainly not stop doing it. Only if she feels safe enough she will use the litter tray again. You should cuddle her and tell her how much you love her. You have to give her confidence.

You might say that many things in life happen out of Fear or out of Love. All bad things originate from fear, all good things originate from love. Love conquers **all** but it has to be there. Punishment always breeds fear. Nobody moves to Anorexia-land for pleasure. It is, as Professor Myriam also says, a strategy of survival. Often a last resort to survive. When you take that away - by forcing someone to eat - **and you do not give her anything in return**, then you deliver her completely into the hands of Satano.

Indeed, Professor Myriam says it so beautifully. 'The chaos in your head is too hard to bear and therefore you flee to Ano-land.' Because there, you don't feel so much pain any more. You will get more and more obsessed by 'eating-not-eating- and- exercising.' There is no more room for other thoughts or matters. The chaos in your head is still there, but now it is limited to those three things. That feels more secure. You think that you have, at last, come to grips with life again. And that is Satano's surreptitious action! He has taken control of your life, but he gives you the illusion that it's you who has life under control again.

In the long term, anorexia always leads to serious problems and possibly even to death! It is the most deadly mental disorder. That says a lot!

Only when someone feels secure she will dare venture into a fight with Satano. But as a result of under nourishment and total exhaustion, her body is constantly in a condition of panic and alert. She certainly does not feel secure! The body needs food and causes you to be seized by panic. And it is right too! It's an extremely dangerous situation you are in. Your body is now in the flee or fight mode. You feel more and more restless. Your body sends you hunting as it were. 'Hurry, go get some food, I need food otherwise I will die!' Your body is wise, so wise. But your mind is under the spell of Satano, who cleverly uses your feelings of agitation to make you exercise. 'Move! Come on, move! And more and more! And no! Certainly don't go hunting for food.' The weaker you get, the stronger Satano gets. Until...until your body gives up. I know, I have been down that road before. I had almost reached the point of no return. Only, I realised in the last moment what was happening to me. I looked into Karma's anxious eyes, he was desperately afraid. My powers continued to diminish. He watched me, when we were walking, and saw me sometimes floating out of my body from exhaustion. Then he came running to me and pushed his head against my hand. 'Mama, please don't leave me,' he implored. 'What will happen to me if you're not there any more? Please, please eat! When I came into your life I was as thin as you are now, and look at me now, I have grown strong and healthy. Only because I ate! Please, start eating more!' I didn't have my pussy-children at that time. If I had, I even might have changed my life sooner. But I felt what Karma was trying to tell me.

For a long time everything went well. I survived on insufficient but healthy food. But those days were over. 'If you have anorexia,' my father's doctor had said, 'you will get into serious trouble. It might be soon or it will be later, but trouble you will get!' How true! I weighed a mere 43 kilos. I had to do something, but oh, the fear to eat more! It was so strong and I was so weakened. I realised I could not manage it by myself. I also didn't know how much food I needed and what kind of food. I only knew all about calories. I was a 'walking calorie-table! So, I consulted an expert, Marleen, a dietician, who became a real friend. I surrendered myself, body and soul, to her. She knew how to control Satano. That was the beginning of my healing process.

It is such a pity that one does not realise that you don't **have** to seek refuge in

Ano-land if you can't bear your life any more. There are other, much better places. You can move to 'Health-land', your own land. The land in which you can live just as safety, also without being forced to do things you don't want to do. It's a land in which you can also stick to an eating-living-scheme, so that you have the same legitimate excuse not to do things you don't like. That was one of the reasons why you went to live in Ano-land, after all. Of course, this time, it is a good and healthy eating-living-scheme. A scheme that you drew up together with the dietician. Take the good things from Ano-land with you and leave the bad and compulsive habits behind. Stay for a while in your 'own land'. From the vantage point there, you can consider moving little by little into the ' big, bad, dangerous world'. Just go slowly and calmly. Realise that you can always move back to your own land. You will read the happiness and joy in the eyes of your fluffies once you start getting healthier and happier. They knew very well that you were ill and they were terrified. Not only for you, but also for themselves. They are really worth fighting for! They need you so!

Only when the anorexic recognises that she has become too weak to fight and is willing to hand over the responsibility for her weight to the expert in that field, the dietician, only then she will escape from Ano-land. Not only you will need someone to tell you what healthy eating is all about, but also your body image is completely distorted. You feel bloated and thick while the others see only skin and bone. You can imagine how horrible you will feel when you are actually putting on weight. And that's not only between the ears. You are really going to feel physically all kinds of strange things. Your hormones get into action again. You feel literally ill, miserable and confused. These are also withdrawal symptoms because you miss the endorphins, the body's own morphine, which the brain produces when you're starving yourself. Another powerful weapon of Satano, because you really have to 'kick the habit' when you start to eat more. Also your feeling about 'hunger' or 'satisfaction' is completely gone. For so long you stopped listening to it, that it has given up and stopped warning you. The dietician can help you with all this and put your mind at rest. It's all part of the healing process and you have to get through it, there's no other way.

Two things are important:

First, start or keep exercising, but with moderation. Doing a lot of sport produces endorphins and so you'll be less troubled by withdrawal symptoms.

Moreover, you'll be less bothered by oedemas. Many girls get oedemas when they start eating more and gain weight. That's such a horror. You feel so puffy and fat! It's disheartening!

Secondly, do try to do something that really interests you. You must have a purpose in life. Working is the best thing to do, because it schedules your day. You could start with volunteer work. Structure is very important, otherwise you'll brood the day away. And...be sure, you can count on Satano to make sure you will brood!

As you grow stronger, you'll better be able to challenge Satano and get him under control. At a given moment, all of a sudden, you'll notice that you are not obsessed by food and weight any more. You will enjoy eating, but many other interesting and thrilling things will have entered your life as well. Now you'll 'eat to live' while in Ano-land you lived to 'have permission' to eat. In your Own Land you will lead your own life, in which you decide what **you** want and what you don't want. You have taken with you the good things from Ano-land and left behind the bad things. You are free!

Why are we so afraid to put on weight?

I think - I'm speaking for myself now - that a feeling of emptiness inside us causes our longing for food. Why it is there, I don't know. Maybe it is some unconscious longing for our previous lives in the hereafter, where everything was so beautiful and peaceful. Maybe this emptiness is the result of abuse in your childhood, of some trauma. Maybe you were often humiliated and you learned to distrust people. You lost the ability to love, while you long, deep down in your heart, for a real friend, a companion for life. Eating helps to fill up that emptiness. But just that makes it so frightening. You can't go on eating. As soon as you stop, the emptiness is back at full force. And then there is no escape from your emptiness any more. It is dangerous to eat to get rid of that feeling. You should eat for your health and because you like your food. Try to get rid of the 'emptiness' in another way. Doing sport will help, for instance.

It is very important for bulimia-patients to be aware of this too. They don't stop eating till they are stuffed with food and then they have to vomit it. Of course they feel awful afterwards and much more 'lonely'. Moreover, it is much more pleasant to be able to eat something every two hours, instead of gorging yourself and then have to wait a long time before you can eat again. Even if you got rid of the food, you dare not eat any more that day. You feel so endlessly dirty, ill and sad then. It really isn't worth it. I tried it for some weeks, but stopped because I found it irresponsible to throw away food while so many stray animals are starving. I saw the wonder in the eyes of my dog and the kitties when I spoilt all that food. 'Mama, what are you doing? Are you ill? Why do you cry?' But I also stopped because this food stuffing didn't solve anything. The emptiness returned with great intensity as soon as I stopped eating.

Miguella, my friend and medium, once gave me a reading. She saw that I was very lonely in one of my previous lives. I tended a herd of sheep. She saw fields and heather. It was in some hilly region in Germany. I had a hard life. My parents had died along the road. A wise herb gatherer brought me up. She had found me and I was helping her in her household. I learned to card wool and to spin. I tended her sheep and learned to help people. That woman has become one of my guardian angels. I have suffered much hunger. Wherever I was, I was always afraid to eat. If I was too expensive to keep, I might be abandoned again. That reading explains a lot. For years, eating was the ultimate joy for me. The only moment when I really could relax. That was the reason why I ate as few calories as possible in as big a volume as possible, so I could take a long time over it. Eating was also the only time when I could forget the problems of and the sorrows about my very ill parents and the other troubles that were hurting me. But eating makes you 'fat', that's what I thought then. And that was the reality in my brainwashed head. Eating was dangerous, because when I ate I lost the 'permission' to eat. And then …then I felt the sadness and the emptiness even more. So I dared to only eat the bare minimum. Only then did I have the certainty that I could, at least always eat **that**. Although it was indeed a minimum, I still had that refuge. If things were rough I could say: 'O.K. Marg, in half an hour you can eat and stop worrying'. I could look forward to it. I ate just enough to survive, but not enough to live. And certainly not enough to enjoy life. And that's what the Good Lord wants us to do, here on earth! I still don't understand where I got that idea! Nobody can forbid me anything, except if I permit it. But I was very sure of it. Inspired by the then dominating 'thin is in, fat is bad'-fancy. I didn't care less about my appearance, but I wanted to please my parents. When I was teenager I had a bit of 'puppy-fat'. Mamma and Papa kept on nagging that I ought to loose some weight. How they regretted that when I had become an anorexic! Of course they could not have foreseen that. They only wanted to be proud of their daughter.

And so I have had ano for years. Now I know how much a person can eat without putting on weight. If you eat well, healthy and regularly, you won't add **more** weight than your 'set-point weight'. This is the weight your body needs to function optimally. It will try to keep this weight, at all costs. 'Yes, but', I can hear you think, 'there are so many fat people!' Indeed, that's correct, but everybody is subject to the law of cause and effect. When somebody stuffs herself often enough with 'bad' food, or starts binge eating, of course her weight will increase. Think of the poor force-fed geese who have to suffer so much, only because some 'hairballs' want to eat their livers. A real shame! The set-point-theory works, but you must observe the rules and be very careful with food that contains white sugar. That's dangerous stuff. You must follow a healthy and good eating-living-scheme. That means: about one and a half-hour of walking every day and a well-balanced diet, drawn up with your dietician.

I believe in the Orthomolecular medicine. It has helped me so much to get healthy again. Orthomolecular medicine describes the practice of preventing and treating disease, by providing the body with optimal amounts of substances, which are natural to the body. The orthomolecular way of living is wonderful. It means that you should eat many vegetables and fruit. Good, healthy carbohydrates, brown bread and things like that. No white bread and no sugar. Fish is very good, not too much meat, preferably poultry and also, this is very important, you should eat enough good fats. Olive oil and linseed oil! They are absolutely necessary for your health. It's nonsense that they make you fat. On the contrary! For decades people got the advice to only eat foods low in calories and fats. Well, three quarters of the population is too fat. It's an epidemic in America. Olive oil, Linseed oil and fish oils do not make you fat. On the contrary. They keep you healthy and slim and keep your cholesterol in order. Margarine is not good for your health, whatever the authorities may tell you. Don't eat it. Marleen explained all that to me. She told me that you have to eat 7000 calories to add one kilo. This means that if I keep my weight by consuming, for instance 2400 calories daily, I will only gradually put on weight if I eat about 500 calories extra daily. In principle I should then add one kilo in two weeks. But our body doesn't function that way! It must first be able and **willing** to absorb the calories. And that can only happen if you consume that extra food in the right proportions: as regards carbohydrates (sugars), lipids (fats) and proteins (albumins) and with sufficient vitamins, minerals and trace elements.

Your metabolism will increase then. You will burn up more calories and so you have to eat more again. Just think of a smouldering fire in a stove that hardly keeps burning, because of the pitiful little coal you throw on it (cold). It doesn't draw because no heat is released. The ashes accumulate (constipation). Suddenly you get the idea to poke the fire and to slowly (otherwise the fire will just be quenched and die) add a quantity of easily combustible (digestible) coal. The fire flickers...will it catch or go out? The stove is cold, the chimney dirty and humid. But then, yes suddenly it feels a warm glow and it starts to hum softly. It gets air, air at last! Pretty soon the stove begins to radiate a salutary warmth. It gets energy. It feels well and happy again. At last! All people and animals sitting around it also feel warm and satisfied. 'More coal!' they call. 'More warmth!' The harder it burns the more coal it consumes. Now, just be honest: did you ever see a stove growing fat? Something to think about, isn't it? More coal, faster combustion, more warmth.

My advice is to consult a competent dietician. Draw up an eating-scheme in consultation with her, by mutual agreement. What I mean is that she will give you a basic scheme to which you add your own preferences in agreement with your dietician. So you will know for sure that your scheme is healthy and that you will still enjoy your food. It must be a scheme about which **you** feel good and that you can follow for the rest of your life. On top of this scheme she'll give you an extra 500 calories that you need to put on weight. If ever you are fortunate enough to reach your set-point weight - that's often terribly difficult - then you might want to cut down on those extra calories. But never ever touch your basic scheme. You will always be able to eat that. Up till now, I never had to cut down on the extras.

You must promise this to yourself! One of Satano's most fruitful tricks is to say: 'O.K., go on and eat your fill! Soon, very soon, you cannot do that any more. You will have grown fat and that means: no more food for you! Hi, hi, hi!' Yes, he feels threatened and will put up a mighty fight. So, you must reply him in kind: 'shut up, you hairball! I will only talk with you when I have reached my set-point weight. Get lost!' Don't argue with the creep, you are too weak still and you will lose at this moment. Just ignore him and stop all your negative thinking. From now on just concentrate …not on having to be thin but on growing delightfully healthy and strong.

Some wonderful weapons to fight Satano are humour and the 'Red-therapy' (Save-therapy). The latter is a variation on Professor Diekstra's Ret-therapy: Not the **incident** determines your feeling and your behaviour, but your **view about it**. That's why it is important that your view about it is based on reality and not on some disorganised concoction by your brains. To find this out, you have to do the four-questions-test. If one or more answers to these questions are negative, your view is wrong and you should think again. ANTS, automatic negative thoughts can really spoil your life. (And I do love those little good organised animals.)

Question 1: Does my view correspond to reality?
Question 2: Does my view bring about the feeling I want?
Question 3: Does my view lead to an effective solution to the problem?
Question 4: Does my view lead to the required behaviour?

You are in charge of your thinking and you can indeed replace negative views by delightful and comforting ones. I allowed myself daily one quarter of an hour for brooding. Than I allowed myself to see everything as black and bleak as possible and to wallow in sadness like a pig in mud on a hot day. But once that 'delightful' quarter was over, I mentally cried **STOP!!!** I picked up a big stop sign and stuck it in the air: Stop!!! Then I replaced those brooding thoughts by better ones.

Those better ones had to be:

- Comforting.
- Easy to call up.
- Preferably always the same scenario.
- They should have nothing to do with the problem.

I forced myself not only to think those thoughts, but also to feel the peace and happiness they caused me when I experienced that situation. I visualised myself sitting in the sun, with Puddie in my lap. Cosily warm and purring he reclined there. I could feel the vibrations of his purring. 'Mieeuwww, purrr, prrr,' I softly heard. I felt his whiskers tickling my cheek when I cuddled him. I smelled the fragrances of flowers and trees, listened to the wind rustling in the trees. A wonderful feeling of happiness flowed through me then. The rotten feelings had melted like snow in bright sunshine!!

It's so important that, once **you have received your scheme, you really stick to it.** You must eat every gram according to your dietician's instructions. Don't eat more either. Otherwise Satano will talk you into cutting down. 'You changed it once so you can change it again.' You must rely completely on your dietician's advice. Ignore the fears and panic you will experience when you start eating well. They will get worse as you gain weight. But, please take my word for it, it is impossible to get healthy and strong without putting on weight. And you cannot put on weight without adding kilos!

- From now on you have surrendered the responsibility for **what** you eat to the dietician. That's not any more your 'department'.
- The responsibility for your weight rests with your body. It is the only one who knows what your set-point weight is.
- Your responsibility - and this will make or break the venture - is to scrupulously eat every gram mentioned in your eating scheme.

Your body will search for its set-point weight and stick to that weight, as long as you eat well. You'll have to adjust your idea about the ideal weight, though. As the media keep on flooding our imagination with horrible skin-and-bone movie stars and fashion models, we've been brainwashed into thinking that we should look like them. Absurd and abnormal! Our Dear Lord did not create us women like that. What goes against nature is always wrong. Besides, it's a battle you can never win. If you will not listen to your body, it will make you listen to it. It will go on strike. It's its last resort! It has to make you realise what you're doing.

My dear friend and psychiatrist Doctor Wim says that everybody has a critical weight. If you go below that weight, things will go wrong! People who don't suffer from anorexia don't have to worry much about that. They will not artificially try to stay below it. But we anorexics and ex-anorexics, we have to watch out. Starvation and underweight make us feel so delightfully secure! My critical weight amounts to 58 kilo. I really feel that is true. Every time I weigh less, I feel ill and tense. I have pain all over, I then feel extremely cold and tired and have a fungus infection. Besides, we women are, when we get on in years, programmed in such a way that we gain weight, maybe to build up some reserve for our old days, or as some protection against osteoporosis. When we, being under Satano's spell and drive, force ourselves with all our strength to keep underweight, we're bound to get into trouble. Serious trouble! Even if that low weight didn't cause any problems when we were younger. The older we get, the less we can stand being underweight.

Doctor Wim told me about a girl who had recovered. She was way deep down in Ano-land, weighing only 38 kilo. She was 1,72 metres tall. She had to be hospitalised. Finally she had come to the conclusion that she could not go on living in that way. It took her two years to get out of Ano-land. Together with her dietician she drew up a good eating-scheme and she stuck to it. She put on weight, but it was sheer hell. She got oedemas and became allergic to just about everything. She was often desperate, but she persevered. Suddenly, about one year after having reached her target weight, she felt better. Now she is a young woman radiating with health and well-being. She weighs 65 kilo and feels euphoric. Most of her allergies have gone too. So indeed, all symptoms will pass away if you persevere. Fortunately I never had oedemas, probably because I resolutely kept doing my walking exercises.

When you have been living for many years in Ano-land, you will have forgotten how wonderful it is to feel well and relaxed. You don't realise any more that it isn't normal to feel compulsion and agitation. Satano is a very cruel tyrant, an implacable enemy. He literally drives you on until you drop with exhaustion. As long as he is in command, you won't be allowed to enjoy yourself. But the stronger you become, the easier it will be to make Satano 'shut up'. Lots of problems, mainly physical in nature, will disappear when you have reached a good weight. The restlessness and the compulsion pass away and you'll feel like enjoying things again. This doesn't mean however that life will just be offered to you as a gift on a golden tray. Problems are inherent in life because we have to gain experiences. That's exactly why we are here on earth. We must learn to convert bad experiences into positive ones. That's how we acquire wisdom. If you can look at things that way, you'll be able to handle your problems and troubles with more ease, even though, of course, it's always nasty the moment they occur.

It's so wonderful to be able to enjoy eating again. To do the things you were not allowed to do during your life of compulsion. Like reading a good book and sitting down quietly in the sun and cuddling your pussy-child. Our Dear Lord gave us those moments of pleasure, to be able to recharge our batteries, so that we will have the power and energy to face the next problem. If we refuse to be nice to ourselves, we make life so much harder. Ask The Lord for help and advice. He can't interfere in your life because you have received the freedom of choice. But he will always help and support you when you ask Him to. His answers will come like whispers in the wind. He talks to you by way of intuition. That tiny voice deep down in your inner self. Suddenly you know!

When you're overcome with fear - and there will be fear when you start eating more, lots of fear - keep on saying over and over again: 'I trust in The Lord and in all that's good. His love is my protection, everywhere and always.' That's my mantra and really, it helps.

Breathing well is very important too. It's the best way to calm down. Try to do the following breathing exercise a couple of times, every day. Sit down in a quiet spot and try to relax. (As soon as I do this, Daimke jumps into my lap). Close your eyes and inhale slowly and deeply through your nose. Picture the fresh air like a clear yellow-white light full of happiness and health that flows softly through your nose into your body. It reaches the bottom of your stomach. Then it stops. (Just like water being thrown from one bucket into the other). First the bottom of you tummy begins to bulge out from this beautiful light. Than the rest of your stomach and your breast follows. You are mighty big now. Hold on to your breath for a few seconds. Then you begin to exhale. You start at the bottom of your stomach again. Slowly you push the light upwards till it flows through your nose out of your body. It takes all the sorrow and the stress you had gathered with it. It's best to count slowly from 1 to 5, then to hold your breath for a moment and then to breathe out in 5 counts again. Then you wait again during a few counts before repeating the exercise. This pause is important to avoid dizziness.

I always do this during my walks. Indeed, the only place where I can really relax is outside. I have to feel the wind and the sun. This exercise has the advantage that you can do it while working or even while driving. Wherever you are, you can always withdraw into yourself and do the breathing-practice. This has helped many cats to survive. They just cut themselves off from the threatening environment they happen to find themselves in.

Try to listen to your intuition as much as possible. That 'little voice' inside you will grow stronger as you let it guide you. Our kitties always let themselves be guided by their intuition. Ask them for advice. They have a direct connection with the Lord. They will help you and support you as much as they can. In their eyes you can read the answers to your questions. Use them as your  model. Listen to them. They did not come to you without purpose. The Lord has sent them! They are our guardian angels, our teachers. When Evelyne, my orthomolecular Doctor saw me for the first time, she gave me the best advice I could get: 'Just do as your kitties do! Enjoy life, be nice to yourself and relax. Try to 'purr' as much as possible.'

The actions against overweight that I see cropping up everywhere in the media make me very angry. It is very irresponsible and downright dangerous to always remind people of the dangers of overweight instead of stressing the advantages of eating well and healthily and getting more exercise. They never talk about the dangers of being too thin. And believe me, that is much more dangerous. Besides, what is overweight anyway? A lumberjack working hard all day and eating plenty grows muscles and may look well-built, but he is one chunk of health and well-being. I remember friends of my parents who rode on horseback till the age of nearly ninety. They were really well rounded. They ate cakes and chocolate and enjoyed life tremendously. No dieting for them. 'In that word is 'to die' included' they said to me, every so often. And they are right. 'Being round and sound', says my dear Chummy-boy, 'is much healthier than being 'thin and ill' and it's so much more pleasant!' Yes, my little man is wise!

Mind you, the best way to get fat is to keep to a rigid diet. As you won't be able to keep to it for long, you will start to yo-yo. (Lose weight, gain weight, lose weight again). Your body will put itself on spare burning and you will get really fat on little food. Listen to your body and not so much to your mind! Eat at least four good healthy meals a day. Make your body strong. Spoil it. It is so tired and has suffered so much. If you act like that, everything will turn out well! Please, love yourself. You are good as you are. Learn to accept yourself as the Lord created you and be thankful for it. You are unique! The only thing that really matters is that you lead the life you want to lead. Then you will be happy. Don't forget that the scheme is there for you and don't start living for the scheme. You must be able to deviate from it, otherwise it will turn into a new obsession.

Dear H and kitties…

I sincerely do hope that this letter has helped you a bit. Read it out aloud to your two lovely kitty-angels and then listen to their reactions! 'Prr prrr! Oh, mama, please start eating again. Oh do!!! Oh, we feel so happy! You're back home! Now we're going to enjoy playing together. Prr purr.'

H.'s reply was very moving:

'Dear Marguerite,

Thank you for your kind and encouraging words. Just like yesterday's sun, shining through the window touched my skin and warmed me, so your light and living power through your letter touched me directly into my heart. Your words have pleased me a lot. It was as if a fresh ray of hope reached out to me through the darkness of Ano-land. I have enjoyed looking at the pictures of your kitties and in your love for animals I recognised myself. When I was a child I begged my parents for a pussy or a doggie, but the reply was always an implacable 'no', up to the time when there was a burglary in our neighbourhood and my father wanted to keep a watchdog. It was a shepherd dog, which had to be trained with much discipline. So I had to watch out not to cuddle him too much in the presence of my father. But secretly I established a wonderful bond with him and finally found a real friend who liked me. I think he felt my pain. I told him everything and he was always happy to be with me. We walked for hours in the nature with which I also had a tremendous bond. I think you have been walking these days as well, with your pussy-child on your shoulder, enjoying the burgeoning of trees and plants? As a result of your texts, the following childlike poem flowed out of my pen yesterday. I wrote it especially for your kitties.

DEAR PUSSYCAT,

Angel of great loving powers,
Always soaking me with smiling showers.
Your love is like a benign breeze,
Bringing warmth to me when I freeze.

You understand my sorrow, you know my pain,
You'll always stay with me, sun or rain.
And on the days when storms start blowing,
Your soft head against my chin is very consoling.

Your feline antics never fail to give me a hand,
When I have to fight Satano forcing me to Ano-land.
And your little voice merrily assures me,
That it won't harm to take a cookie with my tea.

You show me the way to enjoy life day and night,
And to let myself bask in heavenly light.
Your wise eyes say 'I always do mind!'
Indeed, you do and never shall I leave you behind.

Yes, together we can withstand Satano's full force,
That demon who wants me to go from bad to worse.
No, he can no longer drive us apart,
Let's hike together to God's heavenly yard.

© *Heidi*

I understand very well that you have a busy life. You give me a wonderful example of how to take care of myself and not to get drowned in stress, thereby giving Satano more elbowroom again. I am so glad I know you now and I am sure too, that we are connected even, without words, time and space. It's like having the privilege of meeting a soul sister, which gives me the energy to continue. Thanks for the tip to make the change by strictly following an eating-scheme. I have problems with both anorexia and bulimia. I am 1,80 metres tall, but I haven't reached 50 kilos yet. I suffer a lot from binge eating. Often I throw up everything afterwards (I even often throw up small meals). It is as if I hope to spit the pain and filth out of my body, that way. I have been trying this for more than ten years but it doesn't help.

I think the time has come to get rid of these self-destructive habits by means of a scheme to which I can stick. It is frightening because I know how hard that will be. I've tried it innumerable times before but thanks to you there is a new power now which I, against all despair, will grasp. My body has suffered much damage (stomach, digestive system, and teeth), but I remain confident that good food will restore its powers. It's a marvel anyway that it is still functioning after all the misery. A body is indeed a wonderful instrument and I hope that I will return' home' to it again some day.

Should I feel like writing you some words or thoughts, you don't have to feel obliged to read them or to react to them. It's sufficient for me that I can send them and the energy will take care of the rest. I wish you many marvellous moments in everything you do, amidst your six dears. You are doing a fine job by so honestly being yourself and by supporting others with so much love. Please feel free to use my letter, those words are not my possession anyway. It's just like some energy that flowed through me on its way to a new place.

Warm greetings and thousand sunrays.
H...and cat-children.

P.S. I have this strong feeling that somewhere a third kitty-angel is waiting to come to me. Maybe to support me when I take this new step in my fight against Satano, who will defend himself with all his means and powers. At this moment I feel safe, but I know he's a sly fellow who will show up out of the blue to get me under his control again.'

Such wonderful letters. I am very thankful to H. for allowing me to include them in my book. And yes, I know now that a third angel has come to live with her. Little Prince, an Oriental Shorthair who will help her in her fight against Satano! Oh, I do hope she will heal! Anorexia is such a terrible disease! I pray for her and I keep on sending her Light and Love.

And when we bury our face in our hands and wish we had never been born, they don't sit up very straight and observe that we have brought it all upon ourselves. They don't even hope it will be a warning to us. But they come up softly and shove their heads against us.

Jerome K. Jerome 1859-1927

Chapter 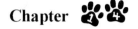 14

Training

Cats are a mysterious kind of folk. There is more passing in their minds than we are aware of.

Sir Walter Scott

As I refuse to talk about a cat or dog as 'it', I really think that an insult. I will speak in this chapter about 'he and him' and in the next chapter about 'she and her', this to prevent Puddie to be hurt again.

My kitties and I do everything by mutual consent. The nice thing about bringing up cats is that you don't have to be the boss. I thoroughly loathe playing the 'pasha'. When I was still living in Numansdorp, I trained dogs. A dog needs a real boss, a leader of the pack who can guarantee his security. This 'being the boss' must be kept up during his whole life. You have to train him and demand that he follows your orders. When a dog doesn't consider you worthy to be his leader, he will take command himself. He has to, because his 'wolf-brain' warns him that a bad leader may cost him his life. The knack is to always be consistent during his whole life. No is No! Training dogs is a nice job and I loved it, but I prefer to do things in consultation. It's great that fluffies don't require such intense training.

Cats are solitary animals. Sometimes though, strays will form a group and then there must be a leader who sees to it that the group functions well socially. He interferes when some of the members have a fight. He scouts for places where food can be found. He gives protection and so on, but he will allow the other cats to be free and he doesn't demand absolute obedience. He does demand respect, though. There are certain rules and the group must observe them, it's for their own good.

When a kitten is introduced in a family, he has to learn to consider his 'straightup-walkers' as his cats-in-command. Fair and protective cats-in-

283

command, for sure, but cats-in-command, who have to be respected all the same. It is very important that the kitten learns that as soon as possible. Of course, when a full-grown cat is introduced, he has to learn that as well. When there are already cats in the household, he must start at the back of the line.

When a kitten plays too roughly with his mother or his siblings, his mother will teach him not to. When people get such a lively ball of fur in their house, they often like it very much when he attacks them, bites their ankles, scratches or hisses. 'How cute and brave!' But then the kitten won't learn to respect you and he will continue acting like that. So, don't play too rough with him and stop immediately when he hurts you. Say No! And hiss. A cat is super smart and learns quickly.

Teach him from the beginning that some things are not allowed and that he just has to accept certain things. Make sure you have it your way but always be friendly and calm. The best way to cure him of something he shouldn't do is by using a plant spray. Don't show him that **you** are using it, that's the most effective thing. Hissing is clear language: 'Mama is angry, this is not allowed!' Always be consistent. Not on the table means Never on the table!

There are some golden rules to observe when training. The most important one is: Rewarding is much more effective than punishing. Try to prevent having to mete out punishment.

- Change yourself into a cat. Think cat. Lie down flat on the floor and look at the world from his position.
- Learn to read his body language. Long before actually doing something, his body betrays it already. The tail starts swishing, the ears move nervously, the eyes change or become glassy.
- Try to be ahead of him. Say 'No' before he jumps on the kitchen sink, for instance. This prevents having to take action.
- Hiss!!! Hissing means 'No!'
- Scowl and correct only on the very moment your cat does something wrong, never afterwards. Even a few seconds after the act he has already forgotten what he did. When you're angry with him then, he won't understand and he will lose confidence in you and will start avoiding you.
- Respect your cat. When he doesn't like something and it's not important for his safety or health, don't order him to do it. The cat-in-command doesn't

require it either. He doesn't demand obedience, only respect. A cat is not a dog.

Catje, no matter how cute and lovely she is, doesn't want to be on my lap. Well, I just let her be. I am certainly not going to force her to do it. It took one year before Mickje was willing to come cuddling on my lap. Now, she spends hours there. She embraces my neck with her paws and pushes her head against me. So cute! Mutual respect and agreement. Oh, if only people would understand that! It would prevent a lot of trouble and misery.

There is a new and very nice training-method: Clicker Training. It is used more and more often. It is learning in a positive way! When the cat does something you want him to do, you click a clicker – a metal device that produces a clicking sound - and immediately afterwards you give a treat. Very soon your cat will learn that 'click' means a treat and he will try to make you click by doing that what you want him to do. There is a good book explaining this method: 'Clicker Training for Cats' by Karen Pryor. See the bibliography at the end of this book.

Cat Problems

There are many cats who don't mind living together with other fluffies or who even like it. But as a matter of fact, cats are solitary animals and some cats do find it difficult to live as a member of a group. Then, it's very important that there are sufficient place for them to withdraw to. And ... that there is not too much unrest around them. My fluffies sense at once when I am nervous and tense myself. They will try to help me by frequently sitting close to me or by laying in my lap and purring. That's so lovely of them! But they take on my stress and will take it out on each other. Taking good care of yourself and making sure you feel all right is therefore very important, not only for yourself but also for your cats. And what an excellent excuse to stop working too much and too long! Restlessness is very annoying, so try to prevent it. I know the feeling only too well! Stress seriously affects and weakens the immune system of our cats and of ourselves.

Something very helpful in this respect for my pussy-children (and also me!) is the Feliway Plug-In. This diffuses pheromones, cat-calming scents. The cat himself produces pheromones when he rubs his chin over things or gives you shoves with his head. When my fluffies are nervous - for instance because of strangers in the house or garden or because it's full moon - and I plug the Feliway plug into the socket, their nervousness quickly decreases. Pheromones are also available as sprays under the same brand name. Very handy, for instance to spray into cat-carriers, so that your cat will be calmer when you take him with you on a trip. Feliway really works! The pheromones convey the message to them: all is well, don't worry!

Uncleanliness

Originally cats were hunters. They bury their droppings to hide their presence from their prey. In the wild they also prevent infection by always using the same location to relieve themselves. The mother cat teaches her kittens to use the litter tray pretty early on. They'll remember those lessons for the rest of their lives. Cats are extremely clean animals. They like clean surroundings. So, when you find urine or droppings outside the tray, there is something wrong with him. Try to find out, as soon as possible what's wrong. Bladder stones may be life threatening and they can be one of the causes making your cat unwilling to use his tray. Cystitis is often another reason.

It is very important to clearly distinguish **spraying** from **urinating**.

When your cat does not **urinate** in the litter tray, he might be ill or there is something making him feel unsure. Your cat is afraid of something. Maybe she or he suddenly took fright. There is a feeling of restlessness and stress stopping him from using the tray. **Spraying** has more to do with territory and status. It's easy to see the difference between spraying and urinating. When your cat sprays, he spreads some urine on clearly visible vertical surfaces. When doing this, his tail is erect and vibrating and his hind legs make kicking movements. You will notice a very concentrated look on his face when he is spraying. When he just does not do it in the litter tray, he will squat down and urinate where he is. Often he will try to hide the puddle afterwards by scratching around it, as if collecting soil to throw on it. So, when you find considerable puddles of urine on horizontal surfaces, it is not the result of your cat's spraying actions. Anyway, even if a cat is in a spraying period, he will still use the litter tray for urinating and defecating.

Why does a cat "forget" his house-training?

Problem 1: **Urinating outside of the tray**

Fear of the tray or fear of its surroundings. Restlessness caused by changes inside the house or its surroundings. The cat wants to feel safe and secure again and leaves its mark accordingly.

You will find puddles of urine and maybe also droppings in various spots inside your house. The droppings are just on the floor and the urine is not spread on a vertical surface, because then it would be the result of spraying.

Causes:

Bladder infection or bladder stones.

When your cat urinates in the tray and he has a bladder infection or stones in the bladder, he will experience a strong and sudden pain. That frightens him and makes him afraid of returning to the place that hurt him so much. You will hear him mewing frequently and walking with a high-arched back because of the pain. Maybe he will still try to urinate in the litter tray a couple of times after his bad experience. So, when you notice that your cat visits his tray frequently but for very short times, you should consult a veterinarian without delay. Tomcats especially may suffer terribly from bladder stones. It may even develop into a life-threatening affliction when the stones block up the urethra. In just a couple of hours this may lead to serious damage of the kidneys and even cause the death of your cat. It is only logical that a cat suffering from a bladder infection will refuse to use the tray. It hurts so much! You wouldn't want to sit down for a second time on a toilet seat full of drawing pins?

Constipation.

The hard faeces can hurt an awful lot when they are forced out. The cat is afraid to return to that place which caused so much pain! In both cases it is fear of the spot where he experienced such pain which forces the cat to relieve himself elsewhere. The solution is simple and obvious. Let your veterinarian find out immediately what's wrong. Medicine or a diet with more fibre might solve this problem. Buying another tray might be a good idea. He will be scared now of the old tray. Even one cat should have more than one tray.

Sometimes it's the other way round.

You have placed a new tray or used a new sort of litter. Your cat doesn't like it and is afraid to use the tray. So, better leave the old tray around when you're introducing a new one. When you want to change the contents, change gradually. Mix the new with the old litter first, before using new litter only.

- The tray has a **cover** but your cat doesn't like to be covered when 'doing his thing'.

- The tray has **no cover** but your cat values privacy when 'doing his thing'.

- Another cat or a dog has **attacked** your cat when he was in the tray or coming out of it. A tray without a cover is useful in this respect: the cat can keep an eye on the surroundings.

- The tray is in a **place** which he doesn't like. For instance there is too much disturbance there. Try to find a quiet spot, some unfrequented corner in a bedroom for instance.

- When the tray is too **close** to his **food and drink,** he may find that unpleasant. We too don't like to take our meals close to the toilet.

- There is a **shortage** of trays. Sometimes a cat likes to use one tray for urinating and another for defecating. Little kittens can't find the tray sometimes because it's too far away and so, out of need, eliminate elsewhere.

- In households with more cats, **more** trays must be provided. Cats are fastidious and sometimes won't use trays frequented by other cats. There should always be as many trays as cats, plus one!

- The tray is **too dirty.** I use clumping litter and every week I empty the trays completely and disinfect them with Hibiscrub, a safe disinfectant. Also, I remove turds and puddles as soon as I find them.

- The tray is **too clean!** Yes, that's also possible. It helps when the tray smells a bit of urine. When you find a turd or a puddle next to the tray, you can pick it up with some paper and deposit it in the tray.

- The cat is **afraid**. There is too much agitation in the house. Other cats pester him. Suddenly something changed in the house. He feels insecure. He is afraid of going to the tray.

The only way to solve this problem is by eliminating the cause of the fear. How? First, eliminate physical causes by having your cat examined by a veterinarian. If he is physically ok, try to figure out what happened by thinking of your cat's point of view. What changes occurred in his life lately? What makes him scared? What might have frightened him? Never punish him! That would have a contrary effect. It would make him feel even more afraid and insecure. Punishing a cat is as absurd as punishing an anorexic because she is afraid to eat. Yet, this still frequently happens!
Your cat must feel safe and secure again in his home. So play with him and cuddle him as much as possible. Tell him that you love him immensely. That will help a lot. Make sure he has many safe retreats and hiding places in the house. See to it that he can eat and sleep in peace and quiet. Most of all, see to it that he can make use of his litter tray without being disturbed.

Problem 2: **Spraying**

Spraying occurs mostly when there are many cats in a household. It is usually a problem of territory and status. It is a cat's way of marking territory and of inter-feline communication. Fortunately our kitties usually use 'visiting cards' which are acceptable to their humans. Like head shoves, whereby the cat rubs his cheek against a human or a thing, so that his scent is transferred to them. Scratching a pole or some other object and so marking them with his scent is also such a 'visiting card'. It makes the cat feel secure and at ease. They have become 'his' things. Spraying will only happen when something serious is the matter. Once in a while a cat will use stools to communicate a message. Mostly, however, he uses urine.

When many cats are living together, there will usually be one who is the leader. He feels himself responsible for the other cats. When, for instance an outsider has strayed into the garden or sprayed against the front door, the leader has to assert himself and therefore must leave his scent everywhere. Especially he will try to cover the scent of the 'bad-boy'. He feels threatened and says: 'This is my place! Get out of here! This is my territory!' He acts so to protect his security and that of his group.

Spraying may also be the result of changes within the group itself. For instance the leader falls ill and so another cat has to take over. Or a cat is on heat. A newcomer has been introduced to the group. Almost all full tomcats and sometimes she-cats on heat spray. A tomcat who is still 'entire' has to spray to tell his rivals: 'Hey man, this is my territory. No trespassing!' He also sprays to inform pussies on heat that 'a beautiful prince consort is at their Catship's service to gladly…' A tomcat has to spray because the sexual urge to propagate is stronger than himself and rightly so! Otherwise the feline race would become extinct. So it is no use punishing him for something he can't help being and doing! Quite the contrary! Punishment will worsen the problem and he will lose his trust in you. A pussy in heat sprays to say that she is in need of a man, and this **very** instant! Moreover, when she is fertile or when she is pregnant and suckling kittens, it also means that she has a higher status. The higher her status, the better she will be able to take care of her kittens. Nature is organised so beautifully! So she will start marking her territory to inform the other cats that she is the boss from now on.

If you don't use your cats for breeding, it is best to have them **neutered.** That usually solves the problems, but not always.

Spraying may also be a sign of insecurity. The cat feels threatened and insecure. By spreading his scent around he reassures himself. When something new comes into the house, for instance a piece of furniture, it often appears as a threat to him, so he will make that horrible thing 'his own' by marking it with his scent, giving it his 'spray'.

Try to 'think cat' and find out why he feels compelled to spray. What message is he trying to communicate to you? It is always an SOS-signal! He is in distress. He would never spray just to upset you. He can't help it. Something is bothering him. What makes him so restless? Has there been a fight in the household? Other cats who have been fighting outside? Maybe some strange, awkward straightup-walker has been in 'his' home? Has his mama had a baby? A new feline was introduced into the household? The house is being renovated or repainted? Has something changed in his surroundings? If he is an outdoor cat, maybe the neighbour's cat attacked him? Maybe a strange cat entered 'his' house through 'his' cat flap, ate his food, so he is hungry which also creates restlessness and stress?

If many cats live together, there is often rivalry. If there is not enough food, they have to fight for it. The higher the status of a cat is, the more food he gets. So, he will try to be or stay the boss. If one of the cats in a group must follow a strict diet, because he has to lose weight for instance, that easily could cause problems.

Try to puzzle out what 'got into him'. Once you understand why he felt the need to mark his surroundings with his scent, you may be able to remove the cause. As soon as he feels secure and safe again, the spraying will stop. As it is in the case of urinating outside the tray, love is also the best therapy in the case of spraying.

Fortunately my kitties seldom spray. Just once in a while they do it. Mostly in springtime. Probably because neighbourhood cats roam around then and leave behind their scents. Daimke is extremely anxious. When, for instance my roof needs repair and someone has to work up there, she is upset for the rest of the day. Then I'll find her 'scents' sometimes. Also when I have lots

291

of work to do and my fluffies get less attention and feel lonely, Donsje especially feels afraid and forlorn then. Maybe she thinks then that I am incapable of defending her and so she sprays to take courage. As soon as I am 'back' again and take the time to play and cuddle with my fluffies, all spraying stops. Maybe Donsje also sprays to keep me from a burnout? Puddie also did some spraying before. Especially when he came into conflict with Daimke. Now he gets homeopathy from Carina and it's over. Homeopathy is really effective provided you apply the right remedy! Puddie has changed completely and most important, he has become calm and happy again. He often comes lying on my lap and is much kinder towards the others. I am so glad. I love him so and hate to see him in distress.

What matters very much both in case of peeing outside the litter tray and in case of spraying, is to **clean up** everything thoroughly. When a cat has the urge to leave marks behind, he will regularly check to make sure that his marks are still strong enough. When the scent is fading, he will add some more. But when the scent is completely gone, he will not feel the urge to add.

Still, never use ammonia or chlorine to clean up the marks. These substances smell a bit like urine and your cat will think: 'Hey, mama also sprays here, so I'm doing the right thing!' Scrub the spot thoroughly with soapsuds from a **biological detergent**. That contains enzymes, which 'eat' the proteins and fats of the urine. Let the spot dry and spray medicinal **alcohol** or methylated spirit on it.
You can also feed your cat on that spot. Cats never spray on places where they eat.
When a cat is doing 'his thing' outside the litter tray and keeps doing that whatever you do, you can try to confine him, part of the day, in an **indoor kennel** or a small room. Of course, only if he doesn't mind that, because stress is the first thing to avoid in this case. He should not experience it as punishment. So, reward him with titbits and cuddles when he goes in there. Make it a cosy place. Put only his tray and his basket inside. He will never soil his own sleeping place and so he will learn again to do it in the tray.

In America, doctors sometimes prescribe antidepressants when there are urinating-problems. Doctor Dodman wrote a book about it. Of course, never administer antidepressants without consulting your veterinarian first. It seems they are sometimes effective.

My friend Carina Smeets, homeopathic veterinarian, will explain on the following pages how to use Bach Flower Remedies to combat pee-problems. I have followed the courses myself and I often use them. They give very good results. Of course, Carina has much more experience in this field. I am very grateful to her for writing these lines for my book. Chapter Nineteen deals with Bach Flower Remedies.

Bach Flower Remedies for Urinating Problems

Our cat pees outside the tray

I regularly receive calls from people whose cats suddenly won't pee in the tray any more. If it is just a cat on heat using the kitchen sink or the washbasin for temporary toilet, the problem is not so serious. If, however, it's about a cat who slowly but steadily is providing unpleasant smells all around the house or, more in particular, around your computer, you may say you have a serious problem.

In the first place, let your veterinarian check out whether this behaviour is not caused by some physical disturbance. It might be that the cat in question is suffering from a serious bladder infection. When this infection has been effectively treated with common or homeopathic medicines, perhaps supported by Bach's **Crab Apple**, the urinating problem will vanish. If there is only one litter tray, the solution may be to add another tray. Many cats prefer to use one tray for defecating and another for urinating.

Another option is to clean the tray more frequently. Some cats are so choosy that only a super clean tray will serve the purpose! In this case you may administer a combination of **Beech and Crab Apple.** When these measures won't solve the problem, I advise you to thoroughly investigate when exactly your cat pees outside the tray. Once you are aware of that, you will quickly find out the 'why' of the problem.

When your cat – for whatever reason – is angry with you or tries to get extra attention, the correct remedy is a combination of **Holly and Chicory**. If she has recently experienced some radical change, you could try **Walnut**. When it's a matter of marking territory, **Chicory, Vervain and Vine** should be considered. It is also possible that your cat urinates out of fear, because another cat in the group pesters her. In that case it is best to treat both the 'underdog' with **Chicory and Mimulus** and the 'pest' with **Vine and Holly**.

About Spraying: No hangover from a spraying rover

Many people, especially those keeping entire tomcats in the house, have to face it sooner or later: spraying!

Not only tomcats but also she-cats sometimes feel like marking an object by - the tail proudly erect and the behind stuck out - squirting some urine on it. Everyone who has experienced this extraordinarily annoying problem also knows that we're dealing here with a very persistent habit, which can't be stopped just like that.

Cats who spray are often self-assured and have dominant characters. They don't spray because they are afraid, but to mark their territory. But also, there are the gentler creatures who spray because they are 'bothered by their hormones.' For the latter neutering may be the solution. The first group however, will often happily continue spreading odorous messages in inconvenient places.

Tomcats have a territory, which can be ten times the size of the territory of a she-cat, with the result that one tomcat may have several she-cats at his service. That's why cause number one of spraying is the confinement of too many not-neutered cats in a too small area. The lack of 'hiding places' for cats can also cause territory-related behaviour. Events like moving, stress, rivals or the presence of she-cats on heat may also trigger spraying.

Sometimes your veterinarian will treat your cat with hormonal remedies. For instance injections with Tardac or the 'pill' for cats. Experience has shown that they might be effective in the beginning, but that the duration of effectiveness of the injections gets gradually shorter. In some cases the spraying gets even worse. Moreover frequent administration of these remedies may lead to unfavourable side effects, for instance the development of mammary-tumours.

Bach Flower Remedies enable us to correct this annoying habit in our cats in a natural way. When your cat starts spraying after moving or after the introduction of a newcomer into the household, you may give **Walnut**, if necessary combined with **Honeysuckle and Star of Bethlehem.** In case of possessive or real dominant cats **Beech, Chicory** and/or **Vine** are possibly good remedies.

When you are not sure why your cat sprays but you notice he has stress, you may begin by administering **Rescue Remedy**. Later you can change to a remedy that better suits the cause. In certain cases however, you'll have to bring up the heavy artillery before its undesirable behaviour will stop. You'll have to treat your cat with homeopathy.

With lots of thanks to my dear friend Carina Smeets.

God made the cat in order that man might have the pleasure of caressing the lion.

Fernand Mery

Chapter

Facts about Cats

With the qualities of cleanliness, affection, patience, dignity and courage that cats have, how many of us, I ask you, would be capable of becoming cats?

Fernand Mery

Care

The best thing that you can do for your kitty is to give lots and lots of TLC (Tender-Loving-Care). Playing, cuddling, **giving much love**, they are the best guarantees for a healthy and happy feline life. Stress is fatal. It impairs the immune system and so creates the ideal conditions for diseases to strike. Try to find out what your cat likes.

Puddie likes being stroked especially under his chin. He can't reach that spot himself. He really comes to ask me to stroke him there. Catje regularly rolls onto her back and wants to be caressed on her belly. But she definitely will not sit on my lap. Chum is no lap cat either but he often comes to be stroked. Mickje wants to be stroked over her back and head. Daimke often lies on her back in my arms and also wants to be stroked on her belly. Donsje greatly enjoys being stroked on the head. And Tommeke...he is now the biggest cuddler of all. He loves to be caressed all over and does not want me to stop. Each one of them wants to be cuddled in a different way.

Animals think in images. You can also say that they also 'feel' in images. They smell and hear them. Professor Temple Grandin from America says so. Animals converse with each other by telepathy and body language. Humans can think both in images and words. When talking with your cat, you should always try to link your words to an image. She will intercept your thoughts. Try also to intercept her thoughts. After some exercise you will be able to. Talking is very important. My fluffies really understand everything I say. The more you talk with them, the more they will understand and the stronger your bond with them will become. The fluffies and I do a lot of mewing with each other.

Leash-Training

Some cats really enjoy walking on a leash, other cats abhor it. Donsje, Catje and Daimke love it. Puddie, Mickje and Chummy loathe it. When your cat doesn't like it, you should never force her to.

The best way to teach her is to start indoors. The first few times you put the harness on inside the house. Begin with half an hour, then longer. If it works well, tie a short leash to the harness and just let the cat drag it. See to it that the leash doesn't get stuck somewhere. She might get frightened if a chair suddenly turns over. Next, you train her to walk while you hold the leash in your hand. Of course, never pull, just hold the leash tight when she walks in the wrong direction and give slack when she walks along with you. Don't forget to reward her. A piece of chicken or a cat-snack just in front of her nose works like magic. Cats are super fast learners, but they must enjoy what they are learning. You should always **stay around** when she is wearing the harness and also never tether your cat outside unless you can watch her. She might become frightened and get tangled in the leash or a dog may approach her. When Puddie is tied outside on the lawn, I am always extra watchful.

When she is doing all this without problems, you can take her out to a quiet spot, for instance a little park without traffic. A pouch bag is a comfortable way to carry her. But also that has to be learned. She should always wear a harness with a leash when you take her in the pouch bag, as she might become scared and jump out. Using the cat-carrier is safer. There are cats who adore walking. The fresh air, the sunlight, oh, how they love it! I find retractable leashes most convenient. I fasten the pulley to my belt so that my hands are free and the leash can never slip out of my hands, not even if I fall.
I immensely enjoy my walks through the garden with the fluffies. They draw my attention to things which I would probably never notice in their absence. A mouse scurrying away, a bird sitting on a branch, a beetle, a strange noise. I visualise myself down to their level and experience the world through their eyes, ears and noses. I try to feel what they feel. It is unbelievable how rich

297

nature is. What they teach me is much more valuable than what I can learn from whatever expensive book about nature. The most beautiful lesson they teach me is that they live in the 'here and now' and don't brood about any past or future. Only 'now' matters and, of course, that's true. Walking with your cat or dog is the best way to find peace.

Brushing. Is very important, especially in the moulting period. If you don't brush regularly, your cat will ingest hair while grooming herself and this may cause hairballs. There is special cat food designed against hairballs and there is also paste which causes the hairballs to dissolve. You should regularly give her a flowerpot with **cat grass**. You can buy it in a pet shop. Your cat will eat the grass to throw up, so that the hairballs come out. Replace the grass frequently. If it grows too ripe and develops seeds, the stalks may get stuck in her throat. In some cases an operation might be necessary to remove them. The grass should not bear seeds.

Brushing the teeth with special toothpaste helps against tartar, yet it is quite a job and not all cats succumb to it. Dry food is much better for the teeth than canned food. There are now special 'teeth-chunks' available, which clean the teeth during the chewing-process. Good food also makes for a balanced environment in the mouth, which prevents tartar development. Chewing is very important.

Fleas are a real pest. Not only do they cause itching and discomfort but they also act as an intermediary host to tapeworms. Some cats are allergic to fleabites and may scratch their skin open after only one bite. Squirting one pipette of Frontline high on their neck once a month can prevent this. Push the hair aside and squirt the drops onto the skin. Very high up in their neck so they can't lick it off. Frontline is effective against **fleas and ticks**. That is a big advantage, especially for outdoor cats, because ticks may cause Lyme disease. There are more effective remedies against fleas, like Program or Advantage, but they don't have any effect on ticks. Some **anti-flea** products contain Permethrin, which is not as innocent as one might think. Permethrin can cause toxic symptoms in cats, such as spasms.
Research has revealed that this mostly happens when dogs and cats are living together and the dogs have been treated with Permethrin. Often the warning on the packets is overlooked. If you use it, it's extremely important to prevent the cats licking the Permethrin from the fur of the dogs. Frontline

contains no Permethrin. The active substance in Frontline is Fipronil, which is very efficient and safe. Once applied, it mixes with the sebum and is spread on the skin up to the sebaceous glands. If Frontline is licked up soon after applying, the cat might happen to have an overproduction of saliva. This is brought about by the solvent and does not matter. Fipronil concentrates in the sebaceous glands and is not sensitive to sunlight, rain, swimming, washing and even shampoo. That's why this product works longer than most other products.

You should also deflea in the winter. Even if it freezes outside, in our houses it's warm and cosy for the fleas to hibernate. I use Frontline every month. One thing is very important: **Never use Frontline for dogs on cats** as the dose is much too strong. I always put the packets for the doggies in another cupboard. Of course, you should regularly wash the cats' blankets and pillows and also frequently vacuum the house. The whole surrounding area must be treated against fleas too.

It is best to **worm** twice yearly. Kittens should be wormed more frequently, when they are still small they are very susceptible. It is recommended to get the wormer from the veterinarian rather than from a pet shop. He can also draw up a worming scheme. Milbemax or Drontal are recommended for outdoor cats, because they are also effective against tapeworms. Mice and fleas may transmit tapeworm. Of course, there are other good remedies. I just read about a new wormer, Profender that works against tapeworms, round worms and hookworms. It is a spot-on and is used just like Frontline by squirting a pipette high in their neck. There are also pastes available, but they don't have any effect on tapeworms.

Nowadays veterinarians recommend **vaccination** against panleucopenia for indoor cats only every two years. My six couldn't agree more! But vaccination against cat flu should be done every year for the time being. Never think: 'My cat doesn't go outside so vaccination is not required.' That's nonsense! It's always possible that visitors bring infection inside. So vaccination is a must! But too much vaccination is not good either. On the Feline Advisory Bureau website you will find all information: site: www.fabcats.org

Pivoting windows are very dangerous. Don't open them! That's the safest. But if you want to take the risk, never ever leave them open when you're away!

Your cat may get her head stuck in it and suffocate. It is a horrible death and it really happens. Make sure your windows are fitted with strong **screens**. Apart from screens I have put plain wire netting in front of my windows. That is strong enough to support the cats when they climb on it.

Never let your cat on the **balcony** unless it is fenced securely with wire netting. In America they have a term for cats who fall out of windows or from balconies 'The Flying cat syndrome'. So often it happens there! The cat is watching a bird or butterfly and loses her balance. Usually a cat will land safely on her feet but the impact of a fall from a high level is so strong that she can fracture her jaw and get internal injuries. Often they also shatter their paws as a result from such a fall-on-her-legs-from-a-high-altitude. Many cats don't survive such a fall. So be careful!

Insecticides are very dangerous of course. Especially the weed killers that are used on grass growing in between gravel or paving stones. They cause many accidents and are not necessary. Twice a year, we spray a salt-solution on the weeds and they wilt completely. Salt is very cheap. After all, it's spread in huge quantities on the roads during winter and it's very effective.

Even more dangerous are chemical granules used for **slug and snail-control.** They are usually very poisonous. There's a new kind of granules on the market, allegedly unattractive to dogs and cats. Still, the Utrecht University has received more than sixteen animals suffering from symptoms of poisoning. These granules contain metaldehyde, a lethal poison for dogs and cats. It's certainly not true that these granules have no taste. It's a fact that dogs and cats have eaten them, even if the cats don't swallow the grains themselves, they may still get the poison into their system. Birds do eat slugs and snails or peck at the granules. Maybe even mice eat them. Cats do sometimes catch birds or mice. Moreover, the poison seeps into the soil and pollutes the environment. Nowadays granules based on iron are available and they really make snails disappear. These granules are not poisonous. This type of granule can be ordered from Brinkman among others. The address is included in the list at the end of this book.

The **snail** itself is not totally without danger for felines. The slime is toxic and may cause intestinal problems. Of course, our cats are aware of this most of the time, but there is always the risk of a curious cat or kitten wanting to find out for herself...

Constipation: in case of constipation it is best to administer vegetable oil. Pour some over the food. Olive oil and the like. It is readily available in every household and serves well as a harmless laxative. Of course in small quantities, just a few drops. Another effective method is to dip a thermometer in oil and place it in the anus. That often suffices to remedy a mild constipation. Dr Liliane advised me to give Puddie, Donsje and Mickje some diluted evaporated milk when they are troubled with constipation. Many cats get diarrhoea from cowmilk, but sometimes they do tolerate evaporated milk and that is a good purgative. It also has the advantage that it is liquid and they like to drink it. Another effective medicine is Katalax, available from the veterinarian.

For drinking, plain **water** is best. Of course you have to replace it often. I always give my fluffies filtered water which I also drink. Tap water tastes of chlorine, cats don't like it and it's bad for them. Since I gave the kitties waterfountains they drink much more. They love them and Catje often plays with the falling water. They have charcoal-filters so the water is always fresh.

When your kittens suffer from **diarrhoea** you have to consult your veterinarian immediately. Kittens dehydrate very quickly, which is very dangerous. When the cat is older you can wait a bit. Don't give her any food for one day except natural yoghurt. You may also add some Isogel or intestinal cleanser to the food. It renders the stools firmer in form but Isogel doesn't heal. You could also give a pinch of 'good' intestinal bacteria, which are also present in natural yoghurt. We have Simfidus capsules, which you can get in the pharmacy. You have to administer them with the food because intestinal bacteria require sugars in order to multiply. Anyway I give yoghurt to my fluffies every day. They are fond of it, especially when it is laced with honey. Norit (Carbo Activatus, Vegetable coal) is a very safe medicine. You can give a pinch of Norit in the yoghurt or over some cooked chicken or dissolve a bit in some boiled cold water. You suck up the solution in a syringe without the needle and spray a few drops inside the pouch of the cat's mouth. Very little because she must never choke herself. That is very dangerous. Norit also cleans the stomach and bowels in case of poisoning. Carbo vegetabelis is a good homeopathic remedy against diarrhoea. Doctor Richard Allport, homeopathic veterinarian and a regular contributor to the cat magazine Cat World, recommends Slippery Elm in case of diarrhoea and chronic intestinal problems. Ginger has a calming effect on the intestines.

Being too **fat** is not good for anyone. Indoor cats especially are prone to "plumpness". When you can't feel your cat's ribs any more, it's time to put him on a diet. But let him **lose weight gradually**. Contrary to dogs, who may slim down quickly, cats must not do so. They may get Fatty Liver Syndrome when losing weight too fast and that is deadly. If your cat really has to lose weight, consult your veterinarian first. He will prescribe you special dry food, low on calories and rich on fibre. Of course she should exercise more. It would be lovely if you could take her for walks on a harness. Playing helps a lot too.

When a cat is **ill** and eats nothing or very **little** for more than a day or two, give her a few times a day some green tea against Fatty liver syndrome, using a syringe without needle and trickle some drops in the pouch of her cheek and wait until you notice her swallowing it. Always give her lukewarm food. The cat prefers it and also it has a stronger smell than cold food. When the cat refuses to eat, it helps sometimes to heat the food. Smelling is very important for a cat and that's the reason why a cat often doesn't eat when she has a stuffy nose. Do go to the Vet if she does not start eating soon. It's dangerous for cats not to eat for longer than a few days because then they can get the fatty-liver-syndrome which is lethal.

Cats are easily sick, but if they **keep on throwing up** you have to pay attention. It could be a blockage of the gastrointestinal tract by an extraneous object like a rubber band, a button, a marble, a pebble and so on. It could be a hairball that's stuck somewhere inside or maybe they are simply ill. So, visit your veterinarian. Sometimes cats eat so fast that they throw up immediately after the meal. Regurgitation that's called. Siamese especially are fast feeders. Puddie is a real guzzler. That's why I now throw a handful of his dry food with a wide arc into the room a few times a day so that he is forced to search them one by one. That prevents his guzzling it in a jiffy and so Mickje has the time to finish her food in peace. Moreover Puddie enjoys it very much.

Elastic bands are life threatening. Cats love playing with them. The things move and it seems they are tasty. Donsje is fond of them. Luckily I have been able to prevent her swallowing elastic bands. In spite of my precautions, it happened that twice an elastic band from the mail ended up on my desk in the office and twice I had to get it out of Donsje's mouth. Since then I have posted a big warning in the kitchen: **No Elastic Bands in this House**! They tend to curl up when swallowed. Gastric juices render them rock-hard. Such an elastic band can then perforate the stomach or intestinal wall like the razor-sharp point of a dagger. It may also get stuck. When you see your cat eating an elastic band or you suspect she has eaten one, take her at once to the veterinarian. Almost always an operation will be necessary. It makes no sense to have X-rays taken because rubber doesn't show on them. The horrible thing is that you cannot always watch your cat and be sure she didn't eat rubber. As a precaution make sure there are no elastic bands in your house. **Elastic makes cats sick**!

When you know that your cat has swallowed an extraneous object, you can **make her vomit** by sprinkling a teaspoonful of kitchen salt at the back of her tongue, but you should only do this when an **object** is involved and it has just happened. If you think your cat has eaten some poison, never force her to vomit because that will force the poison again through the oesophagus, which might then be fatally injured.

Never allow your cat to play with **cotton wool**. A cat's tongue has sharp spines and so she cannot simply spit out a plug of cotton wool that she has licked up. The cat may suffocate. The same is true of threads of wool, string and pieces of knitting. Simply put: anything which will stick to Velcro, will also stick to a cat's tongue. Too bad, because there is nothing more tempting to a cat than a ball or plug of cotton. When you see that your cat has swallowed a thread and it still partly hangs out of the mouth, you can hold it to prevent your cat swallowing more of it but never pull hard. It might already be stuck inside. This is especially true in case of a thread partially coming out when your cat is relieving himself. Don't try to pull on it while it is stuck but go at once to your veterinarian.

The cat's **normal temperature** reads about 38.5° C. A drop in temperature is mortally dangerous. Immediately wrap your cat in a small blanket and put her on a hot-water bottle of about 40° C. and call your veterinarian.
Cats are very sensitive animals, **medicines** which are totally harmless to humans, may be deadly to cats. Never administer medicines without prior consultation with your veterinarian.

Never give **aspirin** to cats. It takes four days before a cat's liver has cleansed the residues of a quarter of an aspirin tablet from the blood. A higher dose may cause poisoning and even death.

Never give **chocolate** to your cat. It contains theobromine, a substance that is poisonous to dogs and cats. Their bodies cannot break it down.

Harmful as well: paracetamol, antifreeze (it has a sweet taste), exhaust gases (for example carbon monoxide in garages), and so on. And, of course, **rat poison**. (Although dogs are more likely to eat this on account of its sweet taste). When a cat eats a poisoned mouse, she normally gets too little poison into her system to provoke bleeding but still, poisoning cannot be ruled out altogether! When her nose is bleeding immediately give her, before taking her to the veterinarian, vitamin K that stimulates coagulation of the blood.

Swiffer Wetjet is dangerous too. It is a cleanser to clean floors etc. It has happened that a dog and a few cats have died after Swiffer Wetjet was used. The poor dog and the cats died of kidney failure and problems with the liver. On the packing it is noted that Swiffer is dangerous for animals and children, but the letters are so small that they are easily overlooked. It seems the product contains antifreeze, which is extremely dangerous for dogs and cats. We only use the wonderful old-fashioned soft soap. We call that green soap. Smells good too!

Now that we are discussing dangers: recently a newspaper published a big warning to cat owners. Passive **smoking** is also very dangerous to the health of your cats. Your pets run the risk of developing serious health problems when they have to inhale the smoke from their people. One more reason to give up smoking!

'Smoke, smoke, smoke...
that cigarette,
Smoke, smoke, smoke...

Your cats

And yourself...
to death.'

This cheerful song was a hit when I was young. It's so true. Smoking is so dangerous. 'A straight-up walker' Puddie says, 'should not smoke. If he were meant to, the Good Lord would have given him a chimney! And we cats, we hate that filthy, black, stinking smoke. It sticks to our fur. Immediately, we wash it of. Horrible stuff! My tail gets really bushy from it. Stupid habit, smoking.'

Puddie is right. It's especially the cleaning of their coats that the cats do that is so dangerous. The wonderful cat magazine Your Cat magazine published a verry good article about smoking. *'Cats who live in a house were the people smoke run twice as much risk of getting a malignant Lymphoma than cats who live in a house free of smoke. That's what Vets from the Tufts University school of Veterinary Medicine in America say. If the cats are not allowed to go outside they are obliged to inhale the smoke too. The dirty sticky black smoke particles full of toxic substances fall on their fur and their pads. Cats are super clean and as soon as possible they lick themselves clean. And than, of course they swallow the poison, which is extremely dangerous.'*

Twice as much risk to get malignant Lymphoma is too much! For cats it's very difficult to heal from this illness. If people really love their dog or cat, they ought to stop smoking! Doctor Danielle Gunn-Moore, BSc BVM&S PhD ILTM MACVSc MRCVS, RCVS, specialist in Feline Medicine who often gives lectures about cat-illnesses in the University of Edinburgh agrees with all her heart with the American view about the dangers of smoking for cats.

'Smoking not only causes malignant Lymphoma for the cats who have to suffer passive smoke, but also illnesses of the respiratory system, such as chronic bronchitis, asthma and disorders of the chronic bronchial tubes or it aggravates them.

So please stop smoking your cats to death!

With many thanks to Sue Parslow from the Your Cat Magazine who gave me permission to use this information. The purrfect little tomcat is designed by my friend Anne Versteyne.

In chapter 18 I include a list of **plants** which are toxic to cats, but **Lilies** are so dangerous that I want to mention them in this chapter too. They are lethal. Even a small dose of the pollen that the cat licks from her fur can make her so ill that she will eventually die. All parts of the plant are poisonous. Just read all about it in chapter 18. It's horrific!

Never feed your cat raw **pork** or meat products made from pork. Cats may get a lethal disease from it. Raw chicken is dangerous as well. Some veterinarians however do recommend raw meat. Just make sure then that you buy the right kind of raw meat. Some producers of cat foods do supply raw meat that has been quality-controlled.

Fat is an absolute necessity for the cat, but never feed him used cooking fat, which is poisonous to them. Watch out for unsaturated (animal) fats, an excess of them may cause liver problems. Eating lots of liver may cause an excess of vitamin A and is therefore dangerous. Don't give more than two spoonfuls a week.

A **wasp's sting** in the throat area or in the mouth may be mortally dangerous. Apis Mellifica, a homeopathic medicine will reduce the swelling immediately. Administer it before going to the veterinarian. Dissolve three grains in some boiled water and trickle it in the pouch of the cheek by means of a syringe without needle.

Catching urine: Some cats will not use a litter tray when it's empty. In the pet shop you can buy a bag of pebbles for aquariums, rinse them thoroughly and dry them so they are completely free from dust particles, which may taint the urine sample. Put the pebbles in the empty tray. The pebbles don't absorb moisture and so you can easily pour the urine out of the tray or suck it up by means of a syringe and put it into a clean bottle. Some veterinarians sell bags with non-absorbent pebbles specifically for this purpose. Katkor for instance www.katkor.com . Holding a spoon under your cat while he is urinating is another way to catch urine for a test.

Administering Pills

First explain to your cat what you are about to do and why. It really matters, otherwise she might put up a fight. Grasp her head with your left hand, put your thumb and index finger on the corners of her mouth and slowly bend her head a little bit upwards and backwards. At the same time push your thumb and index finger against her mouth so that it opens. Pick up the pill

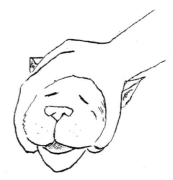

with your other hand and slowly push it as far as possible to the back of the tongue. Quickly close her mouth while keeping her head tilted backwards.

Softly rub her throat up and down and wait till you see the cat swallow. When you see her licking her nose you can be sure she has swallowed the pill. (It also happens that sometimes the cat pretends that she has swallowed the pill but spits it out later.)

Immediately after she swallowed the pill I always give her some water with syringe without needle or a littlebit of butter and some chicken. It 'lubricates' and they love it. So, I am sure that the pill does not stay blocked in the oesophagus, which can cause serious problems. To give butter afterwards is more effective than coating the pill with butter. Then it will slither out of your hands. Of course, you tell her how plucky she has been and you give her some tasty titbits. It is recommended to practise regularly.

For instance while grooming your cat, just open her mouth and insert your finger. Then give her a titbit.

I brush the teeth of my fluffies, that's even a better opportunity to practise. You can also hide the pill, crushed or not, in a snack. A crushed pill might taste bitter. Another way is to dissolve the pill in some water, suck up the solution in a syringe without needle and trickle it inside the cheek pouch. Not very nice for your cat but at least you can be sure he has taken the medicine.

The easiest way to administer a **liquid medicine** is by using a disposable needle-less syringe without needle, available in the pharmacy. Hold your cat's head tilted upwards a bit and slightly pull the cheek pouch to one side. Slowly squirt some liquid into the

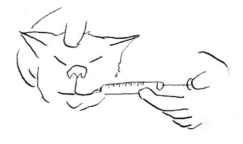

mouth and wait until she swallows. Do give very little at a time to prevent choking, which may cause **pneumonia**.

I have read somewhere that when a cat resists your giving her a pill, you could try to put her with her paws against a screen and softly press your body against the cat's body. She will then cling to the screen and so your hands are free. Wrapping the cat tightly in a towel with only the head sticking out also works.

Toxoplasmosis

It's a pity that there are still women who, out of fear of toxoplasmosis, will part with their kitty when they are pregnant. It's absolutely unnecessary. True, toxoplasmosis is a danger to the foetus when the mother is not immune to the disease. Many people however have already had the infection and you cannot get it twice in your life. You can have yourself tested for it. The toxoplasma parasite is a single-celled organism. Infection may occur in the first place by eating raw or partly cooked **meat**. The disease can also be transmitted through badly washed **vegetables** and through contaminated **soil.**
Cat faeces may cause toxoplasmosis when more than two days old, so
when you clean the tray thoroughly every day there is no risk. In principle cats excrete the oocytes only once in their lifetime, mostly when they are kittens and only for a few weeks. After that they are immune. It is indeed better that a pregnant woman wears gloves when cleaning the litter tray or has someone else do it, but that's the only precaution she has to take to prevent infection. Fresh droppings cannot cause toxoplasmosis. Cats are very clean and immediately lick off any trace of discharge in their fur. It's an injustice to get rid of your cat because a human kitty is on her way! Besides there is nothing more beautiful than children growing up with cats or dogs. They will be the best of friends.

The editorial staff of 'Hart voor Dieren' (Heart for Animals) gave me permission to include the following piece. I am very happy about this because it may save the life of your cat. I do hope you will never need it!

The article, written by Doctor Henk Lommers, was originally published in the magazine 'Hart voor Dieren'. (Heart for Animals)

Artificial Respiration

When your cat has difficulty breathing, her breathing is slow and irregular. She will stretch her neck and exert herself to inhale enough air. The mucous membranes of tongue and eyes turn blue and if the breathing does not provide enough air, unconsciousness may follow. When this happens immediate intervention is of the utmost importance: apply artificial respiration immediately.

So, as **soon** as possible:

First remove anything that squeezes the cat's body. Next, open the mouth and slowly try to pull out the tongue. Use a piece of cloth if the tongue slips away. Check for objects blocking the throat and, if any, remove them as soon as possible. Try sliding the object upwards by pressing the throat from the outside immediately below the location of the object. Try to catch it. Use the cloth when the object slips away.

Lay your cat on her right side on a hard surface. Stretch her legs away from her body so that the chest is free and can expand. Stretch the neck and pull out the tongue as far as possible. All this should be done smoothly and quickly.

Then apply artificial respiration:

Put two fingers next to each other on the left side of the thorax right behind the shoulder blade. Push in the thorax evenly, exert force if necessary but not too much. When the thorax moves downwards release it immediately so that it will spring back to its original position. This will allow air to be sucked in. When the thorax is back in its starting position, push it down again. Pushing down and releasing should be done 12 times per minute.

Push in and count: 1-2.
Release and count: 1-2-3.
Again, push in and count:1-2...
Etc.

Mouth-to-nose resuscitation:

When artificial respiration cannot be applied because, for example the ribs are broken or because of some injury, you have to apply mouth-to-nose resuscitation:

Close her mouth and pull the upper lips tightly over the under lips so no air can escape. Put your lips on both nostrils and blow air into them. Blow hard so you can see the thorax rise as air flows into the lungs. Do this during three counts. **So 1-2-3 blow air inside.**

Remove your lips from the nose and let the cat exhale during two seconds, **count 1-2**.

Then again blow air inside for three seconds.

1-2-3 counts blow air inside.
1-2 counts let him exhale.
1-2-3 blow air inside.
Etc.

In case of cardiac arrest, you should also give heart massage.

In case of cardiac arrest:

Lay the cat on its right side, the left foreleg stretched forwards as far as possible.
Place the palm of your hand on the breastbone right behind the forelegs in such a way that your thumb is on one side and your fingers on the other side of the breast. The heart is immediately below your fingers and by squeezing the chest reasonably firmly, the blood will be squeezed out of the heart. It will fill with blood by itself again afterwards. Don't squeeze too hard.

1 count push down,
1 count release,
1 count push down etc...
About 15 times every minute.

After **2 minutes** verify if the heart starts beating by itself. If not, continue applying resuscitation.

Sometimes **both** have to be applied at the same time.

So: **apply half a minute heart massage and half a minute artificial respiration.**

Check every two minutes whether the heart beats by itself. If it does, continue applying artificial respiration only until the cat starts breathing by itself.

With many thanks to Doctor Henk Lommers.

My friend Anne made the exquisite drawings in this chapter. Thank you so much, Ann, for allowing your tomcat to teach us First Aid Techniques. He is such a sweet fellow!

Beware of people who dislike cats.

Irish proverb

Chapter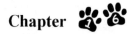

Miscellaneous, Cats Confidential and Animals in the Bible and the Koran

The smallest feline is a masterpeace.

Leonardo da Vinci

This chapter contains some funny and/or interesting facts about cats.

In Chapter 14 and 15 you will have read about the accidents which cats risk getting when they are living with their Straightup-walkers. You know now how to give your cats pills and how to save them by artificial respiration and in case of a cardiac arrest. Also my friend Carina and I told you how to make it easier for the kitties to adjust to the human way of living, which often is not easy for them to understand. You have read about the ways to teach them something. But to be honest, humans could learn much more from their cats. The lessons they give their people are so much more valuable. They are lessons of life!

I am very glad and thankful that I am allowed to use some of the wonderful stories from the Cats Confidential Newsletter. Cats Confidential is the monthly newsletter that reports on the remarkable abilities and accomplishments of cats. The mission of Cats Confidential is to remind cat lovers all over the world how wonderful cats are and how much people can learn from them. To tell about the remarkable and unexplained mental abilities cats possess and how cats have changed the course of history and saved people's lives

All proceeds from the subscriptions to Cats Confidential go to the Grey Rocks Cat Sanctuary. That's where also Smokey and Timothy lived and live. They are two very wise cats indeed! I am sure you will love the stories. The address and how to subscribe is noted in chapter 21.

312

Smokey and Timothy: a friendship that truly deserves immortality

Timothy was born in the cold winter of 2001, somewhere far back under the floor of a house behind the Grey Rocks Cat Sanctuary's main building.
He was one of four kittens, the rest of whom have disappeared and, we presume, have gone to kitty heaven. Timothy was the last of his litter, but he does have two older brothers and an older sister from an earlier litter. The mother of all of them is a beautiful but very feral tortoiseshell/calico whom we were not able to catch and have spayed until she had given birth to three litters.
As a kitten, Timothy, of course, had no father whom he knew. But he adopted a father – Smokey, a long-haired male about eight years old who arrived at the Sanctuary as a kitten after a rough life as a stray.

Timothy became devotedly attached to Smokey, and Smokey, unlike many older cats, was more than willing to accept this little kitten as his friend and spend time with him, groom him and, we are certain, impart to him the knowledge essential to being a cat. These two cats truly loved each other.

Kittens do not remain kittens very long, and Timothy is now four years old. He's used up several of his nine lives, having been accidentally locked in a neighbour's basement for more than two weeks and having had his tail bitten and broken, probably by a predator. The tail became infected and had to be amputated, but Timothy is still healthy and well. Several years ago Smokey disappeared and, we are sure, went to cat heaven, but not before helping Timothy learn the important things about being a cat. We know they had good communication. We know they loved each other. And we think it's important for our best conclusions as to their conversations to continue in our newsletter.

Cat conversations with Smokey and Timothy

The morning sun had just risen above the huge hackberry trees
guarding the eastern border of the Grey Rocks Cat Sanctuary, and Smokey carefully selected a large area of sunshine that would be there a while – at least until mid-afternoon, when the sun would drop down over the top of the mountain. Smokey was a very large cat with long, dark fur that turned reddish in the summer and very light grey in the winter on his back and

underside. In both his ears were noticeable nicks that dated back to ancient battles in his younger days as a stray. Now neutered, he lived a comfortable life at the sanctuary and had become unofficially but unanimously the senior male resident cat. He was loved by all, including not only three of his daughters who also lived there, but also several very young cats like one-year-old Timothy, who were no earthly kin but who revered their adopted father figure.

Timothy, who was shorthaired and solid black with large, innocent, yellow eyes, curled up next to Smokey in the sunshine, and when Smokey rolled on his back with obvious pleasure, Timothy did the same. Cats communicate in many ways – some known, like body language involving tails, ears, whiskers and physical positions. But lacking the human ability to communicate verbally, they make up for it with what can only be called mind-to-mind communication. How this works, nobody knows. But is very clear and specific, and there are rarely any misunderstandings. Timothy sat up and washed his face with his paws and then settled into a crouch.

"Uncle Smokey, so many times I see our humans sad and worried. I know they love us, but why can't they be happy like we are and enjoy life like we do?"
Smokey yawned. "Beats me, buddy. Seems like humans are just too bogged down with a lot o' silly unimportant things that they don't have time to understand what life is all about. I get the feelin' they don't appreciate what they got.
Seems like they're just treadin' water till it's over and wearin' themselves out."
"Do humans ever chase butterflies, Uncle Smokey? I did that this morning, and it was so much fun. I never caught one, but I just had the greatest time. Then I found a shady spot under an azalea bush and took a nap. That was fun too."
"That's what living is about, boy. Enjoyin' everything there is to enjoy in the world. Knowin' what's important. Like right now it's important to get up and walk over to see if anybody left a little canned food on top o' the dry stuff they give us. I sure hope they did, but if they didn't, no big deal. Nothin' to worry about."
He paused and sat up and looked out over the green spring lawn. "Hey, there's your sister Melanie out there. Go sneak up and pounce on her. She'll

314

pop you in the chops and chase you all over the yard, and that ain't just only fun, it's good exercise." He watched as Timothy crouched, ready to spring out and surprise his sister. And he remembered when he was a kitten. Life was fun then, too.

Smokey and Timothy crouched on a wide stone ledge of the large house at the Grey Rocks Cat Sanctuary. They had already eaten their evening meal, and they were watching some of the other cats eat theirs. Smokey sat up and began the after-dinner clean-up of his grey-black fur, then licked his paws and began to wash his face with them. One-year-old Timothy was acutely interested in watching another black cat, not much older than he was, but with longer fur.
He cocked his head and looked at Smokey. "Where did the new cat come from, Uncle Smokey? He doesn't seem to be wild. But he has a funny attitude."

"Blackie? Don't know exactly, buddy. He just appeared one night about a month ago. Scrawny and half-starved, with almost all the hair on his tail and back gone. Just showed up at mealtime and ate and ate and ate. He was so thin you could see his ribs sticking out."
"And our humans let him stay?"
"Sure. They'd do anything in the world for cats. That's how I got here about ten years ago. Just came, and they were glad to feed me."
"He looks very nice now. Getting his fur back. But his feet look funny. And he still has an attitude."
"You'd have one too if somebody'd cut off all your toes."

Timothy was shocked. "Who would do a horrible thing like that?"
"Humans. Who else? Probably stupid ones. He must have belonged to somebody, because when they took him to the vet they found out he'd not only been neutered, but he'd been declawed."
"Declawed? You mean they pulled out his claws?"
"That's what most humans think. But that's not what they do. They cut off his toes, claws and all. Front feet and back feet both."

315

Timothy looked at Blackie as he crouched to eat his supper. "But a cat needs his claws. How on earth can he climb a tree? Or protect himself? Or catch something to eat?"

Smokey gently closed his eyes and then opened them again. "Well, son, he can't. I swear, I don't know how he ever got here alive. He ain't from around here, and he must have been out there a long time to be so starved. After his humans did all that to him, they probably moved away and left him, or just threw him out on his own. But he'll be all right at the sanctuary. Our humans will keep him inside the house and feed him good."
"No wonder he's got a bad attitude."

Smokey licked a paw and rubbed it across his face. "He'll get over it. That's one big difference between cats and humans, buddy. Cats learn to accept whatever life deals 'em and make the best of it. Humans don't seem to be able to do that. Blackie 'll be okay. But it's a good lesson for a young cat like you. We got a good life here, and don't you forget it. So you try hard to make friends with Blackie. He's a pretty nice little cat, and a tough little cat too, to have found this place and survived to get here. Cats without claws don't last long in the wild." Smokey curled himself up for a nap, thinking how starved he was when he arrived at the sanctuary years before. And how thankful he was that he still had his claws.

Cats just know these things

Smokey and Timothy sat in rocking chairs on the porch of the Grey Rocks Cat Sanctuary, watching the tops of tall trees blow in the wind as a thunderstorm moved through. Lightening could be seen occasionally, and a few seconds later came the roll of thunder. Timothy watched the sky with the inquisitive eyes of a kitten and then turned to look at Smokey, whose eyes were half closed.

Uncle Smokey, did you notice that cousin Ferdie came home from his trip yesterday? It was a beautiful day, and the sun was shining, but it seems like he knew there was going to be a storm.

"I've noticed that right after Ferdie comes home from his trips, there's always rain or snow or something a cat wouldn't want to be travelling in. How does he know what's going to happen?"

Smokey shifted his position, making his chair start to rock, and then settled back down again. "Cats just know these things, buddy. It's part of bein' a cat. Don't matter too much to humans. They travel in nice warm, dry cars and carry umbrellas around. But us cats need to know to go home and not get caught way out in the boondocks in a thunderstorm like this one."

Timothy was puzzled. "But I'm a cat, and I didn't know it was going to rain today."

"You will when you get older, Tim. When you start travelin' out in the woods. You'll just get a feelin' that you need to get home pretty quick for your own good. I still get that feelin' myself, but I stay home most o' the time anyway."

Timothy licked a black paw and rubbed it across his nose. "Does that mean we're smarter than humans?"

"It sure means we use our brains more. Humans got bigger brains, but they ain't learned how to use 'em very well. Us cats know how to use our brains to do all kinds of things humans never have been able to do. Did you ever look at our humans and kinda know in advance what they were about to do?"

"I guess so. And then they do it. And sometimes I seem to know when something bad is going to happen...or something good. And, sure enough, it happens. Is that what you mean, Uncle Smokey?"

"Absolutely. Just like we know when there's a big ol' mean dog comin' into the yard, even before we see it or hear it. And we know to skedaddle up a tree or get somewhere where we're safe."

Smokey sat up in his chair as rain continued to pour down.

"Tim, sometimes you may sense that somethin' bad is gonna happen that could hurt our humans, and you need to warn 'em. If you ever get that feelin', do everything you can to get their attention. That's part of our responsibility to our humans. I knew a cat once that got his humans to wake up in the middle of the night and get out of the house because it was on fire, and the humans would have burned up.

Timothy crouched, his eyes half closing. "I think I can tell when our humans are sad about something. I try to rub against them to cheer them up. It works pretty well."

Smokey scratched behind his ear. "There you go, buddy. That's what bein' a cat is all about. It's your job to do what we can to help our humans, because they're good to us and feed us and let us come in the house."

He jumped down from the chair as a big bolt of lightening flashed through the sky and a huge thunder clap followed.

"And that's what I'm gonna do right this minute. Go in the house. That storm's getting too close for comfort."

He pushed his way through the cat door and Timothy followed.

Ferdie, who had arrived the day before, was already sleeping in a hall chair, curled up into a black and white bundle of fur, one paw folded over his eyes, safe from the storm he had known was on the way.

For a cat, life's too short to spend it fighting wars.

Smokey and little Timothy were watching television in the upstairs sitting room of the Grey Rocks Cat Sanctuary. Their humans had left the set on to entertain the cats while they were gone. Usually it was tuned to a channel where animals appeared, but today there was news, with pictures of soldiers and tanks and airplanes and sounds of machine gun fire and explosions.

Timothy's eyes were wide and his ears tuned like two satellite dishes to the noises of battle. "What on earth is going on, Uncle Smokey?"

Smokey yawned. He had seen all this before and had heard his humans talking about it. "It's a bunch o' humans fightin' a war, buddy."

Timothy never took his eyes off the TV screen. "I've heard about wars. But I never realised wars looked and sounded like that."

Smokey had been lying on his side, but now he adjusted to a crouch from which he could see the screen better. "More crazy stuff humans do, Tim. Killin' and destroyin'."

"Why do they do it?"

Smokey half closed his eyes. "Well, s'pose a bunch of orange cats got together and decided to take over a territory of some black and white cats and just run 'em off or kill' em. Just for the heck of it. They'd come swarmin' down, and they'd all fight one another and there'd be dead cats all over the place and those that weren't dead would be so scratched and clawed and bitten that life wouldn't be worth livin'."

Timothy cocked his head in puzzlement. "But cats don't do anything like that, Uncle Smokey. Cats may fight each other now and then, but cats don't fight wars."

"I know, boy, I know. But humans do. Usually because some wild-eyed humans gets 'em together and tells 'em there's a bunch of 'bad' humans out there that don't believe what the 'good' humans believe, and so the best thing is to wipe 'em out. So they get all worked up and go to war. Don't make no sense, but that's what they do. Been doin' it for as long as there've been humans livin' on earth."

"Because one kind of human is different from another?"

"Seems like that has somethin' to do with it. Humans come in different colors, just like cats. But shoot, I'm gray and you're black and we got black and whites and calicos. Most of us have tails, but Bob and Roberta don't have any because they're Manxes. Blackie don't have any claws. But all of us here at Grey Rocks get along just fine."

"If we get along, why can't humans get along?"

"Oh, they'll learn, Tim, they'll learn. It just takes 'em a lot longer to figure out what us cats have known all the time. Life's too short to spend it fightin' wars."

"I wish our humans would come home and get some other kinds of pictures on the screen. Wars are just horrible. I'm so glad I'm a cat."

Smokey rolled over on his back. "Me too, buddy. Me too.

Lessons from cats 1

Cats achieve happiness by not living in fear of the unknown.

Psychologists have said that one of the primary reasons many people are never able to achieve happiness is that they live constantly in fear of the unknown and worry about things that exist only in their imagination. The fear that they may have some terrible illness prompts them to go to the doctor and then worry constantly when the doctor is unable to find anything wrong.

When the economy is bad, they fear they may lose their jobs. And, of course, many religions have prospered because humans have no idea of what happens to them after they die, fear the worst and try to buy their way into heaven.

Cats don't live in fear of the unknown. This doesn't mean cats aren't cautious. And it doesn't mean cats don't experience fear when they are threatened by something real, such as an automobile or a predator. But they are able to enjoy a happiness most humans never achieve because they don't live in fear of the unknown.

There's a big difference between fear of the unknown and caution. Any intelligent person will exercise caution so as to guard against the legitimate possibility of danger. And when something real and dangerous is encountered, fear is an emotion that sends a rush of blood and oxygen to our brains to help us figure out how to protect ourselves. But too many people fear things that exist only in their imaginations, and therefore cannot enjoy the real happiness life is all about. Cats can, because they don't spend their lives imagining things to be afraid of and worry about. We could learn so much from cats.

Lessons from cats 2

Learn to have faith in your body's ability to heal itself

Polls and surveys show that the skyrocketing cost of health care and the continuing controversy over how best to make it available are extremely high on the list of things that concern Americans. Why has the health care situation gotten out of hand? Because Americans do not know, do not believe or refuse to accept one very simple fact: That 90 per cent of all the problems we go to doctors about would cure themselves even if we did not go to doctors.

Cats, even though they've never attended medical school (where that fact is well known, though not too well publicised) are very much aware of this. Cats know that along with the gift of life from their creator, they were given still another marvellous gift: a body which in most cases heals and repairs itself. Exactly the same gift humans were given, but often do not appreciate. Cats get sick the same as we do. They suffer physical injuries just as we do.

320

But they rarely, if ever, complain. They simply adjust their lifestyles to help enable their bodies to heal. And it works.

More than ten years ago a little black and white tabby named Junior showed obvious signs of some kind of illness. His family took him to a veterinarian, who promptly gave him a test and announced that he had feline leukaemia. The vet was astonished when Junior's family decided to take him home instead of letting the vet put him to sleep. As they paid the bill, the woman at the front desk commented quietly to them, "Don't worry too much. My cat was diagnosed with the same thing and given six months to live. That was five years ago, and he's doing fine."

They took Junior home, and he immediately found a spot on a wall where the sun shone a large part of the day. He rested and slept there during the next five of six weeks. His energy returned, and he lived a normal and happy life for more than two years. Junior knew his body would take care of itself if he gave it a chance.

People criticise cats because they sleep a lot. But what they're doing is normal. They're storing up energy for times when they need it, perhaps in sudden bursts, to escape from a dog or jump out of the way of a car. Many health authorities say humans would benefit greatly by doing the same thing, taking "cat naps" in the afternoon or evening.

As it was with little Junior, the warm sunshine can be a great healer for humans as well as for cats. And so can resting in the cool shade on a hot summer's day.

Watch your cat when he or she wakes up. Notice the process of stretching – something at which cats are experts. If you would do the same thing before hopping out of bed, you'd feel much better all day and chances of sore or strained muscles would be reduced significantly.

Many cats throw up more frequently than their humans would prefer, but this is not a reason to rush them to the vet. It is usually a reaction of the cat's body, which may well be protecting it from serious illness. Possibly it had eaten spoiled food or something else that could have caused harm if it had stayed in the cat's stomach.

Watch your cat in the early morning and early evening. Outdoor cats will be racing around the yard, running up trees and chasing one another. Indoor cats will be racing from room to room and leaping on and over the furniture. This is exercise, and it's another way they keep their bodies in shape. Humans would benefit by doing the same. There are, of course, times when cats really need to go to the vet. But there are many more times when they don't. Even after a tough fight leaving cuts and bruises and bite marks and claw marks, the cat will usually survive nicely simply by licking its wounds and being sure it gets enough undisturbed rest.

A recent survey showed that doctors in one city treat an average of 38 patients a day and spend about six minutes with each patient. Multiply that by the 90 per cent of those consultations that were probably not necessary, and you have a tremendous amount of money being spend unnecessarily – often the taxpayers' money. Cats would rather let their marvellous bodies heal themselves as they were intended to do. It's much cheaper. And, best of all, it works.

Lessons from cats 3

The importance of taking life one day at a time

Some years ago there was a very popular gospel-type song called "One day at a time." Among its lyrics were the lines, "Yesterday's gone, and tomorrow may never be mine." One of the hardest things for humans to do is to take life one day at a time without letting their minds drift back to the past or worrying about the future. We could learn so much from cats.

For a cat, today is today, and that's what's important. Cats make the best of each day, enjoying it as much as possible and doing the best they can without worrying about what may happen tomorrow.
For a cat, yesterday's gone, except for any lessons that might have been learned in the past and are carried over in the cat's brain as a safety measure for the future.

But unlike humans, the cat doesn't reminisce about the good old days of the past or let itself be haunted by something bad that happened in the past. And the cat doesn't fantasise about wonderful things that may happen in the future, or worry about bad things that may happen. After all, for cats and people alike, tomorrow may never be. Someone once said, "Today is the first day of the rest of your life." That would seem to make today a very important day. The most important day. A day for cats and people to make the most of.

Lessons from cats 4

Whatever happens, cats will adapt instead of complaining

There's an old saying that you can tell the temperature by the length of the cat.
And it's true. On a hot summer day, you'll probably find your cat lying stretched out to a length you never dreamed possible. And in the winter when it's very cold, your cat will take a nap curled up in a tight little ball, making itself more comfortable by the warmth of its own body. Cats don't waste time feeling sorry for themselves. They know how to adapt. We should do our best to learn from them.

When the weather is hot, we whine about the heat and turn on the air conditioner and then complain about the electric bill. In the winter we whine about the cold, turn up the heat and then complain about the gas bill. In these and many other situations we're too busy feeling sorry for ourselves to adapt – that is, to make the best of whatever situation comes along, especially if it's something we can do nothing about.

If a cat is sick or injured, it will find a quiet place and rest and give its body time to get well or its injury to heal. When we are sick we wonder why this is happening to us and feel sorry for ourselves. Then we fill up our bodies with medicines or pain killers, many of which actually keep our bodies from healing as fast as they would if we simply adapted to our situation and let our bodies heal themselves.

As we and our cats go through life, we come upon unpleasant situations every day that we can do nothing about. Cats don't like these any more than we do, but they don't waste time worrying about them. They adapt. We humans, on the other hand, spend time feeling sorry for ourselves and then spend more time trying to change things that cannot be changed. We could learn so much from cats.

How the unconditional love of a cat helps strengthen our immune systems

In the latter half of the 20th century, medical science, after a long hit-and-miss history of seeking to discover "cures" for all the ailments of the human race, finally figured out that the best way to cure just about anything – from cancer on down – was to utilise the powers of the human body to cure itself. Our bodies cure themselves through our immune system, an amazing mechanism in which cells from the thymus gland travel through our blood vessels, seeking out, attacking and killing the bad things that cause disease and disability.

The answer to many problems, medical science discovered, was to strengthen our immune systems so they could do the best job possible of protecting us.

What does all this have to do with cats? A lot. Studies and many case histories have shown clearly that the love and support of a cat is magnificent stress-fighter, a form of physiological relaxation and preventive medicine. Researchers say this is the way to keep our immunity to certain diseases strong.

Scientists in psycho-neuroimmunology have found connections between states of mind, the brain and the immune system. And the unconditional love which cats have for us is thought to be the most powerful known stimulant of the immune system. Indeed, researchers feel that all disease may be ultimately related to a lack of love and that the resulting exhaustion and depression of the immune system leads to physical vulnerability. Cats provide the unconditional love that has a positive effect on the immune system and thereby enables the thymus cells to do their job more efficiently when our bodies are in danger.

And there's more. Have you ever watched your cat do such ridiculous things that they made you laugh? Well, just a few minutes of laughter lowers stress hormone levels and raises the number of circulating antibodies that fight off disease. Laughter may also stimulate brain chemicals, which can relieve pain and help our bodies relax. Many doctors have concluded that all healing is related to the ability to give and accept unconditional love. And a multitude of case histories have proven that the love and support of cats have helped untold numbers of humans fight off and conquer diseases and other ailments.

What cats do for us

- Warm our laps.
- Give us someone to talk to.
- Help reduce high blood pressure.
- Bring the winter air inside, nestled in their coats.
- Create a kindred feeling with other "cat people".
- Turn common household objects like bottle caps into toys.
- Make us more aware of birds.
- Donate their services as alarm clocks.
- Display daring acrobatic feats right in front of our eyes.
- Contribute to living a longer life.
- Make a window sill more beautiful.
- Keep mice on the run.
- Inspire poets and playwrights.
- Teach us how to land on our feet.
- Let us indulge our desires to really spoil someone.
- Make our homes warmer.
- Remind us that life is mysterious.
- Share with us the all-is-well experience of purring.
- Instruct us in the luxurious art of stretching.
- Show us how to lick our wounds and go on.
- Give us cool cartoon characters.
- Make even an old worn couch look beautiful.
- Open our hearts.

Sir Winston Churchill

Greatest Briton who ever lived' loved cats

 Best Friends Magazine, the excellent publication of the Best Friends Animal Society, contains in its current issue write-ups of some of history's famous cat lovers (ailurophiles) and cat haters who were afraid of cats (ailurophobes). Perhaps the most famous cat lover was Sir Winston Churchill, Prime Minister of Great Britain during World War II.

Sir Winston, who was inspired by his ginger-coloured cat in 1940 to write the words for a famous speech that boosted the morale of the British at a terrible time when London was being bombed almost every night (See Cats Confidential, December 2003), refused to start dinner until his cat, Jock, was present at the table.

Jock, it was reported, also attended wartime cabinet meetings held in an underground war room, and Churchill himself took the cat to the shelters when the air raid sirens sounded. The March issue of Smithsonian Magazine contains an extensive article on Churchill and the opening of a museum in his honour on the 40th anniversary of his death at the age of 90.

Churchill was a truly heroic leader without whom Great Britain might have ceased to exist. All cat lovers should be proud that this man, who, in a recent BBC poll, was voted the greatest Briton who ever lived. Like us, he was a great cat lover!

Doctor Vernon Coleman has written many books, among them some first-rate books about cats, for example The Alice-Series, We Love Cats and his beautiful new ones: The Cat Basket and The Secret Lives of Cats (see the bibliography at the end of this book). 'We love cats' is filled with 'wonderful' cat facts. I got permission to include some in this book.

- Cats' hearing is much more sensitive than that of humans and dogs. (Cats' hearing stops at 65 kHz whereas humans' hearing stops at 20 kHz).

- In ancient Egypt the penalty for killing a cat was death.

- Cats purr when they are feeling any intense emotion - whether it is pleasure or pain.

- Cats have an excellent night vision but cannot see in total darkness.

- When running flat out, a domestic cat can reach about 50 km per hour.

- Cats can be identified by their nose pads. Every cat's nose pad is unique.

- If you are stressed you may be able to lower your blood pressure a little by stroking a cat.

- Cats have eighteen toes - five toes on each front paw, but only four toes on each back paw.

- A cat cannot see directly down. (This is why cats can't see pieces of food which are lying on the floor right under their noses.)

- The cat flap was invented by Sir Isaac Newton. He also invented the kitten flap. It's a smaller version of the cat flap which can be easily pushed open by kittens.

- Cats can get sunburn. White cats especially are susceptible to cancer on their ears when they get too much exposure to the sun.

- An English cat called Puss died in 1939 just one day after her 36th birthday.

- Author Ernest Hemingway shared his life with 30 cats.

- Cats can make 100 different vocal sounds.

- Most tortoiseshell cats are female. The only exceptions are occasional, sterile males.
- A cat has 32 muscles in each ear!

- Florence Nightingale owned 60 cats during her lifetime. She refused to travel anywhere without her cats.

- There is a myth that the first cat appeared when Noah, afraid that the rats might eat all the food on the ark, prayed to God for help. God responded by making the lion sneeze. When the lion sneezed he produced a small cat.

- Frederic Chopin's *Cat Waltz* was partially inspired by his pet cat, which bravely jumped onto his keyboard while he was composing.

Cats tend to have shorter lives than people - and to age more rapidly. The following table shows (roughly) how old a cat is in human terms.

- The cat who is 1 year old is 15 years old in human years.
- The cat who is 2 years old is 25 years old in human years.
- The cat who is 4 years old is 40 years old in human years.
- The cat who is 7 years old is 50 years old in human years.
- The cat who is 10 years old is 60 years old in human years.
- The cat who is 15 years old is 75 years old in human years.
- The cat who is 20 years old is 105 years old in human years.
- The cat who is 30 years old is 120 years old in human years.

With many thanks to Doctor Vernon Coleman.
Taken from the book: We Love Cats by Dr Vernon Coleman.
Chilton Designs Publishers, Publishing House
Copyright 2002

Animals in the Bible

Too often people have used and still use the Bible as an excuse to abuse, torture and kill animals. Allegedly 'animals are inferior beings whose only purpose is to serve us. It says so in the Bible!' What a nonsense! The Bible doesn't say so at all! The Bible is indeed the greatest book ever written, but you can interpret its texts in many ways. That's why bad people will interpret the Holy Book wrongly and distort it to justify their evil doings.

We all come from the same source. We are all here on earth for just a short while before moving on to our next life. Yes, animals too move to a next life!

328

They are certainly not inferior to us. Quite the contrary is true! We can learn such a lot from them. As far as giving love and affection is concerned, animals are much better at that than most people. Animals give unconditional love.

In Taylor Caldwell's fine novels 'Dear and Glorious Physician' (a novel about St Luke) and 'Great Lion of God' (a novel about St Paul), there are many stories about Christ's love for animals. How He always interfered on their behalf. How He enjoyed nature, the birds, the butterflies, the flowers, during His long walks with His followers. After all, was He not born in a stable surrounded by animals? Luke was also very fond of animals and the animals were fond of him. In Taylor Caldwell's book Luke says that animals have the soul of an innocent and simple child and that God loves animals. Luke is my favourite apostle.

True, the Old Testament contains a lot of animal misery but in those days there was also much human misery. Those times were very different from our times and therefore you have to understand the Bible in terms of the times in which it was written. Life then was very tough. I hate to read about the bloody sacrifices of animals but thanks to the coming of Our Lord Jesus the sacrificing is not necessary any more. Jesus sacrificed Himself and so made all further offering unnecessary. Jesus' coming into the world brought Love and Peace. The Christmas message is so marvellous, only some people still don't hear it in their heart.The Lord gave us so many beautiful proverbs. Like these:

'Whenever you did this for one of the least important of these brothers of mine, you did it for me.'
'In everything do to others as you would have them do to you.'
'You shall not murder.'

The Lord intended these proverbs also for the animals. You must also be kind to them. It is incomprehensible that precisely 'in the name of the Lord' so much killing has been done and still is being done. He, who is all Love and Peace!

But even the Old Testament says that God definitely thought well of animals. In the first place it is written that animals clearly have a soul. Many people still deny this.

The following proverbs come from the CD-ROM 'Animals in the Bible' from the Institute Johannes Calvijn and from the Bible (New Revised Standard Version).

Genesis 1:24 And God said, "Let the earth bring forth living creatures of every kind: cattle and creeping things and wild animals of the earth of every kind." And it was so.

Genesis 1:27 So God created humankind in his image,
in the image of God he created them; male and female he created them.
Man and animal have been created on the same day as **fellow creatures**: one is indeed the fellow or companion of the other.

Genesis 1:30 "And to every beast of the earth, and to every bird of the air, and to everything that creeps on the earth, everything that has the breath of life, I have given every green plant for food." And it was so.

Genesis 2:15 The Lord God took the man and put him into the Garden of Eden to till it and keep it.
(To till and to keep is not to destroy and to exterminate!)
And when the Flood came, God also saved the animals and He made the covenant both with Noah and the animals.

Genesis 8:1 But God remembered Noah and all the wild animals and all the domestic animals that were with him in the ark. And God made a wind blow over the earth, and the waters subsided.

Genesis 8:8 Then he sent out the dove from him, to see if the waters had subsided from the face of the ground.

Genesis 8:9 But the dove found no place to set its foot, and it returned to him in the ark, for the waters were still on the face of the whole earth. So he put out his hand and took it and brought it into the ark with him.

Genesis 8:10 He waited another seven days, and again he sent out the dove from the ark.

Genesis 8:11 And the dove came back to him in the evening, and there in its beak was a freshly plucked olive leaf; so Noah knew that the waters had subsided from the earth.

Genesis 9:11 "I establish my covenant with you, that never again shall all flesh be cut off by the waters of a flood, and never again shall there be a flood to destroy the earth."

Genesis 9:16 "When the bow is in the clouds, I will see it and remember the everlasting covenant between God and every living creature of all flesh that is on the earth."

Proverbs 12:10 The righteous know the needs of their animals, but the mercy of the wicked is cruel.

About sacrifice:

Proverbs 21:3 To do righteousness and justice is more acceptable to the Lord than sacrifice.

The following proverbs show that God positively loved animals:

Proverbs 27:23 Know well the condition of your flocks, and give attention to your herds.

Proverbs 30:24 Four things on earth are small, yet they are exceedingly wise:

Proverbs 30:25 The ants are a people without strength, yet they provide their food in the summer;

Proverbs 30:26 The badgers are a people without power, yet they make their home in the rocks;

Proverbs 30:27 The locusts have no king,
yet all of them march in rank;

Proverbs 30:28 The lizard can be grasped in the hand, yet it is found in kings' palaces.

Proverbs 30:29 Three things are stately in their stride; four are stately in their gait:

Proverbs 30:30 The lion, which is mightiest among wild animals and does not turn back before any;

Proverbs 30:31 The strutting rooster, the he-goat, and a king striding before his people.

Ecclesiastes 3:19 For the fate of humans and the fate of animals is the same; as one dies, so dies the other. They all have the same breath, and humans have no advantage over the animals; for all is vanity.

Ecclesiastes 3:21 Who knows whether the human spirit goes upward and the spirit of animals goes downward to the earth?

Isaiah 1:3 The ox knows its owner, and the donkey its master's crib; but Israel does not know, my people do not understand.
(Here the prophet points out the loyalty and attachment of animals in contrast with the people of Israel).

Isaiah 11:6 The wolf shall live with the lamb,
the leopard shall lie down with the kid,
the calf and the lion and the fatling together,
and a little child shall lead them.

Jonah 4:11 "And should I not be concerned about Nineveh, that great city, in which there are more than a hundred and twenty thousand persons who do not know their right hand from their left, and also many animals?" (The Lord loves all of His Creation. Here God blames Jonah for his mercilessness not only with respect to the one hundred and twenty thousand people but also with respect to the cattle).

Psalms 104:24 O Lord, how manifold are your works! In wisdom you have made them all; The earth is full of your creatures.

Luke 12:6 Are not five sparrows sold for two pennies? Yet not one of them is forgotten in God's sight.

Luke 12:24 Consider the ravens: they neither sow nor reap, they have neither storehouse nor barn, and yet God feeds them.

Luke 12:27 Consider the lilies, how they grow: they neither toil nor spin; yet I tell you, even Solomon in all his glory was not clothed like one of these.
(God cares even for a single sparrow, the ravens and the lilies in the field. His love for His Creation is so great!)

Numbers 22:21 So Balaam got up in the morning, saddled his donkey, and went with the officials of Moab.

Numbers 22:23 The donkey saw the angel of the Lord standing in the road, with a drawn sword in his hand; so the donkey turned off the road, and went into the field; and Balaam struck the donkey, to turn it back onto the road.

Balaam struck his donkey another two times...

Numbers 22:28 Then the Lord opened the mouth of the donkey, and it said to Balaam, "What have I done to you, that you have struck me these three times?"

Numbers 22:29 Balaam said to the donkey, "Because you have made a fool of me! I wish I had a sword in my hand! I would kill you right now!"

Numbers 22:30 But the donkey said to Balaam, "Am I not your donkey, which you have ridden all your life to this day? Have I been in the habit of treating you this way?" And he said, "No."

Numbers 22:31 Then the Lord opened the eyes of Balaam, and he saw the angel of the Lord standing in the road, with his sword drawn in his hand; and he bowed down...

Numbers 22:32 The angel of the Lord said to him, "Why have you struck your donkey these three times? I have come out as an adversary, because your way is perverse before me.

Numbers 22:33 The donkey saw me, and turned away from me these three times. If it had not turned away from me, surely just now I would have killed you and let it live."

(So the donkey saved its owner. She saw and she knew what Balaam didn't see and know.)

The donkey has a special place in the Bible. Solomon used horses in his warfare but donkeys were used as beasts of burden and mounts in the Middle East until this day. A light-coloured or white tamed donkey was a new king's mount. Mother Mary sat on a donkey when she travelled to Bethlehem. Even before His birth, Jesus was riding on a donkey. It's a significant sign of the donkey's special animal status that Jesus chose it to enter Jerusalem.

'The Healing Paw', a wonderful book (see the Bibliography at the end of this book), also contains some beautiful quotations:

Animals share with us the privilege of having a soul.
Pythagoras BC 551

The animal world is a manifestation of God's power, and demands respect and consideration. The desire to kill animals, unnecessary harshness and callous cruelty towards them, must always be condemned.
Pope Pius XII

All things are born of the unborn, and from this unity of life flows brotherhood and compassion for all creatures.
Buddha

In Buddhism we are told that animals possessed of the Buddha nature are in time destined for heaven.
Christmas Humpryes

Many people think Islam is cruel to animals. But it was certainly not Mohammed's intention to be cruel towards animals. Mohammed himself had a cat, Muessa, which he loved very much. She was always at his side. And so it happened that one day Mohammed was called to pray while Muessa lay sleeping on the wide sleeve of his robe. Rather than disturb his dear cat in her sleep, he cut off the sleeve. When Mohammed returned from his prayer, Muessa bowed to her master to show her gratitude for his concern. Mohammed patted her three times on her back and promised her a permanent place in paradise. Speaking of love for animals...

No beast is there on earth or fowl that flieth, nothing have we passed over in the book of Eternal Decrees, that shall not be gathered unto the Lord.
Koran

There is not an animal on the earth, nor a flying creature on two wings, but they are people like unto you.
Koran

The greatness of a nation and their moral progress can be judged by the way their animals are treated.

Gandhi

FOR ALL ANIMALS:

Blessed are you, Lord God,
Maker of all living creatures.
On the fifth and sixth days of creation,
You called forth fish in the sea,
Birds in the air and animals on the land.
You inspired St Francis to call all animals
His brothers and sisters.
We ask you to bless this animal.
By the power of your love,
Enable it to live according to your plan.
May we always praise you
For all your beauty in creation.
Blessed are you, Lord our God, in all your Creatures!
Amen.

Source unknown

Chapter

Feline Disorders

Hear our humble prayer, Oh God, for our friends the animals, especially for animals who are suffering. For any that are hunted or lost, or deserted or frightened or hungry. For all that must be put to death. We entreat for them all Thy mercy and pity and for those who deal with them, we ask a heart of compassion and gentle hands and kind words. Make us, ourselves, to be true friends to animals and so to share the blessings of the Merciful.

Albert Schweitzer

I am extremely grateful to The Feline Advisory Bureau for allowing me to use their Catfacts sheets for Purring Angels. FAB is the leading source of information about cat-illnesses in England. They are wonderful. FAB has been providing information on cats and their care in health and sickness for many years. The charity has become synonymous with expertise in feline treatment, both in the veterinary field and cat care in general.

This chapter is far from complete, but I hope it will give some useful information on some rather common cat diseases. It is the most recent information available about these terrible diseases. I hope from the bottom of my heart that the readers of my book will never have to face these diseases.
On the website of FAB www.fabcats.org you will find the complete information about cat disorders and many other things you should know about cats.

I start with Panleukopenia, that mean assassin which almost took the life of Daimke and Catje while killing all their playmates. Panleukopenia is the nightmare of everyone involved in the rescue and shelter of kittens. It is a very cruel disease.

Feline Infectious Enteritis

Feline infectious enteritis (FIE) is also known as feline parvovirus (FPV) and feline panleukopenia (pan = all, leuko = white, penia = lack of) and is probably the greatest disease threat to any rescue facility and has a very high mortality rate, particularly in unvaccinated kittens. It was the first disease of cats to be shown to be caused by a virus. Parvoviruses are very dangerous as they are able to survive long periods, sometimes even years, in the environment. Cats infected with FPV can continue to excrete the virus for at least six weeks following infection. Parvoviruses are resistant to many disinfectants and it is vital that an effective disinfectant is used.

Source and spread of infection

Feline infectious enteritis is spread by direct faecal-oral contact and also indirectly following contamination of the environment or objects by an infected animal, eg, on food dishes, grooming equipment, bedding, floors, clothing or hands. Transplacental spread through the uterus to the unborn kittens can occur. Infection in late pregnancy leads to the underdevelopment of the cerebellum, an area of the brain concerned with coordination of movements. Kittens that are infected as they are developing in the uterus often appear normal at birth but as they become more active, they show uncoordinated movement, walking with their legs wide apart and with muscle tremors frequently present.

Clinical disease

In kittens over three or four weeks of age and adults, the virus causes a severe enteritis, following an incubation period of five to nine days. If the immune response is not adequate to protect the cat, the virus will enter the bloodstream and travel to the bonemarrow and lymph glands, leading to a marked decrease in white blood cells. From there, the virus travels to the intestines where it destroys the rapidly dividing cells of the lining of the gut. Infected cats and kittens usually have a fever, are obviously depressed and will not eat. This phase is rapidly followed by severe vomiting and bloody diarrhoea. Occasionally kittens will be found dead, having shown no signs of the disease previously.

Treatment

No specific treatment is available and it is vital that any suspected cases are nursed in isolation as this is a highly contagious disease. Protective clothing must be worn and hands washed thoroughly after handling any cat or kitten suspected of having the disease. Where possible, one or two people who do not handle any other cats should be assigned as nurses. Cats often die from dehydration and massive secondary infection, so fluids and broad spectrum antibiotics are crucial. Severely dehydrated cats will usually require intravenous fluids and veterinary support is essential. Anti-emetics (to stop vomiting) and vitamin supplements can also be helpful. Good nursing care is vital to help sick cats, especially young kittens recover from the disease.

Control

Feline infectious enteritis is far better prevented than treated. Highly effective vaccines are available and all cats and kittens should be vaccinated. Modified live vaccines should not be used in pregnant queens or cats that are immunosuppressed and, in such cases, dead (inactivated) vaccines are recommended. As with all infectious diseases, vaccination needs to be combined with good management practices, including disinfection and use of isolation procedures. To maintain protection, regular booster vaccination will be required.

Feline Leukaemia virus – FeLV

Feline leukaemia virus (FeLV) is a common and important cause of illness and death in pet cats. Cats that become persistently (permanently) infected with this virus are at risk of developing many severe illnesses such as anaemia and cancer. Between 80 and 90% of infected cats die within three and a half years of being diagnosed as having FeLV.

The most common effect of infection is immunosuppression. The virus infects cells of the immune system (the white blood cells) killing or damaging them. This leaves the cat vulnerable to a wide variety of other diseases and infections (secondary infections). FeLV is a member of the same virus family as feline immunodeficiency virus (FIV).

Who is at risk?

FeLV is a fragile virus which is not able to survive for long in the environment, so the spread of infection between cats relies on prolonged and close contact. For this reason infection is most common in situations where there is a high population density of cats. It is estimated that 1-2% of cats in the UK are infected with FeLV. This figure tends to be higher in more densely populated city cats and lower in rural cat populations. In multi-cat households and catteries where FeLV infection is endemic (constantly present in the household), up to 30% of the cats may be infected.

Young cats, particularly those less than six months old, are especially vulnerable to becoming persistently infected.

How is it spread?

The major source of the virus is in saliva from a persistently infected cat. Virus is spread by activities where saliva is exchanged between cats, such as mutual grooming or sharing of food bowls. Alternatively, FeLV infection of other cats may be caused by biting or contact with urine and faeces containing the virus. It is also possible for the virus to be passed from a queen to her kittens either in the womb or after the kitten is born, via infected milk. However, it is uncommon for FeLV-infected cats to give birth as FeLV usually causes pre-natal death of the kittens which results in reabsorption or abortion.

Not all cats which are exposed to FeLV become persistently infected. Either they have not been exposed to enough virus or their body's immune system is successful in eliminating the infection. The majority of cats become infected with the virus entering the body via the mouth or nose. The virus multiplies at these sites before spreading, in the bloodstream, to the rest of the body and in particular to the bone marrow. If the cat is able to eliminate the virus, this will occur during the initial stages (4 - 12 weeks) of infection. Once significant infection of the bone marrow is present, the cat remains infected for the rest of its life.

Very rarely FeLV infection may be limited to certain parts of the body such as the mammary (breast) tissue. This is known as a 'localised infection'.

Signs and symptoms

A variety of chronic and/or recurrent disease develops in cats persistently infected with FeLV. There is a progressive deterioration in their condition over time. Clinical signs are extremely diverse but include fever, lethargy, poor appetite and weight loss. Respiratory, skin and intestinal signs are also common. Cats may suffer from several illnesses at the same time. Anaemia occurs in about a quarter of infected cats. FeLV can infect the red blood cells in the bone marrow causing a reduction in numbers of these cells or production of abnormal red blood cells which do not work properly. In other cases, FeLV may cause destruction of red blood cells by the cat's own immune system. Anaemic cats show clinical signs such as weakness and lethargy.

Cancer develops in around 15% of cats infected with FeLV. The most common is lymphoma, a cancer of lymphocytes (a type of white blood cell) resulting in solid tumours or leukaemia (tumour cells in the blood stream). Solid tumours can be seen at various sites including the intestine, kidneys, eyes or nasal chambers. In multicentric lymphoma, the tumour involves multiple lymph nodes and other sites.

Treatment of FeLV infection

There is currently no treatment that is able to eliminate a FeLV infection. Treatment must therefore be aimed at maintaining quality of life and managing the effects of infection such as immunosuppression, anaemia and cancer.

Prompt and effective supportive care and management of secondary infections is essential in the ill FeLV-positive cat. Because of the failing immune system, much longer courses of antibiotics are needed. The response to therapy is usually much slower and less successful.

Relief of symptoms may be provided by non-specific therapies such as corticosteroids, anabolic steroids and multivitamins (which encourage appetite). Antiviral agents, such as AZT, which have been used in people with HIV, do not appear to be beneficial in the FeLV-infected cat. A further treatment called recombinant feline interferon has recently been licensed, and there have been anecdotal reports of its use in cases of feline leukaemia. At this point, the value of the drug remains somewhat controversial until further scientific evidence becomes available. Some cats with lymphoma may show temporary improvement when treated with cancer chemotherapy drugs. This usually involves a number of drugs given by mouth and by injection.

Maintaining Health

Cats with FeLV infection should not eat raw meat because of the increased risk of *Toxoplasma gondii* infection. This parasite is usually only a problem in immunosuppressed cats where it can cause uveitis (inflammation of the internal structures of the eyes), neurological signs such as seizures (fits) and ataxia (drunken gait).

Vaccination, particularly for cat 'flu and infectious enteritis, is recommended for any cats staying in a high risk situation such as a veterinary hospital or cattery. Flea treatment is recommended to minimise the risk of *Mycoplasma haemofelis* (a blood parasite which can cause anaemia) transmission. Routine worm treatment is also recommended.

Vaccination

Several vaccines are available for FeLV. The aim of these is to prevent cats exposed to the virus from becoming persistently infected. All of the vaccines aim to do this by stimulating a successful immune response to FeLV. Unfortunately, no vaccine is likely to be 100% effective at protecting against infection. Vaccination is recommended in situations where cats have a high risk of exposure to the virus. This includes free-roaming cats and those in contact with potentially infected individuals.

It is unwise to assume that a vaccinated cat is necessarily free of infection, and where it is important to know the FeLV status of a cat (for example introducing a new cat to a breeding colony) it is vital that a vaccination certificate is not accepted in place of a negative FeLV test. Vaccination of cats does not interfere with the FeLV blood tests.

The lack of a totally effective vaccine means that it is also inadvisable knowingly to mix a FeLV-infected cat with a vaccinated uninfected cat.

Controlling disease

As the virus is highly infectious and readily transmitted by prolonged close contact, other cats in the household are at risk of becoming infected via mutual grooming and sharing of food bowls. Uninfected cats should be kept away from the persistently infected cat where possible. It is also recommended that FeLV-positive cats are kept indoors to minimise spread to other cats in the area. This maybe difficult for some cats who will not tolerate being kept inside permanently. It is important to carefully weigh up the risks (to your own cat and others) with the welfare implications. It is feasible to fence in the garden or to construct a run where cats can go out, thereby preventing any risk to your own or other cats.

In the breeding cattery, the 'test and removal' system has been extremely successful at eliminating FeLV infection. This system relies on FeLV testing of all the cats with separation of any that test positive. After a period of 12 -

16 weeks, all of the cats are tested again as some cats initially testing negative may have been incubating the disease and some of those testing positive may have been transiently infected with subsequent elimination of the virus.

Any cats repeatedly testing positive should be removed from the unit, while only those with two consecutive negative tests are kept. All new additions to the colony, whether vaccinated or not, should be tested for FeLV before joining the cattery. All cats in a breeding colony should be tested every 6 - 12 months in order to maintain the negative status of the colony.

As an aside, single cats that are confined indoors should not be at any risk of exposure to FeLV. It is however possible for an adult cat to succumb to disease from FeLV infection despite having spent their whole life since kittenhood isolated from other cats. This can be explained by the often protracted course of FeLV infection; if a kitten was infected by his/her dam prior to rehoming, the signs of FeLV infection may develop months to years later after the time of initial infection with FeLV. The risk of spread of FeLV at cat shows is minimal.

Blood Test

Vets use test kits to detect one of the viral proteins (p27) present in the bloodstream of FeLV infected cats. Often the kits simultaneously test for FIV, as many of the clinical signs of FIV infection are similar to FeLV infection. Occasional false positive and negative results occur, so it is vital that a confirmatory test is performed if an unexpected result is obtained. This is especially important if a positive result is obtained in a healthy cat and conversely if a negative result is obtained in a sick cat with signs compatible with FeLV infection.

Confirmatory tests include;

Virus isolation - detects the virus within the blood plasma

Immunofluorescence - this tests for viral antigens (proteins) in white blood cells

PCR (polymerase chain reaction) - this test detects the genetic material of the virus, however it can only be performed by selected laboratories

Whilst the results of a confirmatory test are pending the cat should be isolated to avoid any possible risk of transmission to other cats.

The following test protocol is generally followed by vets;

If the cat tests antigen negative on an in-practice test, there is a high probability that it is genuinely negative.

If a healthy cat test is antigen positive on an in-practice test, the cat is retested using a confirmatory test

If the cat tests antigen positive but is negative on a confirmatory test, the cat is retested after 12 weeks to confirm the status

Testing cats in the rescue situation

Ideally all cats entering a rescue centre should be tested for FeLV infection, however this may not be feasible due to the cost implications involved. It is advisable to enquire whether a cat has been tested prior to agreeing to rehome it. A cat that has tested positive to FeLV should only be rehomed when all of the risks have been explained to the new owner.

Prognosis for infected cats

The prognosis for a sick FeLV positive cat is poor; the associated disease problems are usually serious. For cats that have been identified to be FeLV positive but are healthy at the time of diagnosis, the prognosis is guarded. Most of these cats subsequently develop a fatal FeLV-associated problem, however the time course for this to occur can be variable (months-years). It is vital that these cats are isolated to prevent further transmission of FeLV infection to other cats and secondly to reduce the risk of the FeLV positive cat contracting infections; if that cannot be guaranteed, euthanasia should be considered.

Feline immunodeficiency virus - FIV

Feline immunodeficiency virus (FIV) is a significant cause of disease in cats worldwide. It was first discovered during the investigation of a disease outbreak in a previously healthy colony of rescue cats in America that had been showing similar signs to people with acquired immunodeficiency syndrome (AIDS) caused by human immunodeficiency virus (HIV) infection. Although HIV and FIV are very similar, the viruses are species specific, which means that FIV only infects cats and HIV only infects humans. Thus there is no risk of infection for people in contact with FIV-positive cats.

What is FIV and how does it cause disease?

FIV affects the cells of the immune system (white blood cells) killing or damaging them. This causes a gradual decline in the cat's immune function. Early stages of infection may not cause outward signs. The immune system is very important in fighting infections and monitoring the body for cancerous cells and thus FIV–infected cats are at a far greater risk of disease and infection with other viruses, bacteria and other organisms such as *Toxoplasma gondii* or *Haemobartonella felis* (a blood borne parasite which causes anaemia).

Prevalence of FIV

The overall prevalence of FIV in the healthy UK cat population is approximately 6 per cent and estimated to be approximately 14 per cent in the sick cat population. This prevalence varies in different areas of the world and between different cat populations (ie, a housecat compared to a farm or feral cat).

Which cats are at risk?

The most common method of transmission of FIV is via biting during fighting. For this reason entire male cats carry a higher risk of infection and a free-living lifestyle of feral or stray cats increases the prevalence. Any cat can be infected at any age but there is often considerable delay between infection and development of clinical signs and thus the appearance of the disease is more common in middle-aged to elderly cats.

How is FIV spread?

Biting is considered to be the most important method of transmission of FIV. The saliva of an infected cat contains large amounts of virus and a single bite can result in transmission of infection. Infection can also occur by close social contact within a group of cats where there is no overt aggression via the sharing of food bowls and mutual grooming. A small number of kittens born to FIV-infected queens may also become infected in the womb or by drinking infected milk. This is difficult to confirm until several months after birth because of the presence of maternally derived antibodies. Sexual transmission is not thought to be a significant route of infection. It is not known if blood sucking parasites such as fleas can spread infection so it is wise to maintain a regular flea control programme.

What are the clinical signs of an FIV infection?

The disease conditions associated with FIV infection are fairly non-specific

During the primary phase of infection in the first 2-4 months, cats may show short-term signs of illness including malaise, pyrexia (high temperature) and possibly lymph node (the glands that filter blood from the body to check for infection or cancerous cells) enlargement (lymphadenopathy). Most cats will recover from this early phase and enter a second phase when they appear to be healthy. Eventually in the third phase of infection, other signs of disease develop which can be as a direct effect of the virus. One example would be infection of the gastrointestinal tract which may cause diarrhoea. By depressing the immune system and the cat's ability to fight off infection, the FIV infected cat is then prone to other (secondary) infections and diseases. These conditions can take many forms and therefore the clinical signs are quite variable. However the combination of multiple persistent or recurrent disease may point to immunodeficiency. Common signs include malaise, weight loss, inappetence, pyrexia, lymphadenopathy and gingivitis (inflamed gums). Additional problems include rhinitis (inflammation of the tissue lining the nose causing sneezing and nasal discharge), skin infections, anaemia, conjunctivitis (inflammation of the lining of the eyes), uveitis (inflammation of the internal structures of the eye) and diseases of the nervous system which may cause behavioural changes or seizures (fits). Infected queens may abort litters.

How is FIV diagnosed?

There are several test systems available for diagnosing FIV infection. Some of these tests can be performed in your own vet's practice. These tests involve detecting antibodies to the virus. As with most diagnostic tests, this test is not 100 per cent accurate and may produce some false positive or negative results in the following situations:

• Some FIV infected cats produce antibodies which are not detected by the standard test (false negative).
• The sample may be contaminated (false positive).
• In early stages of infection, FIV antibody is not produced (less than two months following infection). It is thus prudent to repeat a negative test result in a suspicious animal eight to 12 weeks later.
• Kittens born to FIV infected queens will receive maternally derived antibodies via the milk and these antibodies are detected when the kitten is tested for FIV. Although all kittens born to a FIV-positive queen will be antibody positive, the virus itself will only be passed on to approximately 30

per cent of the litter. Maternally derived antibodies may be present for up to four months. Kittens should thus not be tested for FIV via an antibody test until they are at least six months old

More specialised tests are also available at external laboratories (which your vet can send samples to) to detect the virus itself and these tests are very sensitive. Virus isolation can also be performed. If the initial antibody test is in any doubt or gives a confusing result then your vet may request an additional confirmatory test is performed to ensure that the correct diagnosis is reached.

Treatment options

To date there is no treatment that has been shown to reverse an established FIV infection.

The main aim of treatment for an FIV-infected cat is to stabilise the patient and maintain a good quality of life. Although not licensed for use in cats, some antiviral medications used in patients with HIV infection (such as azidothymidine, AZT), have provided some improvements in a proportion of FIV-infected cats.

Interferon, a compound that interferes with virus replication, has received a lot of attention recently in the treatment of many viral infections. Recombinant Feline Omega Interferon is the first veterinary interferon available on the European market and has antiviral and immunomodulatory (adjusts the immune response) properties. To date there are no completed scientific studies as to the effectiveness of this product but anecdotally there have been some positive reports of its usefulness in treatment of FIV-infected cats.

Evening primrose oil (550 mg once daily) in mildly affected FIV-positive or asymptomatic cats may produce some improvements such as increases in bodyweight and blood cell counts.

Prompt and effective management of secondary infections is essential in the sick FIV-positive cat. As these cats are immunosuppressed, a much longer course of antibiotics is often required.

Long-term management of the FIV-infected cat

Cats infected with FIV should be confined indoors to prevent spread of the virus to other cats in the neighbourhood and to minimise exposure of affected cats to infectious agents carried by other animals. Good nutrition and husbandry are essential to maintain good health in infected cats. These cats should be fed a nutritionally balanced and complete feline diet. Raw meat, eggs and unpasteurised milk should be avoided, because the risk of food-borne bacterial and parasitic infections is greater in immunosuppressed individuals. A programme for routine control of parasites (fleas, ticks, worms) together with a routine vaccination programme should also be maintained. In FIV infection or in other cases where immunosuppression is suspected or proven, there is a potential risk with the use of live vaccines and potentially a risk that these vaccines may on occasion result in the development of clinical disease. While this is likely to be more of a theoretical than a practical risk, nevertheless, where a choice is available, it may be safer to use a killed/sub-unit vaccine rather than a traditional live vaccine.

Cats infected with FIV should have a vet check at least bi-annually to promptly detect changes in their health status. Your vet will perform a thorough examination of your cat and concentrate particularly on the mouth, skin, lymph nodes and eyes and record your cat's weight. A blood sample should also be performed yearly to check your cat's blood count. If any illness is detected either by the owner or the veterinary surgeon then supportive therapy should be instituted immediately.

Intact male and female cats should be neutered to reduce the stress associated with mating behaviours and seasons. Neutered animals are less likely to roam outside the house or interact aggressively with their housemates.

Prevention and control

A vaccine for FIV has been licensed in the USA but there is limited data on its efficacy. As the vaccine's function is to produce antibodies to the virus, the use of FIV vaccination in this country would invalidate most in
-house testing kits available to your veterinary surgeon.

If one cat in a household is confirmed to be FIV positive then ideally the FIV infected cat should be isolated or rehomed. However, as the risk of transmission by social contact such as sharing food bowls and mutual grooming is very low, many owners elect to keep the household as it is. It may be helpful to feed cats using separate food bowls as large amounts of virus are present in saliva. Litter trays and food bowls should be disinfected after use to kill the virus. Once outside of the cat's body the virus dies within a few minutes, so infection is not easily carried on clothing or other objects.

Advice for breeding colonies

To minimise the risk of introducing FIV into the colony, breeders are advised to prevent their breeding cats having free access outdoors, or having contact with any cats that are allowed outdoors. Annual testing of breeding cats and of new cats before introduction, is advised. If an infected cat is identified then appropriate measures must be taken:- stop breeding, test all other cats and remove or completely separate infected ones. All cats should be retested in 3-6 months, and if still negative then breeding can resume.

Advice for cat rescue centres and organisations

Ideally routine screening should be performed in all cats but financial constraints mean that this is often not possible. In this situation, any symptomatic cats should be tested together with any obviously aggressive cats (often entire male cats). Also any stray or feral cats should be tested.
Ideally cats should be housed separately and if not, then kept in the smallest groups possible. A policy of neutering before rehoming should also be effective in reducing transmission of FIV.

Prognosis for infected cats

The prognosis for FIV-infected cats remains guarded. If the diagnosis of FIV-infection is reached early in the course of the disease, there may be a long period during which the cat is free of clinical signs related to FIV. Although it is not certain that all infected cats go on to develop an immunodeficiency syndrome, the evidence available suggests that the majority do, and in all cats the infection appears to be permanent. Many cats with FIV can remain healthy for extended periods with the above management guidelines.

Feline infectious peritonitis – FIP

Feline infectious peritonitis (FIP) is fatal disease of cats, caused by a feline coronavirus. Infection with coronavirus is actually very common in cats but most of the time it does not cause any problems, other than maybe mild self-limiting diarrhoea. Uncommonly, the virus mutates (changes) within an infected cat, and it is this mutated form that causes the disease of FIP.

How do cats get coronavirus?

Coronavirus is ubiquitous among cats and infection with the virus is particularly common where large numbers of cats are kept together. It is estimated that 25 to 40 per cent of household pet cats are infected. This infection rate increases to 80 to 100 per cent of cats kept in multi-cat households, rescue and breeding colonies. The virus is spread by the faecal-oral route, that is, the virus is shed in faeces into the environment and cats become infected following ingestion when grooming or eating. Most infected cats shed the virus in faeces for a variable period of time and then stop. The cat can then become re-infected from another cat and start shedding virus again. In contrast, some cats shed virus continuously.

Although coronavirus is the cause of FIP, infection with coronavirus does not mean that the cat will go on to develop FIP. In comparison to the number of cats infected with the virus, the number that develop FIP is very small. It is only when the virus mutates that FIP may develop.

What causes the virus to mutate?

While the precise cause of the viral mutation is unknown, several factors are likely to play a role. The majority of cases of FIP develop in younger cats. A poorer immune response together with other stress factors such as rehoming, neutering, vaccination or other concurrent disease may make younger cats more vulnerable to FIP. FIP can, however, develop in any age of cat and predisposing factors or risk factors are not always evident. Genetics may also play a role in some cases as purebred cats appear to be at a greater risk. Sometimes particular lines of a breed have a high rate of developing FIP.

What are the clinical signs of FIP?

FIP has very diverse clinical manifestations, but there are no clinical signs associated that are unique for the disease. The classic form of the disease, often termed 'wet' FIP is characterised by a build up of yellow fluid within the abdomen (resulting in abdominal distension) and/or chest (resulting in breathing difficulties). However, the presence of this fluid is not diagnostic for FIP, and in addition a large number of FIP cases will not have any visible fluid build up. Initial clinical signs are often very vague, consisting of lethargy and loss of appetite. In some forms of the disease inflammatory lesions in the eye and nervous system can occur, resulting in visual disturbances and abnormal behaviour, a wobbly gait or tremors. The disease is usually rapidly progressive and ultimately fatal.

How can FIP be diagnosed?

There is no specific diagnostic test for FIP. Tissue biopsies can confirm a diagnosis, but often the cat is too sick for these procedures to be undertaken and so in many cases a definitive test is only made on post mortem examination.

If FIP is suspected, the veterinary surgeon will perform a thorough clinical examination, including examination of the eyes and neurological assessment. The more findings that are present that are consistent with FIP, the more likely that the cat does have FIP.

If any fluid is present within either the chest, abdomen or both, analysis of this fluid is one of the most useful tests that can be performed. X-rays of the chest and abdomen, and ultrasound examination of the abdomen are very useful to detect very small amounts of fluid when obvious signs of fluid build up are lacking. This fluid can then be sampled via ultrasound guidance. The fluid is most often (but not always) thick and straw-coloured in appearance, and on analysis has a very high protein content and low cell count. The presence of fluid in the abdomen does not confirm a diagnosis of FIP as some other diseases can also lead to the build up of similar fluid. If the fluid is present within both the chest and abdominal cavity, then FIP is even more likely.

Routine blood tests (haematology and biochemistry) are very helpful firstly in trying to exclude other causes for the clinical signs, and secondly to look for changes which may support a suspicion of FIP. Frequently the numbers of one type of white blood cell (lymphocytes) are low, there may be a mild anaemia, blood protein levels are usually very high, and sometimes blood bilirubin (pigment from old red blood cells) levels are high. All these changes are very non-specific and do not make a diagnosis of FIP, but help to increase suspicion of the disease.

Many of these abnormalities may not be present in the early stages of the disease, but may become evident as the disease progresses. Thus some tests that give normal results may have to be repeated later.

Cats can be tested to see if they have been exposed to coronavirus by checking for the presence of specific antibodies. However, such a coronavirus serology test is of very limited use in diagnosing FIP. This test does not distinguish between the coronavirus encountered commonly with few associated problems, and the mutated form that causes FIP. So, as many cats are infected with coronavirus, many cats will be positive with this test. It does not give any information as to whether that cat has or may develop FIP. Furthermore, some cats with confirmed FIP are actually negative for antibodies, so it also can not be used to exclude FIP.

In cats with neurological signs without any other abnormalities, MRI scan of the brain and analysis of CSF fluid can also be useful.

Can FIP be treated?

Once clinical signs of FIP develop, it is generally an incurable and fatal disease. Treatment is given to relieve symptoms and may include anti-inflammatories and appetite stimulants. While there are a handful of anecdotal reports suggesting some success with newer antiviral drugs, studies have yet to show a proven benefit of any such treatments. In most cases euthanasia is the most humane course of action to avoid suffering.

Is there a vaccine for FIP?

There is a commercial vaccine that has been developed and is used in the USA . It is not available in the UK . The efficacy of the vaccine is really unknown with different studies producing very different results. It does not appear to be particularly effective, and is only licensed for use in kittens over 16 weeks of age, by which time most kittens are already infected with the virus anyway.

How can FIP be prevented and controlled?

Household pets

FIP is least common in household pets. The risk can be minimised by obtaining cats from a source with relatively few cats and by keeping cats in small stable groups (less than five cats in a household). Minimising 'stress factors', such as rehoming, worming, vaccination and neutering happening all at once, or while the cat is suffering from another illness, may also help minimise the risk of the disease.

Breeding catteries with endemic FIP

Total eradication of coronavirus infection from catteries is extremely difficult as the virus is so ubiquitous, and it is unsuitable in most cattery situations to attempt this. A more practical approach is to consider elimination of coronavirus infection in newly born kittens, providing the opportunity of re-homing kittens free of coronavirus. If pregnant queens are isolated one to two weeks before they are due to kitten, and then the queen is kept isolated with her kittens (whilst employing good hygiene procedures to prevent environmental spread of infection to the kittens), a substantial number of these kittens with remain negative for coronavirus. Following weaning, the queen can be removed and the kittens still kept isolated and tested at 12 to 16 weeks of age for coronavirus antibodies. If they are negative, the isolation procedure has been successful.

This procedure sometimes fails if the queen is shedding the virus and passes it on to her kittens. It is thought that this is less likely in queens over two years of age, and can be helped by early weaning of the kittens (at five to six weeks of age when maternally derived antibodies are still protective) and removing the queen from the environment. Good hygiene is also an important part of the control of spread of the virus to kittens in these situations. Although these procedures are successful, they require considerable commitment from breeders, and there are some concerns about the behavioural development of kittens when they are reared in isolation up to the age of four months.

Often it is more appropriate to accept that there is endemic coronavirus infection and institute measures to try and minimise its impact. Considering that the virus is spread by the faecal-oral route, practical control measures that can be used include:
• Having at least one litter box for every two cats, located in easy to clean/ disinfect areas
• Litterboxes should be kept away from food and water bowls to prevent cross contamination
• Faeces should be removed from litterboxes at least once daily, and litter should be completely changed as often as possible accompanied by disinfection of the trays
• Cats should be kept in small stable groups of four or less – minimising cross-contamination within a household
• Breeding programmes with more than eight to 10 cats (including kittens)

should not be undertaken in a normal household. Larger numbers require some purpose built facilities to enable proper hygiene and care to be maintained.

• Regular brushing of the coat, particularly of long-hair cats is desirable to reduce contamination with faeces and litter

• Isolation of queens and their kittens can be recommended as a means to controlling spread of coronavirus to the kittens.

Rescue catteries

Adequate hygiene and avoiding overcrowding are essential strategies for minimising the risk of FIP in such situations. Cats should be housed individually, or if this is not possible, they should be batched on arrival, and kept in small stable groups.

Feline upper respiratory tract disease – Catflu

Cat flu is a common cat disease that can be life-threatening. Symptoms include sneezing, nasal discharge, conjunctivitis (inflammation of the lining of the eyes), discharge from the eyes, loss of appetite, fever and depression. Occasionally, mouth and eye ulcers and excessive drooling of saliva may be seen. The very young, very old and immunosuppressed cats are more likely to develop severe disease and possibly die as a result of their flu. Where death occurs this is usually because of secondary infections (infections with bacteria in addition to the flu viruses), lack of nutrition and dehydration.

Who is at risk?

Cat flu is most commonly seen in situations where cats are kept in large groups such as breeding catteries, rescue centres and feral cat colonies, although it can also be seen in pet cat households.

Cats most at risk include unvaccinated cats, kittens, the elderly and cats which are immunosuppressed for any reason. In immunosuppressed cats, damage to the immune system has left them vulnerable to a wide variety of diseases with which they would otherwise be able to cope. Immunosuppression can be seen in cats infected with feline leukaemia virus (FeLV) or feline immunodeficiency virus (FIV), cats with other severe illnesses, or in those receiving treatment with certain medications such as corticosteroids or anti-cancer therapy.

353

Although vaccination helps to reduce the risk of cat flu, this disease can still be seen in vaccinated cats.

Causes and symptoms

The symptoms of cat flu are most frequently caused by infection with one or both of the cat flu viruses - feline herpes virus (formerly known as feline rhinotracheitis virus) and feline calicivirus.

Feline herpes virus (FHV) infection often causes severe and potentially life-threatening illness. Although the majority of cats infected make a full recovery, this often takes several weeks and some cats are left with permanent effects of infection such as chronic rhinitis. Cats with chronic rhinitis are usually well in themselves but have a persistent discharge from the nose and sneeze. Secondary bacterial infection of damaged tissue can cause chronic conjunctivitis, sinusitis and bronchitis (inflammation of the linings of the eye, sinuses and air passages). Antibiotic treatment usually only provides temporary relief of these symptoms.

Feline calcivirus (FCV) infection usually causes a milder form of cat flu with less dramatic nasal discharges. Characteristic mouth ulcers are sometimes the only sign of infection. The ulcers may be present on the tongue, on the roof of the mouth or the nose.

Some strains of FCV cause lameness and fever in young kittens (these can occasionally be seen after vaccination). Affected cats recover over a few days although they may need pain killers through this time. More recently a more virulent strain of FCV has been identified in the USA. This strain causes severe swelling of the face and paws and has a deleterious effect on the whole body with a high mortality rate (40%). Further investigation into this strain is currently ongoing.

Diagnosis and treatment

Diagnosis by the veterinary surgeon is based on symptoms and laboratory tests. Testing for flu viruses requires taking a mouth swab which is then sent to a specialised laboratory where the virus is grown and identified.

Unfortunately there are currently no drugs available to kill these viruses so treatment is aimed at supporting the cat through its illness. This treatment includes antibiotics to treat any secondary bacterial infections as these can be life-threatening, and drugs to help loosen the nasal discharge and make breathing less of a struggle. As cats with flu are often reluctant to eat, they may need to be tempted by offering gently warmed, smelly and palatable food. Syringe feeding of liquid food can be tried if necessary, although caution is advised. Severely ill cats may require hospitalisation for feeding by a tube placed down their nose or directly into their stomach.

Interferon, a compound that interferes with virus replication, has received a lot of attention recently in the treatment of many viral infections. Recombinant Feline Omega Interferon is the first veterinary interferon available on the European market and has antiviral and immunomodulatory properties. To date there is little documented evidence for its success in cats for the treatment of FHV and/or FCV.

Trifluorothymidine is an anti-viral eye drop that is a licensed human product that has been used with some success in cats with severe eye lesions as a result of FHV infection

Acyclovir, a drug given in human herpes virus infections does not seem to have good activity against FHV.

Dehydrated cats may also need fluids given intravenously via a drip. General nursing is also essential. Discharge around the eyes and nose should be gently wiped away using a damp piece of cotton wool and the cat should be kept warm and comfortable.

Carriers

Most cats that recover from cat flu become 'carriers'. Carrier cats usually show no sign of illness themselves but, by shedding virus in their saliva, tears and nasal secretions, are a source of infection to other cats. FHV carriers shed virus in their secretions intermittently. Shedding tends to occur following times of stress, such as a stay in a boarding cattery, and may or may not cause some recurrence of flu signs such as sneezing and nasal discharge in the carrier cat. Treatment for other diseases using corticosteroids may also precipitate an episode of virus shedding. Cats that are FHV carriers remain so for the rest of their life. In contrast, most cats infected with FCV shed the virus continuously for a short time after recovering from flu and then virus shedding stops. In a few cats FCV shedding continues for several years.

Spread

Cat 'flu viruses are spread in three ways.

Direct contact with an infected cat showing signs of flu.

From contact with virus carried on clothing, food bowls and other objects.

Large amounts of virus are present in the saliva, tears and nasal discharges of cats with 'flu. The virus is able to survive in the environment for up to a week.

From contact with a cat that is a carrier of cat flu. Breeding carrier cats are a risk to their kittens as the stress of kittening may precipitate shedding of FHV and infection of the kittens with either FHV or FCV may occur before the kittens are old enough to be vaccinated.

Prevention

The risk of developing cat flu can be reduced by regular vaccination against FHV and FCV. These vaccines stimulate the cat's immune system helping it to fight infection and protect it from developing disease. However, although vaccination usually prevents severe disease developing, they are not always 100% effective against preventing infection and mild disease may still occur in some cats. FCV has several different strains and work is still ongoing to develop more effective vaccines. Recently some newer vaccines have been marketed, which include cover against some of these more recently recognised strains.

It is advisable to vaccinate all household cats, especially if the cat goes outdoors, stays in a cattery or goes to cat shows. If an individual develops cat flu, subsequent stress, such as attending a cat show, should ideally be avoided.

Breeding cats should be vaccinated before they are mated so that they produce high levels of antibody in their milk. These maternal antibodies only protect the kittens until they are about 4 - 8 weeks old, after which the levels of antibody gradually disappear. Kittens can only be vaccinated successfully when the levels of antibody have disappeared at between 6 and 12 weeks of age.

Cats that recover from infection with FHV or FCV may be able to resist future infections (be immune) for up to a year or more. As there are many strains of FCV, a cat that recovers from infection with one FCV strain can still subsequently be infected with another. Vaccines use strains of FCV which give the most cross-protection to other strains, to try to provide as broad a protection as possible against this infection. This is not an issue with FHV as only one virus strain exists.

Barrier nursing

Preventing the spread of infection in a multi-cat environment involves 'barrier nursing' of infected cats. The infected cat should be isolated from the other cats, for example kept in one room of the house, where it can be treated without the risk of spread of virus to other cats in the household. Separate food bowls and litter trays should be used for this cat. These should be disinfected with a product which kills the virus but is safe to cats, as recommended by a veterinary surgeon. In a cattery, one person should look after the ill cat, and they should disinfect their face and hands and change their clothes or overalls when leaving the cat in isolation. If one person cares for all the cats, the infected cat should be handled last of all the cats in the home.

Many many thanks again to FAB who gave me permission to use this wonderful information. I am so proud I am allowed to use it for Purring Angels.

The Feline Advisory Bureau is a charity dedicated to the health and welfare of cats. Founded in 1958, FAB has had a major influence on the health and welfare of cats. By funding veterinary surgeons to specialise in the care of cats, and by gathering information on cat diseases, FAB continues to create a scientific backbone for many of the advances in the treatment of cats. FAB has a comprehensive public information service, runs conferences and seminars and works for higher standards in boarding catteries and the care of cats in veterinary practice. The quarterly FAB Journal covers all aspect of cat diseases and treatments, behaviour, breeding, nursing, case reports and general cat interest.

If this advice has helped you care better for your cat please enable us to help others by making a donation. You can do this via the Website www.fabcats.org or by sending a cheque to the address below (made payable to 'Feline Advisory Bureau')

All information is available on the site www.fabcats.org

Dr. Allard Hendriks, the prop and stay of the Poezenbel Foundation, wrote an instructive piece on problems related to urinating in Poezenbelletje number 33. I received permission to include it in this book.

Help, my cat can't pee

When you see your cat frequently visiting its litter tray (or other locations) to urinate, it is very important to check if there is at least some flow of urine. In the case that there is a common bladder infection, your cat will produce some urine after forcing. However, if all its forcing won't produce any urine, your cat (and you) really are in trouble! Female cats have a short and wide urethra and are, apart from a few exceptions, never troubled by urethral obstructions. They do have, for the same reason, more frequently common bladder infections. Tomcats have a much longer and narrower urethra with an unfortunate constriction immediately before the exit. When your tomcat can't urinate no matter how much he tries, there is probably a blockage.

If you suspect that your tomcat is unable to urinate, you are facing an emergency and you should immediately call your family veterinarian or the veterinarian on duty. It so happens that when the urine cannot be eliminated via the normal channels, it will accumulate in the bladder. At a given moment the bladder will be full and so the kidneys cannot drain urine any more. This will stop the production of urine and then all kinds of waste products will accumulate in the blood with the result that the tomcat will quickly develop uraemia. This process develops so fast that it may cause your tomcat's death within 24 hours!
Urethral obstruction is easy to diagnose by palpating the full and painful bladder in the abdomen. The most prevalent cause of urethral obstruction is bladder stones (uroliths). There are several kinds of bladder stones, but usually it is 'struvite'.
Cats in the wild are real carnivores producing urine with a low degree of acidity. Cheap cat food especially contains many comparatively (cheap) vegetable proteins which cause the cat to produce urine with a high degree of acidity. Now, this high degree of acidity combined with the concentration of certain minerals, especially magnesium, will enhance the formation of struvite. Fat and lazy cats (indoor cats!) and/or cats which don't drink much are easily and more frequently troubled by bladder stones. Your veterinarian will, almost always after applying an anaesthetic, try to insert a small hose, a catheter, into the tomcat's urethra. This catheter usually suffices to flush out

the bladder stones obstructing the constriction of the urethra or to dissolve them through the action of special fluids. Sometimes puncturing of the bladder in the abdominal wall may be necessary to reduce the pressure in the bladder and to facilitate flushing.

In a certain number of cases the urethra is obstructed in such a way that the only remedy is amputation of the penis, in which case the terminal and constricted end of the urethra is removed and the tomcat is more or less rebuilt as a female. If the obstruction can be successfully removed, the bladder is subsequently flushed to remove as many stones as possible. Depending on the seriousness of the obstruction and the time and effort required to remove it, your veterinarian may decide to affix the catheter for some days to guarantee the outflow of urine, so that the bladder and the urethra have some rest to recover from the trauma.

It is important that you put your cat on a stone-dissolving diet as soon as possible to prevent renewed production of bladder stones and to dissolve any residue in the bladder. Stone-dissolving diet food acidifies the urine. It contains low concentrations of magnesium, among others, and should be given for a few weeks only. Afterwards you can change to a stone-preventative diet. Anti-stone diets are only available at the veterinarian's and compare as far as prices and quality are concerned with the so-called 'premium brands' in the pet shops. When you are feeding your cat tinned food and dry food of premium quality, the chances of stone-formation are indeed lower, but there is no guarantee that bladder stones will not be formed.

In view of the high risk of relapse, it makes sense to feed your tomcat a stone-preventative diet as prescribed by your veterinarian for the rest of his life.

Another not so frequent cause of urethral obstruction is an inflammation of the urethra causing the urethra's inner wall to swell so much that it cuts itself off so that the cat can't urinate any more. Catheterising these cats is simple. The catheter simply slides into it. It is especially important with these cats to leave the catheter in place for some days so as to rest the urethra.

Urethral inflammations may be caused among others by: bladder infections, recent catheterising related to troubles caused by bladder stones, but markedly frequently: **pure stress!!** If stress is suspected, it makes sense to -

if it's possible - eliminate possible stress factors. In some cases homeopathy may be helpful. How to prevent all this misery as much as possible? For starters, by keeping your cat happy, slim and moving. Further, it pays to 'invest' in higher priced cat food.

Friendly greetings,

Allard Hendriks, veterinarian.

FOR ALL ANIMALS:

Heavenly father,
You created all things for your glory
And made us stewards of this creature,
If it is your will, restore it to health and strength.
Blessed are you, Lord God,
And holy is your name for ever and ever.
Amen.

St Francis of Assisi

Chapter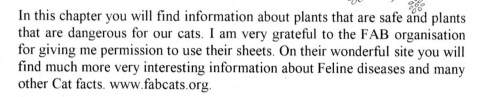

Hazardous and safe plants

A kitten is in the animal world
What a rosebud is in the garden

Robert Southtey 1774-1843

In this chapter you will find information about plants that are safe and plants that are dangerous for our cats. I am very grateful to the FAB organisation for giving me permission to use their sheets. On their wonderful site you will find much more very interesting information about Feline diseases and many other Cat facts. www.fabcats.org.

There are many dangerous plants. Why is it that often the most beautiful plants are the most toxic? Think of digitalis. But the most dangerous species is the Lily. These are lethal for cats.

In the cat magazine Your Cat I read a horrible story about the dangers all varieties of Lilies pose to our cats. When these very beautiful flowers bloom, pollen is produced. A thirteen-year old Siamese died an agonising death after brushing against a vase of lilies. Pollen fell on her fur, she licked it off and died some hours later as a result of liver failure, vomiting and dehydration. She was also struck with sudden blindness.

All varieties of the lily family are dangerous and all parts of the plants are toxic. Cats are the only animals that are so sensitive to this plant. The first symptoms are depression, loss of appetite and vomiting. Failing immediate help, the symptoms will get worse and include bad breath, dehydration, diarrhoea and breathing difficulties. Then the cat will most likely get acute renal failure. Only the vet might be able to save her then, by dialysis, fluid injections under the skin and so on, if it is not too late. There are many poisonous plants but lilies are the most dangerous ones.

I had a group of lilies in front of the living room run and one in front of the office run. I already had my misgivings about the plants and I always trimmed the leaves so they did not reach inside the runs. Of course, after I read this article I removed both groups. I was sorry for the beautiful flowers, they can't help it, but my cats are my first priority.

Cat World's August issue features two extensive articles about this most important topic. Lilies are causing more and more problems as they are becoming more and more popular. It makes no difference whether the plants are growing outside or are cut and kept in vases, they are extremely poisonous! If your cat is poisoned by them, you have to react quickly and get her to the vet as soon as possible or she will die from renal failure. Lilies are rather new to England and not much was known about them, while in America, where this plant is widespread, there have been many warnings against lilies. The problems started in 1990, but last year 275 cases of poisoning were reported. The Animal Protection Agency and the Poison Department now plan an extensive information drive. The Poison Department and the veterinarians have expressed their concern and take the matter very seriously. They confirm the fact that it is one of the worst reactions to poison a cat can get and that its life can only be saved by very aggressive treatment. The experts also say that all parts of the plant are poisonous, not only the pollen.

So, not only elastic bands are lethal for cats, lilies too! (I am very afraid of elastic bands, knowing a few cats that have died after eating them).

Here follows the information from FAB.

Lots of us are surrounded by plants, both wild and cultivated, in our homes and gardens and come to no harm. However, a small percentage of these plants have the potential to cause harm to ourselves and our cats.

Who is at risk?

Most cats are fastidious creatures and are careful what they eat. Poisoning in cats is therefore generally rare. It is the young, inquisitive cat or kitten that is most at risk of eating harmful plants, particularly household ones. Boredom also has a part to play. When a cat is confined to a run or lives entirely indoors hazardous plants should be removed from its environment. Cats given free access to the outside world tend to have other things to occupy their minds than sampling unfamiliar vegetation. But even free roaming adult cats may accidentally ingest needles or seeds that have become entangled in their coat during grooming.

Cats don't eat plants!

All plants, even grass, can have an irritating effect on a cat's gastrointestinal system causing them to vomit. But, given the opportunity, cats like to nibble on grass. When not available their attention may turn to often less suitable household plants. Tender plants are generally a favourite. Particularly dangerous is Diffenbachia (dumb cane).

Preventive action

Remove all potentially hazardous household plants to prevent unnecessary exposure. This is especially important for kittens or cats kept indoors. A list of plants that are unsuitable to grow in a house with cats is given below.
Outdoors the story is not so simple. Free roaming cats have access to many gardens so it will be impossible to prevent all possible contact with potentially harmful plants. You can however remove the most toxic plants from your garden and make a note of any in your neighbour's gardens that are potentially dangerous. List common and Latin names. This list may help your vet if poisoning is suspected.

You can also ensure that any new additions to the garden are safe. The Horticultural Trade Association has a code of practice for its members and most garden centres and nurseries label plants that are toxic or cause skin reactions. Plants are grouped into three categories: A Poisonous; B Toxic if eaten; and C Harmful if eaten. You are unlikely to find a category A plant on sale - Poison Ivy being one example. Category B plants should be avoided. After gardening, never leave hedge clippings or uprooted plants near pets. Their novelty value may encourage inquisitive chewing. Sap from damaged stems can cause skin irritation as well as being poisonous. Bulbs, rhizomes and roots can be the most hazardous parts of some plants.

Has my cat been poisoned?

A veterinary surgeon should be contacted immediately if your cat suddenly collapses, has repeated vomiting or severe diarrhoea or shows signs of excessive irritation (red, swollen, blistering or raw) of skin of the mouth or throat. Cats that are lethargic and off their food for a day or more may also have ingested something unsuitable and professional help should be sought. If you see your cat eat something that you suspect to be poisonous do not attempt to make the cat vomit. Take the cat to the vet with a sample of the plant - or even better a plant label. This will help the vet to find a treatment or antidote to the poison. Make a note of the time of eating and any symptoms. Several days may pass between the ingestion of the undesirable material and the effects.

Skin reactions

It is more common for plants to cause skin irritation in gardeners than to poison them. Contact with the leaves, stems or sap of certain plants can cause rashes and hypersensitivity to sunlight resulting in sunburn. In cats these plants may cause blistering or itching of the mouth and gums. Occasionally this is misdiagnosed as gingivitis. Sneezing and eye problems can also be caused through contact with these plants. Contact with the leaves of food plants such as tomato, strawberry, rhubarb, parsnips, carrot, celery, marrow and cucumbers may all potentially affect the cat in this way. Geranium and Primula leaves can also cause similar skin irritation. Many plants that are poisonous when eaten may also have the potential to cause skin irritation on contact with leaves or sap. These are indicated in the list below.

Hazardous plants

The following is a fairly comprehensive list of plants that are potentially poisonous or harmful to your cat when eaten. Contact with some of the plants listed may be sufficient to cause skin irritation (marked *) It is often the fruit or seeds of plants that are potentially harmful. Many of us are already familiar with plants that carry really toxic berries such as Deadly Nightshade. Only a small quantity of these need to be eaten for a fatal result. Other plants in the list may come as a surprise - Daffodils for example. Here, however, it is the bulb that causes harm if ingested. The fact that the list contains some very common plants should not be cause for concern. Most of these potentially harmful plants taste bad and are unlikely to be eaten in sufficient quantities to cause permanent damage. Woody garden plants are also unlikely to be eaten by your cat - tender household plants pose most risk.

Hazardous plants

House plants

Amaryllis
Aphelandra
Castor Oil Plant, see Ricinus
Christmas Cherry, see Solanum
Chrysanthemum, see Dendranthema
Codiaeum
Croton, see Codiaeum
Cyclamen
Dumb cane, see Dieffenbachia
Dieffenbachia
Devil's Ivy, see Epipremnum aureum
Elephant's Ear, see Alocasia, Caladium
Epipremnum aureum
Ferns
Holly, see Ilex
Hypoestes phyllostachya
Hyacinthus
Ivy, see Hedera
Mistletoe, see Viscum
Nerium oleander
Oleander see Nerium
Ornithogalum
Poinsettia, see Euphorbia
Senecio
Star of Bethlehem, see Ornithogalum umbellatum
Umbrella Plant, see Schefflera
Zebra Plant, see Aphelandra

Garden plants

Abrus precatorius

Aconitum *
Actaea
Aesculus
Agrostemma githago
Aleurites
Allium
Alocasia
Alstroemeria *
Anagallis
Anemone
Angel's Trumpets, see Brugmansia
Angel Wings, see Caladium
Apricot, see Prunus armeniaca
Aquilegia
Arisaema
Arum
Astragalus
Atropa
Avocado, see Persea americana
Azalea, see Rhododendron
Baneberry, see Actaea
Bird of Paradise, see Strelitzia
Black-eyed Susan, see Thunbergia
Bloodroot, see Sanguinaria
Box, see Buxus
Broom, see Cytisus
Brugmansia
Bryony
Buckthorn, see Rhamnus
Burning Bush, see Dictamnus
Buttercup, see Ranunculus
Buxus
Cherry Laurel see Prunus laurocerasus
Chincherinchee see Ornithogalum
Caesalpinia
Caladium
Caltha *
Catharanthus

Celastrus
Centaurea cyanus
Cestrum
Chrysanthemum see Dendranthema
Clematis
Colchicum
Columbine see Aquilegia
Conium
Convallaria majalis
Corncockle, see Agrostemma githago
Cornflower, see Centaurea cyanus
Cotoneaster
Crocus, see Colchicum
Cupressocyparis leylandii *
Cyclamen
Cytisus
Daffodil, see Narcissus
Daphne *
Datura *
Delphinium
Delonix
Dendranthema *
Dicentra
Dictamnus
Digitalis
Echium *
Euonymus
Euphorbia *
Elder, see Sambucus
False acacia, see Robinia
Fems
Ficus
Flax see Linum
Frangula see Rhamnus
Fremontodendron *
Foxglove see Digitalis
Four o'clock: see Mirabilis jalapa
Galanthus

Gaultheria
Giant Hog Weed, see Heracleum mantegazzianum
Gloriosa superba
Glory Lily see Gloriosa
Hedera *
Helleborus *
Hemlock, see Conium
Henbane, see Hyoscyamus
Heracleum mantegazzianum
Hippeastrum
Holly, see Ilex
Horse-chestnut, see Aesculus
Hyacinthus
Hydrangea
Hyoscyamus
Impatiens
Ipomoea
Iris
Ivy, see Hedera
Ilex
Jasminum
Juniperus Sabina
Kalmia
Laburnum
Lantana
Lathyrus
Larkspur, see Delphinium
Lilium
Lily of the Valley, see Convallaria
Linum
Ligustrum
Lobelia (except bedding Lobelia) *
Lords and Ladies (Cuckoo pint), see Arum
Lupinus
Lycopersicon *
Lysichiton
Madagascar periwinkle, see Catharanthus
Marigold, see Tagetes

Melia
Mirabilis jalapa
Monkswood, see Aconitum
Morning Glory, see Ipomoea
Narcissus
Nerium oleander
Nicotiana
Nightshade, deadly, see Atropa
Nightshade, woody, see Solanum
Oak, see Quercus
Onion, see Allium
Oxytropis
Paeonia
Papaver
Parthenocissus
Peach, see Prunus persica
Peony, see Paeonia
Pernettya
Persea americana
Philodendron
Physalis
Phytolacca *
Pokeweed, see Phytolacca
Poppy, see Papaver
Polygonatum
Primula obconica *
Privet see Ligustrum
Prunus armeniaca
Prunus laurocerasus
Prunus persica
Quercus
Rhamus (including R.frangula)
Rhododendron
Rhus *
Ricinus
Robinia
Rosary pea, see Abrus precatorius
Rubber plant, see Ficus

Rudbeckia
Rue, see Ruta
Ruta
Sambucus
Sanguinaria
Schefflera *
Scilla
Skunk cabbage, see Lysichiton
Snowdrop, see Galanthus
Solandra
Solanum
Solomon's seal, see Polygonatum
Spindle Tree, see Euonymus
Spurge, see Euphorbia
Strelitzia
Sumach, see Rhus
Sweet pea, see Lathyrus
Tagetes
Tanacetum
Taxus
Tetradymia
Tobacco, see Nicotiana
Tomato, see Lycopersicon
Thornapple, see Datura
Thuja *
Tulipa *
Veratrum
Viscum
Wisteria
Yew, see Taxus

This information sheet is produced by the Feline Advisory Bureau.
www.fabcats.org

Luckily enough there are also 'safe' plants for our cats to sleep and play in.
It's wonderful to give your cat her own little garden. I put a few drainpipes
with a diameter of about one metre upright in the runs. I filled them with
good soil and planted Catnip and Thyme in them. The cats adore lying in

them on hot summer days. Afterwards they smell lovely. And, at the same time, fleas won't come near them as they hate the smell of Catnip. Yes, cats know very well what's good for them.

I also planted Red Sage, Curry plant, Tarragon and Mint. These plants don't flower much and thus don't attract wasps and bees. Catmint (Nepeta) and lavender do flower profusely but cats love them even more. If you trim the plants just before flowering, you can include them in your garden. We are particularly fond of Calamintha Nepeta. It smells of mint and flowers very late. My fluffies like to wallow in it so they smell deliciously of mint afterwards. It is a delight to watch them.

Also harmless: Bergamot (pear), Catmint, Dame's violet, Evening primrose, Feverfew, Field mint, Lemon balm and of course Roses.
Every issue of the lovely Cat magazine 'Your Cat' has one or two pages about gardening. Much useful information is found in it. I kept all the pages and made a list of the non-toxic plants for cats. Sue was so kind to give me permission to use it for Purring Angels. Here they come:

Safe plants for Cats

Bamboo Fargesia Murieliae (Bamboo)
Thymus Silver Posie (Thyme)
Calendula Officinalis (Pot Marigold)
Chamaerops humilis (Dwarf fan Palm)
Sempervivum Arachnoideum (Cobweb houseleek)
Phormium Tenax Cultivars (New Zealand flax)
Eschscholzia californica (Californian Poppy)
Pansies. For example Four whiskery faced pansies
Pansy Red Leopard
Tiger Eye Violas
Pansy Angel Amber Kiss
Lonicera Nitida (Shrubby Honeysuckle)
'Lemon Beauty'
Low spreading evergreen.
Salvia Officinalis (Sage)
Erica Carnea (Winter Heather)
Helichrysum Italicum (Curry plant)
Evergreen

Choisya 'Sundance'
Hakonechloa Macra
'Alboaurea' (dwarf grass)
Geranium Macrorrhizum
'Bevan's Variety'
This is no common geranium!!!

Vigorous Trailing Bedding Plants

    Helichrysum Petiolare
    Petunia Purple Wave
    Surfinia Petunias
    Tapien Verbenas
    Diascias
    Pelargoniums
    Anagallis

You can order most of those plants at
Mr Fothergill's Seeds Ltd
Gazeley Road
Kentford
Newmarket, Suffolk
CB8 7QB
Email: webmaster(at)mr-fothergills.co.uk
Email: david.thompson@fothergills.co.uk
Telephone: (+44) 01638 751 161
Fax: (+44) 01638 554 084
So there are many plants for our cats and ourselves to love and enjoy without
getting ill.

*He seems the incarnation of everything soft and silky and velvety, without a
sharp edge in his composition, a dreamer whose philosophy is sleep and let
sleep.*

Saki 1870-1916

Chapter

Bach Flower Remedies

AN OLD RUSSIAN PRAYER FOR ANIMALS

Hear our prayer, Lord, for all animals.
May they be well-fed and well trained and happy.
Protect them from hunger and fear and suffering.
And, we pray, protect especially, dear Lord,
the little cat who is the companion of our home,
keep her safe as she goes abroad,
and bring her back to comfort us.

Anonymous

Bach Flower Remedies
By Doctor C. SMEETS
'Vetcare'. Practice for holistic medicine.

Some years ago, in the course of my practice in holistic veterinary medicine, I was regularly asked whether I also used Bach Flower Remedies. I decided to take a closer look at what Bach flower therapy actually meant. The more information I obtained about this therapy, the more it became clear to me that it is an exceptionally suitable method to heal animals. As a matter of fact the use of the remedies is relatively simple while its action is extraordinarily mild and - when correctly applied - very effective. Administering Bach Flower Remedies is easy and there are no side effects.

Edward Bach, an English physician, devoted the last years of his life to the search for natural remedies which could bring about healing in a simple but effective way. And so he developed 38 simple remedies (made from flowers and plant parts) and one compound remedy, the well known (but unfortunately often wrongly used) Rescue Remedy.
The objective of these remedies is to bring disturbed emotions back to balance. The remedies do not add nor repress anything. As such they are pre-eminently

373

suited to remedy problematical behaviour in animals. When an animal's emotional balance is seriously disturbed, physical complaints may also show. But frequently occurring problems like, for example, dirtiness or spraying can also be put right by these remedies.

It is very important to observe your cat attentively so as to find out what exactly causes its problem. Once you have established the cause, you can decide what simple remedy or what combination of several remedies may cure your cat.

Bach Flower Remedies sometimes work incredibly fast, sometimes even after one day, but in any case after 2 to 4 weeks.

Of course, the remedies work both in case of serious mental problems and also in case of the little and not so little everyday worries of the average cat's life: visit to the vet or to a show, gestation, having kittens, trips by car, loss of a companion...

Bach Flower Remedies are available at the pharmacy or any well-assorted (natural) chemist. You buy the remedies you need in so called stock bottles. You can also buy some empty 30 ml droppers at the pharmacy: they will be your 'user bottles'. In the user bottle you put mineral water or tap water that has been boiled and cooled down first. Then you add four drops from the stock bottle to the water in the user bottle. Shake well. This mixture can then be used. In the beginning you can give four drops six times a day. After two weeks you can change over to giving four drops four times a day. It is best to give the drops straight from the user bottle into your pet's mouth, but you can also simply add it to the food or the drinking water. It is important to see to it that the dropper does not touch the mouth.

Do not use too many remedies at the same time. Try to limit yourself to three or maximum seven remedies. The Rescue Remedy counts for one remedy, even though it is itself a compound of five remedies.

When your user bottles are empty, boil them for ten minutes and they are ready for re-use.

Here below the various remedies and for what condition to use them:

374

The Rescue Remedy is a first aid remedy!!!

To be given in case of any form of acute trauma in this word's widest sense.

Emergencies
Accidents
Acute stress
Birth

It may also be given preventively, when you know that your pet is about to experience something it doesn't like. (Visit to the vet, visit to a show).

Rescue Remedy is composed of five remedies:

- Star of Bethlehem
- Clematis
- Rock Rose
- Cherry Plum
- Impatiens

Rescue cream

First aid lotion

All types of wounds, scratches, skin problems
For treatment of insect bites, stitches, light burns, bite and scratch wounds, grazes etc.

N.B. For longhaired animals it may be handier to use a lotion with a base of Rescue Remedy and Crab Apple.

Injuries

For all kinds: Rescue Remedy and Rescue Cream

In case of serious burns/shock
Call your veterinarian immediately!

Drip Rescue Remedy on lips, gums or ears.

Make sure the injured cat keeps warm by covering her.

For the time being, do not remove nails, pieces of glass etc. from the wounds, as that may worsen bleeding. Just apply a rolled compress like a ring around the injured spot.

Insect stings

Dab the area around the sting with cold water and Rescue Remedy.
Administer Rescue Remedy orally against fear.

Burns

Flush with **warm** water!! If necessary, mixed with Rescue Remedy. Administer Rescue Remedy orally, if necessary drip on lips, gums or ears. In case of serious burns, go to the veterinarian immediately.

Pregnancy

Adjusting to a new situation	**Walnut**
Exhaustion	**Olive**
Cat is listless	**Hornbeam**
	Wild Rose
Vomiting while pregnant	**Crab Apple**

Birth

Exhaustion	**Olive**
Complete exhaustion	**Oak**
Cat slow during delivery	**Hornbeam**
	Wild Rose
Shock	**Star of Bethlehem**
	Rescue Remedy
Panic	**Rock Rose**
	Rescue Remedy

Cat threatens kittens	**Cherry Plum**
Adjustment, change	**Walnut**

Kittens

After birth	**Rescue Remedy**
Or	**Walnut**
if necessary with	**Star of Bethlehem**
Exhaustion after long delivery	**Olive**
Kittens hardly move	**Hornbeam**
after an easy delivery	
Kittens barely alive	**Clematis**
Kittens don't go to mother	**Wild Rose**
Kittens are very agitated	**Impatiens**

Going to their new homes

- **Walnut**
- **Honeysuckle**
- **Star of Bethlehem**

In the car
Practice makes perfect!

Carsickness	**Scleranthus**
Afraid of travel basket, car	**Mimulus**
In case of blind panic	**Rescue Remedy**
Bothered by change	**Walnut**
When your cat can't get used to	
travelling in a car	**Chestnut Bud**

Aggression

Related to fear	
Cause clearly demonstrable	**Mimulus**
Loss of self-control	**Cherry Plum**
Related to dominance	
Authority	

Territory	
"Bossing" the other(s)	**Vine**
Jealousy	**Holly**
Complete intolerance to other(s)	**Beech**
Willing to help but	
overstepping the mark	**Vervain**
Related to anger	
Anger comes and goes quickly	
Also: delaying factor	**Impatiens**
Related to changes	
Aggression after change	**Walnut**
Related to kittens	
Possessiveness	**Chicory**
Urge to protect	**Red Chestnut**

Uncleanliness

After a change	**Walnut**
Out of dominance	**Vine**
If necessary, a combination of	**Beech**
	Chicory of Vervain
Stress out of fear	**Mimulus**
	Rock Rose
Wants only a clean tray	**Crab Apple**
if necessary combined with	**Beech**
Cannot find a good spot	**Water Violet**
If necessary (depending on cause)	**Mimulus**
Attracting attention	
Combination of	**Holly**
	Chicory

While the cause is still unknown, you may begin with administering Rescue Remedy for a couple of days.

Life in the group

Intolerance	**Beech**
Hissing, mewing	
Dominance	**Vine**

Submissive is being pestered	**Centaury**
Cannot be alone	**Agrimony**
Will not be alone	**Water Violet**
Jealousy	**Holly**
Timid	**Mimulus**
Lost in the group	**Larch**
Changes in the group	**Walnut**
	Honeysuckle

Hyperactivity

Caused by:
Stress
combination of

Mimulus (fear)
White Chestnut (worrying)
Walnut (changes)

Over enthusiasm
combination of

Vervain (can't stop)
Impatiens (quickly bored)

Obsessive behaviour
Inflicting wounds on itself by
biting, scratching and/or licking
combination of

Crab Apple

Cherry Plum (frustration)
Impatiens (excitement)
Vervain (frustration)

Fear

Cause clearly demonstrable   **Mimulus**
applies to a cat which is timid and/or nervous
Without demonstrable cause   **Aspen**
Cat runs away and hides without any obvious reason
Arising from concern   **Red Chestnut**
Applies to sweet cats who, for example
have kittens
Coupled with loss of self-control   **Cherry Plum**
unpredictable aggressive behaviour

also towards the owner
Panic!   **Rock Rose**
Cat grows rigid with fear

<u>Death</u>

To ease the crossing to the next life:
combination of   **Walnut**
                                              Honeysuckle
                                              Aspen
                                              Olive

With many thanks to my dear friend Carina.

'Vetcare'. Practice for holistic medicine:
Doctor. C. SMEETS
Zwaansweg 26
4247 EX Kedichem
Nederland
Tel: + 31-183-567.150

Email: vetcare@chello.nl

Site: http://vetcare.homestead.com/vetcare.html

AT RAINBOW BRIDGE

There is a bridge connecting Heaven and Earth.
It is called the Rainbow Bridge because of its many colors.
Just this side of the Rainbow Bridge, there is a land of meadows,
hills and valleys with lush green grass.
When a beloved pet dies, the pet goes to this place.
There is always food and water and warm Spring weather.
Those old and frail animals are young again.
Those who have been maimed are made whole again.
They play all day with each other.
Some of them here by the Bridge are different.
These pets were beaten, starved, tortured, and unloved.
They watch wistfully as their friends leave one by one,
to cross the bridge with their special person.
For them there is no one, no special one.
Their time on earth did not give them one.
But one day, as they run and play,
they notice someone standing by the road to the bridge.
This person wistfully watches the reunions of friends,
for during life, this person had no pet.
This person was beaten, starved, tortured, and unloved.
Standing there alone, one of the unloved pets approaches,
curious as to why this one is alone.
And as the unloved pet and the unloved person get nearer to each other, a miracle
occurs, for these are the ones who were meant to be together, the special person and
the beloved pet who never had the chance to meet while on Earth.
Finally, now, at the edge of the Rainbow Bridge, their souls meet,
the pain and the sorrow disappears, and two friends are together.
They cross the Rainbow Bridge together, never again to be separated.

Source Unknown

381

Chapter

Poezenbel Foundation

Founded at Huissen on 18 January 1995

My dear friend and soul sister, Maria and her husband Gé founded Poezenbel to be more able to help kittens in distress. It all started when Maria heard from a farmer that he had drowned his kittens, except for one he could not catch, 'which made him very angry!' Well, Maria was not happy about it either! How horrible that that still happens! She promised to catch the little one and offered to neuter the mother and the other cats on the farm to prevent them having more litters. Of course those kittens were always killed. With much reluctance he agreed. Maria found the very wild but adorable little kitten hidden under a lot of rubbish. She was about six weeks old, a lovely tortoise-shell kitten. Asselijntje she was called. In less than a week she wasn't afraid any more. She became the most cuddleable kitty I have ever seen. It is not true that you can't tame a feral cat. On the contrary! They often become the most lovable cats.

Maria says:
'Kittens are abandoned. What a cowardly act indeed! Unfortunately it is a routine we have to face every year! Kittens are found everywhere, from the banks of brooks to the inside of containers, nothing surprises us any more. It happens too that stray cats can't take care of their own offspring. Of course we help those little ones too.

Hand rearing kittens is far from simple. During the first weeks of their lives, those little ones need special kitten milk. They have to be fed every two hours, day and night. Also, during the first month after their birth the kittens can't eliminate by themselves. They have to be stimulated to be able to pass urine and faeces. Normally the mother does that by licking the anal and genital areas. We stimulate the kittens by rubbing a moist wad of cotton wool over those areas. Kittens cannot regulate their body temperature during the first month of their lives. We have to keep them at the right temperature with hot water bottles.

It is always risky to hand rear the little ones as we never can substitute the mother cat, but it's the only chance they have to stay alive. They miss the antibodies present in the mother's milk. That is why we use the best powdered milk available but...it is very expensive. Every rescuee has to be examined to make sure she does not have a fungal infection. We do that with the Wood's lamp but if there is any doubt we have to send skin tissue to a laboratory for culture and study. On arrival, the kittens are first put in quarantine. If they are healthy they are then moved to the living room. It is very important that the kittens have as normal a life as possible while growing up, so they will become social, cuddleable cats. Often these little kittens have been through a lot of misery already. We have to visit the veterinarian regularly. Often medicines are needed. Of course the kittens have to be wormed and to be freed from fleas. At about four weeks the kittens are weaned. They change the bottle for more solid food. Special canned food and dry-food for kittens is then consumed in huge quantities. Never use inferior food for weaning. It always causes problems. Hill's Science Diet Feline Growth is good, for example.

When the kittens are nine weeks old and healthy, they receive their first vaccination and a chip (a subcutaneously implanted identification number) to have some protection when they leave for their new owners. We ask a small contribution to help in covering the expenses. On average the foundation spends 125 euros to raise a kitten. The new owner is required to have the cat neutered. We are not raising abandoned kittens in order that they put, in their turn, more kittens into the world. When our finances are sufficient, we set up programmes to neuter stray and farm cats. We also enter into arrangements to prevent a recurrence of kitten problems.

The foundation's objectives are to act as a mediator in the homing or re-homing of stray cats and cats that need a new home, so as to prevent any feline suffering.

- We mediate between humans and stray kittens.
- We try to prevent kittens being killed on farms and help in finding them good new homes.
- We shelter motherless kittens and bottle-feed them (of course, depending on availability of space).
- We keep a register of lost and found cats and advise what to do.

- We match supply and demand between cats and human beings and keep track of the situation and we try to prevent any unnecessary suffering.
- We advise (and if necessary assist) persons when kittens have to be handreared. We have a practical booklet **'What to do if mother cat cannot or will not take care of her kittens'** which is available on request.
- We shelter kittens below 6 weeks or when extra care is required.
- After a period of quarantine, our kittens mature in the living room together with our other cats and dogs so that they get all possible opportunities to develop into social cats. Our kittens have a very high 'cuddleability-factor.'
- When the bottle-fed kittens are healthy and are a minimum of ten weeks old, we will home them with people where they are truly welcome.
- When our kittens leave us, they are vaccinated, wormed, free from fleas and chip-implanted.
- Our kittens are only homed under contract, in which the new owner commits himself to have them neutered.
- We assist people when they have questions or problems with their cats or refer them to the proper person or authority which can help them.
- We devote ourselves to having stray cats and farm cats neutered. That is the best way to prevent a lot of misery.
- By way of the internet we inform and educate.

We devote our time to all these objectives, with love, with pleasure but also often with grief. We can only do this thanks to the support of our members and sponsors!

If you are willing to support us, we'll gladly welcome you as member. Of course gifts are also welcome. Please mention when transferring the amount, whether it is a once-only gift or whether you want to be a regular member.

For a minimum of 13 euros per year, you will become a member. Every four months you will receive our member magazine Poezenbelletje. In this magazine you will read what happened in the past quarter. It also contains regular features by veterinarians Allard Hendriks and Carina Smeets, Tomcat

Stapper from Zoetermeer, Tomcat Puddie from Belgium, cats' purrs from a Belgian friend, quarterly news from Maria and also many useful tips and other purrs about cats.

Each kitten that is born has a right to life.

Be a responsible owner,
Have your cat neutered!

Maria van Aalten
Gravekamp 71
6851 NJ Huissen
Tel/Fax: + 31-26-3255752 (workdays
13.00-17.00 p.m.)
For kittens in distress: 06-509.11.803
(day and night)
E-mail: info@poezenbel.nl
www.poezenbel.nl

Radobank no: 12.40.79.970 or account: 7176970
Sterilization Fund: Radobank no: 12.40.85.113

Appendix

Addresses

Books, Magazines & Websites

Angel Animals Network
Allen and Linda Anderson
P.O. Box 26354, Minneapolis MN 55426, U.S.A
E-mail: angelanimals@angelanimals.net, Website:
www.angelanimals.net

Animals and the afterlife
C/o EnLighthouse Publishing
1835A S.Centre City Pkwy 181, Escondido CA 92025,
USA
Website: www.AnimalsAndTheAfterlife.com
E-mail: StorySubmissions@AnimalsAndTheAfterlife.com

Animalwriting
Chantal Greeve en Balou
Havengrafstraat 26, B-8300 Knokke-Heist, Belgium
tel-0475-94.96.24
E-mail: animalwriting@love4animals.be, Website: www.love4animals.be

Cats Confidential Newsletter
WR Corp. Publishing, P.O. Box 108, Chattanooga, Tennessee 37401, USA
Tel 001-423-265-4571, Fax 001-423-265-4574
Email: wrcorp@mindspring.com

Cat World
Laura Quiggan
Ashdown.co.uk, Avalon Court, Star Road
Partridge Green.West Sussex RH13 8RY, England
01403 711511, extension 113, fax 01403 711521
E-mail: info@ashdown.co.uk, Website: www.catworld.co.uk

Book *Feline Online*
By Elyse Cregar, ISBN 0-9621292-1-6
www.felineonline.net
Book Clearing House, 46 Purdy Street, Harrison, NY 10528, USA

For Every Cat an Angel
Chris Davis, Lighthearted Press Inc.
P.O. Box 90125, Portland Oregon 97290, USA
Tel: 503-786-3085, Fax: 503-786-0315
E-mail: davis@lighthearted.com, Website: www.lightharted.com

A cat lover lives here
Forge Rosemary
1 Beaumont Road, Worthing. Sussex, BN14 8HF, England

Moon Cottage Cats
Marilyn Edwards Website: www.thecatsofmooncottage.co.uk

Een snoepje van een poesje
Claes Patsy
Rijschoolstraat 53/1, B-3800 St. Truiden, Belgium

New World Library
Danielle Gotchet, Administrative Assistant
14 Pamaron Way, Novato, CA 94949, USA
(415) 884-2100, ext. 10
E-mail: Danielle@newworldlibrary.com or ami@newworldlibrary.com

To order the lovely book *Ophelia*:
www.authorhouse.com
Marilyn A.K.A. Sarah Ann Hill & O & S 2506 Cherokee Avenue, Charleston, West Virgina
25301-1018, USA
E-mail: MSS1048@aol.com

Paw Tracks In the Moonlight
Coon Cat Books, Denis O'Connor
Ivy Cottage , West Thriston, Morpeth, Northumberland NE 65 9 EF, England
Tel: 0044-1670 787885

There is eternal life for animals
Pete Publishing
Pete Publishing, P.O. Box 282, Tyngsborough, MA 01879, USA
E-mail: hickory4@world.std.om, Website: www.eternalanimals.com
Niki Behrikis Shanahan
Old Hickory Road, Tyngsborough Ma 01879, USA

Doctor Vernon Coleman
Trinity Place, Barnstaple, Devon EX 32 9HJ, England
Tel: +44-1271-32.88.92,
Website: www.vernoncoleman.com

Over the Rainbowbridge
Wendy and Steve, Penlleinau Blaencaron, Tregaron, Ceredigion
Wales SY25 6HL, United Kingdom
Tel 0044-1974-299000, E-mail: rynchanon@nightwing.fsbusiness.co.uk

Smarter than Jack Limited
Location: Level 4, 61-63 Thorndon Quay, Wellington, New Zealand
Post: PO Box 27 003, Wellington, New Zealand
Phone: 64-4-473 7005
E-mail: jenny@smarterthanjack.com, Website: www.smarterthanjack.com

Traditional and Classic Cat International
Randi S. Briggs
7615 Clyde Way, Smartsville CA. 95977, USA
Website: www.tccat.org, E-mail: www.tccat.org

Traditional Cat Association
Diana Fineran
PO Box 178
Heisson WA 98622
USA
www.traditionalcats.com

Sheelagh Lecocq Traditional Siamese
2 Sydenham Villas, Janvrinroad, St. Helier, Jersey JE2 4LF, England
Tel: +44-1534 73.68.20
E-mail: traditionalsiameseuk@yahoo.co.uk ,
Website: www.members.tripod.com/tsca.uk/

Your Cat Magazine
Editor: Sue Parslow
Roebuck House, 33 Broad Street, Stamford, Lincs PE9 1RB, England
Tel: +44-(0)1780 766199, Fax : +44-(0)1780 766416
E-mail: s.parslow@bournepublishinggroup.co.uk
Website: www.yourcat.co.uk

Your Cat Bookshop
PO Box 60, Helston, Cornwall ,TR13 0TP England
Tel: 08700 708071
E-mail: yourcatbookshop@sparkledirect.co.uk

Hans Sevenhoven (He gave me the information about St Francis)
http://home.hetnet.nl/~sevenhoven/francis/francis2.htm

Catshelter and other Cat- or animal welfare organisations

APMA

Preventive Action against the Martyrdom of Laboratory Animals
De Burletlaan 4, B-2650 Edegem, Belgium
Tel: +32-3-449.49.08
E-mail: apma@telenet.be, Website: www.apma.be

Foundation Amivedi, National foundation for registration Lost and found animals,
Postbus 53018, NL-AA 's Gravenhage, The Netherlands
Tel: +31-70-368.28.41, Centraal registratienr: +31-40-243.28.11

Foundation Brooke Hospital for Animals Nederland
Van Baerlestraat 13-C, NL-1071 AM Amsterdam, The Netherlands
Tel: 020 670 92 29, Fax: 020 679 28 00
E-mail info@brooke.nl , Website: www.brooke.nl

C.A.D. Coordinatie Antwerpse Dierenbescherming VZW
Animal Protection. Databank for lost and found pets.
Pets for adoption.
Tel: 0032-3-440.05.48, Fax: 0032-3-448.29.81
E-mail: cad-dieren@telenet.be, Website: www.cad-dieren.be

Dierenbevrijdingsorganisatie Poezenboot Caprice
Animal Liberation Organisation Cat-shelter boat Caprice
Mieke Schuddinck, Nieuwevaart 245, B-9000 Gent, Belgium
Tel: +32-9-236.19.07
E-mail: poezenboot@pandora.be,
Site: www.poezenboot.be

Het Felix Project
Els en André Engelen, Schansstraat 3, B-3665 As, Belgium
E-mail: elsan@yucom.be
Website: http://home.scarlet.be/~ae973514/index1.htm

GAIA Global Action in the Interest of Animals
Ravensteingalerij 27, B-1000 Brussel, Belgium
E-mail: info@gaia.be, Website: www.gaia.be

International Fund for Animal Welfare (IFAW)
Mariëlle van Enckevort
Bezuidenhoutseweg 225, NL-2594 AL Den Haag, The Netherlands
Tel: 070 - 3355011 Fax: 070- 3850940, Website: www.ifaw.nl

LSOH (Landelijke Stichting Ouderen en Huisdieren) (National Foundation Elderly people and pets)
Prins Johan Frisostraat 7, NL-3466 LZ Waarder, The Netherlands
Tel: +31-348-50.16.01

Poezenbel Foundation
Maria van Aalten
Gravekamp 71, NL-6851 NJ Huissen, The Netherlands
Tel/fax: +31-26-325.57.52
E-mail: info@poezenbel.nl, Website: www.poezenbel.nl

De Rietkat Foundation, Postaddress: Mishagen 43, B-2930 Brasschaat,
Belgium, Tel: +32-3-633.29.71, Fax: +32-3-633.03.96
E-mail: info@rietkat.be, Website: www.rietkat.be

Torre Argentina
C/o Silvia Viviani
Via Marco Papio 15, 00175 Rome, Italy
E-mail: torreargentina@tiscali.be, Website: www.romancats.com

Gerda Thys
Vanheetveldelei 92, B-Deurne 2100, Belgium

Felissana Foundation
Bloemstraat 45, NL-1975 EM IJmuiden, The Netherlands
E-mail: mienie.mouw@worldonline.nl, Website: www.felissana.nl

Sabine van der Meer
VZW Zwerfkat in Nood 11
Postbus 58, NL-3630 Maasmechelen
E-mail: Info@zwerfkat.com, Website: www.zwerfkat.com

Artists

Gallery de kat z'n viool (the cat and the fiddle)
residence of poet *Tomcat Slaapmuts* and the artist that illustrated this book
Anne Versteyne, Kastanjestraat 36, NL- 8021 XT Zwolle, The Netherlands
Tel: +31-(0)38-452.54.96
Website: www.dekatzijnviool.com E-mail : info@dekatzijnviool.com

Catgallery La Dame Bastet
Various cat artists, gallery established 1994
c/o **Meta Dame**
Aaltenseweg 21, NL-7025 CJ Halle, the Netherlands
Website: www.dame-bastet.com E-mail: info@dame-bastet.com

Cats in watercolour
Yvonne Hamaker-Bontrop
E-mail: aquavon@hetnet.nl, Website: http://home.hetnet.nl/~von46/index.html

Renate Leijen &
Noorse Boskatten Cattery 'Zihuatanejo's' (Norwegian Forest Cats)
Mina Krusemansstraat 56, NL-3207 DE Spijkenisse, The Netherlands
E-mail: artphoto@hetnet.nl
Website : http://www.artphotonfc.nl
Animal Art and Photography

Margreet van der Wart
Espelerpad 10b, 8311 PS Espel The Netherlands
E-mail: silverdunizel@live.nl, Website: www.silverdunizel.nl

Monos
Monique Schampaert, Schotensesteenweg 67, B-2100 Deurne, Belgium
Tel : 03-325.27.58
E-mail: Monos.art@telenet.be, Website: www.monos-art.be

Francien van Westering
E-mail: francien@francienskatten.nl, Website: www.francienskatten.nl

Medical Adresses

Medium Miguella Boessen
Vrangendael 16, NL-6137 BB Sittard, The Netherlands

Petal Cleanse
Bio-Life International
1-3 Upper Grove End Farm Business Units, Brailes, Oxon OX15 5BA, England
Tel: +44-1608-68.66.26, Website: www.bio-life.co.uk

The Margrit Coates Foundation for Animal Healing
PO Box No 1826, Salisbury, Wiltshire SP 5 2 BH, **England**
Website: www.theanimalhealer.com

Telepathisch Communiceren Met Dieren (telepathic communication with animals)
Animal communicator

Cecilia van der Drift
Zuiderstraat 8, NL-3742 BD Baarn, The Netherlands
E-mail: cecilia.d@planet.nl, Website: www.telepathiemetdieren.nl

FAB - *Feline Advisory Bureau*
Taeselbury
High Street, Salisbury, Wiltshire SP3 6LD, England
Tel: +44-870-742.2278
Website: www.fabcats.org

'Vetcare' Praktijk voor Holistische Geneeskunde (Practice for Holistic Veterinarian science)
Drs. Carina Smeets
Zwaansweg 26, NL-4247 EX Kedichem, The Netherlands
Tel : +31-183-567.151
E-mail: vetcare@chello.nl, Website: http://vetcare.homestead.com/vetcare.html

Cat Products & Products with Cat designs

Betty´s Hotel for Cats and Shop
Betty Hoogstad-Netze, Prins Hendrikkade 51, 1501 AD Zaandam
tel. 075-670 38 83, fax 075-77 18 117, mobile phone 06-21 22 54 24
website Cat Hotel: www.bettyshotel.nl,
website on-line catshop: www.bettyswinkel.nl

Happy Cats
For the greatest fleece beds and more for your cat(s)!
E-mail: info@happycats.nl, Website: www.happycats.nl

The Cat Gallery
Peter Hanson, Fax: 0044-1904-61.10.53
Website: www.thecatgallery.co.uk, E-mail: sales@thecatgallery.co.uk

Appendix

Bibliography

Cat Books

Adamson, Lydia	A Cat with no Regrets	P
Adamson, Lydia	A Cat in the Manger	P
Adamson, Lydia	A Cat by any other Name	P
Adamson, Lydia	A Cat in the Wings	P
Adamson, Lydia	A Cat of different Color	P
Adamson, Lydia	A Cat in Wolf's Clothing	P
Adamson, Lydia	A Cat with a Fiddle	P
Adamson, Lydia	A Cat in the Glass House	P
Amory, Cleveland	The Cat who came for Christmas	Li
Amory, Cleveland	The Best Cat Ever	Li
Amory, Cleveland	The Cat and the Curmudgeon	Li
Anderson, Allen and Linda	God's Messengers	N
Anderson, Allen and Linda	Angel Animals	Pl
Anderson, Allen and Linda	Angel Cats	Pl
Anderson, Allen and Linda	Angel Dogs	Pl
Anderson, Allen and Linda	Memorial Kit	Pl
Ballner, Maryjean	Cat Massage	St
Bayley, Nicola	The Necessary Cat	
Bessant, Claire	The Cat Whisperer	Jo
Bessant, Claire	The nine Live Cat	Jo
Bessant, Claire	What Cats Want	M
Behrikis Shanahan, Niki	There is Eternal Life for Animals	Pe
Behrikis Shanahan, Niki	Animal Prayer Guide	Pe
Bloomfield, Betty	Nursing and Hand Rearing Newborn Kittens	Ab
Bloomfield, Betty		
Briant, Keith	A Kitten for Christmas	Mi
Campbell Jenny	Cats are Smarter than Jack	Av
Corey, Paul	Do Cats Think?	Ca
Coates, Margrit	Hands-on Healing for Pets	Ri
Coleman, Vernon	We love Cats	Ch
Coleman, Vernon	Alice's Diary	Ch
Coleman, Vernon	Alice's Adventures	Ch

Coleman
Coleman
Coleman
Coleman
Capuzzo
Capuzzo
Chernak

Chernak

Cregar,
Caldwel
D'Alessa
Daniels,
Daniels,
Daniels,
Daniels,
Daniels,
Davis, C
Davis, C
Dixon, J
Dodman
Dolan, k

Dohany
Edwards
Edwards
Edwards
Forge, R
Friends
Gallico,
Gallico,
Gethers.
Hill, Sai
Jackon I
Johnson
Johnson
Johnson
King, G
King, G
King, G
King, G
Kreislei
Kurz, G
Lessing
Loxton,

Vernon	Alice and other Friends	Chilton Designs Publ
Vernon	Cats' Own Annual	Chilton Designs Publ
Vernon	The Secret lives of Cats	Chilton Designs Publ
Vernon	The Cat Basket	Chilton Designs Publ
Michael and Teresa Banik	Cat Caught My Heart	Bantam books
McElroy, Susan	Animals as Teachers and Healers	Ballantine Publishing Group
McElroy, Susan	Animals as Guides for the Soul	Ballantine Publishing Group
yse	Feline Online	Book Clearing House
Taylor	Dear and Glorious Physician	Reback & Reback
dro, Deborah	Nelson (Torre Argentino)	Sinnos
ucy	Cat Companion	Hodder Books Ltd
ucy	Cat Crazy	Hodder Books Ltd
ucy	Kitten in the Cold	Hodder Books Ltd
ucy	Nine Lives : Amber	Hodder Books Ltd
ucy	Clever Cat	Hodder Books Ltd
ristine	For every Cat an Angel	Lighthearted Press
ristine	For every Dog an Angel	Lighthearted Press
ne	Do Cats have ESP?	Running Press
Dr. Nicolas	The Cat who cried forHelp	Bantam Books
ren	Best True Cat Stories	Michael O'Mara Books Ltd
, Franklin	The Cats of Our Lives	Carol Publishing Group
Marilyn	The Cats of Moon Cottage	Hodder and Stoughton
Marilyn	More Tales from Moon Cottage	Hodder and Stoughton
Marilyn	The Cats on Hutton Roof	Hodder and Stoughton
semary	A Cat Lover Lives Here	Blackie & Co
a Roman Cats	Cat Tales	Barbara Palmer
aul	Honourable Cat	Pan Books
aul	The Silent Miauw	Pan Books
Peter	The Cat who went to Paris	
h Ann	Ophelia's Winter	Authorhouse
aun, Lilian	The Cat Who	
Bennett, Pam	Hiss and Tell	Penguin Books
Bennett, Pam	Think like a Cat	Penguin Books
Bennett, Pam	Cat vs Cat	Penguin Books
oriel	The Wild Road	Century London
oriel	The Golden Cat	Century London
oriel	The Knot Garden	Century London
oriel	None Such	Century London
on, Kristin	The Compassion of Animals	Three Rivers Press
ry	Cold Noses at the Pearly Gates	
Doris	Particularly Cats	
Ioward	99 Lives of Cats	Duncan Baird

Mallinson, Jeremy	The Count's Cats	Llumina Press
Mancuso, Theresa	Cats do it better than People	Adams Media
Melmoth, Jenny	A Cat in my Lap	Alfresco Books
	Amber	
O'Boyle, Jane	Catnip for the Soul	Quill William Morrow
O'Connor, Denis	Paw Tracks in the Moonlight	Coon Cat Books
O'Mara, Lesley	Greatest Cat Stories	Michael O'Mara Books Ltd
Various writers	Favourite Cat Stories	Pan Books
Pryor, Karen	Clicker Training for Cats	Ringpress Books
Roberts, Billy	The Healing Paw	Thorsons
Radford, Roy and Gregory, Eveline	Eternally-Yours Faithfully	Capall Bann Publishing
Sheridan, Kim	Animals and the Afterlife	Lighthouse Publishing
Schoen, Allen and Proctor, Pam	Love, Miracles and Animal Healing	Simon & Schuster
Schoen, Allen and Proctor, Pam	Kindred Spirits	Souvenir Press London
Steiger Brad & Sherry Hansen Steiger	Cat Miracles	Adams Media Corporation
Samek Stefanie	A Cat's Christmas	A Dutton Book
	Purring in the Light	A Plume Book
Thornton, Helene	Cat Chat	Virgin Books
Tovey, Doreen	Cats in May	Summersdale Publishers Ltd
Tovey, Doreen	Cats in the Belfry	
Tugby, Wendy M.	Over the Rainbow Bridge	Publ. Wendy M. Tugby printed Gomer Press
Van der Wart, Margreet	Purrings	
Vlielander, Marg	Wonderen op pootjes	De Rietkat
Webb, Cheryl Renee	Do Pets and other Animals go to Heaven?	Brite Books
Whitelaw, Stella	Favorite Cat Stories	Michael O'Mara Books Ltd
Williams, Marta	Learning their Language	New World Library
Williams, Tom	The Politicats	Professional Press
Wood Deborah	The Tao of Meow	Dell Trade

Medical Books

Hamilton, Don	Homeopathic Care for Cats and Dogs	North Atlantic Books
Morrison, Roger	Desktop Guide	Hahnemann Clinic
Pitcairn and Pitcairn	Natural Health for Dogs and Cats	Rodale Press

Turner, Trevor and Turner, Jean	Veterinary Notes For Cat Owners	Stanley Paul
Wilde, Clare	Natural Healing for Animals	Cathie Limited
Zidonis, N. and A. Snow	Acu-Cat	TallGrass

Spiritual Books

Althea, Rosemary	The Eagle and the Rose	Warner Books
Althea, Rosemary	Proud Spirit	Morrow N.Y.
Char	Questions from Earth, Answers from Heaven	St. Martin's Press
Praagh, James van	Talking to Heaven	Dutton
Praagh, James van	Reaching to Heaven	Dutton
Schlemmer, Phyllis V.	The Only Planet Of Choice	Mary Benett

MIRACLES ON LITTLE FEET

When you live all day in the company of six
"miracles on little feet", enjoying their love,
warmth, humour and loyalty, sooner or later
you will want to write a book about them.
That's how my book "Miracles on little Feet "
came into being.

Since my childhood I have been in close and
special contact with animals. Animals were not
just playmates; they were my most important
teachers. They taught me the real meaning of
friendship, unconditional love and loyalty.
They paid attention to me, they worried about
me. They taught me the real value of life. Their
love is Love with a capital L. My dearest wish
was to have a cat. This dream only materialised five years ago when Puddie
came into my life. Puddie, my beautiful grey half-Siamese king-cat!

From Day One we had a strong bond. Puddie jumped on my desk and in his
huge beautiful green eyes I discovered the mystical powers of the cat, the
animal that originally descended from Bastet, the Cat-Goddess. So much I
learned from Puddie and my other furry friends. Then Luckje came, a born
wanderer who clearly was 'sent' to me to support me in one of the most difficult
periods in my life. When his mission was accomplished and I felt stronger
again, Luckje suddenly left, no doubt to comfort another person in need. I still
miss him and I always will because "a friend in need is a friend indeed". Just
before Luckje left Donsje came into our lives. This cute little kitten was found
in the middle of a wheat-field. Maria, founder of the Poezenbel foundation - a
foundation that takes care of abandoned kittens and cats - nursed Donsje and
then brought her to me.

Luckje must have realised that I missed him, for soon after his disappearance
he sent us Mickje, a sick and starving she-cat thrown over the fence into my
garden. I took care of her and nursed her into the healthy and happy cat now
frolicking with the others in and around my house. In " Miracles on little Feet"

you will read all the details of the lives and experiences of Puddie, Luckje, Donsje and Mickje.

Frequently, animals are considered as "lower beings", inferior to us humans. I think the truth is different. Animals are equal to us. Sometimes they are even superior to us! They are still close in touch with Nature, the Almighty, the All. In "Miracles on little Feet", I also discuss this theme.

I have had anorexia for thirty years and I show how this silent killer "ambushes" lives and secretly takes control. My book also discusses themes like reincarnation, the return of cats to their masters after death. The fact that cats do not just appear into our lives but come with some purpose, like Luckje who helped me make it through some very tough days. I talk about castration, the disadvantages of letting cats run free and the advantages of keeping them safe in runs. I tell about the dangers threatening our cats in - and outside of the house. In a separate chapter, Maria van Aalten tells all about the care of orphaned kittens. The book ends with a mix of interesting facts related to cats and cat-people.

Last but not least, my friend Anne Versteyne has beautifully illustrated my book. Anne is an artist who knows how to render the inner power and humour of our cats in her lively drawings. Part of the proceeds of the sale of my book will be donated to the Poezenbel Foundation.

Purring Angels is illustrated by my dear friend Anne Versteyne. www.dekatzijnviool.com . All the drawings are made by her with the exception of the drawings on:

Marg's World has been made by my dear friend Monique
It's an oil painting 60x40 cm.
Monos.art@telenet.be   www.monos-art.be

Vernon Colerman's prayer for cats: This beautiful sad kitty is from Vernon Coleman
www.vernoncoleman.com

Page 36: The Logo from the FSC has been made by Tomcat Stapper, Pudje's pen pal. He also wrote the beautiful poem 'Litter Tray'. Of course his mum Dede did help him a bit.

Pages 98, 99, 100, 123: All the drawings in this wonderful story are from Wayne Pond http://www.eatel.net/~meme

Page 143: This lovely painting is made by Renate Leijen
http://www.artphotonfc.nl

Page 166: I found this beautiful, oh so sad kitty when I was 14 years old. For me she is the personification of all the poor cats who are badly treated. That moment I decided to dedicate my life to cats in distress. For all those years I kept her with me. She travelled with me to France and Belgium and is now sitting on the cupboard. She will stop crying the day that all strays are neutered and living a happy life with full tummies.

ISBN 142512202-7